'*Services Marketing* (third edition) is packed full of interesting, up-to-date case studies from all over the world. It is written in a refreshing style that peppers theory with practical scenarios. It is a tremendous read as the examples bring the book to life.'
— **Alexandra J. Kenyon**, *Chartered Marketer, Centre for Hospitality and Retailing, Leeds Metropolitan University, UK*

'The authors have clearly developed and updated sections to provide a better understanding of how services today conduct their business. Both the "Postcards from Practice" and the "It's in the News" articles are excellent new additions.'
— **David Ratcliffe**, *Senior Lecturer in Marketing, Northampton Business School, UK*

'*Services Marketing* (third edition) is relevant, topical and student friendly. With its in-depth case studies and novel features, "It's in the News" and "Postcards from Practice", it should prove a popular text for lecturers and students.'
— **Isabelle Szmigin**, *Professor of Marketing, Birmingham Business School, University of Birmingham, UK*

'An excellent combination of real-world case studies and services marketing theory. Good for practitioners and students alike.'
— **Simon Kelly**, *Senior Lecturer in Marketing, Sheffield Hallam University, UK*

'This book should be read by all academics, students and practitioners interested in service marketing. It is rich in models, theories and cases and offers an insight into the operations of many different service industries.'
— **Prof Okoso-Amaa**, *Dar es Salaam Business School, Mzumbe University, Tanzania*

'A well-written and accessible text, rigorously underpinned with theory and copious references. I particularly liked the emphasis on small-scale businesses.'
— **Adrian Palmer**, *Professor of Marketing, School of Business and Economics, University of Wales Swansea, UK*

Services Marketing

Text and Cases

Third Edition

Steve Baron
Kim Harris
Toni Hilton

First published 2009 by
PALGRAVE MACMILLAN

Palgrave Macmillan in the UK is an imprint of Macmillan Publishers Limited,
registered in England, company number 785998, of Houndmills, Basingstoke,
Hampshire RG21 6XS.

Palgrave Macmillan in the US is a division of St Martin's Press LLC,
175 Fifth Avenue, New York, NY 10010.

Palgrave Macmillan is the global academic imprint of the above companies
and has companies and representatives throughout the world.

Palgrave® and Macmillan® are registered trademarks in the United States,
the United Kingdom, Europe and other countries.

ISBN-13: 978–0–230–52093–6 paperback
ISBN-10: 0–230–52093–6 paperback

This book is printed on paper suitable for recycling and made from fully
managed and sustained forest sources. Logging, pulping and manufacturing
processes are expected to conform to the environmental regulations of the
country of origin.

A catalogue record for this book is available from the British Library.

A catalog record for this book is available from the Library of Congress.

Contents

List of Figures

List of Tables and Exhibits

Tables

Exhibits

Postcards from Practice

It's in the News!

List of Case Study Figures

Preface to the Third Edition

In the Preface to the second edition, in 2003, we noted how technology and Internet usage had radically changed learning opportunities since the first edition of the book was published in 1995. Now, a further six years on, we acknowledge how the discipline of services marketing has itself progressed significantly in tandem with the increased availability and usage of information and communication technology. Whereas, in the earlier editions, the book may have been slightly unusual with its concentration on people and experiences, the current debates on the service-dominant logic of marketing, with emphasis on operant resources, co-creation of value, relationships and consumer experiences, places it firmly in the mainstream of services marketing and service research.

We are grateful for the feedback on the first two editions from students and fellow lecturers, and from the reviewers of the current edition. The second edition sold well in Australasia, and we now have a third author from New Zealand (Toni Hilton) who has made a major contribution to this edition. We have nearly 14 years experience of using the book with mainly undergraduate and multinational MBA cohorts of students, and that has determined some of the changes we have made in order to enhance the pedagogical aspects.

New Features of the Third Edition

The structure of the book has proved to be robust and has not changed significantly. Nevertheless, there are new chapter headings and significant additions and deletions of content that reflect a move towards a terminology and exposition that is in keeping with the service-dominant logic of marketing. The chapter heading changes are not cosmetic, but are indicative of a different way of thinking about service and services. For example, we believe that a change in chapter title from 'Service Encounters' to 'Customer Interactions in Service' reinforces the notion of customers as co-creators of service value.

Only four case studies have been retained from the second edition, and a further seven have been added. There are three reasons for this. First, some of the features of the deleted case studies were no longer appropriate to customer experiences in 2008–09. These case studies do, however, have good learning elements in them, and are being made available separately on the companion website.

Second, a number of the new case studies are from out of the UK, and so add an international dimension. Third, the new cases acknowledge the choices available to consumers, through technology, more readily. The majority of case studies still have a small-business focus.

Four other features are new to this edition. 'Postcards from Practice' are included in each of the first ten chapters. They are reflections by practitioners on aspects of service as seen from an organisational and work experience perspective. 'It's in the News!' items are included in all eleven chapters. They demonstrate the prevalence and relevance of service issues in our everyday lives as reported by the media. We have chosen items under each heading which we believe are interesting and instructive. From experience, they can be used as introductions to a chapter or topic, or as a kind of mini-case study that stimulates classroom debate. We have also added an extensive glossary to help readers master the terminology associated with this exciting field of study. Finally, we would like to draw your attention to the companion website that accompanies this edition: www.palgrave.com/business/baron.

Acknowledgements

Once again we have received tremendous support during the preparation of this third edition of this book. Most notably we would like to thank those who have contributed a 'postcard from practice' or worked with us on the development of the case studies.

Phil Ashton	Olivia Blaylock	Corina Crisan	Elaine Eades
Graham Eades	Charlotte Fairhurst	Emma Featherstone	Norman Gordan
Neha Gudka	Richard Handley	Yves Hausammann	Emily Hilton
Darryl King	Robert Kingstone	Stuart Lees	Justin Newcombe
Julie Nolan	Lindsay Rocke	Martin Rocke	John Robinson
Sara Simmonds	Chris Storey	Mike Waterston	Sally Waterston
Grant Wilson	Hui Zhong		

To all these people we express our sincere thanks. Finally, we would like to thank our families for their encouragement and support throughout this endeavour.

The authors and publishers are grateful to the following for kindly allowing the use of copyright material: American Marketing Association, publishers of the *Journal of Marketing*, for Figures 6.7, 6.8, 6.9 and Table 11.2; MCB Publishers of the *International Journal of Service Industry Management* for Figure 6.5; Emerald Group publishers of the *Journal of Services Marketing* for Figure 9.2; Sage, publishers of the *Journal of Service Research* for Figure 10.2; *Harvard Business Review* for Figure 10.4; Every effort has been made to contact all the copyright-holders, but if any have been inadvertently overlooked the publishers will be pleased to make the necessary arrangement at the earliest opportunity.

STEVE BARON
KIM HARRIS
TONI HILTON

1

Introduction

Why study services marketing? Why pick up a textbook on services marketing?

There may be a variety of reasons – you are working in a service business, you are representing consumers, you have 'got to' because you are a student, and it is part of your course. Whichever direction you start from, however, we believe that, like us, you will find services marketing a fascinating field of academic study, firmly embedded in the real world.

It is real, because we all *consume* services as part of our everyday life. A day in our life may involve, for example, listening to a favourite radio programme, travelling on a train or bus, visiting the shops and buying a snack at lunchtime, arranging a dental appointment, attending lectures and tutorials, buying a book via the Internet and calling into the pub for a drink in the evening. At work, we may rely on administrative, technical and clerical support services, and come to expect that offices, toilets and other rooms are regularly cleaned. Furthermore, we probably have an opinion on the level of service offered in all these areas, and are quite prepared to share our feelings of satisfaction/dissatisfaction (with the services) with others. When we consume certain types of services on a less frequent basis – for example, going on a package holiday, eating in an expensive restaurant, making a claim on an insurance policy – we are usually highly attuned to the service provided, and perhaps even more likely to express our opinions of the quality of service.

📖 It's in the News! 1.1

Increased Affluence

According to the UK's *Sunday Times* of 24 February 2008,

> ... we are being dubbed as a nation of butlers. How true – the super-rich require a fleet of staff to cater to their increasingly complex needs, and it's gone beyond the traditional nanny, housekeeper and driver. These are mere skeleton staff: now, a new brighter phalanx of personal helpers is assuming the white gloves as well. Pilots, publicists, art dealers and bodyguards have become *de rigueur*, as well as more niche service providers such as fake-eyelash technicians, personal record producers, and jewellery curators.

📖 It's in the News! 1.1   (Continued)

The article goes on to identify other services being employed by affluent consumers.

- Private tutors (art, history, languages – whatever. Does it matter?)
- A super-stylist (for party appearances and private dinners)
- A concierge (sits in your house and sorts your mail when you are away)
- A television crew (someone documenting your life)
- The log man (for £10,000, this Chelsea-based artist will style your fireplace).

Postcard from Practice 1.1

Service Leads to Customer Loyalty

Banking in New Zealand was highly regulated until the mid-1980s. Banks could borrow only at strictly controlled rates and similarly lend only with carefully regulated margins. There was little to differentiate the service of the main banks and their customer bases were stable and therefore ostensibly 'loyal' as there was little incentive to change. However, it was widely accepted that customer service levels were generally poor. With deregulation that all changed. New banking products were available almost overnight and customer service levels were improved enormously in response to the open market. Competition forced a huge change on the banking industry. Customers suddenly had a choice of a wide range of innovative products, many of which could be tailored to their specific needs. They started to move to competitor banks at alarming rates, often for marginal financial benefit, but motivated by the lure of improved service standards and personalised products. Banks started to realise that the 'customers come first' slogan was more than a slogan – it was the reality on which the financial performance of their business rested. They undertook big investments in people, product development and infrastructure.

Source: Richard Handley.

But for many of us, we are not simply service consumers (or customers); we also *provide* service. We are both consumers and providers of services. If you are reading this book, it is likely that you work full-time in a service industry or that you have had some part-time jobs in the service industry. This is a wonderful position from which to appreciate the issues involved with the marketing and management of services. In addition, you may well find that you have played several different service roles. In our own case, for example, although our service job may be described as 'teaching' or 'lecturing', we have played other roles such as researching, student counselling, consulting and editing, with varying degrees of success.

In the course of your study of services marketing, you can, and should, make use of your experiences of consuming and providing services. Your experiences will enable you to be constructively critical of the theory and to add creatively to theory. We believe that in building an understanding of services, and hence of services marketing and management, you should wherever possible draw on experiences and intuitions. In so doing, this ensures a more interactive and lively vehicle for learning.

So our answer to the question 'why study services marketing?' is that it is an invigorating exercise in combining theory and practical knowledge to further an understanding of something which is an important part of life.

If we look at the historical development of services marketing, it has been acknowledged that 'services marketing developed academically because it filled a need in marketing practice'.[1] Service executives persuaded academics that a different approach was required to understand the marketing of services from that used for the marketing of goods. It may not be obvious immediately, but it will soon become apparent that many services are incredibly complex, and provide different challenges for marketing practitioners and academics alike. The complexity is illustrated by a story of a particular service experience and the analysis that follows.

Service Experience Services are experienced and evaluated as a series of processes which, while frequently intangible, leave concrete impressions and memories.

A 'Service' Experience

To introduce many of the features of service provision, and identify the exchange relationships between the service provider organisation and its customers, we start with a story of a service experience. The story is fictional. It is an amalgam of several personal and reported experiences. However, the incidents described in the story should strike a chord with you, and hence provide an understandable scenario for a more general discussion.

To encourage a more purposeful reading of the story, we suggest that you consider the following questions about the nature of the service itself and the service experiences of the main characters.

- What is the service the passengers (the Townsends) are paying for? How might the service be defined? When does the service start and finish?

- Is the service *provision* different for the two passengers (John and Jack Townsend)? Is the service *experience* different for them? To what extent might the service experience be affected by employees of the service providers? By the physical settings in which the service takes place? By other customers (passengers)?

The Story

John Townsend and his son Jack (aged 14) were travelling to Singapore to join John's wife Jane, who was completing a spell as a visiting lecturer at the National

University of Singapore. They had chosen to fly with Singapore Airlines. John had booked the flights through the Internet. He was also very pleased with himself that his websearch had unearthed lots of information about Singapore. In particular, he had been able to book a Sunday 'brunch' at the Raffles Hotel in Singapore for the three of them – an experience a friend had told him not to miss. John had never flown on 'long haul' before. His only experience of a scheduled flight was a British Airways flight to Geneva. Jack had flown on package holidays to Menorca and Crete with the family and definitely did not like flying. The 13-hour flight from Manchester to Singapore was viewed with mixed feelings. John regarded it as part of a wonderful, never likely to be repeated, experience (with the bonus of seeing Jane after three months apart). Jack just wanted to get it over.

They arrived at Manchester Airport's Terminal 1 three hours before the flight time (as instructed on their tickets). The reception hall was very crowded and noisy but it was clear from the information on the handily placed multiple monitors that they should check in at Desk 21. The next problem was actually finding Desk 21. They could see plenty of desks with destination indicators above them, but they could not spot that particular number. An armed security guard was the only airport official around, so they asked him for assistance. He directed them politely to Desk 21. After passing several long queues of passengers with trolleys full of baggage, they were pleasantly surprised to see a small queue of only two passenger groups. The surprise turned to frustration when they were informed that they had mistakenly joined the 'Raffles Class' (i.e., first class) passenger queue – the red carpet should have been the giveaway – and had to join, instead, the much longer economy class queue at Desk 22.

In the queue, John spent the time talking to a couple of Manchester University female students who were flying home to Singapore. He learnt a lot about the types of food and the places to eat, and about which tourist attractions were good value for money (and which were not). Whilst checking in the baggage, John and Jack were asked a number of security-related questions. Although they were the standard practice, the questions added a hijacker dimension to Jack's fear of flying. Finally, they were able to secure plane seats in an aisle seat and adjacent seat in the middle four seats of the plane, which was very important to both of them in view of the length of the flight. Despite his economy class status, John felt quite pleased that he was travelling with an airline that to him was a symbol of exotic travel. Jack could not have cared less.

Baggage successfully despatched, and with over two hours still to wait, they made their way to the main concourse. It was brightly lit with a variety of shops (including, John was surprised to see, a branch of Harrods), located around a central seated area. The seats were arranged so that only about 20 per cent of the passengers could see flight information monitors clearly. Yet passengers needed this information to know when to proceed to passport control. This situation seemed to increase congestion, with passengers frequently vacating their seats to look at the monitors, leaving their partners to spread out luggage to hold on to seats. This clearly irritated many passengers, and John shared a mutual moan about the lack of information with a family travelling to Dubai. John found the hour's wait before proceeding to passport control interminable. Jack, with heavy metal music blasting through his 'iPod', and many friends to chat to on his mobile phone, was unperturbed.

After an uneventful passage through Customs, they entered the departure lounge. There were some tables covered with uncollected crockery and glasses, an expensive coffee bar, a self-service snack bar and several shops, including duty-free outlets. It was very crowded. Passenger information was provided on monitors at various locations in the lounge, hypnotically flashing messages about the departure times and instructions to proceed to 'gates'. Occasional flurries of passenger activity meant that instructions to proceed to appropriate gates had flashed up. Jack, with the common sense of youth, had spotted the two Singaporean students sitting in front of one of the monitors. 'Relax dad,' he said, 'just follow them when they move.'

It turned out to be Gate 2 which was a good ten minutes away, even on the moveable walkway. Through the windows they could see several planes waiting to depart. John was pleased and reassured to see that their plane was one of the biggest. However, when they got on board, although the interior was bigger that any they had seen before – eight seats to each row, and two corridors – the individual space per seat was disappointingly small, particularly for John's 6ft 3in. frame. They were both very impressed with the in-flight entertainment system. Each passenger had individual controls and his/her own monitor on the seat in front. Not only were up-to-date films available for viewing, but the system was interactive! Jack immediately sought out the flight magazine to find out the range of video games available. John soon stopped worrying about where to put his feet as he started to look around at the fellow passengers. There was a mix of families, couples, ages and ethnic groupings, but quite a few empty seats as well. The children of the family in front appeared to be very worldly wise, and were already talking about Changi airport and making plans to 'get one of the free toothbrushes from the toilet before they are all taken'. John mused to himself that he had already experienced so much and yet they had not even started on the flight.

Jack stiffened during the cabin crew's demonstration of emergency procedures, but relaxed visibly when the pilot calmly described the flight route. John began to relax after the complimentary drink and Jack worked out his personalised programme of movie watching. The cabin crew, one man and three women, all very elegantly dressed, were extremely polite and helpful. Nothing was apparently too much trouble. At one stage, they searched the complete economy section looking for a passenger who would be prepared to swap seats with another passenger who wished to sit with a friend. They even found out the English football results at the request of a passenger. Jack decided that he needed to go to the toilet at the very time when the cabin crew had started to serve dinner, but there was no way past the meal trolley for the next 30 minutes. He had to sit and suffer. John and

Jack tucked into the 'Shrimp Newburg', and listened to the co-pilot explain how they could follow the route on their video system. As the pins and needles in his legs increased, John thought enviously of the business-class passengers, not to mention 'Raffles' class passengers, in their spacious seats. When the plane was over Calcutta, he even wished he had paid twice as much for the extra comfort.

Analysing the Experience

Almost all the incidents described in the story could happen to air travellers irrespective of their point of departure or of airline used. Therefore, this is not a story specifically about Manchester Airport or about Singapore Airlines, but describes the feelings and apprehensions of the service customers as well as the facilities offered by the service providers. It contains elements and issues that are common to most types of services (not just air travel). These elements and issues form the content of much of the services marketing academic and practical literature. We start with an examination of three fundamental aspects of services – process, people and physical evidence, the management of which contributes to the success, or otherwise, of the marketing of the services. We then take a different perspective by focusing on the visible and invisible (to the passenger) elements of air transport service provision to highlight issues of relevance to the marketing of all services.

The Process

Shostack, in the early 1980s, affirmed that service is not a thing but a process – 'the process is the product'.[2] Services are processes that occur over time. The very way that the story of John and Jack's flight to Singapore is told emphasises the process elements. 'They entered the concourse, *then* they looked at the information screen, *then* they asked the way to Desk 21, *then* . . . '. The complexity of the service experience can be appreciated very clearly when it is broken down into the many process components. Even what may appear, at first glance, to be a relatively simple service, for example, a gent's barber, can be seen to be quite complex when viewed as a complete process (see Chapter 6). It is always surprising to discover how many distinct process elements there are for a service – try counting the number of clicks on the mouse for a straightforward service by the Internet, such as checking your current account balance using your bank's website.

The fact that a process has many elements can have several implications for service managers.

First, while there may be a 'core' service that the customers are paying for, there are also many 'peripheral' elements to the service. The core service offering is the 'necessary outputs of the organisation which are intended to provide the intangible benefits customers are looking for'. Peripheral services are those which are either 'indispensable for the execution of the core service or available only to improve quality of the service bundle'.[3] In the airport scenario, the

Core Service
The service that customers pay for and frequently comprises the intangible element of the service experience.

Peripheral Service
Service elements that support the delivery of the service paid for. Many peripheral services provide the tangible elements of the service experience.

flight itself is obviously a major component; that is, the means of travelling quickly and safely from Manchester to Singapore. This could be described as the core element in this context. There are, however, a range of extra components of the service which are still highly valued, such as meals and drinks on the plane, in-flight entertainment, and pillows, blankets and toothbrushes for passenger comfort (the peripheral elements). Of course, passengers may not think this way, and may give more weight to some of the peripheral elements than to the core service. How often have you heard people voicing complaints about the food served on a plane or the (lack of) drinks, even though the flight was on time with smooth takeoff and landing? Furthermore, *each separate element* in the process, whether it is core or peripheral, can be a cause of customer (dis)satisfaction.

Second, when does the service begin and end for the customer? For the Townsends, the first contact with the service provider (Singapore Airlines) was via their website. The last contact (for this journey at least) would probably be at Changi airport in Singapore, where a whole new set of services would have been provided. As will be discussed in Chapter 4, certain encounters with the service organisation may be more important than others from the customers' perspective, especially the first encounter! The website has to be easy to use.

Third, the Townsends had a relatively stress-free service experience. It is not unknown, however, for various elements in the flight process to result in service 'failures' – for example, the flight is delayed, the baggage goes missing, the available food on the flight does not correspond with the menu. Passengers, in the main, will understand the reasons for service failures, but will also expect the service providers to 'recover' the situation to their satisfaction. Service organisations study the service process in great detail to ensure that they have sound 'service recovery' strategies in place. Service recovery is a very important aspect of services marketing and is dealt with in both Chapter 6 and Chapter 9.

Service Failure
Dissatisfaction arising from an unanticipated service outcome or performance.

Service Recovery
Steps that a service provider and their contact personnel take to move a customer evaluation of the service from dissatisfaction to satisfaction.

Fourth, unlike physical goods, 'time' cannot be stored and used later. The empty seats on the Manchester to Singapore flight cannot be resold. With processes, appropriate management of supply and demand is crucial to business success. Service organisations, therefore, are often concerned with capacity management, a feature that is discussed and illustrated in Chapter 2.

Finally, the process is not exactly the same for all passengers. The Raffles first-class passengers, for instance, were given different treatment both before and during the flight. They would have faster check-in, a wider choice of food and drinks, more leg room, greater speed of service and so on. The design of a higher level of customisation of service for Raffles passengers relates to the design of the process.

The People

The story highlights the importance of people involved in the service, in terms of their individual behaviour and attitudes, and their interactions with each other. The people in this context are the customers (passengers) and the contact personnel (the people providing the service for John and Jack). There were several different contact personnel involved in the story. John and Jack came into contact with the pilot and co-pilot, the cabin crew, the baggage checkout personnel and the security guard. The latter, although not employed by the airline, is still a contributor to passengers' service experiences. The appearance and manner of contact personnel, as well as the words they actually speak, their 'scripts' (to use a drama analogy), can significantly affect the passengers' overall perception of the service. Their status will also influence the extent to which they can vary the nature of the interaction with the passengers or are constrained by a predetermined script. For example, the baggage checkout employees must go through their set security script even if it is distressing to Jack, whereas the senior cabin crew steward may be allowed to use initiative and improvisation to calm a nervous passenger.

It is a major challenge for many service organisations to train all employees to promote their ideals of customer service, especially if some contact personnel are employed by other companies (e.g., security guards, restaurant staff or cleaners). The issues are covered in more detail in Chapters 7 and 9. The important role played by the contact personnel is emphasised by Bateson,[4] who notes that 'the contact personnel can be a source of differentiation'. This is particularly appropriate with a service such as an airline where, because 'many airlines offer similar bundles of benefits and fly the same planes from the same airports, their only hope of a competitive advantage is from the service level'.

Just as the different personal characteristics of the contact personnel will influence the nature of the service, so too will the different personalities of the customers. The customers typically experiencing a particular service may differ according to characteristics such as age, gender and socio-economic group. The Townsends' fellow passengers tended to be well-off families from many ethnic groups – quite a different mix from those on the package holiday to Crete. Fellow customers in the service setting can clearly influence a service experience. They may be acquainted (e.g. John and Jack) or strangers, so-called 'unacquainted influencers'.[5]

The story of John and Jack Townsend illustrates that *customer perceptions* of a service differ, even if the customers receive the same core and peripheral services. Personal and situational factors govern the service perceptions. John was looking forward to the flight and had planned to make the most of the whole experience. Jack, on the other hand, was nervous about flying and just wanted the flight to be over as soon as possible. Various cognitive, emotional and physiological responses affect their service experience. John believed that a long-haul scheduled flight would be better than a charter flight, had categorised Singapore Airlines as exotic, and both he and Jack had been reassured by the size of the plane. John felt frustrated by the lack of available information (and thus the lack of control) in the departure lounge. Jack, although becoming increasingly anxious by virtue of security checks and guards, was happy to sit and listen to

Service Scripts
These are frequently used to standardise the customer experience by ensuring that contact personnel know what behaviours are expected of them. Some service scripts specify words as well as behaviours to be used when interacting with customers.

Customer Perceptions
Customer views and opinions.

personal music in the lounges. Both were affected by the lack of space on the plane. In John's case, it was proving very uncomfortable. On a related issue, customer *expectations* of service can vary. The Townsends' expectations stemmed from previous flight experiences, Singapore Airlines advertisements and website, and Jane's account of her flight. In contrast, the Singapore student seasoned travellers had far more experience with the airline on which to form their expectations. Customer expectations and perceptions of services are key components of the measures of customer satisfaction and service quality; they are covered in detail in Chapter 8.

From the above, it can be seen that, unlike physical goods that can often be mass-produced and standardised, services will always vary because of the people element. No two coffees will be served exactly the same, even by the same cabin crew member. No two customers will interpret the crew member's manner or demeanour in exactly the same way. No two cabin crew members will have responded to their training in exactly the same way. Of course, part of the variation in services is due to the customer's participation in the service, either physically (lifting baggage on to the scales, walking to the correct gate) or verbally (stating the requirement to sit in a non-smoking area, ordering the flight meal). Customers help *produce*, and can even *create* the service, as well as *consume* it.

The Physical Evidence

By physical evidence, we mean the exterior and the interior environment to the service setting and the equipment and technology that customers may encounter in their dealings with the service provider. Although the core service for the Townsends – quick, safe transport from Manchester to Singapore – is essentially intangible, the story clearly shows that there are many tangible aspects that may affect their perceptions of the total service experience. The exterior and the interior environmental dimensions of the service would include the ambient conditions of the airport and aeroplane (temperature, air quality, music, noise etc.), the utilisation of space (equipment, layout, furnishings) as well as signs, symbols and artefacts. These elements make up what has been labelled the 'servicescape'.[6] In our story, the Townsends noticed noise and heat at the airport and the lack of signage and seating arrangements at the terminal. The lack of space inside the plane itself affected both the passengers and the cabin crew. The service provider has a great deal of control over this part of the service package. For example, designing individual, interactive entertainment systems for passengers with monitors on the seat in front gives the passengers more control and improves their flight experience. Airlines also recognise the importance of tangible mementoes for the passengers to take away with them to remind them of the occasion, for example in-flight magazines, toothbrushes and printed meal menus. These are often determinants of repeat purchase. In Chapter 6, we

Customer Expectations
The ways in which customers anticipate the service performance and outcomes.

Servicescape
The physical built environment in which service encounters take place.

look at the design of the physical evidence of services as well as the design of the service process.

The equipment and technology which the Townsends encountered include the Internet, an in-flight entertainment system and moving walkways, each of which have been designed to operate independently of any contact persons. They are examples of technology-based services[7] that were unavailable until the 1990s. These forms of self-service are of great interest to all service providers, as they increase hours of business (e.g., ATMs, 'pay at the pump' petrol/gas stations, flight ticket machines), and may reduce the inherent (human) variability of the service provider. John and Jack are more likely to take notice of other equipment in the servicescape if it does not work as it should. Broken baggage return conveyor belt systems cause delays and a lot of ill feeling.

Technology-based Services
Services that rely more heavily on customers interacting with machines than with contact personnel.

Visible and Invisible Elements of Services

The extended service experience of the Townsends is determined by the elements that are visible to them (e.g., the behaviour of a contact person, or the layout of the aeroplane) and those which are invisible to them (e.g., the staff training programmes, the computerisation of the baggage handling system, the catering preparation). Using the analogy of a service being like a drama performance,[8] the visible elements are 'front-stage' whereas the invisible elements are 'back-stage'.

Front-stage
Service elements that are visible to customers.

Back-stage
Service elements that are invisible to customers and are frequently undertaken by non-contact personnel.

The elements that are visible to John and Jack are essentially people and physical evidence as demonstrated above. However, it is their *interactions* with people and the physical evidence that determine the service experience. They engage in interpersonal interactions with each other and with other customers (e.g., students in the queue, family from Dubai in the main concourse). These are known collectively as *customer-to-customer interactions*. They engage in interpersonal interactions with the many contact personnel – *customer–employee* interactions. They engage in interactions with the physical environment, equipment and technology.

The visible elements (people and physical evidence) are common to most services (hospitals, education, restaurants, hotels, sporting occasions, retail outlets, banks, package holidays, hairdressers etc.), and, likewise, the resulting interactions are determinants of the customer experience in these services, albeit with varying degrees of relative importance. Chapter 4 is devoted to an understanding of customer interactions in services. It also highlights the importance of efforts made by service providers to control the interactions. With customer-to-customer interactions, for example, most managerial emphasis has been on reducing the possibility of negative exchanges between one customer and another. This can be achieved by, for example, allocating 'quiet' carriages on trains for passengers who do not wish to be disturbed by other passengers carrying out conversations on their mobile (cell) phones. Some strategies have been put forward, however, to encourage positive interactions by 'rewarding' customers who give useful advice to other customers.[9] A resulting, pleasant conversation with a fellow traveller is both satisfying and makes the time pass more quickly.

The invisible elements largely support the service process as described above. Although the invisible components are not valued directly by customers, they are recognised by writers and managers alike as being important components of the service package.[10] Airport and airline services spend huge sums of money on improving and enhancing computerised systems and other technology in order to move passengers more efficiently through the process. (For example, Terminal 5, in London's Heathrow airport, opened in 2008, is reputed to have cost £4.2 billion.) Jack, who wanted to get the 'ordeal' over with as quickly as possible, would no doubt appreciate the management concentration on the back-stage.

The language used in understanding and writing about services, and services marketing, employs two metaphors – the factory metaphor and the drama/theatre metaphor, each of which relates to different goals of a service organisation. If the goal is efficiency (probably with a concentration on the invisible elements of a service operation) then service is likened to a factory, with an emphasis on inputs and outputs to the process. If, however, the goal is the customer 'experience' (probably with a concentration on the visible elements – the people and the setting), then service is likened to a theatrical production, with an emphasis on the performance. What may be particularly exasperating to the people charged with the marketing and management of services is that a goal of efficiency may suit one customer (e.g., Jack), but not another. John, for example, may prefer more of an experience to remember, savouring every moment. Service goals and the use of metaphors are considered in Chapter 3.

The Structure of the Book

The story has provided specific examples of many of the issues and key areas of services marketing. Clearly, a single scenario will not address all the issues. However, the story and our brief discussion of the elements that make up the service experience provide a useful starting point for explaining the structure of the remainder of the book.

In Chapter 2, we set the context by examining the ways in which services can be defined and the potential range of application of services marketing theory. As will be seen, it is not just businesses that refer to themselves as 'services businesses' that can make use of the theory. The importance of services in many economies is increasing rapidly and some national and global statistics are provided to emphasise the scope of development of the service economy. Some fundamental building blocks of the theory – characteristics of services, perceived risk of services and the services marketing mix – are introduced. All can be related back to the story above, but clearly have widespread applications, which will be illustrated with examples from a range of services. The chapter also charts the evolution of services marketing as an academic sub-discipline and outlines the key elements of the service-dominant logic of marketing, a twenty-first century approach to marketing that underpins our concentration on people and, in particular, customer and consumer experiences.

The use of metaphors in services marketing is well recognised by academics and practitioners alike. The two most common metaphors for services are 'factory' and 'drama/theatre'. With the former, we happily use expressions such as 'service delivery', 'service productivity', 'efficiency' and 'process'. With the latter, we talk of 'service performance', 'roles and scripts' (for employees and customers), 'front- and back-stage' and 'service setting'. Both metaphors are helpful in understanding services and providing a language of communication. In Chapter 3, we explore the use of the metaphors in some detail, especially relating to the service goals (to mix metaphors!). We firmly believe that the metaphor usage is important in constructing how service is perceived by customers and service organisations (is the service goal efficiency or performance?), but equally, we are aware of its limitations.

Our airline passengers interacted with contact personnel, the built environment (represented by the airport and the aeroplane) and with other passengers. They benefited from efficient, but invisible, service elements such as flight meal preparation and computerised reservation systems. Their encounter with the service was for a finite period. These features are common to many services. In Chapter 4, we concentrate on customer interactions in services and their central role in the marketing of services. The personal, situational, cognitive, emotional and physiological factors peculiar to particular customers are relevant here, and affect the *content* of the service encounter. Interpersonal service encounters are extremely important, but the Internet in particular has rapidly increased the need to learn more about technology-based service encounters.

Service Encounter
Occurs when customers directly interact with any aspect of the service delivery system.

In the late 1990s and early 2000s, there has been a great interest, by practitioners and academics, in providing holistic service *experiences* for consumers. In the story, we see, for example, that John was expecting more than a routine flight between two destinations, and also that the flight was perhaps only a component of a never-to-be-repeated overall travel experience. In other contexts, such as shopping mall[11] and store[12] design, the intended consumer experience is paramount in planning the setting and activities. There are even claims that the service economy is being replaced by an experience economy.[13] Chapter 5 builds on the drama/theatre metaphor to explore the consumer experience.

The factory metaphor emphasises service as a process. The design of service processes is covered in Chapter 6, with a special focus on service blueprinting. This approach ensures that the invisible elements supporting service delivery are understood and fully integrated. We have found that the service blueprint is not only integral to service design and positioning, but it also provides a useful visual tool for creative service ideas.

In Chapter 7, we explicitly acknowledge the *people* aspects of services, particularly the roles of the contact personnel. As the story demonstrates, customers (passengers) may make contact with several people who are providing the service, some of whom are more empowered than others to improvise, but all of whom should, as far as the company is concerned, be offering passengers the service which is promised. This represents a great challenge to most service organisations, large or small. Finally, theory and practice are brought together through the discussion of the elements of a research instrument, SERV*OR, which companies can use to measure service orientation: Are they really structured to provide good, or even excellent service?

John and Jack Townsend each had their own prior expectations of air travel service. On meeting Jane in Singapore, each could recount his actual perceptions of that same service. What did they think about the quality of service? Were they satisfied with the service? Or even delighted? Did their views differ? If their expectations were exceeded, it is likely that they would be satisfied and would give a high-quality verdict. Service quality and customer satisfaction are recognised as important service output measures. To increase service quality and/or customer satisfaction, within an appropriate budget, is normally part of the mission of a service organisation. Chapter 8 examines the current work and debates on service quality and customer satisfaction, and looks at the models that are based on 'gaps' between customers' expectations and subsequent perceptions of a service.

Given Jane's working relationship in Singapore, there is a possibility that the Townsends may visit Singapore again in the future. Both Manchester Airport and Singapore Airlines would wish them to travel with them again. In other words, they wish to retain them as customers. A concentration on customer retention, through a marketing policy which merges marketing, customer service and quality elements, is termed 'relationship marketing'. This is covered in Chapter 9 and builds on the material in earlier chapters, particularly Chapters 7 and 8.

Implicit in the management and marketing of services is the desire for the organisation to make a profit (or break even, in the case of not-for-profit services) and to achieve certain levels of productivity. Perhaps surprisingly though, there remains limited explicit reference in the services marketing literature to the issues of service profitability and productivity. Chapter 10 looks at work in this area.

Finally, in Chapter 11, we look forward and outline some potential futures and associated research issues. We are made aware regularly of the interest in services marketing by the number of students at undergraduate and postgraduate level who undertake dissertations in the field. This chapter contains ideas for such work.

The Relationship between Theory and Practice

New to this edition is the inclusion of two features that highlight the everyday relevance of services marketing theory for practitioners and customers alike: 'postcards from practice' and 'It's in the news!'. Our purpose is to demonstrate the pervasive nature of services within our daily lives and assist readers to draw upon their own experiences to make sense of theories discussed within this text. We hope to encourage readers to become more critically aware of the good and bad service practices they encounter and therefore be more confident when determining managerial responses to improve service practice. In essence that is the philosophy behind this text: drawing upon personal understandings of how customers evaluate their experiences to learn how organisations might best respond managerially.

Characteristics of Case Studies in the Book

The book has 11 case studies. The case studies enable practice, theory and personal experience to be integrated. They are different from, but complement the case studies that are in many of the other textbooks on services marketing. Most cases in this book share the characteristics outlined below.

Small-scale Operators

First, the majority of the case studies describe the issues and concerns that affect *small-scale* service operators that are generally neglected in the wider services marketing literature. Although these businesses may not make such a significant financial contribution to the service economy as the large-scale operators frequently cited in the literature (e.g., banks, building societies, insurance agencies, telecommunications organisations, hotel chains), they often make a significant social contribution to the welfare of the communities in which they operate.[14]

The social role performed by the services covered in this book is an important theme running through the cases. As Czepiel *et al.* point out: 'Service encounters are a form of human interaction important not only to their direct participants (clients and providers) and the service organizations that sponsor them, but also to society as a whole.'[15]

Human Involvement in the Service Experience

The services selected involve a high level of human interaction. Most commonly this consists of interaction between contact personnel and customers, but it may also be between fellow customers during the service experience. This perspective enables us to focus on the whole range of problems faced by service managers struggling to control human involvement in the service delivery process. The human involvement may be facilitated by increased consumer accessibility to information and communication technologies. Solomon in Czepiel *et al.* uses

quotations from service managers to illustrate the unpredictability and importance of human exchanges in the service experience in their article on service
encounters.[16]

> In a service business, you're dealing with something that is primarily delivered by peo-
> ple to people. Your people are as much of your product in the consumer's mind as
> any other attribute of the service. People's performance day in and day out fluctuates
> up and down. Therefore, the level of consistency that you can count on and try to
> communicate to the consumer is not a certain thing.

The cases illustrate the importance of the development of long-term personal
relationships to the continued success of many service operations.

Easily Replicated Format

Although reading, studying and analysing written case studies provides an effective means for matching theory and practice, it is not the same as actively
studying a real service organisation. We have found that undergraduate and postgraduate students can gain enormous benefits from *writing their own case study*
of a small service business. Indeed, three of the case studies in this book were
written by student groups we have supervised in the past three years.

An in-depth study of a real (small) service organisation can often be achieved
over a period of two months or so, and any interviews with the service
owners/managers can be guided by the checklist of questions below (Table 1.1).
We highly recommend it.

Table 1.1   Checklist for gathering suitable information from owners/managers of small service
businesses

History of the business
When was the business founded?
By whom?
How has it developed/changed?
Location(s)?

Staffing
How many?
Who?
Personal details; age, qualifications, experience, attitudes/beliefs?

Nature of the business
What sort of business are you in?
How do you define the service you offer?
Who are your competitors?

Location
If important, collect maps, diagrams.

Physical environment
Ask to look around 'outlet' of interest (front- and back-stage).

Table 1.1 (Continued)

___

Method of payment
How do customers pay for the services?
What variety of methods are offered?

Making contact with customers
How do you make contact with new customers; advertising, promotion, PR?
How do you retain contact with existing customers?

Relationships (other than with customers)
What other parties do you deal with; suppliers, accountants, agencies, societies?
What was in your diary over the last month? Refer to key telephone/fax numbers, addresses,
    email, etc.

Invisible elements
Typical transactions with business associates?
What equipment has to be purchased? Why?
How are records kept?
Try to obtain flow diagram from first customer contact to final purchase.

Peripheral services
What else is offered on-site to improve overall service?
Any examples of special services offered to particular customers?

Customers (1)
Who are the typical customer variations?
If I wished to become a customer, how would I go about it? (*repeats, but important*). How do
    you build up good relationships with customers?
Which customers are most likely to repeat buy?
Can you give examples of where your service exceeded/did not meet customer
    expectations?

Customers (2)
Describe some examples of staff interactions with customers
(a) incidents that went well
(b) incidents that went badly for whatever reason.

Customers (3)
Describe some positive/negative incidents of customers interacting with other customers

(a) conversations
(b) altercations
(c) cooperations

How do they affect the business?

Contact personnel
How are they trained/prepared for the job?
How much initiative can/should they use? Give examples.
What are the attributes of a very good member of your staff?
What are the minimum requirements of a member of staff?

Recovery
Give examples of an incident which was going wrong, but which was recovered to the
    customer's satisfaction (more than one if possible).

General
How do you define service quality in the context of your business?
Do you have a mission statement and/or company objectives?

___

Overall Learning Outcomes

Having read the chapters and undertaken the case studies, you will be able to

1. *Identify the theoretical aspects of services marketing.* In particular, you will be able to

   - critically evaluate the theoretical contributions to services marketing
   - interrelate consumer, customer and provider perceptions of services.

2. *Understand how theory translates into service practice.* In particular, you will be able to

   - choose appropriate services marketing frameworks to analyse a service business
   - apply flexibility in your study of new and developing service practices.

Discussion Questions and Exercises

1. Think of three services you have used in the last seven days. What are the *processes* involved with these services from your (customer) perspective?
2. Name two services where companies have attempted to replace contact personnel with machines. To what extent has the changeover been successful?
3. Why is physical evidence important in services?
4. In what type of services might it be an option to make the invisible elements of the service more visible?
5. What small service businesses are run by members of your family or by friends?

Notes and References

1. Berry, L. L. and Parasuraman, A., 'Building a New Academic Field: The Case of Services Marketing,' *Journal of Retailing,* 69(1), Spring 1993, pp. 13–60.
2. Shostack, G. L., 'Breaking Free from Product Marketing,' *Journal of Marketing,* 41, April 1977, pp. 73–80.
3. Carman, J. M. and Langeard, E., 'Growth Strategies for Service Firms,' *Strategic Management Journal,* 1, 1980, pp. 7–22.
4. Bateson, J. E. G., *Managing Services Marketing: Text and Readings,* 2nd edn., Dryden Press, London, 1992.
5. McGrath, M. A. and Otnes, C., 'Unacquainted Influencers: When Strangers Interact in the Retail Setting,' *Journal of Business Research,* 32, 1995, pp. 261–72.
6. Bitner, M. J., 'Servicescapes: The Impact of Physical Surroundings on Customers and Employees,' *Journal of Marketing,* 56, April 1992, pp. 57–71.
7. Meuter, M. L., Ostrom, A. L., Roundtree, R. I. and Bitner, M. J., 'Self-Service Technologies: Understanding Customer Satisfaction with Technology-Based Service Encounters,' *Journal of Marketing,* 64, July 2000, pp. 50–64.
8. Grove, S. J. and Fisk, R. P., 'The Dramaturgy of Services Exchange: An Analytical Framework for Services Marketing,' in L. L. Berry, G. L. Shostack and G. D. Upah (eds), *Emerging Perspectives on Services Marketing,* American Marketing Association, Chicago, 1983.
9. Pranter, C. A. and Martin, C. L., 'Compatibility Management: Roles in Service Performances,' *Journal of Services Marketing,* 5, Spring 1991, pp. 43–53.
10. The 'servuction' model of service delivery systems explicitly recognises 'invisible' components: see Langeard, E., Bateson, J., Lovelock, C. and Eiglier, P., *Marketing of Services: New Insights from Consumers and Managers,* report no. 81–104, Marketing Science Institute, Cambridge, Mass., 1981.
11. The Mills Corporation, for example, wishes to draw consumers into its malls 'who are not only ready to shop, but are also ready to have an experience'. http://www.millscorp.com/
12. See, for example, ImagiCorps, and its offer of 'Retail Theater'. http://www.imagicorps.com/retail.html.

13. Pine, B. J. II and Gilmore, J. H., *The Experience Economy: Work is Theater and Every Business a Stage,* HBS Press, Boston, Mass., 1999.
14. Baron, S., Leaver, D., Oldfield, B. M. and Cassidy, K., *Independent Food and Grocery Retailers: Attitudes and Opinions in the Year 2000,* Manchester Metropolitan University, Manchester, June 2000.
15. Czepiel, J. A., Solomon, M. R. and Surprenant, C. F. (eds), *The Service Encounter: Managing Employee/Customer Interaction in Service Businesses,* Lexington Books, Lexington, Mass., 1985.
16. Ibid.

2

The Contemporary Context

Learning Objectives

Overall Aim of the Chapter

To provide an overview of, and background to, services in modern economies, and the basic building blocks of services marketing research.

In particular, the *chapter objectives* are

- to emphasise the economic importance and growth of services in advanced economies

- to provide a summary of the evolution of services marketing thought and draw attention to the current debate around service-dominant logic

- to demonstrate the scope and characteristics of service provision

- to introduce the management implications arising from the characteristics associated with services along with the services marketing mix.

Services Marketing Mix
The 3 additional Ps: People, Process and Physical Evidence making 7Ps in total.

In the previous chapter, through use of the story, we identified a number of important components of a service experience. Interest in these components has resulted in research and an established body of knowledge of services marketing. A key feature of much of the research has been the clear link between theory and practice. We now set the context for the more detailed study of theory and practice in services marketing.

This chapter is divided into four sections. First, we look at *the importance of services* within many of today's economies. Second, we examine the *evolution of the sub-discipline of services marketing* over time and reflect on its current status. Third, we consider the *scope of service provision* and the *characteristics* upon which the study of services marketing is founded. Finally, we introduce the *management implications* that arise from the characteristics associated with services.

Economic Importance of Services

In many advanced economies, consumers spend more on services than on tangible goods. Depending on definitions, service industries account for around 75 per cent of gross domestic product, and the labour force, in the United States, Western Europe, Australasia and Japan. In Hong Kong, the figure is nearer to 85 per cent.

Here are some statistics that present a perspective on just how important services are:

- One of the biggest employers in the United Kingdom – the Royal Mail Group – employs around 193,000 people;
- 80 per cent of employees within the United Kingdom work in service industries and one in every five UK workers are employed within the public sector;
- The tourism industry in the United Kingdom employs 2 million people; more than agriculture, coal mining, steel, car manufacturers, aircraft, food production and textiles together;
- The 'take-away' sandwich industry contributes more to UK net gross domestic product than farming;
- On a global level, during 2007 PriceWaterhouseCoopers employed 146,000 people in 766 offices across 150 countries and earned in excess of US$ 25 billion.[1]

Postcard from Practice 2.1

When do Patients become Customers? Marketing in the UK National Health Service

The UK National Health Service is the world's largest publicly funded health service, originally based, from its inception in 1948, on the ideal that good healthcare should be available to all. Most NHS health services are free at the point of use for all 60,000,000 UK residents. The service employs more than 1.5 million staff, and at the time of writing this is the fourth largest employer in the world – only the Chinese People's Liberation Army, the Wal-Mart supermarket chain and the Indian Railways directly employ more staff.

The service is basically funded from national taxation and in 2007/8 it cost £90 billion. In recent years the UK Government has announced its intention to drive up quality of services, improve choice for patients, reduce waiting lists for operations and generally improve efficiency in the service, and there have been a range of initiatives to support this. Two of these are 'Patient Choice' and 'Payment by results'.

'Patient Choice' has been expanded so that patients referred by their local General Practitioner to see a specialist in a hospital are able to choose for themselves where they receive that treatment, and in many cases book that appointment themselves directly using the 'choose and book' system. In order to exercise choice, patients will need to have accurate information about services available to them, and the 'NHS Choices' website provides some relatively minimal information to help patients to compare hospitals, including comments from patients about the services they have received.

'Payment by results' is also expected to have a major impact on the NHS. Historically, hospitals were paid according to 'block contracts'. The money paid to the hospitals providers by the primary care trusts (commissioners) was broadly based on historical data, that is how many such operations were carried out the previous year (with estimates about any likely changes) and how much this had cost the hospitals to deliver. There was no incentive for hospitals to increase the numbers of patients treated: quite the opposite, as in most cases they would receive no more funds. Payment by results aimed to reduce waiting times and increase the amount of work done, by linking payment directly to the actual 'care episodes' completed. There would be one 'tariff' for every specific type of treatment, based on the national average cost – so if it had traditionally cost a hospital more than this, it would need to find a way to reduce costs by being more efficient. Fundamentally, money would only come with patients.

The combination of the patient choice agenda and payment by results has meant that hospitals, for perhaps the first time, have to address the issue of marketing their services – a concept which to some health professionals is difficult to accept.

Hospitals have to now involve themselves in gathering market intelligence, about customers and also about their competitors (other hospitals and private providers). They have to find out what their patients think of their services, and what their expectations are. They have to consider their organisation's reputation, and branding issues. Customer service training is now on the agenda. They need to understand the reasons why patients choose particular hospitals; Transport links? Reputation? Car parking? Recommendation of the local GP? Hospital website? Cleanliness? Waiting times? They may also need to re-consider which services they offer.

In 2007, David Thorp, director of research and information at the Chartered Institute of Marketing, in a master class to the Association of Healthcare Communicators, commented on the reluctance of hospitals to understand what marketing is and what it can do. 'If NHS managers do not understand how marketing can help, they are working with one arm tied behind their backs . . . to be commercial they have to put the patient first; to do this means understanding patients needs and delivering on them . . .'

Source: Elaine Eades.

There has been a substantial growth in services in the last two decades. Healthcare services, business services, personal services, legal services, amusement and recreation services, accounting, engineering and architectural services, automotive services and hospitality services have grown at approximately double the rate of other industries since the mid-1980s.[2] Some of the reasons for the growth in many countries are:

- *Deregulation*: Major service industries such as legal services, financial services and transport services have been deregulated, resulting in increases in the numbers and types of service providers in these sectors.

- *Increased affluence*: In general, people with more disposable income consider purchasing services previously undertaken in the home such as ironing, cooking, cleaning, children's parties. This has resulted in increases in service businesses offering dry-cleaning, takeaway meals, domestic cleaning and the generation of novel ways to provide birthday party experiences out of the home.[3]

- *Increased free time*: People fill their time with leisure pursuits, travel, 'surfing the net' and so on. David Lloyd Leisure, for example, opened up 32 clubs across the United Kingdom between 1995 and 2000 claiming that the 'unique club environment has been specifically designed to offer a wide range of sporting and social activities to ensure that members enjoy their most valuable leisure time'.

- *Changing demographics*: The increase in both the number of working women and the number of people aged over 55 years in the United Kingdom has resulted in the increase of specific services which recognise the changes; for example, nanny/baby-minding services and pre-school nurseries, off-peak holiday packages and social activities such as 'bingo'.

- *Information and digital technology in the home*: Service companies have set up or have attained a presence on the Internet in recognition of the potential for online service purchases made at home. The Internet can assist customers to search for and compare products or services they seek. Many companies, such as airlines, provide discounts for purchases made through the Internet. Retailers, in particular, are keen to seek opportunities of shopping from home. Some retailers have used the Internet to extend their store-based business. For example, by 2007 online grocery sales for Tesco, the UK Grocery retailer, exceeded £1 billion. At that point Tesco had 850,000 active online customers placing more than 250,000 orders per week delivered by 1860 vans operating out of 294 stores.[4] New retail businesses have emerged that use the Internet as their only means of selling products to consumers. A good example is Amazon, launched in 1994. A further category of Internet-based service organisation has developed where the purpose of the business is to provide a new marketplace where buyers and sellers gain direct access to each other. eBay would be the leading global example here although there are others such as TradeMe in New Zealand. Increased leisure time, combined with increased availability of the Internet, has spawned the development of virtual worlds such as online multi-user games and Second Life as well as providing a new 'venue' for social networking (FaceBook, MySpace, YouTube). Our dependence upon the Internet has resulted in the development of new retail businesses that provide the Internet as a service: the Internet café.

📖 **It's in the News! 2.1**

Services in the Digital World

According to the *Chicago Tribune* (8 February 2008),

When David Hui found himself stranded in the middle of nowhere on a broken-down Amtrak train on the East Coast [of the USA], he called for help – to his personal assistant in India. Working over the Internet, the assistant figured out where Hui was, based on the last street signs Hui had seen from the train, then tracked down a rental car to come pick him up. In the end, the train started moving again before the car arrived, but Hui, 30, was no less impressed by the effort on his behalf from half a world away.

'I've been surprised at how much personal ownership they take to make my tasks a success,' said the Cambridge, Mass-based management consultant, who for the past year and a half has been a client of Get Friday, a Bangalore personal and small-business services outsourcing company. 'They go the extra mile for me.'

In the latest twist on globalization, it is now possible to hire a personal assistant – in India – to take care of just about anything you don't have time to do and that can be accomplished via phone or the Internet. Need your daughter's birthday party organized? A snowplow to clear your driveway? Your resume and cover letter sent out to potential employers? How about a romantic vegan dinner for two delivered to your home, complete with live music? A personal assistant working from a cubicle in Bangalore or Hyderabad now can arrange all that and a whole lot more, and not just for the long-pampered uber-rich but for a much bigger market: America's exhausted middle class.

'Anything that's illegal or in bad taste we will not do. Other than that, bring it on,' said T. T. Venkatash, a senior manager for Get Friday.

The service economy can be seen to be very important, but even so, Pine and Gilmore[5] see it being replaced by an 'experience economy'. They say that consumers of the twenty-first century are looking to purchase experiences, and that businesses should be geared up to selling experiences. Their argument is that, over time, economies have moved from primarily trading commodities to primarily selling manufactured goods, to primarily selling services, to a position where businesses selling experiences will be the profitable ones.

They use the commodity, the coffee bean, to illustrate their point. People who harvest and sell coffee beans on the futures market receive the equivalent of 2 cents a cup. Once the beans are ground and packaged by the manufacturers, the customer pays the equivalent of 5–25 cents per cup at the grocery store. If the ground beans are brewed in the most basic of cafes and served to customers, the cost per cup moves up to, say, 50 cents per cup. If the coffee is served in a five-star restaurant or an idyllic location, the price per cup may be $5, or even as much as $15, in, for example, one of the cafes in St Mark's Square in

Venice. They argue that customers will gladly pay the $15, because an hour-long stay in an open-air café in Venice represents an 'experience' well worth the extra money.

Whether you accept their argument or not, more and more retail and service businesses are claiming that they provide experiences for consumers. Belinda Earl, on being appointed Chief Executive of Debenhams, a UK Department Store chain, claimed that she wanted to boost 'interactive services with cus-tomers... by creating different experiences for customers in the store, such as offering makeovers'. As a result of creating the experiences, she expects to 'persuade women to purchase six times more products, stay with us longer, and spend more'.[6] In the United States, the Mills Corporation, which develops shop-ping malls, claims on its website that 'creating memorable experiences' is the key element of their competitive advantage. We will return to this theme in Chapter 5.

The Evolution of the Sub-discipline of Services Marketing

In an article entitled 'Tracking the Evolution of the Services Marketing Litera-ture', written in 1993, Fisk, Brown and Bitner[7] identified three distinct stages in the evolution of services marketing. This list has recently been extended to include developments during the last 15 years[8]:

1. the 'Crawling Out' stage which took place prior to 1980;

2. the 'Scurrying About' stage between 1980 and 1986;

3. the 'Walking Erect' stage from 1986 to 1992;

4. the 'Making Tools'stage from 1993 to 2000;

5. the 'Creating Language' stage from 2000 to now;

6. the 'Building Communities' stage which is associated with future develop-ments.

Each of the stages will be explained, so that you can evaluate the research work and practice in services marketing in the context of its evolutionary stage. We also draw your attention to the emergence of what is called the Service-dominant logic which we believe will shape the future development of the discipline of marketing as well as services marketing.

Crawling out

In the 'crawling out' stage, discussion centred around the need for a separate body of literature to deal with the specific problems of the service sector. Papers considered whether there was anything significantly different about operating a service business that would necessitate a distinct body of marketing theory. To address this issue, writers clearly had to take into consideration the full range of marketing theories that existed and reflect on their usefulness in a service context. Specific areas of marketing theory were examined and found to be insufficient or inappropriate when it came to handling service sector problems and concerns. Donnelly,[9] for example, highlighted the differences between the marketing 'channels' used for services and those used for physical goods and implications for marketing strategy.

Criticisms were aimed at the existing discipline of marketing with its 'product' orientation. 'Can corporate banking services really be marketed according to the same basic blueprint that made TIDE a success?', asked Shostack in her provocative article in 1977.[10] She criticised traditional marketing for being 'myopic' in having failed to create relevant paradigms for the service sector. In response to these criticisms, marketing traditionalists argued that service organisations did not need a separate body of theory, and that existing marketing theories could, and should, be applied to service organisations. They argued that services could not be defined tightly enough to deserve special treatment and, in many instances, were so closely linked to the physical product that they needed to be considered as part of the 'offer' when developing marketing strategy. For example, the after-sales service guarantee supplied with a motor car could be valued as highly as the interior design features of the car itself.

Scurrying about

In the 'scurrying about' stage between 1980 and 1985 the quantity of academic literature produced about services marketing increased considerably. Efforts were made to classify services more clearly[11] and attention focused heavily on the crucial issue of managing quality in service operations. Zeithaml, Berry and Parasuraman developed their pioneering 'gaps model' of service quality,[12] which highlighted the importance of efforts made to assess quality in services. Other topics emerged as being particularly important to the management of service organisations, including a better understanding of the components of the 'service encounter' (i.e., the interpersonal aspects of the service), 'relationship marketing' and 'internal marketing'. For the first time textbooks on services marketing began to be produced, establishing it more firmly as a legitimate field of academic study.

Booms and Bitner[13] developed their expanded 'marketing mix' for services that took into account the distinctive characteristics of services: intangibility, inseparability, heterogeneity and perishability. The 'marketing mix' is the term traditionally used to describe a specific set of tools available to managers to help them shape the offer they present to consumers. McCarthy[14] presented one of the most commonly used 'mixes' in 1960; the 'four Ps', highlighting Product, Price, Promotion and Place decisions as being the most critical areas for consideration. Booms and Bitner added three more Ps to this original mix to make it

Intangibility
The inability of services to be seen, heard, smelt, touched or tasted in the same way that products are used or consumed.

Inseparability
Consumption by the customer at the same time as the service is produced, performed or delivered by contact personnel.

Heterogeneity
The variable nature of service performance or delivery by contact personnel.

Perishability
Services cannot be stored and are therefore time-sensitive and subject to peaks and troughs in demand.

more appropriate to services: People, Process and Physical Evidence. This became the *services marketing mix* :

- Product
- Price
- Promotion
- Place
- People
- Process
- Physical evidence.

The relevance and importance of people, process and physical evidence is re-emphasised every time consumers are asked to relate critical incidents of services (memorably good incidents, or memorably bad incidents) in their own words. Exhibit 2.1 provides examples of critical incidents, related by mature students. They are typical of all the stories provided by the student group. For consumers, good/bad experiences with people, processes, and physical evidence often dominate their evaluations of the experience.

Exhibit 2.1   Critical Service Incidents Described by Consumers

Memorably Good Incidents:

Last year, we booked a discount holiday – an all-inclusive trip to Kenya – 10 days before we were due to go, via teletext. I booked over the telephone, and within 24 hours had tickets, luggage labels, books on Kenya and safaris, complimentary passes to local places, a travel bag, and all the information we could possibly have wanted. The travel company phoned four days before we went, to check everything was OK. The holiday service was absolutely excellent. The travel company sent us a questionnaire when we returned, and a 'welcome home' pack. We have raved about it ever since.

On arriving at the restaurant, we were offered seats at the bar to wait for a table. Within 10 minutes we were shown to one by an exceptionally good waitress, who went through the menu with us before getting more drinks and taking orders. Both the starter and main course arrived within five minutes, and were of superb quality. The waitress regularly checked that we were OK, fetching drinks, etc., as and when required. The overall experience was a pleasurable one, from entering the restaurant to taking the mints on the way out.

Memorably Bad Incidents

Prior to going on holiday, I had my purse stolen, with all the usual cards inside. I went to my bank branch with my cheque book (which had not been stolen) and thought that they would allow me to draw out some money from my account.

In order to save myself some embarrassment, I first checked at the enquiry desk whether it would be OK to draw money from my account with only my cheque book. The gentleman said it would be OK. I then queued to speak to a cashier. I explained my situation, and told her what the man at 'Enquiries' had said. She asked me for further identification, and I explained that it had been stolen. She said 'Sorry, no money can be drawn from your account, without further proof of identity.' I suggested that she phoned a helpline as we do in retail stores under such circumstances, to check information such as mother's maiden name. She said the helpline was not available as it was a Saturday. By this time, I was very annoyed . . . it seemed ludicrous that the bank has no such facilities. She said that she could not help me and that I would have to wait until Monday . . .

I took my car to XYZ on a Saturday, as the exhaust was blowing. They said they would check on the computer if the part was in stock, but they couldn't replace it for an hour. They confirmed that the part was in stock, so I left the car with them. I returned in 90 minutes, and the car was still outside, not repaired. I asked when it would be ready, and they said 'Oh, about another hour, mate.' I returned after an hour. The car had been moved, so my hopes were raised. However, on asking, it became apparent that the part wasn't in stock, and my original exhaust had been removed, and cut in two. I asked what they were going to do, and they said they were expecting a delivery on Tuesday morning, 'would that be OK?' I explained that I worked Sunday and Monday, and needed my car. They said they would try and get a part locally, and promised to ring at 5.30 PM with an outcome. No phone call . . .

Walking erect

In the 'walking erect' stage, Fisk, Brown and Bitner note that there was 'almost no discussion of whether services are different from goods, but rather the literature has focused on specific marketing problems of service organisations'. Services Marketing became an established field of study within the Marketing Discipline with an increasing number of academics and academic journals interested in developing theories to assist in the understanding and management of the practical issues facing services organisations. This generated cross-functional research as academics and practitioners grappled with problems associated with managing quality when quality depends upon customer-determined criteria; designing, managing and evaluating intangible processes; managing supply and demand when capacity is time-constrained; and the need to combine the Marketing, Human Resource and Operations business functions to address these problems.

The Fisk, Brown and Bitner article was published in 1993 and there has been much development within the dynamic field of services marketing which has now resulted in recognition of three further periods with distinct characteristics.

Making tools

This period is characterised by the further development of research to understand and resolve the problems that service organisations face. The emphasis was on quantifying the problems previously identified and measuring the impact of specific management interventions as well as recognising that effective service performance requires a multi-disciplinary approach and draws on knowledge of consumer behaviour, Human Resources Management as well as traditional marketing. Of particular note is that research into service design, delivery (especially service supply chains) and quality was of interest to academics within Operations Management as well as within Services Marketing, as Services Operations emerged as a sub-discipline within Operations Management. This period is characterised by the emergence of research interest from a range of disciplines including service computing. This multi-disciplinary approach has expanded our understanding of the experiences of service employees as well as services consumers through a focus on: service design, service delivery and service experiences (see Chapters 4, 5 and 6); service quality, customer satisfaction and service recovery (see Chapter 8); operant resources, relationship marketing and profitability (see Chapters 7, 9 and 10).

Operant Resources
The knowledge, skills, capabilities and competencies that an organisation can draw upon to create value including those of their customers who co-create value. The current focus on operant resources as a result of the Service-Dominant Logic debate highlights the importance of the people involved in value co-creation.

Service Science
A term used to identify the emerging discipline of Service Science Management and Engineering (SSME) which seeks to integrate knowledge from a range of disciplines such as: economics, business, design, IT and engineering.

SSME
The recognition of Service Science, Management and Engineering as an emerging field of study that seeks to develop inter-disciplinary knowledge of service.

Creating language

In contrast to previous periods of development, technology-based services – machines providing services to people – are receiving greater attention. This rise in the use of technology to deliver service, and particularly self-service, experiences has led to a greater need to integrate IT and engineering perspectives when designing modern services. As a result, the current period of development has become associated with a fundamental shift in thought which is conceptualising service as a field of study that integrates knowledge from information technology and engineering as well as the business disciplines that have previously been interested in service provision. New phrases are emerging to encourage this broad inter-disciplinary approach such as service system and service science. This does not mean that the knowledge of services that we have gained within the marketing discipline will be redundant, rather that other disciplines are likely to be more interested in learning what we know in order to ensure that they are able to improve customer service experiences. Indeed, the emergence of a field of study which requires other business and non-business disciplines to focus on delivering value to customers can only be music to the ears of marketers!

The future: building communities

A symposium was held at Cambridge University, UK in July 2007 to recognise Service Science, Management and Engineering (SSME) as an emerging field of study. There are also predictions[15] of a future where 'private embedded devices' will allow *things to provide services to things*. For example, electrical items such as fridges will be able to purchase their own electricity and insurance and share data on their owner's activities, cars will renew their road tax and so on. The suggestion is that future service innovations will require greater integration of knowledge from the management, design, IT and engineering disciplines. There is talk of the need to develop T-shaped practitioners who are able to integrate their discipline expertise with that from other disciplines in order to resolve performance problems within service organisations.

📖 It's in the News! 2.2

Service Science

According to *Business News*, 25 January 2005,

The new discipline of Service Science is a melding of technology with an understanding of business processes and organization – and is crucial to the economy's next wave. Services have come to represent more than 75% of the U.S. economy, and the field is growing rapidly. In the information-technology business, services have become even more important... The IT-services sector is in dire need of people who are talented in the application of technologies to help businesses, governments, and other organizations improve what they do now – plus tap into totally new areas. The complex issues surrounding the transformation of businesses at such a fundamental level require the simultaneous development of both business methods and the technology that supports those methods. This is the seedbed for a new discipline that industry and academia are coming to call 'service science'.

Service science would merge technology with an understanding of business processes and organization, a combination of recognizing a company's pain points and the tools that can be applied to correct them. To thrive in this environment, an IT-services expert will need to understand how that capability can be delivered in an efficient and profitable way, how the services should be designed, and how to measure their effectiveness.

This new academic discipline would bring together ongoing work in the more established fields of computer science, operations research, industrial engineering, management sciences, and social and legal sciences, in order to develop the skills required in a services-led economy.

Service-dominant Logic

What is evident from the discussion above is that services marketing sought and gained credibility as a sub-discipline of the marketing discipline. The process outlined above implies that the marketing discipline is, or has been, primarily concerned with non-services, that is goods and manufactured products.

A brief audit of text books currently used on core marketing programmes in UK Business Schools would certainly support this view.[16] However, an influential article by Vargo and Lusch, published in the *Journal of* Marketing,[17] has generated considerable debate among marketing academics.

Vargo and Lusch remind us that marketing is fundamentally concerned with processes of exchange. They acknowledge that the majority of marketing exchanges concern service, but they go further than that the sub-discipline of services marketing has gone in demonstrating the importance of service within the total economy (as we have done above). It is important to note their distinction between services, as outputs, from service which they define as a process of using one's resources for the benefit of another person or entity. Vargo and Lusch argue that service (singular) is the basis for *all* exchanges; that manufactured products exist only to facilitate service provision and that, as a result, it is more appropriate to consider the marketing of products to be the special case or sub-discipline of marketing. This view implies that products only exist to increase service efficiency or facilitate service performance. We buy washing machines to perform a laundry service and cars to facilitate our transportation needs. As consumers we demonstrate choices in the way we use products to perform our service needs. The attributes that manufacturers build into their products seek to differentiate their product from others in the same category based upon how their product performs the underlying service for which the product is bought. Washing machines are manufactured with different spin speeds or are made to launder a range of different fabrics. Some cars provide a safer drive, faster drive, or more economical drive than others.

Service-dominant (S-D) logic proposes that value is delivered to customers through co-creation, and *occurs at the time of use, consumption or experience* of the product or service. It is important to distinguish between co-creation and co-production. The terms are not interchangeable within the S-D logic perspective. Co-creation relates to the value received by the customer through usage, consumption or experience. Co-production relates to specific tasks undertaken by customers which may occur prior to or during the usage, consumption or experience stage. As consumers, we chose the degree to which we are willing to perform or co-produce the service ourselves, thereby co-creating the value we experience. We can eat at restaurants or prepare our food at home using products and ingredients that we have bought to enable us to perform those services ourselves. We drive our own cars or choose public transport.

Another aspect of the S-D logic worth noting is the emphasis on *operant* resources as a means of competitive advantage. Operant resources can be defined as the knowledge, skills, expertise, capacity and time of people and, in the context of S-D logic, relate to both co-creation parties: customers as well as the service organisation. This aspect is particularly relevant to a number of discussions within this textbook given the rapid rise in the prevelance of self-service.

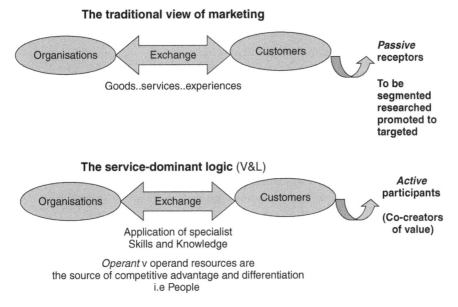

The traditional view of marketing

Organisations ← Exchange → Customers

Goods..services..experiences

Passive
receptors

**To be
segmented
researched
promoted to
targeted**

The service-dominant logic (V&L)

Organisations ← Exchange → Customers

Application of specialist
Skills and Knowledge

Operant v operand resources are
the source of competitive advantage and differentiation
i.e People

Active
participants

**(Co-creators
of value)**

Figure 2.1 Comparing the traditional view of marketing with Service-Dominant Logic adapted by the authors from the ideas within S-D Logic (Vargo and Lusch ref 17)

Given that the Vargo and Lusch proposals have been hailed as a paradigm shift for marketing, we expect these ideas to influence the way in which services marketing is understood, researched and taught during the early part of the 21st Century. We anticipate that many of the principles of services marketing discussed within this book will gradually become the fundamental principles of the marketing discipline as a result. Certainly these principles have wider application across a broader range of organisations than those traditionally associated with 'business' such as non-profit and public sector organisations.

Figure 2.1 summarises the key differences between the traditional view of marketing and the ideas captured within S-D logic. In particular it emphasises the importance of 'people' within the services marketing system, both *customers* (as co-creators of value and operant resources) and *employees* (as operant resources).

Scope and Characteristics of Service Provision

It is difficult to think of organisations that are not involved with service in some form or other.

- Some organisations declare the *whole* business to be a service business.

   There are many examples. In the *private sector*, this would include consultancy business (e.g., IT, public relations, accounting), airlines, estate agents, hairdressers, dry-cleaners and travel agents. In the *public sector*, for many countries, it would include, for example, health or education. In the *not-for-profit sector,* it would include charities, and many local government services. In the *business-to-business sector,* it would include delivery services, technical services, maintenance services and recruitment services.

- Some organisations declare services to be *part* of their business.

Many organisations have service providers within their business. Multiple retailers, for example, rely on administrative services and technical services from within their own organisation. There is always a decision to be made as to whether these services are better provided within an organisation, or whether they should be 'out-sourced'. The use of information technology by business, for example, is being transformed by the growth of 'pay-as-you-go' services; that is, application service providers who hold software at data centres and allow customers to use it over the Internet or a private network.[18]

- Some organisations declare services as an *augmentation* of manufactured goods.

This is seen extensively with sales of traditional manufactured goods. For example, a new car comes with warranties, free delivery and so on, or the purchase of a new carpet includes a fitting service. The majority of organisations today will use a website as an additional sales channel or to enhance communication with customers or for both purposes.

The categorisation above is probably familiar to most readers. It demonstrates the wide and varied number of services that are carried out, typically, each and every day by organisations of all sizes. The body of knowledge built up in services marketing will apply whether service is the whole business, part of a business or an augmentation of manufactured goods. In particular, there are certain common characteristics of services that apply in all these cases. These characteristics – intangibility, heterogeneity, inseparability and perishability – which distinguish services from physical goods, have 'become the fundamental building blocks of most services marketing research, and are as fundamental to the study of services marketing as the 4Ps (Product, Price, Promotion and Place) are to the field of marketing in general'.[19]

Given their importance, we consider each characteristic in turn.

Intangibility

Pure services, such as a consultancy session with a psychiatrist, cannot be touched. Nor can travel on a train or aeroplane, although the train and aeroplane are themselves tangible. Nor can you touch the 'atmosphere' on a train or aeroplane, nor can you touch the conversations with fellow passengers. You cannot touch an aerobics class and can only make a full assessment of the quality of the service offered after having attended the class. A service is 'something which can be bought and sold, but which you cannot drop on your foot'.[20] This clearly differs from the purchase of a nectarine, for example, where the customer can touch the product beforehand and decide whether or not to buy it based on its colour and/or texture. Different aspects of marketing become more important in the service context. For example, a customer may rely heavily on the advice of a friend when considering whether to take part in the aerobics class, whereas a special price promotion that could more easily influence the decision to buy a nectarine.

The intangibility characteristic of services often increases risk for the purchaser. Some services are perceived to be riskier than others depending on whether they are high in

- search factors
- experience factors, or
- credence factors.

A service that is high in search factors is one about which customers can get some (prior) information as to what they will receive. For example, the sun-tanning shop may promise that after five sessions you will look as brown as the person on the photograph, or the breakdown service may claim to provide assistance within two hours for any part of the country. In each case, your search has provided some information that affects your perception of the risk involved with the purchase.

A service that is high in experience factors is one that customers must try out (experience) before they can decide whether or not it is a good deal. Paying for a holiday package, for example, is high in experience factors as it involves so much more than can be conveyed by the holiday brochure. Paying for the experience of a bungee jump is a more extreme example. Purchase of these services is perceived to be more risky than of those that are high in search factors.

A service that is high in credence factors is one that is difficult to evaluate even after experiencing it. These are services that are often offered by professionals or experts in their field. For many of us, it would be difficult to evaluate whether services offered by doctors, lawyers, vets, car mechanics, plumbers or surveyors are value for money, simply because we do not have the knowledge to question them. Services such as these are perceived to be very risky, and require high degrees of reassurance from the service providers.

Heterogeneity

Organisations providing services to customers know that no two service provisions are exactly the same, whatever the attempts to standardise them. In the story in the previous chapter, it was recognised that serving meals on an aeroplane to different passengers would differ not only in the delivery but also in the evaluations by different passengers. Similarly, train operators recognise the great differences both in the service provided and in passengers' perceptions of the service provided, between trains running off-peak and those running in the rush hours. The quality of any service will vary when offered by different employees, probably at different times of the day. Customers who cannot distinguish between physical goods (say, television sets off the same production line) will normally be able to distinguish between services (say, that provided by receptionists in the same hotel).

Inseparability

Inseparability refers to the notion that, in many service operations, production and consumption cannot be separated; that is, a service is to a great extent consumed at the same time as it is produced. For example, although the hairdresser may prepare in advance to carry out the service (i.e., gather the necessary equipment, undergo specialised training, and so on), most of the hairdressing service is produced simultaneously as the customer consumes the service (i.e., sits in the chair).

This characteristic raises various marketing problems primarily related to the fact that customers (who cannot be controlled totally by the service provider) are *involved and participate in the production process*. This is completely different from physical goods, where production and consumption are separated, and the customer has no involvement with the production process. The inseparability of production and consumption in services means that quality is more difficult to measure and ultimately control. Unlike the car factory, where production is out-of-bounds to consumers, and where potential quality failures can often be dealt with out of their sight, the production of many services is in the full spotlight of the consumer.

Perishability

This refers to the fact that, unlike physical goods, services cannot be stored. Even nectarines, which have a relatively short life, can be stored by the retailer for several days and sold at any point during that time to the consumer. An appointment with a dentist, in contrast, at a given time on a given day, cannot be stored and offered again to customers. If a customer cancels an appointment at the last minute, that particular service opportunity is lost and the dentist will have lost valuable revenue.

The problem of perishability is frequently compounded by the fact that the demand for many services is characterised by distinct peaks and troughs. Although trains are overloaded with customers between 7.30 AM and 9.00 AM most weekdays, expensive rolling stock will lay idle at midday and weekends. To overcome problems associated with perishability and uneven demand for services, careful attention is paid to production scheduling and demand forecasting. Pricing and promotion are used extensively to encourage customers to utilise services at a time convenient to the service operator.

While these four characteristics are certainly the ones most commonly associated with services, there is another view. Beaven and Scotti suggest that these four characteristics arise from manufacturing oriented thinking rather than service oriented thinking.[21] They propose an alternative list of characteristics that describe services in a way that does not seek comparison with, or differentiation from, manufactured products (see Exhibit 2.2). Although Beaven and Scotti propose these characteristics as an alternative perspective, the substance behind the characteristics they propose is essentially the same. However, it is useful to highlight the fact that personal perceptions of service experiences leave very concrete impressions on customers. This is something we will explore in more depth in Chapter 8. The benefit of understanding the characteristics of services is to provide managers with a useful checklist of practical implications which will require consideration.

Exhibit 2.2   Manufacturing vs. Service Oriented Thinking

Manufacturing-oriented thinking	Service oriented thinking
1. Services are abstract and intangible products.	1. Services are processes with outcomes that can be perceived directly and indirectly, leaving concrete impressions.
2. Services are non-standardized heterogeneous outputs.	2. Services are personal experiences that can be uniquely tailored to meet individual needs, and expectations.
3. Services are instantly perishable and cannot be produced in advance or stored for future sale.	3. Services are processes that are created and experienced, with outcomes that are often distinct, direct, and imperishable.
4. Services are simultaneously produced and consumed; customer involvement often interrupts operations and interferes with efficiency.	4. Services are encounters that afford opportunities for greater satisfaction through participation, shared responsibility, and timely feedback.

Source: Adapted from Beaven and Scotti (see note 21).

Management Implications Arising from the Characteristics of Services

Some management implications and potential actions resulting from the characteristics of services are first outlined here. They will be reinforced in the theory and case studies later.

First, the intangibility of services is recognised often by firms *stressing the tangible elements* of the service. So the conference organisers will ensure that delegates receive a clear programme of events with copies of important papers presented. The airline company will aim to provide good quality food during the journey. Service firms will also try to *facilitate positive word-of-mouth*. The car mechanic will encourage the satisfied customer to tell friends of his location, or the travel company will include stories of satisfied customers in the newsletter or brochures.

Word-of-mouth
Information provided by one customer to another customer or potential customer.

The heterogeneity of services is often addressed by companies through *service design* methods which reduce variability. In particular, they will try to standard-ise parts of the service that are invisible. For example, in hospital out-patients departments, a carefully designed and fully understood (by the nurses) system for ensuring that patients are seen in the appropriate order will reduce patient feelings of unfairness due to variability in waiting room management. Also, it is argued that *empowerment of front-line staff* can improve the demeanour of cus-tomers who suffer the consequences of unseen variation in service provision. Pas-sengers on a delayed train, for example, may feel better if the rail staff can provide information and even offer free drinks without needing management approval.

The implication of the inseparability characteristic of services is that customers take part in the production of services. This has been embraced by some service companies who *view their customers as partial employees*. They will pay as much attention to letting customers know what to do in order to participate in the service production as they do to employees. Students, for example, are informed as to their expected levels of participation in different formats: lectures, tutorials, seminars. Many services take place in the presence of other customers, who may also be partly responsible for the production of your service. The *management of customer-to-customer interactions* then becomes important. For example, the swim-ming pool staff can institute separate 'lane swimming' and 'fun swimming' areas so that the 'production' needs of both groups of swimmers can be met. Similarly, the design of restaurants to include appropriate smoking and non-smoking areas reduces the likely incompatibilities of different customer groups.

Service issues brought about by the perishability characteristic require man-agement to have contingencies that allow them to *stimulate/reduce demand or increase/reduce supply*. In the travel business, when supply exceeds demand, there are empty seats on trains/aeroplanes that cannot be stored and resold. Like-wise, gaps in the appointments books of hairdressers/dentists are lost business. Table 2.1 provides an example of how a budget airline, RyanAir, manages capac-ity through a pricing system that offers passengers lower prices when the aircraft is relatively empty (flights offered in a month's time, say) and charges higher prices when the aircraft is almost full (i.e. for next day flights).

Indeed, service pricing, or discount offers, are often the means for service organisations to manage their capacities in the light of fluctuating demand – as long as this does not result in pricing policies that confuse the customer (see 'It's in the News!' 2.3).

Table 2.1 'Low-cost airline style' Pricing: Example – Booking a flight from Dublin to Barcelona with RyanAir

Direction	Date of flight	Price (Euros)
Dublin to Barcelona	26 April 2008	123
Barcelona to Dublin	27 April 2008	137
Dublin to Barcelona	26 May 2008	43
Barcelona to Dublin	27 May 2008	47

Using website http://www.ryanair.com/site/EN/, accessed 16.40 on 25 April 2008.

Conversely, when demand exceeds supply, customers invariably have to wait for services. Delays are often not only inevitable, but also are a major source of dissatisfaction for customers. The management of service waits can focus on reducing *actual* waiting times, reducing *perceptions* of waiting times or managing the *impact* of the delay.[22]

Reducing actual waiting times. To attempt to reduce actual waiting times, companies would look to techniques for forecasting customer demand, and employ employee resource allocation techniques to deal with the variations in hourly, daily and weekly demand.[23] Alternatively, they may invest in technology that will speed up customer throughput. The potential success of these operational approaches will depend on the accuracy of the forecasts (which for many services is very difficult to achieve), the availability of part-time and full-time staff to work at short notice, and the available funds for investment.

Reducing perceptions of waiting times. There is some evidence that when customers are entertained or distracted during a wait, they perceive that they have waited for less time. Here, *impression management* methods may be used to reduce customer irritations with queueing/waiting. In Disney theme parks, for example, where visitors can spend half the day waiting in lines, there are many devices for reducing irritation. The queueing areas are designed so that people are nearly always moving (which is better that standing for some time in the same place), monitors at regular intervals show films/videos which are related to Disney or the particular attraction, signs showing likely waiting times are prominently displayed (and which routinely overestimate the time, so that visitors feel good that they have queued for less time than expected), and there is a clear 'first in first out' system to reduce anxiety.

Managing the impact of delay. Despite the attention given to the two approaches above, delays still occur in the majority of services and so any sustainable and effective service recovery system must also be able to deal with the impact of the delay on the customer. The organisation will need to manage how waits are interpreted by customers and the way that they respond. Two aspects are very important here. First, employee efforts during a delay may well determine customer reactions. Where employees are perceived to be showing genuine empathy, customers may forgive the company for the delay. However, if employees are perceived as uncaring, through, for example, carrying on other tasks which have no effect on the reduction of the waiting times, then this converts a delay into a service failure. Second, apologies for the wait, made by employees, are known to affect customer demeanour. A sincere apology is expected and welcomed by most customers. Conversely, a scripted and seemingly insincere apology, such as the standard scripts adopted by rail and airline employees, can be counterproductive and generate angry customer responses.[24]

Branding is felt to be more difficult to achieve for services, largely as a result of the combination of intangibility and heterogeneity. A service brand is said to be a promise about the nature of a future experience with a service organisation or an individual representative of that organisation.[25] It is based on consumers' experience-based perceptions. For many services, consumer experiences are with people employed by the service organisation, and this has resulted in the view that 'employees are the brand'.[26] A desired criterion for succeeding with a service brand is consistency.[27] However, heterogeneity, brought about through service employees with varying skills, emotions and motivations, can harm a service brand. A hotel employee losing patience with an errant child guest can damage the child-friendly brand image the hotel is attempting to foster. There is even evidence, in some organisations, of employee saboteurs, where employees are 'deliberately deviant or intentionally dysfunctional'.[28] They, in turn, have been termed 'brand saboteurs', characterised by deviance, underperformance and service failures.[29] Examples exist in the literature of the creation of successful service brands, but it is generally acknowledged that research into the criteria for successful service brands is in its infancy. The interested reader is referred to the paper by de Chernatony and Segal-Horn.[30]

Finally, in discussing management implications and actions associated with the characteristics of services, it is easy to overlook how *complex* the management of service provision may be. Often there is a range of influences on decision-making in services, making it difficult for some businesses to focus on service delivery issues. Consider train travel service. There are many stakeholders – the Shadow Strategic Rail Authority, the individual rail operators, Railtrack (who manage the infrastructure) and the groups representing rail passengers – each of whom have their own views as to what the service for passengers should be, and what the pricing structure should be.

📖 **It's in the News! 2.3**

Pricing a Service

According to the UK's *Daily Mail* of 24 April 2008,

Rail companies are to simplify fares with three new tickets to end confusion over deals . . . For confused rail passengers trying to find a way through the maze of tickets on offer, help is at hand. Instead of dozens of deals such as Apex, Supersaver,

Megadeal, White Day and Value tickets, train companies have agreed to simplify their range of tickets into just three types.

Passengers will be able to choose between advance, off peak and anytime fares.

Under the new system, advance tickets can be bought the day before travel or earlier and will be sold at a substantial discount. The anytime and off peak fares will be available on the day of travel. Anytime tickets can be used on any service during the day, including peak hours. Off-peak tickets will have restrictions on when they can be used and which services they can be used on but will cost less.

The new system is being brought in by the Association of Train Operating Companies following criticism of the over-complex fare structure and a demand for action in the Government's rail White Paper last year.

ATOC commercial director David Mapp said: 'This is the biggest shake-up in the fares and ticketing system for many years.' 'Passengers have told us they want a simpler fares system. We are listening and responding.' Although the range of tickets has been cut, fares will still vary according to when the ticket is to be used as train companies switch increasingly to 'airlinestyle' pricing. ATOC insisted fares will not be increased as a result of the new structure.

He added: 'Passengers are already used to doing this when they fly on budget airlines. It will become increasingly the norm on the railways.'

Summary

In this chapter, we have provided a contemporary and historical context for the study of services marketing. Given the importance of services in many economies, few people will question the attempts by academics and practitioners to improve the understanding and practice of the marketing and management of services. Although knowledge and understanding of services marketing is increasing, and technology is changing the service offer in many cases, there are ideas from the 'crawling out' and 'scurrying about' stages which are still very influential.

In particular, the four characteristics of services – intangibility, heterogeneity, inseparability and perishability – are as fundamental today as in the 1970s and 1980s. Equally, the services marketing mix (and especially the people, process and physical evidence elements) provides a tremendously useful focus for important consumer service concerns in the twenty-first century.

The current debate around the S-D logic for marketing, along with the emergence of service science and inter-disciplinary emphasis on service systems, is likely to result in more organisations incorporating services marketing principles into their business strategies.

Learning Outcomes

Having read this chapter, you should be able to

- appreciate that the application of services marketing ideas can be useful in all businesses – those that manufacture products, as well as purer service businesses
- appreciate the development of services marketing thought and how the current service-dominant logic debate is likely to contribute towards future developments
- understand, and appreciate the managerial implications of the 'four characteristics of services' – intangibility, inseparability, heterogeneity and perishability
- appreciate the value and relevance of the expanded marketing mix for services and especially the importance given to people, process and physical evidence.

Discussion Questions and Exercises

1. Provide further examples of services that are high in search, experience and credence factors.
2. Take the story in Chapter 1 and identify instances that reflect the four characteristics of services.
3. Identify the different ways in which you use the Internet as a service.
4. Identify the people, process and physical evidence elements that occur in the critical incident stories in Exhibit 2.1.

Notes and References

1. The PriceWaterhouseCoopers 'Global Annual Review, 2007' can be accessed from www.pwc.com.
2. Rodie, A. R. and Martin, C. L., 'Competing in the Service Sector: the Entrepreneurial Challenge,' *International Journal of Entrepreneurial Behaviour and Research*, 7(1), 2001, pp. 5–21.
3. Freely, M., 'Party Politics,' *Sunday Times,* 5 November 2000.
4. Details of current Tesco activities can be accessed at www.tescocorporate.com.
5. Pine II, J. B. and Gilmore, J. H., *The Experience Economy: Work is Theater and Every Business a Stage,* Harvard Business School Press, Boston, Mass., 1999.
6. Steiner, R., 'Debenham's girl who bagged the top job,' *Sunday Times,* 17 September 2000.
7. Fisk, R. P., Brown, S. W. and Bitner, M. J., 'Tracking the Evolution of the Services Marketing Literature,' *Journal of Retailing,* 69(1), 1993, pp. 61–91.
8. IfM and IBM, *Succeeding through Service Innovation: A Discussion Paper,* Cambridge, UK: University of Cambridge Institute for Manufacturing. 2007, ISBN: 978-1-902546-59-8.
9. Donnelly J. H. Jr, 'Marketing Intermediaries in Channels of Distribution for Services,' *Journal of Marketing,* 40 (January), 1976, pp. 57–70.
10. Shostack, G. L., 'Breaking Free from Product Marketing,' *Journal of Marketing,* 41 (April), 1977, pp. 73–80.
11. Lovelock, C. H., 'Classifying Services to Gain Strategic Marketing Insights,' *Journal of Marketing,* 47 (Summer), 1983, pp. 9–20.
12. Zeithaml, V. A., Berry, L. L. and Parasuraman, A., 'A Conceptual Model of Service Quality and its Implications for Future Research,' *The Journal of Marketing,* 49 (Fall), 1985, pp. 41–50.
13. Booms, B. H. and Bitner, M. J., 'Marketing Strategies and Organisation Structures for Service Firms,' in J. Donnelly and W. R. George (eds), *Marketing of Services,* American Marketing Association, Chicago, 1981, pp. 51–67.
14. McCarthy, J. E., *Basic Marketing: A Management Approach,* Irwin, Homewood, Ill., 1960.
15. Barnatt, C., 'Customer Organisation Interfaces,' Cyber Business Centre Briefing Paper, 2000. http://www.nottingham.ac.uk/cyber/Cbp-cim1.html.

16. Hilton, T., Hughes, T. and McDowell, R., 'Does the Marketing Curriculum Reflect the Importance of Services Marketing for Practitioners?,' *The Marketing Review,* 7(2), 2007, pp. 171–184.

17. Vargo, S. L. and Lusch, R. F., 'Evolving to a New Dominant Logic for Marketing,' *The Journal of Marketing,* 68(1), 2004, pp. 1–17. A good source for learning more about the ensuing debate is: Lusch, R. F. and Vargo, S. L., *The Service Dominant Logic of Marketing: Dialog, Debate and Directions,* M.E. Sharpe, Armonk, New York, 2006.

18. Sumner-Smith, D., 'Pay-as-you-go Software Slashes Bill for Information Technology,' *Sunday Times: Business,* 12 November 2000.

19. Martin, C. L., 'The History, Evolution and Principles of Services Marketing: Poised for the New Millennium,' *Marketing Intelligence and Planning,* 17(7), 1999, pp. 324–28.

20. Gummesson, Evert, as quoted in 'Services Marketing: A European Perspective,' Christopher Lovelock, Sandra Vandermerwe, Barbara Lewis, Prentice Hall, Englewood Cliffs, NJ, 1996, p. 7.

21. Beaven, M. H. and Scotti, D. J., 'Service-Oriented Thinking And Its Implications For The Marketing Mix,' *The Journal of Services Marketing,* 4(4), 1990, pp. 5–19.

22. Sarel, D. and Marmorstein, H., 'Managing the Delayed Service Encounter: The Role of Employee Action and Customer Prior Experience,' *Journal of Services Marketing,* 12(3), 1998, pp. 195–208.

23. Slack, N., Chambers, S., Howland, C., Harrison, A. and Johnston, R., *Operations Management,* Financial Times Pitman Publishing, London UK (2nd edn) 1998.

24. Sarel and Marmorstein, 'Managing the Delayed Service Encounter'.

25. Berry, L.L. and Seltman, K.D., 'Building a Strong Services Brand,' *Business Horizons*, 50, 2007, pp. 199–209.

26. Wilson, A., Zeithaml, V.A., Bitner, M.J. and Gremler, D.D., *Services Marketing: Integrating Customer Focus Acroos the Firm*, McGraw Hill, Maidenhead, UK, 2008.

27. de Chernatony, L. and Segal-Horn, S., 'The Criteria for Successful Service Brands,' *European Journal of Marketing* , 37(7/8), 2003, pp. 1096–118.

28. Harris, L. and Ogbonna, E., 'Service Sabotage: A Sudy of Antecedents and Consequences,' *Journal of the Academy of Marketing Science*, 34(4), 2006, pp. 543–58.

29. Wallace, E. and de Chernatony, L., 'Classifying, Identifying and Managing the Service Brand Saboteur,' *The Service Industries Journal* , 28(2), 2008, pp. 151–65.

30. de Chernatony and Segal- Horn, 'The Criteria for Successful Service Brands'.

3

Service Goals: The Use of Metaphors

Learning Objectives

Overall Aim of the Chapter:
To provide an understanding of the importance of the factory and drama/ theatre metaphors in the study of service processes and content.

In particular, the *chapter objectives* are

- to outline the uses (and limitations) of metaphors in services marketing/management theory development

- to explore the structural 'services marketing system' model which adopts the service factory concept and to examine a range of practical service issues arising from the application of the model

- to explore the notions of customer roles and 'intended effects' on customers arising from the transposition of the drama/theatre metaphor into retail and service management.

- to provide a summary of the potential uses and range of applications of the factory and drama/theatre metaphors.

We have emphasised the importance of linking theory with practice in the study of services marketing. In this chapter some theoretical frameworks are introduced which guide practical thinking. The theory results from the creative use of metaphors in services, especially the factory and drama theatre metaphors. We start with a brief discussion of the uses and limitations of metaphors in marketing and management. A *structural* framework – the services marketing system – that is based primarily on the factory metaphor is then presented. This is followed by a demonstration, based on the theatre metaphor, of how the intended effect (of the service performance) on the consumer can be varied by the staging of the *content*. In each case, the implications for service management are given.

Service Performance
The way in which contact personnel provide or deliver the service to a customer.

The Uses and Limitations of Metaphors in Marketing and Management

Metaphors have been adopted widely by management academics and practitioners to achieve a variety of outcomes, most notably to:

- develop new perspectives on situations through evocative imagery
- clarify areas of uncertainty
- direct employees' behaviour in particular ways.[1]

Service Encounter
Occurs when customers directly interact with any aspect of the service delivery system.

Aristotle's dictum was that the greatest thing by far is to be the master of the metaphor.[2] In the field of services marketing, the contribution of the factory and drama metaphors to help researchers explicate service encounters and service delivery and the contribution of the marriage metaphor to help clarify relationship marketing have been highlighted.[3,4] There is little doubt, as we shall see, that metaphor usage has helped academics and practitioners increase their understanding of services marketing.

However, concerns have been expressed about the (over)use of metaphors in business and other contexts,[5] leading to inappropriate decision-making. For example, one of the most frequently used metaphors is the war metaphor. While this metaphor may provide evocative language – 'strategy', 'tactics', 'battles', 'outflanking' – it assumes that the business has a particular goal; that is, winning. It does not have as its main goal, 'building and sustaining relationships', which is a goal more appropriate to the marriage metaphor. It has even been argued that far from us being masters of the metaphor, powerful metaphors can be masters of us. A chilling account of the use of the war metaphor in sport (rugby union) provides a reminder of the care that needs to be exercised in metaphor usage.[6]

We concentrate here on the factory and drama/theatre metaphor usage in services marketing and management.

What are the goals of the factory and drama/theatre metaphors? What insights about services and service customers will the metaphors yield?

Using the Factory Metaphor: The Service as a System

Servuction System
A model that identifies benefits customers gain from their interactions with visible elements of the service experience and places the customer within the service delivery system.

The use of the factory metaphor leads to some very helpful structural models of service systems that apply to a range of different services.

The 'servuction system' model

According to the 'servuction system' model (presented by Bateson, but originally developed by Eric Langeard and Pierre Eiglier[7]), customers receive a bundle of 'benefits' from each service experience as a result of their interaction with visible elements of the service system. Visible elements would include

- all contact personnel employed by the service provider
- aspects of the inanimate environment and
- other customers within the service system.

When receiving a haircut, for example, customers come into contact with receptionists and stylists, the physical dimensions of the salon itself, heating, seating and so on, and other customers within the salon. The model draws the distinction between visible elements and invisible components of the system. The latter would include all the other organisational activities taking place out of sight of the customers, for instance, staff training and administration. According to the model, in order to receive the benefits from the service experience, the customer must be part of the system thus explicitly acknowledging the inseparability characteristic of services.

The services marketing system

Building on the original components of the 'servuction system', Lovelock[8] presents the 'services marketing system', in which service businesses are conceptualised as comprising three overlapping systems:

1. the service operations system;
2. the service delivery system; and
3. the service marketing system.

The model illustrates how the three functional areas – marketing, operations and human resources of the service business – are integrated together.

Figure 3.1 identifies the various components of the services marketing system as related to a hairdressing service. While this particular service is used for illustration, it should become obvious that the structure can be applied to services ranging from theme parks to rail travel, hospitals, retail stores and higher education courses, to name a few.

The service operations system

The service operations system comprises activities which are invisible to the customer, such as staff training, stock replenishment and so on, as well as the visible aspects of the operation experienced directly by the customer, such as how they are treated by employees as soon as they enter the salon or how quickly they are moved around from the washbasins to the cutting chair (if they are receiving a cut and blow-dry, for example). Although there is generally no need for the customer to see most aspects of service operations (therefore they are kept invisible), some service providers deliberately expose customers to 'back-stage' activities in an attempt to influence positively their perceptions of the quality

Contact Personnel
The people who are the point of contact between the service organisation and customers.

Service Marketing System
A model that integrates the Marketing, Operations and Human Resource business functions.

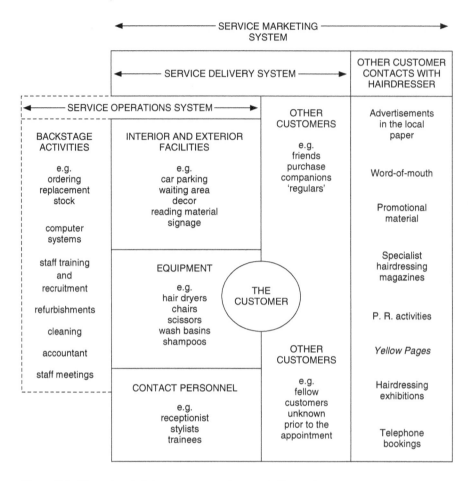

Figure 3.1   The unisex hairdresser as a services marketing system
Source: Adapted from Lovelock (see note 8).

of the service provided. Restaurants frequently invite customers to visit kitchens where the food is being prepared either before or after they have eaten. This is designed to reinforce an image of fresh food prepared in a hygienic cooking environment that may influence their perception of the overall quality of their experience.

Exhibit 3.1   Increasing Prevalence of Information Technology to Support Service Delivery

A Good Experience

IT certainly facilitated my move to New Zealand from the UK in 2005. Needing to rent an apartment I searched the internet from my home in Bristol. The *New Zealand Herald* newspaper was available on-line including the classified section.

A brief skim through that identified a short list of Real Estate Agents for the Auckland area. Logging onto each of their sites I was able to register as interested in renting property of a particular nature within specific suburbs and weekly price brackets. I worked out which suburbs were most appropriate through a website that provides street maps of New Zealand cities. Once the apartment was secured the agent provided me with the names of the leading utilities companies for Auckland and I logged onto their sites. I registered with a Telecom company and an electricity company through their websites entering the address of the apartment and the date from which I wanted the service to commence. I was astonished to find emails from both companies confirming my account number and, in the case of the telecom company, my new telephone number immediately upon completing my registration as a customer. Upon arrival in Auckland I signed the contract for the apartment and collected the keys. Arriving at the apartment I was able to boil the kettle for a cup of coffee while I telephoned my new employer to announce my arrival. I also found a bill from both companies in the mail box.

Room for Improvement?

Desperate for a domestic cleaner I googled, 'domestic cleaning services'. I clicked into the first company which, being top of the list, means that it is a 'sponsored link' and the company is paying per click (see the RAD9 case study for details). Reading through the page it seemed to provide exactly what I wanted. I completed the 'contact us' e-form and clicked to send. Nothing happened. I tried again. Nothing happened. Something was wrong with the website. Nevermind, I will ring instead. However a thorough search of the page did not reveal a telephone number or a fax number. The only means of contacting this company was through the website e-form which would not work. I clicked back to the google page and contacted another company.

The service delivery system

The service delivery system not only encompasses the visible elements of the service operating system, employees and the physical facilities, but also includes exposure to other customers. In many service businesses, positive onsite interaction can have a significant impact on customers' overall perception of their experience. In the hairdressing salon, customers may find themselves waiting for a period of time for their particular stylist in a communal reception area. Conversations frequently take place at this point between customers who have never met prior to entering the delivery system. Although the discussions may consist largely of banter and pleasantries not directly connected with the hairdressing service (e.g., conversations about the weather, traffic in town), the exchanges can for many customers improve their overall experience by making the time pass more quickly. Occasionally, when conversations turn to the service itself, the provider can benefit positively from the exchange. For instance, one customer who has visited the salon several times may comment on the skill and expertise of a certain stylist and the generally professional attitude of all employees. To new customers attending for the first time the comments might have a positive influence on their opinion of the salon.

The service marketing system

The service marketing system incorporates elements of the service experience that may contribute to the customer's overall view of the organisation but are not specifically part of the delivery system. Clearly, many of these are the elements which the organisation may not be able to control, such as the conversations customers may have about the salon with friends or relatives at home, or exposure to the service they may get from reading a hairdressing editorial in the local paper.

Lovelock feels that by conceptualising the service experience as three overlapping systems, services managers are forced to consider their business from a customer perspective rather than a purely operations perspective. It highlights the importance of managing all elements of the business that are visible to customers.

Using the Structural Models to Understand Services

A number of issues for service managers arise directly from a consideration of the structures above.

- How can/should we manage customer participation in the service?
- What attention should we give to contact personnel?
- How do we deal with customers' multiple points of contact in the service delivery system?
- How do we maintain a balance between marketing effectiveness and operational efficiency?
- Given that a service is provided at a specific time and over time, how do we manage the timing of consumption?
- What limitations to growth may be implied by the structural elements of services?

We deal with each of these questions in turn.

Managing customer participation in the service

The models highlight the participation of the customer in the service experience. As Bateson[9] points out, consumers are always involved in the factory, and although their participation may be active or passive, they are always there. In an aerobics class, for example, to get maximum benefit from the experience, customers are expected to exert a degree of physical effort during the class, as well as engage in cognitive activity beforehand, selecting the most appropriate class to attend. As a result, much of management's attention in service organisations is devoted to devising strategies for managing customer participation. Different tactics may be used by the instructor, for example, to influence both forms of participation. Loud music might be played to encourage physical participation during the class, and an advertisement is placed in the local paper to encourage people to attend.

As customers themselves can play such a crucial role in the delivery process, a number of writers advocate that they should be treated as 'partial employees' and the same strategies that are used to manage and motivate employees should be used with customers; they should be given clear instructions as to what is expected of them and appropriate rewards for their contribution. Another strategy for controlling the level of customer involvement in the service delivery system is simply to replace human with machine-based inputs. Although machines are generally more predictable than humans, this is not an option considered by many of the service providers described in this book, as human contact is considered by customers to be a key component of service quality.

Partial Employees
External Customers who's participation in the service process is actively managed and motivated by the service organisation.

Strategies used to manage customer participation are discussed in more detail in Chapter 4.

Attention to contact personnel

Contact personnel feature prominently in the service system and are perceived as being part of the service product. With many services there is often little or no tangible evidence available to the consumer before purchase to help them make an assessment about the quality of what they are paying for. Where this is the case, customers often use the appearance and manner of service employees as a first point of reference when deciding whether or not to make a purchase. Door 2 Door Airbus is a taxi company operating between the airports, hotels and theme parks on the Gold Coast of Australia. There are many competitors for this business which relies on the tourist trade. One of the ways in which Door 2 Door differentiates itself is through the appearance of its staff who all wear a smart and distinctive dark blue Door 2 Door shirt. This makes it easy for customers to locate them in busy places, such as airport arrival halls, and is a short, simple message to communicate to potential customers through the website (www.Door2Doorairbus.co.au) and other promotional material, including the back of tickets. Although a restaurant may be listed in the *Yellow Pages*, a new customer cannot make an assessment about the quality of the food or the standard of service simply from the telephone listing. However, a brief telephone conversation with a restaurant employee can have a vital impact on the customer's decision to visit that restaurant instead of another. Faced with uncertainty about the purchase decision, customers turn to service employees for reassurance and to form quality perceptions before, during and after the service experience. Effective human resource management strategies are therefore very important in service organisations and are considered in more detail in Chapter 7. The task of managing employees is clearly problematic. Bateson[10] notes that 'unlike physical goods people are not inanimate objects but have feelings and emotions'.

One approach to managing the human resources of the organisation (both service employees and, to a certain extent, customers) is to present them with 'scripts' to follow during the service encounter, to ensure that they know exactly what to expect and how to behave. Many organisations favour the use of a set 'script' by employees in an effort to standardise the quality of service delivery (e.g., servers at McDonald's who are encouraged to invite all customers to 'have a nice day'). (McGrath[11] notes, in her study of service encounters in a small gift shop, how employees frequently have different scripts for their front-stage and back-stage activities which, although they may be contradictory in content, are considered to be acceptable business practice and part of their role as sales assistants. She notes how, onstage, sales assistants reassure customers about their purchase with comments like 'that's wonderful' or 'lovely', yet as soon as they go back-stage they comment to fellow employees 'I didn't think we'd ever sell that!' and 'That is one of the few things in this store that I personally cannot stand.') Other service organisations may 'empower' employees to adapt their script to the behaviour and personality of the individual customers in an effort to improve the quality of the service encounter. This is where the theatre/drama metaphor can help clarify the strategies of service managers (see next section). Empowerment of employees is discussed in more detail in Chapter 7.

Multiple points of contact

Although clearly the customers' contact with employees is very important, the structural models highlight the importance of every 'point of contact' in the delivery system. Where these are considered by customers to be especially satisfying or dissatisfying, they have been defined as 'critical' incidents.[12] All points of contact in this context present customers with an opportunity to evaluate the service provider and form an opinion of service quality. In a restaurant, the 'critical' dissatisfying incident could be a telephone call with an employee, the smell of food being prepared in the kitchen or the seating arrangements inside. A critical incident for one customer may go unnoticed by another. The exterior decor may be enough to prevent some customers from entering a restaurant, while others will not make an assessment of service quality until they actually taste the food. It becomes very important that the service provider is aware of each point of contact in the system and, more importantly, the impact it has on the customer's perception of service quality.

Critical Incident
Point of service situation that gives rise to customer evaluations of the experience as either particularly satisfying or dissatisfying.

Exhibit 3.2   Jill's Story – the Role of Personal Disclosure as a Critical Incident

Jill's story is fictitious but draws on real examples gathered through researching the private client 'personal disclosure experience'.

'Jill' is in her late 40s with two children attending University. Jill and her husband are divorcing after 27 years of marriage. Jill visits a lawyer. As she is shown into a messy office, Jill notes the piles of files scattered on every surface, including the floor, and is surprised to find that each file carries a clearly readable name. The lawyer stretches across his desk to shake her hand, introducing himself as Mr. Smith and addresses her as Mrs Jones. Jill suddenly realises that even her name will change soon.

Although sitting in a comfortable chair, Jill realises that she is quite on edge when Mr. Smith opens a new file, already emblazoned with 'Jill Jones', and starts firing questions at her. Jill feels quite intimidated when told for the third time to 'stick to the facts please'. On this occasion it was followed by an almost apologetic explanation along the lines of, 'we only have 30 minutes to deal with this so we need to crack on'. Jill is now confused. He keeps asking her to explain why she finds her husband's behaviour unreasonable to live with, but when she tries he seems to reject her explanation, rephrasing it in some high-sounding legal jargon so she is not quite sure has the same meaning as her words and it certainly does not seem to convey the feelings she intends.

Jill asks what the process is, what should she expect, and what happens to the information she has just given. Mr. Smith hands her a leaflet produced by the local court telling her to read that, 'at her leisure' and that if she has any questions his secretary can probably help.

Jill asks about the likely financial implications of the divorce and how it might affect the children. The lawyer replies that it is too early to talk about financial implications because he has no idea of the husband's position on the matter and says that because they are both over 18 years, it is unlikely to matter much.

At that point Mr. Smith snaps the file shut, stands up and walks to the office door announcing that he will draft a letter to send to her husband. Jill leaves wondering what on earth the letter will say.

Jill visits a financial planner. She had been offered the choice between a 'home visit' or attending the office and had opted to visit the office in part because Phil had stressed how important the first meeting was because it would give Jill an opportunity to see how she felt about doing business with Phil and his company. Phil had stressed that there was no obligation to progress, or costs incurred at this stage – or right up until Jill authorises a financial plan to be written.

Phil introduces himself and greets her with a warm handshake, introducing a number of colleagues to her – all on first name basis. Sitting down, Jill hesitantly

Exhibit 3.2   (Continued)

explains that she is not entirely sure whether or not she really needs a financial planning adviser and that she does not really have a lot of money to invest but that she is about to divorce and feels she needs some advice particularly around maintaining adequate provision for her adult children to complete their education and support them into work. She also admits to feeling a little apprehensive about her personal financial future and would appreciate a little advice and wonders if this is the sort of thing Phil does.

Phil tells Jill that it is not unusual for people to seek out a financial planning advisor while divorcing, as it may be the first time they have to really think about their financial future. He also reveals that he divorced at a time when his adult children were still studying, so he understands her particular concerns on that matter.

Phil explains that there is quite a bit of preparatory fact-finding work to do to support the planning process because it is tailored to individual needs. There is a 'personal inventory' questionnaire that will document her personal circumstances including short-term and long-term aspirations and here he mentions that this is where her desire to support her children through education will become important. Another questionnaire will assess her attitude towards risk so that any investment recommendations will take account of her financial needs including the degree of risk. He mentions that although much of the information is quite personal it is necessary because without knowing exactly what she wants to do with her life the financial plan has no goal or meaning. Similarly knowing more about the way Jill lives her life, particularly her spending priorities, helps Phil design a personal investment plan.

Jill finds herself answering many personal questions and revealing things that she would not even tell her best friend. During the course of the discussion they discovered that they had vacationed in the same place in Greece, both had a hankering to visit the Pyramids, and swapped notes on a couple of local restaurants.

Many firms underestimate the number of potentially critical incidents that exist within the system. A simple analysis of the points of contact between a client and an accountant, for example, reveals the following pattern of critical incidents and highlights potential problem areas that relate to other elements of the service besides interaction with contact personnel.

Initial enquiry:

- Google 'accounting services' on Internet or read advertisement in local paper
- Complete e-form on website and wait for firm to make contact or telephone the firm now
- contact with receptionist
- contact with accountant's building/offices.

First meeting:

- exposure of interior of building and facilities
- second contact with receptionist
- meeting with accountant
- contact with other employees of the firm
- exposure to physical evidence of service quality (e.g. accounts prepared for other clients).

Subsequent meetings:

- receive completed work
- further telephone conversations with employees of firm
- exposure to word-of-mouth from other clients
- contact with related suppliers and buyers
- exposure to payment schemes.

Although this is clearly not a comprehensive list of potential interactions, and will vary from one client to another, it illustrates the number of opportunities that the client has to make an assessment of the quality of the service being provided. The growth in use of the Internet means that all organisations need to consider how they will use their website to support their service provision. Customers can use the website to retrieve more traditional contact information which will result in a telephone call, made by the customer into the service provider. Most service providers are used to dealing with this situation. They are at work ready and willing to respond to customers telephoning in at their convenience. However, organisation websites now frequently include a 'contact us' e-form or an email address. Both options require the organisation to process these contacts and take responsibility for responding. When doing so, the service provider needs to remember that an outbound telephone call made to the customer may not arrive at a convenient time for them. Even the need to arrange a mutually convenient time to recall the customer, and then ensure that the telephone call occurs, adds additional steps and complexity to the service process. The process of service design, discussed in Chapter 6, explicitly acknowledges the many points of contact in a visual form. It is one way of identifying, and designing out, potential service failure points.

📖 **It's in the News! 3.1**

Dealing with Multiple Points of Customer Contact

According to the *Liverpool Echo* of 1 November 2007,

A city-wide campaign was launched today to get Liverpool looking great for 2008. Officials want to make sure Liverpool makes the best impression possible on

📖 It's in the News! 3.1   (Continued)

tourists coming from other parts of the UK and abroad. Liverpool council has already unveiled its 'Look Of The City' programme to wipe out grotspots and disguise construction sites with artwork. Now city leaders are also calling on residents to keep a smile on their faces and improve their behaviour by making sure they do not drop litter or chewing gum on the street.

Transport organisation Merseytravel is involved, today revealing plans to tidy up tatty facilities and make sure motorists can easily get in and out of Liverpool. Businesses are being urged to take advantage of 'welcome to Liverpool' training so their staff make a great impression on visitors.

Cllr Mike Storey, executive member for regeneration, said: 'The message is definitely getting through that 2008 is a once-in-a-lifetime opportunity to showcase this city. The events programme is full of festivals and cultural events, which I think are stunning and will be incredibly successful. But if people come to a fantastic concert or exhibition and have to go through dirty, unkempt streets, or get poor service in a cafe or restaurant, there is a danger they will remember that rather than their cultural experience. One of this city's main strengths is that it is a friendly place. Everyone talks about that, whether it is the taxi drivers or people helping out with directions in the street'.

CITY eyesore Concourse House is to be wrapped in huge banners advertising Capital of Culture year [photograph]. The derelict 13-storey tower, once voted Liverpool's worst grot spot by ECHO readers, is awaiting demolition as part of multi-million pound improvements to Lime Street station. But the building will not be demolished before the end of the year, so regeneration officials have decided to mask it from the view. Two sides of Concourse House are likely to be wrapped in adverts for Capital of Culture, while the other two will probably feature commercial promotions. If the deal is finalised, the eyesore should vanish from view later this month.

Marketing effectiveness versus operational efficiency

A trade-off has to be made, in many service organisations, between marketing effectiveness and operational efficiency. Looking at Figure 3.1, where should investments or savings be made – in the Service Marketing System or the Service Operation System?

The success of many of the small operators described in the cases in this book depends on providing a personal service for customers; that is, a concentration on the service marketing system. This clearly has benefits from a marketing perspective as it enables the service provider to respond quickly to the changing needs and requirements of individual customers. However, the greater the degree of customisation in the service offer, the less opportunity there is for cross-utilisation of resources. If there is a loss of production efficiency caused by the provision of tailor-made services (e.g., where a first-class restaurant provides a personalised menu for special client groups), large organisations will often compensate for this by charging a higher price. This is a simple concept that is often forgotten by smaller operators who struggle to identify the real costs associated with the service operation system and consequently find it difficult to price accordingly.

Another area that service organisations frequently overlook is the effort that the customer puts into receiving the service provision. In contrast to the consumption of manufactured products where customers can be viewed as passive, service customers generally play an active role. By the time a customer arrives at a service provider they will already have put some effort into the consumption process. In addition to the actual price of the service provision, customers frequently have to travel to a specified location to gain access to the service providers which will add both time and money to the cost of the service. They will have planned the visit into their day, maybe taken time off work. Not all customers want to participate in the service and do so reluctantly and with great trepidation. This would be true for many customers seeking medical, dental and legal services. Beaven and Scotti[13] refer to the financial and non-financial costs of participating in services as 'outlay'. Beaven and Scotti also urge service providers to consider the need for 'accommodation' by which they mean the need to provide the service in the most convenient way, to reduce customer outlay, and to encourage customer participation. Although we will return to outlay and accommodation when considering service design in Chapter 6, they are both relevant when managing the timing of consumption and the opportunities for growing service businesses.

Concern with timing of consumption: capacity management

The service manager needs to be concerned about when the customer consumes the service as he/she is part of the system when consuming. A manufacturer of chocolate bars, in contrast, is more concerned about the location of purchase

Service Operation System
Activities and processes that generally occur back-stage and are therefore invisible to the customer.

Outlay
All financial and non-financial costs incurred by customers when accessing, participating in and consuming services many of which are in addition to the price paid to the service provider for the service product. These include costs of travel, time involved and psychological costs.

than the time of ultimate consumption (except perhaps to assist in the new product development process), as it has no immediate impact on the production process. The timing of consumption becomes a problem for many service organisations, as demand levels are rarely stable and predictable. Most services experience fluctuations in demand that often vary from week to week and year to year. For example, although a tour operator may plan for an increase in demand for holidays to Turkey during the summer months, a sudden change in the stability of the economy in the country in May could dramatically change the level of demand. Unlike a manufacturing organisation, the tour operator cannot store up holidays to Turkey until the economy stabilises and demand returns. Strategies have to be devised to retain customers during the summer months, perhaps by offering alternative holiday destinations. This would be one example of how service organisations manage the supply of their service to match the pattern of demand. Similarly, the hairdresser can reschedule working hours of staff to account for the fact that few customers want their hair cutting on a Monday. Top stylists are given a day off on Monday in return for working on Saturday, one of the hairdresser's busiest days of the week. An alternative strategic option for a service business is to attempt to influence the pattern of customer demand to suit supply. The hairdresser might reduce the price of haircuts between 9 and 12 on a Tuesday morning. A restaurant might offer 'two meals for the price of one' between 6 PM and 7 PM. Theme parks and tourist attractions frequently operate 'peak' and 'off peak' pricing structures. Sometimes it is simply not possible to change customer behaviour because their need for the service provision is predictable and entrenched. In such circumstances there is a need to ensure that the service provision is available at the time when customer need is most likely to arise even if that requires the service provider to adapt the way in which they normally do business. A law firm in Bristol opened an emergency helpline for victims of domestic violence which they manned during office hours. During the first few months of operation they received few calls, so they extended the operating hours of the service to include the late evening and early hours of the morning. The level of calls to the helpline, and the consequent number of cases they dealt with, rose dramatically.

Many service providers find it very difficult to match demand and supply on all occasions and, where demand exceeds supply, queuing and reservation systems are put into operation. Customer feedback highlights the fact that delays in service delivery, often characterised by long queues, can have a negative impact on customer evaluations of the service.[14,15] The ideal solution would be to eliminate queues completely by careful operations management. However, where this is not possible, service providers are advised to 'change the customer's wait experience (by perceptions management) so that it results in less uncertainty and anger'.[16] Customers become most annoyed and frustrated when they are forced to wait for a service without being given an explanation for the delay. Service providers are advised to communicate to customers as quickly as possible why they are being asked to wait. Where the reason can be clearly identified by customers themselves, for example, waiting for a ride at a funfair or to pay for goods at a supermarket checkout, strategies must be put in place to make the wait as pleasant as possible for customers. Magazines that are provided in dentists' waiting rooms for customers to read and videos played to customers waiting in a queue for a funfair ride are both examples of tactics used by service organisations to help consumers pass the inevitable 'waiting' time pleasurably. It is all too easy for service providers to overlook the waiting process as an integral part of the service provision, and ignore opportunities to improve the customer experience, as the example in Exhibit 3.3 highlights.

Exhibit 3.3   Entry to Dreamworld

A recent visit to theme parks in Australia's Gold Coast revealed how little attention was paid to the entry process compared with themeparks in the USA or the UK. Arriving 30 minutes before Dreamworld was due to open, none of the ticket booths were open. Although we had pre-paid for our tickets and had been informed that we needed to go to the pre-paid booth it was not clear which booth that might be. It was the first day of the Australian school holiday period so many people were turning up early, being deposited by various tour buses and taxi services. Before long the queues were winding back to the car parks. There was no park information, such as maps, available while we waited, so it was not possible to use the wait time to plan the rides we would take or discuss rendezvous places should our group become separated. There was no information on each of the attractions or pictures (still or video) of anyone enjoying the attractions. There was no view into the park at ground level, so all that could be seen were the tallest parts of some of the nearest rides. There were no 'characters' walking around to attract the attention of young children. The patience of children and their parents were being pushed to the limit. There was nowhere to buy drinks, food or sun block. There seemed to be no attempt at all to manage the gathering crowds, the waiting process or to provide information. The only way to obtain any information at all seemed to be via an office door marked 'customer services'. Suddenly that door was slammed shut and locked from inside. Clearly too many customers were seeking service outside of the designated time period. The only information available during the 30-minute wait was a list of attractions that would be unavailable that day. Finally, at 10 AM exactly, the ticket booths opened and people were let into the park. This experience was repeated at each of the other parks visited.

Growth limitation

Customer participation in the system limits the growth opportunities available to the service firm. Where customers have to travel to the service organisation to benefit from the service (e.g., hairdresser, colour consultant), the location of the service becomes critically important and a major source of competitive advantage. Where there is very little perceived difference between the components of the offer (e.g., dry cleaning), a convenient location can make all the difference. Customers consider the time, and cost, of travel by car and parking. Alternatively, walking distance from public transport access can be an issue. Service providers need to consider how their customers will travel to their location and how they can provide customers with greater value from that visit. It is now quite common to find supermarkets renting space to other service providers, such as travel agents and dry cleaners, as both parties seek to provide customers with more reason to visit the one location.

Although it may be possible to open several physically identical hairdressing studios in different locations, it is not possible to replicate the personality and skills of one particular stylist in all the salons. As a result, organisations are constantly looking for ways to expand their target market that do not involve a physical change in location. George Ball and Son, the funeral director (Case Study 2), for example, has become the nominated funeral director for the UK's largest prepayment plan 'Chosen Heritage'. This enables the company to gain access to a new target market without physically having to move location.

Another way of expanding service businesses from a fixed location is to increase the number of customers who are able to access the location. UK supermarkets provide exclusive bus services to ensure that customers without their own transport can get to their stores easily. Equally it is becoming more common for tourist attractions to include transport to and from hotels as part of the experience to make it easy to visit. Growth of small service operations will always be limited by the number of additional customers they can attract to the location and the number of servers able to perform the service.

📖 It's in the News! 3.2

The Service Factory Metaphor Applied to Health Services

According to the Bloomberg.com: UK and Ireland (29 January 2008),

Productivity in Britain's hospitals and surgeries declined every year between 2001 and 2005 after the Labour government, now led by Prime Minister Gordon Brown, more than doubled spending growth on health. Productivity fell by 2 percent each year even though the government took account of improvements to the quality of care, the National Statistics office said in London today. Productivity was little changed between 1995 and 2001. 'The rise in output has not kept pace with the rise in spending,' Karen Dunnell, the head of the statistics office, said in a statement in London today.

The findings give ammunition to critics of Brown, including the Conservative opposition, who say the government has wasted billions of pounds without ensuring the money is well spent. Spending on health increased by 9 percent during the period while output, such as the number of operations and doctors appointments, increased by 4.4 percent. The statistics office said the figures aren't able to measure all aspects of improvements in the quality of healthcare, a key element to measuring productivity. The government said the figures fail to fully capture those improvements and aren't a fair reflection on the National Health Service (NHS). One example cited was that the data counts extra time spent with patients as a decline rather than an increase in productivity.

'As the Office of National Statistics itself admits, any single measure of productivity is unlikely to capture all the costs and benefits of health-care services,' said David Nicholson, chief executive of the National Health Service. 'An ideal measure of NHS output and productivity must include the quality of patient care.'

Conservatives attacked the government's record, saying it had done too little to improve productivity in hospitals. They cited a study published in September by Derek Wanless who said that the NHS had 'failed' to improve its productivity. 'Labour has invested lots and achieved too little,' said Andrew Lansley, a lawmaker who speaks for the Conservative Party on health. 'Taxpayers will be unhappy that the money invested has been squandered by a prime minister who has forced more paperwork and top-down targets on doctors and nurses.'

The statistics office in 2003 commissioned Tony Atkinson of Nuffield College at the University of Oxford to look at ways of improving measurement of output and productivity in public services such as health and education. Atkinson's report said in January 2005 that statistics should capture changes in the quality of services and reflect their growing value to society. Phillip Lee, the government statistician who compiled today's figures, said he was unable to give an account of how close his office is to capturing improved quality in the statistics.

Using the Theatre/Drama Metaphor: The Service as a Performance

Grove and Fisk[17] present a perspective that considers services as 'drama', with features present at a service encounter being likened to those contributing to a theatrical production. They identify the key components of the service experience as being the setting, the actors, the audience and the performance. The actors and audience are the various human participants (e.g., the salon employees and customers, in a hairdressing context), the setting is the physical environment (e.g., the salon itself, decor, lighting, and so on) and the performance, the process of service assembly. All three components are closely interrelated.

In the context of the funeral service, management attention would need to focus on the parts played by the various players in the team – the ministers, doctors, gravediggers, as well as direct employees of the company – in order to control the whole performance. While the actual funeral itself might only last for a few hours, as with a play, the audience has difficulty appreciating the amount of preparation that has gone on back-stage to get ready for the 'performance', namely coffin engraving, bereavement counselling, gown hire and so on. All too often customers relate the price charged solely to the actual funeral ceremony itself without considering the costs of the back-stage activities.

Although Grove and Fisk acknowledge that the service as drama metaphor cannot be applied equally well to all service businesses, they consider it to be a simpler and more powerful concept than the service factory. It draws management attention to the importance of managing customer (audience) involvement in the service experience, as well as managing the production itself – the stage design, layout and the performance of the actors (employees). The notion of 'role playing' can be used in this context to examine the inter-personal relationships between service customers and employees. Both sets of participants can be seen to be working to a script that is determined by their respective role expectations. Coffin bearers, for example, are expected by their employer to dress and speak to customers in a manner that is appropriate to their role. Their script is closely controlled to ensure that it conforms to customer expectations. In these circumstances, although the unpredictability of demand for the service itself necessitates the use of casual labour for such jobs, a disproportionate amount of time is spent recruiting bearers because of the importance of their contribution in terms of meeting customer expectations. If just one coffin bearer were to act 'out of character' for a small part of the ceremony, it could significantly lower the customers' perception of the quality of the entire service.

Postcard from Practice 3.1

Performing at Wagamama

Reading this chapter reminds me of when I worked as a waitress in a very busy restaurant in New Zealand. We had lots of 'scripts' in this restaurant, and everything we did had to conform to certain timings. For example, we would have to have greeted and offered drinks to each group of new customers within two minutes of their arrival, food had to be delivered to the table within eight minutes of it being ordered and we always had to offer water and side dishes.

There were regular assessments of how well we adhered to our performance 'scripts' and how accurate our timings were with frequent 'mystery diner' visits. A member of the public would come to the restaurant to eat and, unbeknownst to us, would be timing how long everything took to arrive and noting if we offered all the extras we were supposed to. I believe the relevance of the 'script' was first to keep the feel of the restaurant as similar as possible to the other restaurants worldwide and secondly to make sure the serving staff was giving a good level of service.

With regard to the 'back-stage/front-stage' concepts discussed, our performance scripts were obviously unknown to our customers. Our responsibility as serving staff was to keep strictly to the script with regard to timings and offering extras, but also to appear to the customers as if there was no script at all, and as if we were treating each group of diners as individuals. This proved the key to keeping them happy, as the timings were designed to have diners waiting for the smallest amount of time possible, but they all wanted to feel as if they were receiving a special, tailor-made service. I found it was doing little things that really raised customers' opinions of the service – from giving a child in the group a straw with their drink to closing the front door of the restaurant after noticing a diner was cold.

Source: Emily Hilton.

Postcard from Practice 3.2

All on Board and Ready to Learn: King's School Band Programme

I wanted to create a programme that provided students with an outlet for musical creativity, performance opportunities and to address the perceived notion that music was for a certain stereotype. We know from research that music education is good for children. It enhances brain activity and promotes learning in other areas. It is not just about the music but what musical understanding can offer the individual.

My personal belief is that in New Zealand we underestimate children's musical intelligence and ability so creating a programme where by every student learns to play a band instrument was revolutionary for not only the school but for the country.

The key stakeholders who I needed on side for this programme to succeed were the boys. How could I ensure from the start that they have a voice and take part with pride and effort? These questions lead me to some research conducted by Edwin (1986), who discovered that playing an instrument for which a child has a timbre (tone colour) preference aids in the success as a musician. The students in the experimental group were given instruments which they preferred the timbre of. Edwin found that the experimental group demonstrated a higher rate of success and also retained more students over the period of study than the control group. He concluded that students were more likely to be successful in music if they not only got to choose the instrument themselves, but also got to hear what the instruments sounded like and felt like to play before they chose.

To this end I created band night – an evening for the boys to come along and listen to the instruments being played – flute, clarinet, trumpet, trombone, baritone, saxophone, tuba. After listening to the sound of each instrument each boy is given the opportunity to try and make a sound on the instruments.

Postcard from Practice 3.2   (Continued)

The option to simply give the students an instrument or for them, or their parents, to simply tick a list was the easy way to go, but not the most effective. Ensuring that all students had the chance to hear and play the instruments was an imperative to ensure the success of the band programme and the on-going interest of the boys.

Source: Emma Featherstone, Director of Music, King's School, Auckland, New Zealand.

Lessons from the Theatre

Services marketing can learn from the many different theatrical movements that have been developed to create distinct audience responses. Many retail organisations, in particular, do claim to be offering 'retail theatre', but their public statements betray a lack of awareness of true theatre.[18] Table 3.1 demonstrates that a study of the main theatrical movements of the twentieth century – theatrical realism, political realism, surrealism and absurd theatre – can provide a focus for retail service managers who acknowledge the

Table 3.1   Classification of customer roles and intended effects: retail applications

Theatrical movement	Role of the customer	Intended effect	Retail management focus
Theatrical realism (practitioner: Stanislavski)	Voyeur	The customer recognises a realistic setting. 'I am observing "a slice of real life".'	Present merchandise in a realistic setting.
		The customer has no sense of involvement. 'I am observing the performance from a distance.'	Maintain a distance between the customer and the presentation.
Political realism (practitioner: Brecht)	Spect-actor	The customer's role is transparent and clearly understood by both parties. 'I am fully aware that this retailer is trying to sell me something.'	Present merchandise in a simple, open and honest environment. Empower employees to be open and honest about their roles and feelings towards the merchandise.
		The customer has the opportunity on-site, to be critical of the offer and the way that it is presented. 'I feel comfortable challenging any aspect of what's on offer.'	Provide extensive opportunities for customer participation. Develop mechanisms to encourage customers to be critical of merchandise.

Surrealism (practitioner: Artaud)	Sense-ceptor	The customer has a sensory experience. 'I feel as if I have been through this experience. I know what it feels like.'	Provide opportunities for customers to 'experience' events. Provide stimulus to arouse depth of affective response.
Absurd theatre (practitioner: Craig)	Connoisseur	The customer is intellectually challenged by what is presented. 'I don't know what this means but I will try to make sense of it.'	Present merchandise in a 'thought provoking', but minimalist, way. No attempt to be made to explain logic behind the presentation. Little information to be provided.
		The customer response is an individual response. 'In my opinion this is about . . . but I will keep it to myself.'	No opportunities to be provided for customer-employee or customer-customer interactions.

Source: Adapted from Baron, Harris and Harris (2001) (see note 17).

potentially different customer roles, and aim to create appropriate intended effects to match them.

Table 3.1 can help retail and service management to focus their offer according to what they would like to be the intended effect of the 'performance' on their customers. Take, for example, the retailing of computer software. Traditionally, the merchandising of such products has simply involved making shelves and shelves of CDs and manuals accessible to the self-service customer. In the Microsoft store in San Francisco, they have tried a different formula. According to the business manager, the store is an attempt to get the software out of the box and present it in a lifestyle environment. The store is split into 'successful living', 'small business', 'creative publishing' and 'road warrior' areas. In the 'successful living' area, for instance, boxes of software (e.g., 'Family Lawyer') are placed on shelves with silk, beanbag wrist rests, etched glass vases and mugs with definitions of 'passionate' written on them.

Using Table 3.1, managers could consider strategies for merchandising such products, based on each of the four theatrical movements, and the corresponding *defined* customer role.

- Customer as voyeur.

  For the customers to adopt this role, they must see a totally realistic setting from a safe distance. This could be achieved through introducing even more realism in working, living, learning and playing areas in the store, with employees playing appropriate parts – for example, drinking coffee in the living area, playing computer and other games in the playing area. Guidelines as to how to create the 'customer as voyeur' role can be gained from a study of Stanislavski's use of theatrical stage settings in theatrical realism.

- Customer as spect-actor.

  For the customers to adopt this role (i.e., of critical participants in the service), their role must be transparent and understood by both parties, and they must have the on-site opportunity to be critical of the product and merchandising. This could be achieved by creating rooms in the store explicitly for debates about the product, where customers can share knowledge about the products, and by having regular on-site IT educational sessions. Guidelines as to how to create the 'customer as spect-actor' role can be gained from a study of Brecht's use of theatrical stage settings in political realism.

- Customer as sense-ceptor.

  For the customers to adopt this role, they must receive and be immersed in a sensory experience. This could most readily be achieved by a section of the software store entirely devoted to virtual reality experiences. However, care must be taken to ensure that all the activities contribute to an unambiguous intended effect. Guidelines as to how to create the 'customer as sense-ceptor' role can be gained from a study of Artaud's use of theatrical stage settings in surrealist theatre.

- Customer as connoisseur.

  For the customers to adopt this role, they must be intellectually challenged by what is presented, and be able to give an individual interpretation of the performance. This could be achieved by ensuring that the combination of artefacts in the display area has no real explanation, and customers could be challenged (electronically) to reach their purchase goals. Guidelines as to how to create the 'customer as connoisseur' role can be gained from a study of Craig's use of theatrical stage settings in absurd theatre.

The example of retailing of software shows how, by using the theatre metaphor, the service experience surrounding the display of physical products can be varied. The same principles can be applied to the retailing of other goods and services. Some formats may more readily lend themselves to particular customer roles. For example, retailers of sports goods, such as Niketown, are giving customers a sensory experience – what it is like to be a top sportsperson. The theatre/drama metaphor, and Table 3.1, provides ideas for innovation in service content, and segmentation of customers, which can complement the structural insights provided in Figure 3.1. To paraphrase Goodwin,[19] drama can be moved into the service factory.

📖 **It's in the News! 3.3**

Service as a Performance

According to *The Philadelphia Inquirer* in the USA (22 January 2008),

Excitement pervades historic Gettysburg, Pa., as National Park Service officials prepare for the April opening of the new museum and visitor center. Licensed battlefield guides share that excitement, as most guided tours will begin at the center.

Gettysburg is American history at its grandest. To help visitors experience it, the park service tests and licenses battlefield guides. More than 150 men and women currently hold licenses, conducting about 22,000 guided tours per year. Since 1915, guides have specialized in the 'personalized tour,' conducted in the visitor's own vehicle. In basic two-hour tours, guides provide a running narrative of the battle while driving 15 miles or more. By answering visitor questions and tailoring each tour to individual interests, guides craft unique and personalized tours. At the visitor's request, the two-hour tour can be extended to a full day.

Summary

Some fundamental theory and frameworks for the marketing of services have been inspired by two common metaphors: the factory metaphor and the theatre/drama metaphor. If the metaphors are understood, and used appropriately, they add to our understanding of services marketing. The metaphors can even be mixed as argued in the previous section. In this way, both the structure and content of services are given due regard. A summary of the use of these two popular metaphors is provided in Table 3.2.

Summarising the Factory Metaphor

It is assumed that the goal of a service is efficiency. Therefore, we try to get consumers through the system quickly, reduce bottlenecks and queues, and acknowledge the importance of quality control. The focus of attention is the structure and total process through the system. For example, with rail

Table 3.2   The use of the factory and theatre/drama metaphors

	Factory metaphor	Theatre/drama metaphor
Strategic goals	Efficiency	Rave reviews from audiences
Focus of attention	Structure and process	Performance
Assumptions about consumers	Inputs contributing to production	Audience requiring cues from actors
Assumptions about the	Automated factory	Stage play service
Recommendations to management	Design systems and procedures	Coach actors and write scripts
Potential areas of application	Airlines, fast food, rail travel	Theme parks, pubs, restaurants, retailers

travel, we should examine all the points of contact the passenger has with the service, from the purchase of the ticket right through to the ordering of the taxi at the destination point. The consumers are assumed to be the contributors to production, but also the cause of bottlenecks. They are seen as 'partial employees' who can help with service production. For example, regular hospital patients can help new patients familiarise themselves with the environment and systems. The service itself is likened to an automatic factory and terms such as 'inputs', 'process', 'outputs' and 'productivity' become part of the language.

Summarising the Theatre/Drama Metaphor

It is assumed that the goal of the service is to receive 'rave reviews' from the audience (customers). There is a need to acknowledge explicitly that customers evaluate their experiences individually. The focus of attention is on the content of the service; that is, the interactions that take place involving the actors (contact personnel) and audience. Roles and scripts of both actors and audience are of prime importance, as is the design of the service setting. The consumers, being likened to an audience, require cues, leading to stimulation and an 'experience'. The service itself is compared to a stage play, incorporating all the hedonistic elements of service consumption, with attention being drawn to the performance, rather than the process. Terms such as 'front- and back-stage', 'settings', 'roles' and 'scripts' become part of the language.

As is seen in the final two rows of Table 3.2, the recommendations to management may depend on the features of a particular service which determine which of these two metaphors is predominant.

Learning Outcomes

Having read this chapter, you should be able to

- apply conceptual frameworks, emanating from the use of factory and drama/theatre metaphors, to explore key issues affecting service management
- understand the implications, for strategy, HRM and operations, of adopting the factory or drama/theatre metaphors, and the assumptions made about the customers
- appreciate the origin of terms, such as delivery, process, productivity, setting, roles and scripts, which are part of the language of services marketing and management research.

Discussion Questions and Exercises

1. Draw a Services Marketing System for George Ball and Son (Case Study 2). What difficulties did you experience in employing the Services Marketing System for a funeral service?
2. Outline some 'scripts' that employees have employed with you in service encounters.
3. How would you manage the entry into a theme park using the two metaphors discussed in the chapter: (a) factory (service as a system) and (b) theatre (service as a performance).

4. To what extent do customers in an open street market play the role of 'spectactor'?

5. What should the goal of lectures be – efficiency or the subject of rave reviews?

Notes and References

1. Morgan, G., *Imaginization: The Creative Art of Management,* Sage Publications, Newbury Park, CA., 1993.
2. Monin, M. and Monin, D. J., 'Rhetoric and Action: When a Literary Drama Tells the Organization's Story,' *Journal of Organizational Change Management,* 10(1), 1997, pp. 47–60.
3. Goodwin, C., 'Moving the Drama into the Factory: The Contribution of Metaphors to Services Research,' *European Journal of Marketing,* 30(9), 1996, pp. 13–36.
4. Tynan, C., 'A Review of the Marriage Analogy in Relationship Marketing,' *Journal of Marketing Management,* 13(7), pp. 695–704.
5. Hunt, S. D. and Menon, A., 'Metaphors and Competitive Advantage: Evaluating the Use of Metaphors in Theories of Competitive Strategy,' *Journal of Business Research,* 33, 1995, pp. 81–90.
6. Monin, M. and Monin, D. J., 'Rhetoric and Action: When a Literary Drama Tells the Organization's Story'.
7. Bateson, J. E. G., *Managing Services Marketing: Text and Readings*, 2nd edn., The Dryden Press 1992.
8. Lovelock, C. H., *Managing Services Marketing, Operations, and Human Resources,* 2nd edn., Prentice Hall International, Englewood Cliffs, NJ, 1992.
9. Bateson, J. E. G., *Managing Services Marketing: Text and Readings*, 2nd edn., The Dryden Press 1992.
10. Ibid.
11. McGrath, M. A., 'An Ethnography of a Gift Store: Trappings, Wrappings and Rapture,' *Journal of Retailing,* 65(4), 1989, pp. 421–49.
12. Bitner, M. J., Booms, B. H. and Tetreault, M. S., 'The Service Encounter: Diagnosing Favourable and Unfavourable Incidents,' *Journal of Marketing,* 54, January 1990.
13. Beaven, M. H. and Scotti, D. J., 'Service-Oriented Thinking and Its Implications For The Marketing Mix,' *The Journal of Services Marketing,* 4(4), 1990, pp. 5–19.
14. Scotland, R., 'Customer Service: A Waiting Game,' *Marketing,* 11 March 1992, pp. 1–3.
15. Taylor, S., 'Waiting for Service: The Relationship Between Delays and Evaluations of Service,' *Journal of Marketing,* 58, April 1994, pp. 56–69.
16. Ibid.
17. Grove, S. J. and Fisk, R. P., 'The Dramaturgy of Services Exchange: An Analytical Framework for Services Marketing,' in L. L. Berry, G. L. Shostack and G. D. Upah (eds), *Emerging Perspectives on Services Marketing,* American Marketing Association, Chicago, 1983.
18. Baron, S., Harris, K and Harris, R. 'Retail Theatre: The Intended Effect of the Performance,' *Journal of Service Research*, 4(2), pp. 102–117.
19. Goodwin, C., 'Moving the Drama into the Factory: The Contribution of Metaphors to Services Research'.

4

Customer Interactions in Services

Learning Objectives

Overall Aim of the Chapter

To provide a comprehensive evaluation of the encounters that a customer has, in a service context, with contact personnel, other customers and equipment/technology.

In particular, the *chapter objectives* are

- to demonstrate both the frequency and the variety of interactions faced by a customer in the service encounter

- to emphasise the significance of managerial implications associated with customer interactions in the service encounter

- to outline the principal causes of satisfaction and dissatisfaction with interpersonal interactions between customers and employees

- to provide an insight into the frequency and importance of customer-to-customer interactions, and some methods for compatibility management

- to present research on customer interactions with technology-based self-services and the principal causes of satisfaction and dissatisfaction with the interactions.

Introduction

'Service encounters' has been identified as a key component of the current agenda for service marketers.[1] As noted in the previous chapter, every time customers come into contact with any aspect of the service delivery system they are presented with an opportunity to evaluate the service provider and form an opinion of service quality. A customer may form an impression about the quality of a dentist's work, for example, from a brief conversation with another patient in the waiting room, or simply from a glance at the wallpaper in the surgery. Irrespective of the nature and length of the contact, each 'encounter' represents an important 'moment of truth' for the customer. The latter term, originally introduced by Normann,[2] has more recently been termed the 'bullfight metaphor' by Mattsson,[3] as it underlines strongly 'the uniqueness and the importance of every encounter between the customer and the service provider'.

📖 It's in the News! 4.1

Service Encounter – First Impressions

According to the BBC News (7 February, 2008)

In a wide-ranging review on the future of policing by Sir Ronnie Flanagan, the UK's Chief Inspector of Constabulary, he criticises the service provided when people turn up at police stations.

Sir Ronnie calls for a 'radical overhaul' of police station reception areas and the service provided to the public. 'Dingy surroundings, out-of-date posters and poor or slow service' he says, 'have a negative impact on public satisfaction and confidence.'

Shostack[4] provides a helpful definition of the service encounter, referring to it as the 'period of time during which a customer directly interacts with a service'. This acknowledges the notion, from Chapter 3, that customers have multiple points of contact. Furthermore, customers relate to the 'period of time' when asked to recall incidents with the service. Two examples are now given.

Example 1 – Mother takes five-year-old daughter to 'kiddies' fun and fitness class' at a leisure centre.

- Saw details of kiddies' fun and fitness class on leisure centre website
- Rang leisure centre to enquire about this 'new' service
- Parked the car outside the leisure centre
- Met the girl running the class, and talked about what would happen
- Saw new fitness studio
- Met other kids in the class
- Sat outside with other mothers, while the class took place.

Example 2 – Adult male requires quick repair on car.

- Rang the dealer where the car last serviced, found new dealership taken over
- Rang the new dealership
- Dropped car off at dealership, parking spaces available
- Explained problem to man at dealership (his role not clear)
- Rang up later – not contacted as promised
- Saw female receptionist

- Chatted to another customer while receptionist was in back office
- Talked over repairs, bill less than expected, exhaust adjusted 'free of charge'
- Picked up car and drove home.

The examples fit Shostack's definition of the encounter. Her definition includes interpersonal interactions and also customer contact with physical facilities, technology and other tangible elements – interactions that were highlighted in the Service Delivery System in Chapter 3. Because of the inseparability characteristic of services, encounters will be *frequent* in the service delivery system as customers and service employees co-create the service experience. The nature of service consumption means that customers frequently interact with other customers as they co-consume and co-create the service. Because of the intangibility characteristic of services, the *tangible* aspects are important, that is, the people the customers meet, as well as the physical surroundings and equipment. Because of the heterogeneity characteristic of services, there will be *differences* in the nature and customer perceptions of encounters.

Customer Perceptions
Customer views and opinions.

In this chapter we examine the significance of service encounters, as well as the related managerial issues. This is followed by a detailed look at the first three of the following types of interactions:

- customer with service employees
- customer with fellow customers
- customer with technology/equipment
- customer with the physical environment.

The customer interactions with the physical environment will be covered in Chapter 6, as part of service design.

Given the nature of the four types of interaction, the theory on service encounters draws on elements of communication theory, interpersonal skills, sociology, environmental and cognitive psychology, ergonomics and human–machine interfaces.

Significance of Service Encounters

Why, then, has 'service encounters' been identified as such a key component of the current agenda? It is because:

- service encounters are seen to influence customers' perceptions of service quality
- service encounters create lasting memories that influence customer expectations of future service performance
- there are opportunities to *manage* service encounters.

All the interactions that take place during the 'period of time' have the potential to influence quality perceptions, and the greater the number of interactions, the more chances there are for customers to judge the service (and spot mistakes!). Even relatively straightforward services, such as those described in Examples 1 and 2, consist of a mix of customer interactions with service employees, fellow customers, technology and physical surroundings. If services are designed to reduce the potential number of customer interactions, those that remain are critical. The words of advice to webpage designers are apt. Go for fewer clicks, but enhance the encounters.

Not all the interactions are equally critical. In Example 1, according to the mother, the two things that really mattered were the manner of the girl instructor (who checked the daughter's prior experience, and treated her as someone special) and her daughter's interaction with the other children. In Example 2, the most important elements were the attitude of the person on the phone at the new dealership (welcoming), and the explanation of the bill at the end, which helped recover some ill feeling about not being contacted when the car was ready to be picked up. At a more extreme level, a bad landing in an aeroplane is likely to be the most critical memory, however good the rest of the flight had been – good food, pleasant conversation and polite airline staff.

An interaction that is critical for one customer may be less critical or even insignificant for another. In part this may be due to previous experiences of the same or similar service provision in the past which leads a customer to expect how the service will be performed. The Auckland Airport Arrivals (Case Study 4) provides a good illustration of this: Terri is unable to forget the feelings associated with 'being caught' previously by biosecurity officers whereas other passengers may take little notice of the biosecurity measures. For the young boy who has had his ear accidentally cut on a visit to the Barber's the critical interaction is whether or not the Barber draws blood! No matter what criteria parents use to select a dentist for their children the critical interaction for many children will be the sticker and/or lollipop given to them for being good! The critical nature of an interaction may also arise as a result of personal characteristics. In the case of the airline story in Chapter 1, John thinks nothing of the routine security questions at check-in although that interaction added to Jack's fear of flying.

Despite the mix and some of the complexities of the interactions in service encounters, there are seemingly obvious ways of managing them. Employees can be trained to act and react appropriately. Physical surroundings and equipment/technology can be designed to create appropriate environments and way-finding. Even customer–customer interactions can be encouraged or discouraged. Most research on service encounters, therefore, is significant in that there are easily understood management implications resulting from it.

Before examining the different types of customer interactions in more detail, we outline some of the more general managerial issues associated with each of them.

Customer Interacts with Service Employee(s) – Managerial Issues

- How do we train employees to increase customers' levels of satisfaction and perceived quality of the service?

First of all, we need to know what *customers themselves* find satisfying and dissatisfying about services. There is a variety of consumer research techniques that can be used; qualitative methods such as interviews, observation, critical incident stories, and quantitative methods such as surveys and controlled experiments. Second, we need to assess whether the incidents that customers find (dis)satisfying are generic across a range of services, or whether they are situation specific. Third, we need to examine different styles of employee training methods. Some are appropriate for training employees to 'follow the rule book'. Others are more appropriate for encouraging improvisation.

- To what extent, and in what circumstances, should employees be empowered?

As customers, we can often feel frustrated when a service employee seems unable to carry out what seems like a very straightforward adaptation to a service element without first gaining authority from a more senior person. For example, the railway train guard may not be empowered to allow passengers to use empty first-class carriages even when they are causing potentially dangerous congestion by having to stand up in the aisles of the economy class. Or the administrative assistant may not be authorised to accept a student assignment after the 'due time', whatever be the circumstances. Clearly, as these examples imply, there is often a trade-off between employees applying rigidly a set of fair rules and employees adapting and improvising without the need for higher-level approval.

Postcard from Practice 4.1

Canadian Doctor's Interaction with Patients

I tend to use the phrase 'It all depends' a lot. And I think about a quote attributed to Paracelsus 'The dose makes the poison'.

It used to be that patients would consult with relatives and friends for medical information and bring such information to my attention. This would drive me crazy. Now, it is given that patients will regularly go to the Internet and other media outlets to obtain the 'latest' regarding their symptoms, investigations, medications and treatment options. Armed with all this information that they have collected, they do question me and often request and direct the kind of medical care that they feel they should have. I expect such. I rather like that they have become more active participants in their health care. I think that is a positive development. I have never liked the 'paternalistic' stance of medicine.

Postcard from Practice 4.1   (Continued)

Unfortunately, the information patients have obtained can do more than educate or inform. It may create unnecessary worry and stress for them. For I know, and they know, that they are not able to really evaluate their new-found information. They cannot really assess issues of appropriateness of information, statistics, specificity, sensitivity, or evaluate the information in relation to evidence-based medicine. Many physicians have trouble doing so as well. So, I point out to them that 'It all depends' – then we proceed to do medicine.

Source: Robert Kingstone.

Customer Interacts with Fellow Customers – Managerial Issues

Customer Compatibility
Customers with similar tastes and behaviours.

• How can we manage customer compatibility?

As many services take place in the presence of other customers, the fellow customers (often strangers) may affect perceptions of the service. This is quite normal in services such as air travel, aerobics classes, coach tour holidays and tutorials. It is in the interest of service management to keep together customers with similar behaviours and tastes, and separate those with different behaviours and tastes.

• To what extent do customer-to-customer interactions determine the service experience?

Although it may be more difficult for service providers to identify and control interpersonal exchanges between customers in the service environment, such exchanges have the potential to affect the customer's perception of the quality[5] of the service provided and are easily recalled by customers.[6,7]

• To what extent can/should we encourage/discourage customer-to-customer interactions?

Martin and Pranter[8] are anxious to point out that compatibility management is more important in some service environments than others. For example, careful management of the encounter is needed when customers are expected to share time, space or service equipment with one another. Where the service experience necessitates that customers are in close proximity with each other for a period of time, there may be advantages to be gained by encouraging customer-to-customer interactions. Customers travelling on long train journeys often hold conversations with the person sitting in the seat next to them, which passes the time pleasantly. As we see later, the extent to which managers should encourage or discourage customer-to-customer interactions is linked with customer involvement and participation in services.

□ It's in the News! 4.2

Managing Unruly Customers

According to the *Los Angeles Times* (9 February, 2008),

Three police officers in two cars brought home 12-year-old Jeffrey Probasco Jr. crying in the back seat of one of the cruisers, His offense? Violation of California Penal Code Section 640, subsection B4. Specifically, eating 'Doritos' on a bus in Diamond Bar. Jeffrey was snagged in an undercover operation by the Los Angeles County Sheriff's Department and Foothill Transit Police. He was fingered by a plainclothes officer posing as a passenger. That got him kicked of the bus, questioned, issued a ticket and hauled home by police.

'I think it's ridiculous, to be honest', says his mother, Laverne, 'There are other things the police can be doing, rather than writing a 12-year-old up for eating chips'.

Los Angeles County Sheriff's Lt. Kevin Hannigan said the department often assigns undercover officers to bus lines that serve middle and high school campuses. 'We go out whenever the drivers have problems – fare evasion, talking loud, eating, playing music... Unruly children scare away the regular customers who ride the bus'.

Even Jeffrey said his fellow passengers were a rowdy bunch – yelling, shimmying up the poles, doing pull-ups on the overhead grab bar – until the officers arrived.

□ It's in the News! 4.3

Customer-to-customer Interactions

According to Natalie Walsh, writing for the UK's *Daily Telegraph*, 20 March 2007,

Fancy a brief encounter of the French kind? Then book yourself a trip to Nice, Cannes or maybe Marseille. Any destination on the Côte d'Azur will do – as long as you travel by train. The country that gave the world the philosophy café has now launched the train of thought – dedicated carriages on long-distance high-speed TGV trains for supposedly intellectual rendezvous.

For a surcharge of £1, you can arrange to sit next to other passengers with similar interests. Fancy discussing the finer points of Freud, Wittgenstein or the socio-economic impact of the Kama Sutra on rural society? Or how about a game of cards, a serious chat about football or a Sudoko challenge? All possibilities save one are available to passengers who log on to www.idtgvandco.com and surf profiles of other passengers already booked on their train.

TGV insists this is not a matchmaking service. 'We do not encourage amorous meetings,' I was told. But this is France, the land that invented furtive glances, five-minute affairs and illicit rendezvous. This has to be a ruse for romantic encounters if ever there was one.

Customer Interacts with Technology/Equipment – Managerial Issues

- What are the gains and losses involved in replacing interpersonal service with self-service?

The heterogeneity characteristic of services arises mainly from variations associated with the human service employee. Much of this variation could be eliminated by replacing the human-based contribution with technology-based services. There has been a rapid rise in the use of Technology-Based Self-Service (TBSS) options such as 'pay at the pump', 'self-scanning' grocery shopping or the 'self-check-in' kiosk at airports. TBSS systems require support from self-service technology (SST) interfaces such as the Internet, scanning equipment, colour monitors, voice recognition systems and touchscreens. While there are gains in the consistency, and possibly reliability through the use of TBSS, many customers do value human contact,[9] and attention must be given to clarifying the customer roles with self-service systems.[10] Given the need for service organisations to provide value to customers, there is a requirement to determine how customers might value the use of technology within the service provision. TBSS may be entirely appropriate where it can provide benefits of greater access, speed or convenience through 24/7 availability. However, research indicates that service providers may need to be particularly careful when seeking to switch customers to TBSS when they are used to and are happy with their interactions with service employees.Curran and Meuter suggest that service providers wishing to replace personal interactions between customers and employees with TBSS interactions may need to inject greater customer enjoyment.[11]

- What are the attitudes and behaviours of customers with regard to technology-based services (especially the Internet)?

It has been suggested that customers' sources of satisfaction and dissatisfaction with technology-based services may be different from those associated with interpersonal services.[12] With the increasing use of the Internet (see It's in the News! 4.4) in particular, there is a need for management to use creative research techniques to understand more fully the customer needs of and experiences with the technology.

TBSS
Technology-based self-service options.

SST
Self-service technology.

📖 **It's in the News! 4.4**

Internet Retail Sales Growth

According to the *Financial Times*, 1st April 2008,

Led by UK shoppers, Europe has finally started clicking the 'buy now' button. Total online retail spending in the UK, France, Germany, Spain and Italy reached almost €41bn last year, up by a third in the UK and France, and somewhat less elsewhere.

The UK is by far the most internet savvy of the big European economies – shoppers did about 5 per cent of all their retail spending online last year, compared with 1.6 per cent in France and 0.5 per cent in Spain, according to Mintel. That is largely because UK online supermarkets have enjoyed great success. Three of the top 20 European internet retailers are UK grocers, led by Tesco in fourth place.

Internet shopping is also rising because more shoppers are choosing to stay home. Visits to internet shopping sites rose 2.2 per cent year-on-year in March, while high street foot traffic fell 2.7 per cent, Experian Footfall said on Tuesday.

Most of Europe still lags behind the US in adopting the broadband internet services crucial for making online shopping sites function effectively. US e-retail sales totalled $137bn or 3.4 per cent of all retail spending in 2007, according to the US Census Bureau. There are similar trends for travel purchases, where eMarketer estimates US 2007 online spending to be $94bn versus an aggregate $49bn in the big European economies.

Looking ahead, Mintel forecasts online retail spending in France and the United Kingdom will triple by 2012. Germany, where usage of both credit cards and computers is lower, is expected to grow more slowly. High street names such as Carrefour and DSG International are coming to dominate European e-retailing as their US peers do in their domestic market. Amazon is grabbing share in Europe and is the only pure-play among the top 10 online sellers. So the European rankings are likely to change. The German mail order specialists, such as Otto and Arcandor, Europe's top two internet sellers, will soon be displaced.

Building on the discussion in Chapter 3 it is worth noting that technology and machines can help service organisations manage operational efficiency but that there will always be situations where marketing effectiveness requires performance by service employees. It would therefore be important for organisations to determine customer expectations from the service delivery when considering the use of technology and machines to deliver aspects of the service. Where customers associate satisfactory service provision with personal interactions it may be foolish for an organisation to install TBSS provision.

Customer Interacts with the Physical Surroundings – Managerial Issues

• How do we design the physical setting of a service to encourage 'approach' rather than 'avoidance' behaviours of customers?

As consumers, we encounter many types of designed 'servicescapes'. Some are designed to create experiences for us (e.g., 'theme bars'). Some are designed to support direction finding (e.g., airports). Some are designed to support the comfort of the occupants (e.g., children's wards in hospitals). Some are designed to suit the purposes of an event (e.g., the layout of a seminar room or lecture theatre). Some are designed to attract and retain potential customers (e.g., shopping malls and retail stores). We have all probably avoided certain service settings, or wished to leave them at the earliest opportunity, or in contrast 'felt at home' in other settings. The design of the 'servicescape' can be particularly important, as customers' *first* encounter with a service is often with the physical environment.

- Can 'servicescape' design ideas be transferable across different types of services?

The majority of servicescapes cater for interpersonal services, with both customers and employees on-site. Others cater for self-service operations, where only customers are on-site. There are also remote services, such as 'helplines', where only employees are on-site.[13] Rather than each type of service 'starting from scratch', can ideas from one type of service be transferred to another where on-site presence is similar? Examples of transfer of ideas can be seen with some interpersonal services: 'theatre' being applied to retail stores, and theme park activities present in shopping malls.

Customer Interactions in Service Encounters

The managerial issues raised in the previous section have resulted in research that has been undertaken to increase our understanding of customer interactions in services. We now summarise some of the work relating to customer interactions with *service employees, fellow customers* and *technology/equipment.*

Interactions between Customers and Employees

Features of satisfactory and unsatisfactory incidents

According to Bitner *et al.*,[14] 'effective management of the service encounter involves understanding the often complex behaviours of employees that can distinguish a highly satisfactory service encounter from a dissatisfactory one, and then training, motivating and rewarding employees to exhibit those behaviours'.

In this context, one of the first tasks facing service management is to identify which encounters with service personnel customers find most satisfying and/or dissatisfying. Bitner *et al.* used *the 'critical incident' technique* to identify the sources of satisfaction and dissatisfaction. Customers across three 'high contact' service industries (hotels, restaurants and airlines) were asked to describe a specific instance, during the service that they had received, in which particularly good or poor service interaction had occurred. The study identified 699 incidents; 347 satisfactory and 352 dissatisfactory. Of the 347 satisfactory incidents, 86 were from airlines, 165 from restaurants and 96 from hotels. Of the

Critical Incident Technique
A research method that identifies sources of satisfaction and dissatisfaction for customers in their encounters with contact personnel.

352 dissatisfactory incidents, 77 were from airlines, 191 from restaurants and 84 from hotels.

The analysis of the results revealed a number of *employee behaviours* that directly influenced customer satisfaction and dissatisfaction with their service experience. The largest proportion of *satisfying* incidents occurred as a result of unprompted and unsolicited actions by employees which generally gave customers a pleasant surprise; for example, going to your regular restaurant to find that the seating has been arranged in advance especially for you, just as you would want it. On other occasions customers unexpectedly received special or individual treatment for another reason. For instance, they may have been given a vegan menu even though the restaurant had not been notified beforehand of special requirements. The largest proportion of *dissatisfactory* encounters related to 'employees inability or unwillingness to respond in service failure situations'. To illustrate this, if customers had been allocated an unsuitable hotel room by mistake, employees did not appear to be either concerned about the situation or prepared to do anything about it. They would frequently communicate their reluctance to act by non-verbal as well as verbal communication, shrugging their shoulders, for example, to indicate that there was nothing that they could do about the situation.

In general, most of the satisfactory and unsatisfactory incidents related to the presence or absence, respectively, of employees' abilities to:

- recover service delivery system failures
- be adaptable in responding to special customer needs or requests
- take spontaneous actions.

Table 4.1 provides examples of appropriate and inappropriate employee actions relating to the three categories.

In a follow-up survey which analysed *employees'* critical incidents,[15] the same three categories above were identified, together with a fourth category, 'coping with difficult customers'. It is reassuring to service managers that similar sources of satisfaction and dissatisfaction have been confirmed by both customers and employees. Furthermore, each category represents a source of *both satisfaction and dissatisfaction*. Management effort can be channelled into improving customer satisfaction by concentrating on these categories. Critical incident studies can provide a lot more detail about specific events and behaviours that underlie service encounter dissatisfaction than can standard customer satisfaction surveys. However, the technique only tends to focus on incidents leading to customer delight, at the top end of the scale, and dissatisfaction at the bottom, and may miss out the merely satisfactory encounters in the middle.

The next stage in the successful management of this form of encounter is to train, motivate and reward staff to exhibit the behaviours that lead to the satisfying encounter. The results of the above study highlight the important role employees have to play in keeping customers informed about what is happening

Table 4.1 Customer sources of satisfaction and dissatisfaction with customer–employee interactions

Category	Type of service issue facing employee	Exemplar	Example of a satisfactory employee response	Example of an un-satisfactory employee response
Recovery of service system failure	• Unavailable service.	Customer tries to pick up hire car. The one ordered is not available.	Upgrade the car (often followed by positive word-of-mouth).	Imply it was the customer's fault – didn't fill in the necessary paperwork.
	• Unreason-ably slow service.	Train delayed one hour.	Offer free tea/coffee and biscuits while waiting; allow free phone calls.	Standard script: 'We apologise for the delay in service…a buffet service is available on the train for the sale of hot drinks.'
	• Other core service failures.	Dead mouse found in hotel swimming pool.	Move to another hotel (upgrade).	'Will get rid of it when I finish serving dinner for other guests.'
Responding to special customer needs or requests	• Customer has 'special' needs.	Child with nut allergy at restaurant. Parents ask which meals are OK.	Check with chef or manager and run through menu with customers.	Don't know the answer and unable to find out.
	• Customer has preferences.	Customer wants a Big Mac breakfast with no egg.	Adapt, and give two sausages and no egg.	'Sorry, you'll have to pick the eggs out yourself.'
	• Customer admits to making an error.	Customer misses flight through misreading check-in time.	Put on next available flight.	Missed the flight. Tough!
Taking spontaneous actions	• Opportunity for unprompted or unsolicited action.	Waiter notices that customer has a cold.	Brings over a 'hot toddy on the house'.	Asks customer to leave if he cannot stop coughing.
	• Opportunity for demonstrating extraordinary behaviour.	Customer conversation with hotel employee.	Give hotel guest a vase of flowers she admired.	Show exasperation through swearing, yelling or rudeness.

Source: Adapted from Bitner *et al.*, 1990 (see note 14).

in the service system. In order to be able to do this effectively, employees themselves need to know what is going on and have a shared understanding of what the organisation is trying to achieve. They need to possess knowledge about the service provided as well being able to demonstrate a wide range of interpersonal skills. In order to be able to respond appropriately in service failure situations, front-line employees need to be given the power to take action without continued reference to a higher authority. Many of these ideas are encapsulated in the notion of employee empowerment that is discussed more fully in Chapter 7. In their capacity as 'relationship managers', employees have the power to significantly reduce perceived uncertainty for the customer and consequently improve 'relationship quality'.[16]

Employee Empowerment
The ability of employees to adopt a responsive approach to ensure customer satisfaction.

Managerial implications

Arising out of the research above, there are two actions, in particular, which should lead to an improvement in customer satisfaction.

1. *Plan* for effective service recovery.

   Interestingly, 23 per cent of the accounts of *satisfactory* incidents relate to employee responses to service failures. Even if there was initial customer disappointment with a service failure, a successful recovery of the situation by an employee can lead to a high level of ultimate customer satisfaction. An important part of the planning for service recovery process is the need to gain an accurate picture of dissatisfying incidents. Providing mechanisms to capture customer comments, particularly complaints, is critical. Such information is valuable to a service organisation and many spend considerable sums of money on expensive market research yet ignore the 'free' advice their customers gladly provide! Clearly, service failures should be avoided, but equally clearly they do happen. Service recovery policies can be designed and procedures planned in advance so that contact employees can be briefed, trained and rewarded accordingly.

   Customers who perceive that an organisation has not thought through its responses to service failures are likely to become dissatisfied and may spread negative comments to others. For example, it is not unusual for UK railway trains to break down or be delayed. Given the frequency of such occurrences, passengers expect the train operators to have effective recovery systems in place. If they do not, the negative word-of-mouth that follows affects the whole transport system.

   Elliott, Harris and Baron[17] observe that the current focus on service recovery in services marketing has a tendency to analyse the outcomes of individual encounters occurring at the front-stage with less attention to organisational errors occurring back-stage. They highlight the limitations of this approach in providing management with sufficient evidence of an accumulation of failures that might indicate a potential organisational crisis.

2. Communicate with employees about *all* parts of the business.

Employees need to be flexible and give flexible responses when anything even slightly unusual occurs in interactions with customers. To do so, employees need to know the implications of their actions on all parts of the business. For example, the kind gesture of giving the hotel guest a vase of flowers (Table 4.1) may not be wise unless the employee knows who pays for another one, whether there is a budget code, and who is responsible for the replacement. Similarly, the new schoolteacher could be given the flexibility to rearrange a classroom in an open-plan environment to meet pupil needs, but only in the full knowledge of its effect on other classes, teachers and administrative staff.

Customer-to-customer Interactions

Although it may be more difficult for service providers to identify and control interpersonal exchanges between customers in the service environment, such exchanges have the potential to affect the customer's perception of the quality[18] of the service provided and therefore merit some consideration. As many services take place in the presence of other customers, customer-to-customer interactions inevitably occur. It may be just a casual conversation, such as the chat at the desk in the car showroom (Example 2, p. 70). However, it may be the key to a service purchase, as in Example 1, p. 70, where the demonstration by the daughter of the enjoyment of being with the other children was a very important element of the service encounter. Despite the potentially significant effect on service encounters, customer-to-customer interactions have tended to be the neglected dimension of the service experience.[19] However, there are helpful research findings in this area, which yield a number of managerial implications.

We start with a summary of research findings.

Forms of customer-to-customer interactions

There are two types of participation:

1. Interactions between acquaintances.

People often consume services with friends and/or relatives. They carry out shopping with 'purchase pals'.[20] In the context of furniture shopping, for example, a survey showed that only 27.3 per cent of the sample of consumers shopped alone, while over 50 per cent shopped in pairs.[21] For some people, interacting with acquaintances is an integral part of a service. 'Regulars' sit in the same seats at the bar or pub every night, or sit at the same table in the bingo hall every Thursday night. In these cases, service organisations provide the premises for the 'third places' for acquaintances to meet.[22]

The behaviour of acquaintances in a given service setting may vary in different countries. This can be observed with respect to the role of the male partner in female clothing outlets. In Marks & Spencer in the United Kingdom, for example, males will sit in a waiting area outside the female fitting rooms, and in many cases may not even see the proposed purchase being tried on by their female partner. In contrast, in Greece, the couples wish the male to have a more active say in the purchase, and a waiting area for the males would be redundant.

There is some evidence that service companies may wish to facilitate interactions between acquaintances. For example, hairdressers will encourage you to bring a friend to enhance the social aspects of the service. Equally, the provision of 'adult crèches', where people can wait while their companions are trying on garments, is an acknowledgement that people often shop in pairs or groups. However, there is surprisingly little published research on the interactions between purchase pals and the effect of such interactions on purchase behaviour, despite the fact that it is acknowledged that 'one purchase behaviour that it is easy for salespeople to identify . . . is the utilisation of a shopping/buying companion or "purchase pal" '.[23] In the car salesroom context, for example, it is believed that customer utilisation of a companion indicates a lack of experience and a greater susceptibility to salesperson influence.[24]

2. Interactions between strangers (or unacquainted influencers).

People often consume services in the presence of other consumers and interact with them. A stranger may recommend a certain type of beer in a public house or a holiday destination in a travel agent. More annoyingly, a stranger may blow smoke in your face in a restaurant. Often strangers are very knowledgeable about services that you are sharing or about the products available in a service environment. For example, a lady who was thinking of buying a puppy obtained sufficient quality advice from fellow customers in the waiting room at a veterinary practice that the risk of purchase was reduced considerably. She was advised on issues such as 'hip counts', reliable local breeders and insurance plans and it only took half an hour.

Some consumers are more likely to interact with fellow consumers than others. McGrath and Otnes[25] identified categories of consumers who are the most likely to engage in on-site conversations with strangers in retail settings. The 'overt interpersonal influencers' were categorised as being 'helpseekers', 'reactive helpers' and 'proactive helpers'. Helpseekers actively seek information by questioning other shoppers. Reactive helpers respond readily to requests from other shoppers for information. Proactive helpers go out of their way to engage in conversations and offer advice to fellow shoppers. Some shoppers play more than one of these roles. Interestingly, there is some evidence that people who regularly find themselves acting in the role of reactive helper do, in fact, have the ability to respond to requests by other shoppers for product-related information.[26] Consumers seem to be able to identify responsive and knowledgeable fellow shoppers.

Interactions between strangers can be viewed positively or negatively by the participants. In a study of interactions in Florida theme parks, consumers were asked to recall, in their own words, any critical incidents they had encountered with strangers.[27] There were almost equal numbers of positive (49 per cent) and negative (51 per cent) interactions. Many of the incidents described related to sociability (meeting another couple, and spending some time with them in the pub) or to matters of protocol (annoyance with queue-jumpers). In a garden centre context in the United Kingdom, conversations with fellow customers were almost always viewed positively.[28]

In the remainder of this section, we concentrate on *customer-to-customer interactions between strangers.*[29]

Frequency of occurrence of customer-to-customer interactions

There are several types of services for which customer-to-customer interactions are central to successful operation. Services such as group coach or walking holidays, aerobic or language classes, and spectator sports or music concerts depend on interactions between customers to provide a social dimension, share knowledge/experience or simply create an atmosphere.

However, customer-to-customer interactions occur frequently in service environments that are not necessarily designed to encourage them. In a study of a US shopping mall, it was found that 23 per cent of a sample of consumers had had a conversation with a person that they had just met in the mall that day. In the United Kingdom, 13 per cent of a sample of consumers had talked to 'stranger' consumers in a garden centre on the day of the survey, and almost 33 per cent of consumers could recall such conversations on previous visits.[30] The percentages, when multiplied by consumer throughput in these environments and the many similar ones, demonstrate that there are millions of, often spontaneous, customer-to-customer interactions taking place each day in service settings.

Factors stimulating customer-to-customer interactions

Risk reduction is often a stimulus for engaging in on-site conversations with strangers in service settings, with consumers, adopting the role of help-seeker, seeking credible opinions and information – Does this scarf go with this top? Is this the right platform for the train to the airport? Do I sit here to wait for the doctor?

Quite often, interactions start with some form of physical assistance. It is common in train or air travel for passengers to help others with bags and luggage, and this acts as an 'ice-breaker' for prolonged conversations which can last the length of the journey. Hospital patients use the pretext of lending a newspaper or helping to clear up the food trays to start conversations with new arrivals on the ward. In each of these examples, it is possible for strangers to get to know each other in a 'safe conversation' about the service environment. Travel-related conversations are very common between passengers on a train or plane, whereas accounts of illnesses are commonplace between patients in a hospital ward. It is not unusual for people in such environments to share negative experiences about the service. To be able to have a mutual moan about train delays, hospital food or queueing for service is often beneficial to the people concerned, and these interactions can act as 'safety valves' for the service organisations. A study of a UK rail passenger service by Harris and Baron found that conversations among highly dissatisfied customers were of the 'we're all in it together, so let's make the best of it' nature and had a stabilising affect on customer expectations and perceptions of their experience.

Just as the service environment itself can be a stimulus for customer-to-customer interactions, so can physical products on display. In a customer survey in an IKEA store in the north-west of England, almost 50 per cent of conversations between strangers were product-related.[32] For example, one customer would ask another if a bed quilt would suit a certain room setting, or where she purchased the product she was carrying in her bag.

Managerial implications

From the research findings, especially those on customer-to-customer interactions between strangers, there are actions that service organisations can take which recognise the customer satisfaction to be gained from positive interactions and the dissatisfaction associated with negative interactions.

1. View consumers as a human resource.

   In a discussion of social support in the service sector, it has been maintained that, by supporting each other, consumers may carry out functions normally associated with employees. 'Sometimes consumers will be even more effective than paid employees; they are more readily available, and the absence of a profit motive will lend credibility to their advice.'[33] Retail and service managers will need to accept that on-site consumers represent a credible, willing and able human resource, and that their own employees can learn from consumers.[34] Rather than directing their management efforts at keeping consumers apart, or at training employees to intervene to make a sale, service companies could concentrate on training staff to be facilitators of consumer-to-consumer interactions and how *not* to intervene in consumer conversations.[35]

2. Plan to facilitate interactions.

   The process of actively managing customer-to-customer encounters in such a way as to enhance satisfying encounters and minimise dissatisfying encounters is one part of what Martin and Pranter[36] call 'compatibility management'. They identify a number of roles a service provider may play in managing customer compatibility.[37]

- Rifleman

  This role involves targeting the organisation's marketing activity at customer segments that are likely to demonstrate 'compatible behaviours' during the service experience. Holiday companies, for example, stress in their brochures that certain resort destinations are 'quiet and particularly suitable for young children'. This is designed to discourage younger travellers who might be looking for exciting nightlife and the opportunity to meet others of a similar age with the same interests. Tour operators realise that even a few negative encounters between these two customer groups could potentially damage their perception of the quality of the service provided.

- Environmental engineer

  Assuming this role, the service provider would design the service setting before the customers arrive to produce compatible behaviours when they are present. This might include offering separate seating to smokers and non-smokers in a restaurant, and dimmed lights and special booths for romantic meetings between couples.

- Legislator

  In this role, the service provider lays down certain rules that customers have to abide by to receive the service. For instance, a golf club may expect all its members to sign a 'members book' every time they use the course and wear evening dress for all official club functions. Having a clearly defined set of behavioural rules immediately gives members a point of reference for their dealings with others in the club.

- Matchmaker

  Here the service provider actively promotes the service to specific groups that are likely to share common experiences and problems, and consequently are more likely to benefit in the same way from the service experience. A beauty consultant, for example, offers a special consultancy service to young mothers with newborn babies. They are often uncertain about how to make the most of their appearance when trying to regain their shape after childbirth. They frequently also experience the same skin problems and benefit from specialist make-up advice. The consultant is able to use the experiences of the group members when presenting her material.

- Teacher

  Teachers have the responsibility of educating customers into their role in the service encounter, thus avoiding any confusion or potential conflict between customers. Flight attendants, for example, play the role of teacher when they transfer customers from the waiting lounge onto the plane. They request that customers board the plane in order of the row number allocated on the ticket. Although this clearly has operational benefits, it also avoids potential interpersonal conflict between waiting passengers who might accuse each other of queue-jumping.

- Santa Claus

   In this role the service provider rewards customers who exhibit behaviour that results in positive encounters between customers. For example, one customer found telling another how to place a monetary deposit in a shopping trolley to release it for use might be rewarded with a discount on his/her own grocery purchases. Alternatively, a customer recommending a product to another in the store might be rewarded with a free gift.

- Police officer

   Here the service provider is responsible for ensuring that the designated rules and codes of conduct are being followed by all customers. The doorman at a nightclub, for instance, might operate in this capacity, turning away customers who do not conform to the appropriate dress code.

- Cheerleader

   As the title suggests, this role involves encouraging customers in the service environment to work together and share common experiences that relate to the service being provided. For example, the receptionist in the dentist's waiting room might be asked by an anxious patient whether a particular treatment is painful. If the receptionist has never had the treatment she might ask another patient who has had the treatment to offer reassurance to the first customer. The receptionist is acting as a 'facilitator' in the exchange between the two customers. A more overt example of cheerleader behaviour is demonstrated by holiday couriers, whose main task is to encourage a 'good time' atmosphere among customers sharing the same holiday package.

   As customers are involved in both forms of interpersonal encounter identified above – in exchanges with employees and with other customers – service managers are concerned about what motivates customers to take part in the encounter and how their general contribution can be controlled and managed. The nature and extent of customer participation in service delivery systems is clearly very important, as are the strategies to manage customer contributions. These issues are discussed in Chapter 5.

Postcard from Practice 4.2

Managing Financial Planning Client to Client Encounters

We have found client functions to work well for us but we are careful to select similar clients when arranging the events. We invite our most financially sophisticated clients, who are generally our more profitable clients too, to technical events where we will have a formal speaker (often from our head office or one of the fund managers) and lay on quite a structured evening. Our clients have the chance to ask questions and discuss portfolios and options. We take the same approach to organising our social events too because our clients want to know that they are a 'typical' client. They take comfort in seeing other people like them around.

Postcard from Practice 4.2   (Continued)

They feel that we must understand and cater for people like them when they see that our business is made up of lots of people like them. Often our clients know each other before they realise they are our clients. They recognise people from their suburb and they feel comfortable when they notice people driving similar cars. They feel comfortable with their decision to use us when they see that other 'solid people' have made a reasoned decision to work with us too. We also invite prospective clients because it helps them make the decision if they see people they know and feel comfortable with.

Source: Rutherford Rede.

Interactions between Customers and Technology/Equipment

Interpersonal interactions have received the most attention in the services marketing literature. However, advances in technology and equipment have resulted in a greater likelihood that customers will interact with technology to facilitate 'self-service' activities during the period of time they are in contact with a service (as in Example 2, p. 70, where the first interaction was with the website of the leisure club). Indeed, as was described in Chapter 2, one of the key dimensions of a service-oriented business is that it should enhance service capabilities through the use of 'state-of-the-art' technology. Self-service technologies (SSTs) and TBSS are growing areas of interest for many researchers and practitioners within service-based industries, not just marketers, as we discussed in Chapter 3. The rapid rise in the use of SSTs and TBSS has led to a need for service organisations to consider how their customers perceive the value and quality delivered when balanced against the extent to which their labour directly replaces that of the service provider and therefore contributes towards the service outcome. Substituting customer labour for employee labour is not quite the same thing as increasing customer involvement or participation in the service provision and has recently become associated with the idea of customer productivity which has received little research attention to date.[38]

The impact of the Internet on service provision is wide-ranging. In the service sector, it is used most for travel, entertainment and financial services purchases. In the retail sector, it is used most for purchases of books and music, office products, toys and computers.[39]

We concentrate here, therefore, on:

- consumer sources of satisfaction and dissatisfaction with technology-based service delivery (TBSS and SST), and the managerial implications
- strategies for services via the Internet.

Consumer sources of satisfaction and dissatisfaction with technology-based services

A critical incident research study sought to determine consumer sources of satisfaction and dissatisfaction with technology-based services.[40] Technologies included in the survey were automated airline ticket machines, automated hotel checkouts, car rental machines, ATMs, Internet shopping, Internet information searches and 'pay at the pump' terminals. An analysis of the critical incidents revealed three categories of sources of satisfaction and four categories of sources of dissatisfaction (see Table 4.2).

The most frequently cited source of satisfaction with TBSS was the perception that it was better than the interpersonal alternative (68 per cent). Consumers perceived savings in time and/or money, especially when they did not find the need to deal with a salesperson, for example at the 'pay at the pump' terminal. A further 21 per cent of the incidents were described as satisfactory because the technology performed the service operation successfully; that is, it did what it was supposed to do. That this is a source of satisfaction is probably a reflection of relief (or even mistrust in technology). As expectations with technology and machines change over time, this particular source of satisfaction may become less frequent. The other source of satisfaction was the solving of an immediate problem (11 per cent). For example, birthday greetings can be emailed to a friend/relative even after the last post has gone, or money can be drawn out of an ATM to pay for the midnight taxi home.

The most frequently cited source of dissatisfaction with technology-based services was the failure of the technology (43 per cent). The airline ticket machine was out of order, for example, or the ATM swallowed the card for no apparent reason. 'Poor design', especially of Internet websites, was cited in 36 per cent of the unsatisfactory incidents. Either the system was confusing to the consumer, resulting, for example, in ordering the same book twice, or it was inflexible, for example giving the option of gift deliveries only to the cardholder's address. Process failures (17 per cent) occurred where the technology was fine, but there were other problems such as items that were ordered over the Internet being delivered to the wrong address, or on the wrong day. Occasionally, consumers admit responsibility for unsatisfactory incidents. Customer-driven

Table 4.2 Sources of satisfaction and dissatisfaction with technology-based self-service

Sources of satisfaction	Sources of dissatisfaction
• Solves an immediate problem	• Technology failure
• Perceived as better than the interpersonal alternative	• Process failure
• Performed operation successfully	• Poor design
	• Customer driven failure

Source: Adapted from Meuter et al., 2000 (see note 12).

failures (4 per cent) have resulted from demagnetised strips on credit cards, and annoyance/carelessness with a music ordering website (resulting in 200 copies of the same CD!).

Managerial implications

Managers can learn not only from the categories in Table 4.2, but also from a comparison with the sources of (dis)satisfaction with interpersonal services outlined in Table 4.1. Three implications for managers of technology-based services are now discussed.

1. Plan for effective *service recovery.*

    If it is accepted that some breakdowns or failures are inevitable, strategies for service recovery need to be in place. It was seen that empowerment of employees was an option with interpersonal interactions, and also that effective service recovery resulted in customer satisfaction. With TBSS (and the absence of service employees), the key to service recovery will lie in enabling the customers themselves to resolve the problems. To do this, service organisations require an in-depth understanding of problem situations experienced by consumers. What are their frustrations? What are the issues associated with remembering order numbers, account names and passwords? What are the main navigation problems consumers have with Internet shopping? To obtain such depth of understanding, and the subsequent development of self-recovery systems, is likely to require 'shopping with consumers' style research[41] in the context of Internet or other technology-based encounters, rather than survey-based research.

2. *Involve* customers.

    The inseparability characteristic of services entails levels of customer involvement in service encounters. In interpersonal encounters in retail environments, it has been established that customers often have product and process knowledge that is better than that of employees, and are prepared to share the expertise under certain conditions.[42] Actively encouraging customer involvement can be advantageous to the service provider. But do customers understand *how* they are expected to perform? Are they *able* to perform as expected? Are there valued rewards for performing as expected?

    There is evidence that those who design the technologies to support self-service by consumers do not appreciate the lack of consumer understanding of how they are expected to perform. There is even a designated website for 'silly' consumer queries received at computer help lines.[43] Some of the stories are very amusing, but the overriding impression, on reading them, is of a lack of empathy with consumer role clarity, abilities and motivations. There is a consumer experience gap.[44] Where consumers want simplicity, they may get complexity. Where they want service, they may get technology. Where they want to accomplish their goals, they may get 'compelling features'. With TBSS, it is even more important to view customers as human resources for the service organisation, empathise with them, and involve them in the human resource strategies, in order to reduce the consumer experience gap. We anticipate one of the benefits of the emergence of the interdisciplinary SSME (Service Science, Management and Engineering) approach to service development being the design of self-service technologies that emphasise the sources of satisfaction (table 4.2) while reducing the sources of dissatisfaction and thereby providing more satisfying customer interactions.

3. *Customise* the service.

   With interpersonal services, many of the recorded sources of customer satisfaction are related to employees' abilities to respond to *special* customer needs or requests, or to employees acting spontaneously for *individual* customers. Customers are highly satisfied where it has been demonstrated that the service organisation, or its representatives, has tailored the service to them. With TBSS, there is an opportunity for services to be customised as a matter of course, which may lead to them being perceived as better than the interpersonal alternative. The most obvious examples of customised services are the Internet book retailers who will notify individual customers when a book has arrived in their preferred category. Customisation is an option, however, with all TBSS where a particular customer's frequency and types of purchases are routinely recorded. Service providers need to ensure that the SST that supports the TBSS is designed to facilitate customisation.

The danger here is one of complacency. Is the TBSS really providing customisation that leads to satisfaction and repeat purchases? Service companies will still need to carry out research into sources of customer loyalty, as well as customer satisfaction, with TBSS.

Strategies for services via the Internet

For some products (services and/or goods) the potential for selling over the Internet is much greater than that for others. What are the criteria that make a product a candidate for successful Internet selling? Rosen and Howard[45] list the following:

- tactility less important
- generally unpleasant in-store experience
- customisation important
- personal nature
- high margin
- cheap to ship
- instant gratification less important

- standard
- price sensitive
- gift oriented
- info-intense.

Financial and travel services fit most of the criteria, as do goods such as music and books. Other services, such as medical or educational, and other goods, such as clothing or furniture, tend to fit fewer of the criteria, and consequently have less of a presence on the Internet.

Where a service or good does have potential for Internet selling, companies' strategies for Internet usage can vary. Largely, they fall into two camps:

- online or on-site, that is 'clicks *or* bricks'
- online and on-site, that is 'clicks *and* bricks'.

With a 'clicks or bricks' strategy, companies favour either on-line or on-site product selling. The online option offers the advantages of 24-hour access times for customers, and a global customer base. However, for physical goods, the selection and picking service is once again the responsibility of the retailer. There are still consumer trust problems to do with security of payment, and the lack of sensory experience (sight, smell, human contact) may be a disadvantage. For retailers of goods, the back-stage logistics and delivery systems are complex and costly.[46]

With a 'clicks and bricks' strategy, companies are using the Internet as an effective shop window to support on-site retail or service offers. The Internet is integrated into retail and services marketing strategy, as opposed to being an alternative channel for direct sales. Borders Bookstores, for example, make their Internet service available in their stores to facilitate ordering. B&Q in the United Kingdom, use their websites to provide general DIY help, and information as to which products can be bought in-store, to both the general public and the traders. In the United States, there is some evidence that retailers expanding virtually through an Internet presence are also growing physically through store expansion.[47]

Summary

The service encounter has received considerable attention from academics and managers alike because it is believed that:

- a single interaction can affect a customer's total perception of a service organisation
- the service encounter has distinct elements which can be controlled and managed.

The rapid growth in use of technology to facilitate self-service by customers requires service organisations to consider the sources of satisfaction and dissatisfaction with TBSS, which are different to those associated with interpersonal services. Companies, particularly those adopting 'clicks and bricks' strategies, can benefit from understanding the differences. Service organisations that require customers to use TBSS will also benefit from understanding the impact that increasing customer productivity will have on perceptions of the overall value and quality of the service provision.

Customer interactions, in service encounters, with the physical environment, or servicescape, are discussed in Chapter 6.

Learning Outcomes

Having read this chapter, you should be able to

- define the service encounter and categorise the various types of interaction the customer may have during the encounter
- break down service encounters into the multiple points of contact the customer has with the service
- appreciate the managerial implications associated with customer interactions with employees, with other customers and with self-service technologies and equipment
- categorise the causes of customer satisfaction and dissatisfaction through interactions with employees and TBSS
- understand the significance of 'other customers' as part of the human resource present in service encounters.

Discussion Questions and Exercises

1. Can increased empowerment of employees lead to customer dissatisfaction?
2. Name three types of service where customer compatibility is an important issue.
3. Social networking sites are a contemporary example of both customer-to-customer and customer-to-technology interactions. Using your experiences of these sites, evaluate how well you think your experiences are managed.
4. Provide an example of service recovery that you have experienced as a customer. How did the manner of the recovery affect your view of the service organisation?
5. Provide specific, personal examples that illustrate the three sources of satisfaction and four sources of dissatisfaction associated with TBSS and listed in Table 4.2.

Notes and References

1. Martin, C. L., 'The History, Evolution and Principles of Services Marketing: Poised for the New Millennium,' *Marketing Intelligence and Planning,* 17(7), 1999, pp. 324–8.
2. Normann, R., *Service Management,* Wiley, New York, 1984.
3. Mattsson, J., 'Improving Service Quality in Person-to-Person Encounters: Integrating Findings from a Multidisciplinary Review,' *Service Industries Journal,* vol. 14, 1994.
4. Shostack, G. L., 'Planning the Service Encounter,' in J. A. Czepiel, M. R. Solomon and C. F. Surprenant (eds), *The Service Encounter,* Lexington Books, Lexington, Mass., 1985.

5. Bitner, M. J., 'Evaluating Service Encounters: The Effects of Physical Surroundings and Employee Responses.' *Journal of Marketing,* vol. 54, April 1990, pp. 69–82.
6. Harris, K., Baron, S. and Ratcliffe, J., 'Customers as Oral Participants in a Service Setting,' *Journal of Services Marketing,* 9(4), 1995, pp. 64–76.
7. Parker, C. and Ward, P., 'An Analysis of Role Adoptions and Scripts During Customer-to-Customer Encounters,' *European Journal of Marketing,* 34(3–4), 2000, pp. 341–58.
8. Martin, C. L. and Pranter, C. A., 'Compatibility Management: Customer to Customer Relationships in Service Environments,' *Journal of Services Marketing,* 3(3), Summer 1989, pp. 5–15.
9. Milne, J., 'Someone to talk to,' *Internet Business,* March 2000, pp. 75–83.
10. Bowen, D. E., 'Customers as Human Resources in Service Organisations,' *Human Resource Management,* 25(3), Fall 1986, pp. 371–83.
11. Curran, J. M. and Meuter, M. L., 'Encouraging Existing Customers to Switch to Self-Service Technologies: Put a Little Fun in Their Lives,' *Journal of Marketing Theory and Practice,* 15(4), Fall 2007, pp. 283–98.
12. Meuter, M. L., Ostrom, A. L., Roundtree, R. I. and Bitner, M. J., 'Self-Service Technologies: Understanding Customer Satisfaction with Technology-Based Service Encounters,' *Journal of Marketing,* vol. 64, July 2000, pp. 50–64.
13. Bitner, M. J., 'Servicescapes: The Impact of Physical Surroundings on Customers and Employees,' *Journal of Marketing,* 56(2), pp. 57–71.
14. Bitner, M. J., Booms, B. H. and Tetreault, M., 'The Service Encounter: Diagnosing Favourable and Unfavourable Incidents,' *Journal of Marketing,* vol. 54, January 1990, pp. 71–84.
15. Bitner, M. J., Booms, B. H. and Mohr, L. A., 'Critical Service Encounters: The Employee's View,' *Journal of Marketing,* vol. 58, October 1994, pp. 95–106.
16. Crosby, L. A., Evans, K. R. and Cowles, D., 'Relationship Quality in Services Selling: An Interpersonal Influence Perspective,' *Journal of Marketing,* vol. 54, July 1990, pp. 68–81.
17. Elliott, D., Harris, K. and Baron, S., 'Crisis management and services marketing,' *Journal of Services Marketing,* 19(5), 2005, pp. 336–45.
18. Bitner, 'Evaluating Service Encounters'.
19. Baron, S., 'Customer Interactions: A Neglected Dimension of Service Encounters,' Inaugural Professorial Lecture, Manchester Metropolitan University, February 2000.
20. Woodside, A. G. and Sims, T. J., 'Retail Sales Transactions and Customer "Purchase Pal" Effects on Buying Behavior,' *Journal of Retailing,* vol. 52, Fall 1976, pp. 57–64.
21. Baron, Harris, and Davies, 'Oral Participation in Retail Service Delivery'.
22. Oldenburg, R., *The Great Good Place,* Marlowe and Company, New York, 1999.
23. Goff, B. G., Bellenger, D. N. and Stojack, C., 'Cues to Consumer Susceptibility To Salesperson Influence: Implications for Adaptive Retail Selling,' *Journal of Personal Selling and Sales Management,* xiv(2), Spring 1994, pp. 25–39.
24. Ibid.
25. McGrath, M. A. and Otnes, C., 'Unacquainted Influencers: When Strangers Interact in the Retail Setting,' *Journal of Business Research,* vol. 32, 1995, pp. 261–72.
26. Harris, K., Baron, S. and Davies, B., 'What Sort of Soil Do Rhododendrons Like? Comparing Customer and Employee Responses to Requests for Product-Related Information,' *Journal of Services Marketing,* 13(1), 1999, pp. 21–37.
27. Grove, S. J. and Fisk, R. P., 'The Impact of Other Customers on Service Exchanges: A Critical Incident Examination of "Getting Along," ' *Journal of Retailing,* 73(1), 1997, pp. 63–85.
28. Parker, C. and Ward, P., 'An Analysis of Role Adoptions and Scripts During Customer-to-Customer Encounters'.
29. More details on this section can be found in Harris, K., Baron, S. and Parker, D., 'Understanding the Consumer Experience: It's "Good to Talk," ' *Journal of Marketing Management,* 16(1–3), 2000, pp. 111–27.
30. Parker, C. and Ward, P., 'An Analysis of Role Adoptions and Scripts During Customer-to-Customer Encounters'.

31. Harris, K. and Baron, S., 'Consumer-to-consumer conversations in service settings,' *Journal of Service Research,* 6(3), 2004, pp. 287–303.
32. Baron, Harris, and Davies, 'Oral Participation in Retail Service Delivery'.
33. Adelman, M. B., Ahuvia, A. and Goodwin, C., 'Beyond Smiling: Social Support and Service Quality,' in *Service Quality: New Directions in Theory and Practice.* R. Rust and R. Oliver (eds), Sage, Thousand Oaks, Cal., 1994, pp. 139–72.
34. Harris, Baron, and Davies, 'What Sort of Soil do Rhododendrons Like?'.
35. McGrath and Otnes, 'Unacquainted Influencers'.
36. Pranter, C. A. and Martin, C. L., 'Compatibility Management: Roles in Service Performers,' *Journal of Services Marketing,* 5(2), Spring 1991, pp. 143–53.
37. Pranter and Martin, 'Compatibility Management'.
38. Anitsal, I. and Schumann, D. W., 'Toward a Conceptualisation of Customer Productivity: The Customer's Perspective on Transforming Customer Labor into Customer Outcomes using Technology-Based Self-Service Options,' *Journal of Marketing Theory and Practice,* 15(4), Fall 2007, pp. 349–63.
39. Rosen, K. T. and Howard, A. L., 'E-Retail: Gold Rush or Fool's Gold?,' *California Management Review,* 42(3), Spring 2000, pp. 72–100.
40. Meuter, Ostrom, Roundtree and Bitner, 'Self-Service Technologies'.
41. Otnes, C., McGrath, M. A. and Lowrey, T. M., 'Shopping with Consumers: Usage as Past, Present and Future Research Technique,' *Journal of Retailing and Consumer Services,* 2(2), 1995, pp. 97–110.
42. Harris, Baron, and Davies, 'What Sort of Soil do Rhododendrons Like?'
43. http://rinkworks.com.
44. www.zdinternet.com.
45. Rosen and Howard, 'E-Retail: Gold Rush or Fool's Gold?'.
46. Burt, S., 'E-Commerce and the High Street: Threat or Hype?' *Contemporary Issues in Retail Marketing,* Manchester Metropolitan University, September 2000.
47. Rosen and Howard, 'E-Retail: Gold Rush or Fool's Gold?'.

5

Consumer Experiences

Learning Objectives

Overall Aim of the Chapter

To create an awareness of the notion of the consumer experience, and the reasons for the increased interest in the notion by both academics and practitioners.

In particular, the *chapter objectives* are

- to illustrate the notion of a memorable service 'experience'

- to outline the three main reasons for the current interest in consumer experiences

- to compare and contrast the perspectives on the consumer experience of consumers, services marketers and academics

- to summarise the implications for service management who wish to create and stage consumer experiences.

Introduction

After receiving services, consumers sometimes simply forget them or regard them as so 'ordinary' that they just do not talk about them, even when the services have been regarded positively. Yet, after receiving other services, they feel they want to recount their service story to anyone who will listen. So what is it that can make a consumer service into an *experience* worth recounting? In Chapter 4, we discussed at length the value of the critical incident technique as a way of uncovering particularly good or particularly bad service encounters. In this chapter we build on this by exploring how a simple service encounter might become a memorable service 'experience'.

Since the late 1990s, there has been a significant interest in consumer experiences within the field of marketing.[1-3] It has been claimed that two texts *The Experience Economy* and *Experiential Marketing: How to get Customers to sense, feel, think, act and relate* relaunched the 'consumer experience' bandwagon,[4] an interest which had orginally been stimulated in the field of consumer behaviour with Holbrook and Hirschman's[5] reference to the importance of 'fantasies, feelings and fun'. In this chapter, we begin by providing two examples of service 'experiences'. The first example is an experience created by the provider, in this case Hewlett Packard. The second is a memorable experience as defined by consumers. The examples serve as reference points for the later sections of the chapter. Next we identify the reasons for the renewed interest in experiences and explore different perspectives on the consumer experience. The chapter concludes with a discussion of the implications for service management, including ideas for how managers might measure the impact of the experiences they try to create.

Service 'Experiences'

An organisational perspective

The following 'It's in the News!' item (5.1) illustrates how an organisation might view the concept of a service experience.

📖 **It's in the News! 5.1**

The Hewlett Packard Experience Store

According to ITWeb, South Africa, on 12 May 2008,

The world's first Hewlett Packard (HP) Experience store has opened in South Africa.

HP, in partnership with Digital Planet, has announced the official opening of the HP Experience store in Sandton City. HP Experience is the first concept retail store of its kind in the world. Operated and owned by Digital Planet, the store will sell HP's entire portfolio of consumer offerings – from personal computing to imaging and printing products. In addition, consumers will have an opportunity to view and experience the latest HP technology in the store.

'The store is organised around experiences and solutions, not products. We want to provide consumers with an opportunity to interact with the latest HP technology,' said Neil Watson, director and co-founder of Digital Planet. HP Experience consists of various digital lifestyle zones, including a Guru Bar, where trained HP experts provide consumers with in-depth information, assistance and education as part of their shopping experience.

According to Paul Boshoff, General Manager of HP's Personal Systems Group, the store meets consumers' demands of an engaging experience, quality products that perform and solutions that meet their needs. 'We are very excited about the opening of the first HP Experience store and confident that it will pave the way for consumers to further embrace the digital entertainment evolution,' added Boshoff.

A consumer experience

Exhibit 5.1 provides an illustration of a consumer experience where a considerable amount of money was paid for a service that proved to be memorable. It is written by Peter, who, with his wife Christine, flew from the United Kingdom for an Easter holiday in Las Vegas with the tour operator 'Airtours'. It starts with the Airtours welcome meeting, held in the 'Planet Hollywood' store.

Exhibit 5.1   Consumer Account of the 'Sunset Trail Ride and Barbecue Dinner' Experience

At the welcome meeting, we were given details of all the tours/shows we could book through Airtours – flight over the Grand Canyon, visit to the Hoover Dam, and various variety shows. The Airtours rep. went through them all in a presentation, complete with slides. The particular tour that she really got excited about, however, was the 'Sunset trail ride' tour.[6] It involved a short drive to the Red Rock Canyons to a ranch, followed by a 2-hour horse ride with the cowboys, and then a meal of barbecued steak, beans and corn on the cob, enjoyed whilst sitting around the campfire under the desert stars. We had originally planned to revisit the Grand Canyon, but Christine and I both liked the idea of the canyon ride, although neither of us had ever ridden a horse before. It seemed like many others at the presentation had the same idea and similar reservations. Most of the questions were about the canyon ride, and we were reassured that it was possible for novices 'from four to 94 years of age'. Being in our fifties, therefore, appeared not to be a drawback. It seemed, however, quite expensive at $139 per person, so we didn't book on the spot. Two days later, we decided to opt for the canyon ride and sacrifice the Grand Canyon tour (which we were told, by another couple, was a bit disappointing with just a flight for 20 minutes around a small part of the Grand Canyon).

The day came, and we arrived at the pick-up point at the Excalibur Hotel. The bus driver handed out two-page insurance disclaimers to us all, and we had to tick and sign at least 20 boxes. We began to wonder what we'd let ourselves in for. He went on to warn us not to over-claim our riding skills as the cowboys might put us on a horse that we could not control. This seemed to cause a stir, and so he quickly responded by saying complete novices would get the gentle horses, such as 'Buttercup' and 'Smiler', rather than 'Thunder' or 'Bullet'. With hindsight, this was part of the experience – a wind-up of the group to get them talking. Soon the scenery became spectacular, with the beautiful red rocks, and we arrived at the ranch. The driver could not resist one last dig at us, by pointing out a trail high into the mountains that we were going to ride on. At the ranch, we all had to pay up front (it seemed strange to be paying by credit card in such an environment), including a generous tip to the, as yet, unknown cowboys/girls. They then came along and introduced themselves – Big Jim, Hawk, Randy, Jodie, etc. – ten in all, all wearing hats and with spurs on their boots. There were 50 customers on this

Exhibit 5.1 (Continued)

trail ride. Others were turned away whilst we were there. We could see the horses in a fenced area. This was it, then. No turning back. Big Jim asked if anyone was nervous. Five women, including Christine, confessed, and were made a fuss of, and fixed up with horses. No men confessed any trepidation and I wasn't going to be the first. Big Jim, did, however, draw attention to the lack of male honesty, which relieved the tension a bit. Christine was on 'Dusty', and I was given 'Cherokee', but we were separated, and could not share our misgivings. The cowboys/girls briefly demonstrated how we should steer and stop the horse with the reins. This was hard to take in, and quite scary. When we set off, I over-used the reins, and was shouted at 'Don't pull hard on Cherokee. He's got a sensitive mouth.' Not a good start. The next part is taken from Christine's diary of the holiday.

My horse was an Albino with blue eyes called Dusty, Peter's a brown one with piebald markings (Cherokee). We had to ride on *our own* (no-one walking beside us) up a very steep hill, along very rocky and sometimes sandy terrain. Very frightening at first, and my stirrups were too high (+ one higher than the other), so my legs were really aching and rigid the whole time. Stopped for photos on the way up, and at the top for one with Peter. My horse was right at the end of a sheer drop. Stunning views, but sunset hampered by a few clouds. At top, Nicole (cowgirl) adjusted my stirrups, but I was still aching. Saw a coyote. When we got back, I couldn't get off the horse, so Peter and a cowboy lifted me off – my legs were like jelly. Then we had enormous steaks, corn on the cob, jacket potato, beans and lettuce, and then toasted marshmallows on the camp-fire. Finally, a drive back with a view of Las Vegas lights, quite spectacular.

The whole account seems fairly negative, but our legs began to function properly only five minutes after getting off the horse, and round the camp-fire, everyone was in high spirits sharing their experiences and fears. Christine said that we would get a lot of mileage out of this, back home. The photos have been out with all our friends, embellished with stories of our ride up the canyon. It was certainly the highlight of the Las Vegas holiday. Even silly things take on a greater meaning – such as cowboys on horseback communicating by mobile phone, and us sitting around the campfire (after singing 'Home on the range') and being given the ranch's website.

In both of these examples, there is recognition that, in order for the experience to be memorable, consumers need to be given the opportunity to *engage* in the service, not merely to be a player in a service transaction. HP, for example, gives consumers the opportunity to experience the latest technology in store. Christine and Peter were actually required to ride along the trail in the sunset. The scenery and context will have made the experience possible, but their participation and engagement in the service was the key to their evaluations. The photographs, taken by the cowboys/girls, were the tangible items that jogged the memories.

The other aspect which made the second experience so memorable was that it touched the *emotions and feelings* of the participants. The pain and fear associated with the ride (the latter no doubt orchestrated to a certain extent by the service provider) contributed greatly to Christine and Peter's experiences. The satisfaction and relief of conquering the pain and fear, and sharing it with other customers, however was positive.

The fact that both experiences are very 'unusual' also makes them a talking point. How long they will continue to be 'unusual', however, is debatable as more and more companies focus on creating new and different experiences to capture the consumers' attention. Even UK high street retailers, who have traditionally focused on selling merchandise, have begun to devote display space to sell packaged experiences. For example, UK shoppers can buy a James Bond Experience from Boots, or a Big Boys Toy adventure from WH Smith. These, perhaps, are the most obvious examples of services becoming consumer experience; that is, when consumers engage in something *out of the ordinary*.[7]

These three characteristics will be discussed in more detail in the remainder of this chapter. At this stage, however, you may feel that what has been said so far is probably not too surprising. So why is the topic of consumer experience capturing the interest of academics and practitioners at the start of the twenty-first century?

Reasons for the Interest in Consumer Experiences

There are three main, interrelated reasons for the upsurge in interest in consumer experiences:

- the economics of selling experiences
- the move towards providing 'theatrical' retail/service offers
- the closure of 'third' or 'great good places'.

The economics of selling experiences

As was mentioned briefly in Chapter 1, Pine and Gilmore[8] have advocated that advanced economies have moved to what they call the *Experience Economy*. The arrival at this position is via a historical progression of economic value from extracting commodities to making goods, to delivering services, to staging experiences (see, e.g., the coffee example discussed in Chapter 2). This progression is shown in Figure 5.1.

As we move along Figure 5.1, from left to right, Pine and Gilmore argue that the offer moves from being undifferentiated to being differentiated, and from being irrelevant to customer needs to being relevant to customer needs. But, importantly for them, it moves from cheap (market) pricing to premium

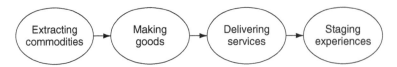

Figure 5.1   The progression of economic value
Source: Adapted from Pine and Gilmore, 1999 (see note 2).

pricing. One can charge a premium price in the experience economy for staging a differentiated experience which is relevant to customer needs. Support for their argument can be seen, for example, in the 'Christmas service' being offered by event planners to families in the United States. For prices of up to £30,000, families can 'enjoy the Christmas festivities, by avoiding the fuss'.[9] For around £27,000 the deal may include three Christmas trees, decoration of seven fireplaces, crystal tableware, shopping for presents, cooking the turkey and signing Christmas cards with a look-alike signature. This is to provide what the purchasers regard as the real Christmas experience; something they could not provide for themselves. According to the providers, the business had taken off in December 2000 'as never before'.

Similarly, customers are willing to pay $139 each for a trail ride in the canyons, with all the cowboy, camp-fire ambience (an experience), whereas a two-hour horse ride (a service) could normally be purchased for less than half that amount.

A UK consumer behaviourist consultant advises that 'people are telling us that they're oversupplied with merchandise and undersupplied with experiences...their houses are full of the stuff. And there's a feeling that an experience lasts a lifetime, while a product wears out.'[10] If, indeed, consumers are expressing needs for staged experiences rather than manufactured goods, then Pine and Gilmore reckon that organisations, such as retailers or shopping centre managers, could stage consumer experiences and *charge an entry fee*. This may not be too far-fetched given the propensity of consumers to pay for tangible mementoes, such as 'Rainforest Café' tee shirts after a dining experience, despite being oversupplied with merchandise. It is quite possible that Peter, Christine or any of their fellow customers would have purchased Red Rock Canyon Trail Ride tee shirts or cowboy hats, had they been available, in their post-ride euphoria (or even via the Internet!).

The move towards providing 'theatrical' retail/service offers

According to a Verdict Report,

> *Retail theatre is more than a fancy layout and slick decoration. The most successful involve real inter-activity with the consumer, making them active, rather than passive, participants. Only in this way can consumers actually feel involved and the shopping experience made more memorable and interesting. For the retailer there are significant bonuses to be gained as a result – shoppers stay in the store for longer, they come back more often and they (probably) tell their friends about the experience.*[11]

Consumer experiences are often seen as the outcome of the offer of 'theatre' in services, none more so than in the retail sector where many firms across the whole spectrum of retailing claim to be offering *retail theatre*.[12] The use of the theatre metaphor in services has been discussed in Chapter 3.[13] Some examples of the claims of retail theatre show superficiality, in that the idea of theatre seems indistinguishable from selling (e.g., the US home furnishing retailer, Tag's Hardware, state 'We treat retail like theater: come in, be entertained and spend money on your way out'), or merchandising (e.g., the UK supermarket group Safeway where they are reported to want 'to bring in the idea of retail theatre, where you have such a fantastic display of apples, for example, that you cannot resist loading into your trolley').

Nevertheless, others do acknowledge that 'theatre' includes the engagement of the consumer and the encouragement of consumer participation in the creation of consumer experiences, as advocated in the Verdict report above. For example, the key to retail theatre for the UK electrical retailer, Comet, is to allow 'the customer to touch, feel and experience the product', and the Levi's jeans retail store in San Francisco, with children in mind, 'hopes to captivate youthful shoppers partly through sensory immersion (surround sound! flickering video projections! DJ/VJ listening stations! tub of warm water)'.[14]

A catalyst for the creation of on-site retail consumer experiences has been the competition of online shopping alternatives (see Chapter 4). Through Internet shopping, consumers can meet convenience, speed of purchase and low price needs when shopping for many types of goods. On-site shopping, therefore, has to provide something different – experiences through theatre – in order to encourage longer stays, repatronage and positive word-of-mouth. In parallel with consumer experiences with on-site retail/service providers, research is being undertaken on consumer experiences with retail/service websites, the E-Xperience.[15] Here the emphasis is on creating hassle-free, seamless experiences for consumers.

It is not only in retail, however, where theatrical techniques are used to create consumer experiences. The most blatant example in the hotel sector is the Venetian Hotel in Las Vegas, which is said to have cost $2 billion to build.[16] As with other Las Vegas hotels, it has a Casino and over 5000 bedrooms. It also has 17 restaurants, and a spectacular themed presence on Las Vegas Boulevard, complete with Rialto Bridge, a canal and a replica of the St Mark's Campanile bell tower. The main experience for consumers, most of whom are visitors not residents, is to be found, however, in the 'Grand Canal Shoppes' inside the hotel. The shops are in a themed setting, with gondola rides (at $15 per person) on the canal running through them to a replica St Mark's Square complete with cafes, bars and so on, all under a painted blue sky with small white clouds. The gondoliers are all trained singers, dressed authentically, who serenade their passengers at the canal turning point, heard, of course, by all the passing shoppers. There are scheduled operatic performances and concerts on the canal bridges and in the square, and mime artists act as statues in the wider spaces of the shopping mall.

The closure of 'third' or 'great good places'

It may seem, from the above, that the creation and provision of consumer experiences is only available to well-funded service organisations in the retail and leisure service sectors. However, it is recognised that many much smaller service organisations provide a social consumer experience, playing the role of a 'third place', or what has become to be known as a 'great good place'[17] – a meeting place for people (whose other two places are home and work). Consider the following report[18] on the reaction of the American public to the end of a television series:

> When the final episode of Cheers aired in 1993 after 11 years of warming America's barstools, 80 million people tuned in to bid farewell to the cozy saloon where, as the theme song had it, 'everyone knows your name'. The audience wasn't just saying good-bye to a TV show; it was mourning the passing of 'the great good place' of modern life, as sociologist Ray Oldenburg called the gathering places where communities refresh and sustain themselves. Yes, the old-time saloon and lodges and even the barbershops that once provided places for socializing are mostly gone.

It would seem that the end of a fictitious bar had been mourned in a nostalgic reflection on the reduction in places to meet and socialise, most of which were made available by service providers. Oldenburg[19] listed these great good places:

- cafés
- coffee shops
- bookstores
- bars
- hair salons
- other hangouts at the heart of a community.

In great good places, Oldenburg points out, 'the entertainment is provided by the people themselves. The sustaining activity is conversation, which is variously passionate and light-hearted, serious and witty, informative and silly.'

The notion of the consumer engaging with the service to create an experience again is paramount.

Some service organisations have reacted to the public mourning of the demise of great good places by proclaiming positively that they are a great good place, standing up for the values that Oldenburg proclaims they possess. For example, Bobby Byrne's restaurants and pubs,[20] in Cape Cod, USA, refer to themselves as 'An Eating, Drinking and Talking Establishment' and as 'Cape Cod's "great good place" to raise a glass, break bread, and share a great good thought'. Their message to the 'gentle customer' is that 'the pub is about more than food and drink...we hope that we nourish your spirit and enable you to experience not only another great place but also a great good thought'.

In the United Kingdom, 'other hangouts at the heart of a community' would include the thousands of small shops and service businesses that serve the communities with their 'high streets'.[21] They provide the locations for consumer experiences brought about through social conversations.[22] Their numbers are decreasing year by year, and there are calls for government intervention to maintain a healthy independent retail sector, as independent retailers contribute significantly to the preservation of local communities.[23] The potential closure of these great good places has raised awareness of what would be missing, much of which relates to the perceived lack of opportunities for consumers to have the experience of socialising.

Perspectives on the Consumer Experience

To what extent is there a common understanding of a consumer experience?

As you will have already observed from this chapter, both the word 'experience' and the phrase 'consumer experience' are used often in the context of services marketing, but the meanings and connotations may differ according to the user.

The consumer perspective

Taking the perspective of consumers and their representatives, it is noticeable that, on balance, a consumer experience means a *bad experience* with the purchase of a good or service. On the Internet, for example, one of the well-known search engines, Yahoo!, lists 30 websites dealing with consumer experiences. Some of them, such as 'weBBBox.com', acknowledge that consumers have both good and bad stories to relate – 'If you tell us about your good and bad experiences, with your favorite and not-so-favorite businesses, we'll post them here in the webBbox for all the world to read.' However, the majority of the websites, by their very name, assume a negative stance on consumer experiences, and their addresses vary, from the obvious 'complaints.com' or 'The Complaint Station' to the more provocative 'bitchaboutit.com', 'Gripenet' and 'MadNow.com'.

Even in government reports consumer experiences are juxtaposed with consumers' rights of complaint. A report by the General Consumer Council for Northern Ireland,[24] for example, states that 'we tracked the *experiences* of Northern Ireland consumers in the previous 12 months from having reason to complain to seeking advice and taking action in relation to their complaint . . .'.

This commonly held view of a consumer experience regards experience as relating to *a particular incident that a consumer has undergone with a service provider,* and furthermore, often one that may have been unpleasant. The voicing and sharing of complaints also implies that different consumers may have similar experiences with the same service provider. The bad experience of purchasing a VCR from Company X with malfunctioning remote control, and the subsequent hassle in replacing it, may be a familiar story for several consumers. In Peter and Christine's story of the trail ride, there were many separate incidents, and their particular interchange with the service providers over the issue of 'tips' would have been a (rather negative) consumer experience, according to the view above.

The services marketer perspective

In contrast, service marketers take the perspective that a consumer experience is a *memorable episode based on a consumer's direct personal participation or observation.*

Pine and Gilmore distinguish experiences from the other elements of Figure 5.1 as follows (see Table 5.1).

They emphasise that experiences 'occur within any individual who has been engaged on an emotional, physical, intellectual, or even spiritual level. Theresult? No two people can have the same experience.'[25] From their perspective, experiences are not simply particular incidents that consumers undergo with service providers, they are memorable events that engage the consumers. So, Peter and Christine's consumer experiences would relate to their engagement with the trail ride on the emotional (fear, sense of achievement), physical (discomfort on ride, satisfied hunger) and intellectual (learnt riding skills, knowledge of the terrain flora and fauna) levels over the whole event. Furthermore, they would each have different experiences.

Experiential Marketing
The creation of a memorable episode based on a customer's direct personal participation or observation.

Schmitt,[26] a proponent of 'experiential marketing', agrees with Pine and Gilmore's definition of experience, pointing out that experiences require some stimulation, and that the marketer needs to provide the stimulant in order to create desired customer experiences. He argues that 'as a manager, rather than being concerned with any particular individual experience, you need to ask yourself the more important strategic question of what type of experiences you want to provide and how you can provide them with perpetually fresh appeal'. Such a strategic underpinning of experiential marketing can, he believes, be achieved by addressing five components of customer experiences:

- sense
- feel
- think
- act
- relate.

Table 5.1 Distinctive characteristics of experiences

Economic units	Distinctive characteristics
Commodities	Basic materials extracted from the natural world
Goods	Tangible products that companies standardise and then inventory
Services	Intangible activities performed for a particular customer
Experiences	Memorable events that engage individuals in a personal way

Table 5.2 Schmitt's five components of the customer experience

Component	Description
Sense	Creation of sensory experiences through sight, touch, sound, taste and smell
Feel	Creation of affective experiences during consumption
Think	Creation of cognitive, problem-solving experiences that engage customers creatively
Act	Enhancement of customers' physical experiences
Relate	Creation of 'individual experiences' relating the customer to his or her ideal self, other people, or cultures

Source: Adapted from Schmitt, 1999 (see note 3).

Table 5.2 gives a brief contextual description of the components, which are derived from the consumer behaviour field. The trail ride experience in Exhibit 5.1 can be analysed according to the five components.

Sensory experiences of all types were demonstrated on the trail ride. The service providers had quite a lot of control over this aspect. They chose the particular route or trail to provide stunning views. They gave instructions on how to ride. They ensured trail ride sounds of horses going over authentic terrain, and encouraged singing and 'hollering'. They cooked huge barbecued steaks, and they ensured that all consumers experienced the smell of the camp-fire.

According to both Peter's account and Christine's diary, there were many individual emotions and feelings experienced during the whole event, ranging from feelings of fear to relief and high spirits. The learning to ride a horse was certainly a problem-solving exercise that challenged them, especially when the horse was walking next to the sheer drop. Similarly the two-hour ride was a physical ordeal that neither of them had previously experienced. At the end they had learnt something about a different culture and enjoyed recounting their stories back home in the United Kingdom.

Academic perspectives

There is an academic interest in examining how individuals describe their own experiences.[27] There is value in understanding the symbolic meanings attached to consumer experiences in the act of consumption. Here, the assumption is that consumers' 'reality' is complicated by a reliance on sign perceptions, interpretations and uses. An understanding of how individual consumers perceive marketing stimuli, and how they interpret and use them, should then provide insights for marketing management. In a study of the consumer experience of the British pub, for example, a semiotic analysis of consumers' experiences in and of public houses concluded that the pub concept is associated (by consumers) with individuality and personal choice, rather than a mass-marketing approach.[28] The strategies of the multiple pub operators, that involved uniform pub brands, were therefore seriously questioned in the light of these interpretations of consumers' accounts of their pub experiences. Another study chronicled consumer experiences (in the form of subjective personal responses) of 232 undergraduate students in relation to a retail Department store, Lewis's in the United Kingdom (see Exhibit 5.2). The rich insights provided through the students' descriptions of their expectations and perceptions of the store experience not only identified strategic and operational issues that might have been actioned (respondent 1) but their narrative also foretold the future closure of the store (respondent 2).[29] The experiences were gathered in September 2005 and Lewis's ceased trading in 2007.

Exhibit 5.2   Consumer Experiences of Lewis's Department Store

Respondent 1

I had ideas of a delicatessen with bowls overflowing with edible delights, olives, hummus, real coffee, tea imported from India. Edible delights of the highest standard, fresh and maybe even fair-trade, like those you find at Harrods. As they get closer I Start to squint, no surely, no it can't be. Disbelief gives way to disappointment. It's like an Aldi, cardboard crates of cans, German biscuits, Space invader crisps, and Mr Greedy hotdogs, precariously stacked. A far cry from Knightsbridge (male, 24) page 34.

Respondent 2

Perhaps Lewis's simply goes with the flow because it doesn't have much competition in the Liverpool area. In order for the store to have survived as long as it has it must be making a profit. Although, it would seem that little of this profit has been reinvested into the business in order to update its appearance and image . . . I fear its days may be numbered (female 19) page 41.

We have seen reference, in Chapter 1, to services which have *experience attributes,* as distinct from search or credence attributes. In this sense, experience refers to the accumulated knowledge consumers gain through undertaking a service that allows them to evaluate the service after the event. However, from an academic perspective, the notion of *a consumer experience as Gestalt* tends to prevail over the notion of it being related to a particular incident with a service provider, or to the accumulation of knowledge only. This is why theatre, in its true sense, can aid service marketers in the creation of experiences for consumers. In theatre, each performance is designed to achieve a specific audience reaction, with a detailed consideration given to *all the elements* that create the reaction (improvisation, casting, role play and rehearsal associated with actors, together with stage management, lighting, sound, and costume and props associated with the setting) and to how they work together. The role of the audience, in addition to the role of the actors, is always considered explicitly, and the audience role is different in different forms of theatre.[30] We have seen, from Chapter 3, that audience roles in theatre can be transposed to customer roles in services (refer back to Table 3.1). The experiences of customers playing the role of voyeurs, for example, would be different from those playing the roles of spect-actors, sense-ceptors or connoisseurs. This brings us back to Schmitt's strategic question about what type of experiences you should provide and how you can provide them.

The use of theatrical techniques to create consumer experiences provides an opportunity to go beyond the superficiality that surrounds much of the popular conception of retail or service theatre, and at the same time explore a type of experience in some detail, together with the ways of providing it. To illustrate, let us suppose a retail or service provider wishes to provide an experience with consumers in the role of spect-actor. As a spect-actor

- the customer's role is transparent and clearly understood by both the customer and the service provider(s)

- the customer has the opportunity on-site to be critical of the offer and the way it is presented.

It is seen from Table 3.1 that the role of the consumer as spect-actor was informed by the work of the theatre practitioner Bertolt Brecht. A rich source of ideas can be generated for service providers, that wish to offer different, engaging experiences to consumers (in their roles as spect-actors), from a detailed examination of three aspects of theatre that Brecht directed:

1. methods for managing and developing the roles and performances of actors,

2. techniques for providing planned opportunities for audiences to influence performances, and

3. arrangement of the staging and mechanics for stimulating audience participation.[31]

There are parallels in human resource management (with aspects (1) and (2) above) and operations management (with aspect (3) above) in the creation of these experiences with large organisations, such as the Venetian Hotel, or with smaller operations such as the Trail Ride or even the UK corner shop.

Implications for Service Management

Whether or not we are living in an experience economy, there is evidence that consumers are willing and able to pay for experiences. Three implications for service managers who wish to create consumer experiences arise from the discussion above.

1. *There seem to be different perspectives on the meaning of experience, and these perspectives need to be acknowledged and addressed by management.* There is evidence

that, in popular parlance, a consumer experience is synonymous with a critical incident of the type described in Chapter 4, and as with consumer accounts of critical incidents, the majority of such experiences are 'bad'. Bad experiences lead to complaints and an 'us and them' mentality between the consumer and the provider. Notions of co-production of an experience between consumer and producer are undermined. It is therefore in the interests of service management to reinforce the view of their offered experience as an engaging event or episode – something to which consumers contribute part of themselves. An eating and drinking establishment may be an adequate descriptor, but an eating, drinking and talking establishment may change the perception of dining at Bobby Byrnes from a functional service (with many incidents and encounters) to a place where the consumer is an integral part of an experience.

Postcard from Practice 5.1

The Need for a Student Centred Campus

A tertiary institution needs to provide for students needs over the total student lifecycle – the 'student experience' must be an enjoyable and positive learning experience in a holistic way over the time a student is enrolled. Students need to be supported when they are downcast or under pressure, celebrated when they are successful, encouraged when they are stressed and entertained when they need a break. All these aspects must be provided by a University which is truly committed to being centred on the success of its students.

Source: Richard Handley.

---

2. *All the evidence suggests that the creation of an experience should be highly focused, with great attention to detail.* The intended effect on the consumer must be absolutely clear with all stimuli reinforcing the effect. This applies equally to theme-related virtual experiences, such as the Grand Canal Shoppes in the Venetian Hotel, and social experiences in places such as the local butcher's shop. In the former case, the shops, restaurants and the 'actors' must conform to visitors' perceptions of Venice; for example, pasta restaurants in 'St Mark's Square'. In the latter, employees can be trained to talk to customers and encourage customer-to-customer interactions in the shop to provide the opportunity for social exchanges and the dissemination of local news. Help in creating and sustaining a focus can be gained through reproducing ideas that emanate from theatre practice for generating audience reactions, or by using the components in Table 5.2 as a checklist for engaging individuals on emotional, physical and intellectual levels. The 'It's in the news!' (5.2) illustrates how technology can be used to create focused 'experiences'.

> ### 📖 It's in the News! 5.2
>
> **Technology and the Consumer Experience**
>
> According to the CNN Money News (13 January 2008),
>
> At the US National Retail Federation Annual Convention, IBM is demonstrating future innovations which could help retailers create unique consumer experiences. Through the use of 3-D technology, virtual worlds and some imagination, IBM is showing how retailing is moving beyond the walls of the store into the hands of the consumers. For example, new 'Immersive Retailing' technologies which immerse consumers into an experience are one example of how retailers could augment their strategies to attract and interact with customers in ways which build loyalty.
>
> One of the 'Immersive Retailing' demonstrations IBM shared with customers is the IBM Multi-Sensory Experience. Through the use of 3-D glasses, participants are treated to a fashion show from Europe complete with music and smells. For example, as a model walks down the runway her perfume will be noticeably in the air. Also, when she holds out the very expensive leather purse, viewers will get a 3-D view of it, and will be able to smell the fine leather.
>
> IBM treated customers to another 'Immersive Retailing' demonstration called the IBM Cave. Meant to complement a multi-channel retailing experience, this demonstration brings the user into a virtual reality experience, using a 3-D virtual world and stereoscopic goggles. These goggles react with the head movement of the user and create 360 degree view of a virtual reality room. IBM uses the technology as part of a scenario which has a consumer redesigning a room in his house into an entertainment room.

3. *Much can still be learnt about the pricing of experiences.* Pine and Gilmore argue strongly that organisations can charge premium prices. But how much can/should organisations charge? Could the Trail Ride operators have charged more than $139, given that potential customers were being turned away? It should be noted that prices for the Gondola rides in the Venetian Hotel went up by 50 per cent, from $10 to $15 between two visits to the website in April and May 2001. There does seem to be the potential for companies to charge premium prices, as for many experiences that are on offer, demand is exceeding supply. The record amount paid for an experience no doubt goes to American businessman, Dennis Tito – £14 million for a week's holiday on the Russian Soyuz spacecraft in May 2001. It was to be 'the fulfilment of a life's dream to fly into space'.[32]

Pricing strategies such as cost-plus, or prepayment plans, which tend to be associated with services that are personnel based and which rely on 'experience evaluations',[33] do not appear to be appropriate for Gestalt experiences. It seems to depend on what consumers are prepared to pay, and inventive market research is needed to establish pricing structures that reflect consumers' spending thresholds.

There is value in trying to measure the impact of consumer experiences. Staging and creating memorable experiences is an expensive undertaking and as with other areas of the business, service providers are constantly being asked to assess the value gained from this spend. This poses a number of problems for something which is highly intangible from the consumers' point of view. In Chapter 8, we review the use of 'servqual' and its antecedents as a mechanism for measuring the various dimensions of the service offer. Although these instruments can be applied to some degree to 'experience' evaluation, it has been suggested recently that methods used to evaluate 'theatrical' performances, drawn from the theatre domain, might help develop understanding in this area.[34] For example, Harris *et al* have recently drawn on the work of leading French theatre critique, Patrice Pavis,[35] to illustrate how an alternative 'questionnaire' used in the theatre to stimulate critical discourse around the semiotics of a performance can offer service providers new insights into 'experience' evaluation. In addition, building on the four experience realms identified by Pine and Gilmore, a recent study in the Tourism industry[36] used a measurement scale to assess the extent to which bed and breakfast operators provided entertainment, education, aesthetics and escapism in their 'experience' offer. Although the authors acknowledge that the instrument they developed requires 'further validations across different consumption situations and staged experiences' (p.129), it does start to offer some insights into how we might begin to measure the impact of various 'experience' dimensions.

Summary

It has been argued that consumers wish to purchase experiences and that we may be at the beginning of an experience economy. For the service provider, there are benefits to be gained, in creating differentiated (out-of-the-ordinary) experiences that meet consumer needs, through premium pricing. The interest in creating on-site 'theatre' for consumers is a response to this challenge and also to the competition of online services. In parallel, there is evidence that consumers also value traditional social experiences provided by the great good places which are managed by service providers.

An experience may relate to a particular incident with a service provider, to accumulated knowledge, or to the Gestalt. In the latter case, the *engagement* of the consumer is the distinguishing feature. Organisations wishing to offer an experience therefore must consider in detail how to focus on creating a clear intended effect on consumers. Lessons on how to do this can be borrowed from theatre practice, with especial attention being given to engaging consumers on an emotional, physical and intellectual level. The pricing and measurement of out-of-the-ordinary experiences is neither straightforward nor easy to justify, and requires further research.

Learning Outcomes

Having read this chapter, you should be able to

- appreciate and critically evaluate the reasons for the upsurge in interest in consumer experiences
- understand the distinctive characteristics of experiences and the components that make up such experiences
- distinguish between various definitions of 'experience', and how they offer different perspectives on consumer experiences
- evaluate the implications for service management arising from the discussion of consumer experiences.

Discussion Questions and Exercises

1. What makes a consumer *experience*?
2. Use search engines with the words 'retail theatre' or 'retail theater'. From the results of the search, what appear to be the elements of theatre as applied in retailing?
3. What great good places do you frequent?
4. Explain the different perspectives on the meaning of 'experience'.
5. What advantages might there be for customers to be active, rather than passive participants?

Notes and References

1. Pine, B. H. II and Gilmore, J. H., 'Welcome to the Experience Economy', *Harvard Business Review,* July–August 1998, pp. 97–105.
2. Pine, B. H. II and Gilmore, J. H., *The Experience Economy: Work is Theater and Every Business a Stage,* HBS Press, Boston Mass., 1999.
3. Schmitt, B. H., *Experiential Marketing,* The Free Press, New York, 1999.
4. Patterson, A., Hodgson, J. and Shi, J., 'Chronicles of "Customer Experience": The Downfall of Lewis's Foretold', *Journal of Marketing Management,* 24(1–2), 2008, pp. 29–45.
5. Holbrook, M. B. and Hirschman, E. C., 'The Experiential Aspects of Consumption: Consumer Fantasies, Feelings and Fun', *Journal of Consumer Research*, 9 (September), 1982, pp.132–40.
6. Can be seen on the website http://rockytrails.com/trail.html
7. Arnould, E. J. and Price, L. L., 'River Magic: Extraordinary Experience and the Extended Service Encounter', *Journal of Consumer Research,* vol. 20, June 1993, pp. 24–45.
8. Pine and Gilmore, *The Experience Economy.*
9. Rhodes, T., 'US Buys Off-the-shelf Christmas', *The Sunday Times,* London, 24 December 2000.
10. Bray, P., 'Times Change, but People Don't', *The Sunday Times,* London, 13 June 2000.
11. Retail Verdict UK A Monthly Newsletter, 'Retail Theatre: Interaction Ups Footfall', Verdict Research Limited, October 1999.
12. Baron, S., Harris, K. and Harris, R., 'Retail Theatre: The "Intended Effect" of the Performance', *Journal of Service Research,* November 2001.
13. Pine and Gilmore argue, however, that 'work *is* theater', and would not want to present work *as* theater, i.e. in a metaphorical sense (Pine and Gilmore, *The Experience Economy,* chapter 6).
14. These and other quotes of retail theatre can be found in Baron, Harris and Harris, 'Retail Theatre: The "Intended Effect" of the Performance'.

15. Notes by Doug Hoffman, as circulated to SERVNET subscribers on 1 May 2001 from *Doug.Hoffman@mail.biz.colostate.edu*

16. See http://www.venetian.com

17. Oldenburg, R., *The Great Good Place,* Marlowe & Company, New York, 1999.

18. Levine, J., 'A Place to Chat', *Forbes,* 9 September 1996.

19. Oldenburg, R., *The Great Good Place.*

20. See http://www.bobbybyrnes.com

21. Parker, C. and Byrom, J., 'Towards a Healthy High Street: Training the Independent Retailer', Manchester Metropolitan University, Summer 2000.

22. Baron, S., Leaver, D., Oldfield, B. M. and Cassidy, K., 'Independent Food and Grocery Retailers: Attitudes and Opinions in the Year 2000', Manchester Metropolitan University, June 2000.

23. Pickering, J. F., Greene, F. J. and Cockerill, T. A. J., 'The Future of the Neighbourhood Store', Durham University Business School Publications, September 1998.

24. General Consumer Council for Northern Ireland, *Consumers in the Dark: Rights, Redress and Proficiency,* 1998.

25. Pine and Gilmore, *The Experience Economy,* p. 12.

26. Schmitt, *Experiential Marketing.*

27. Giorgi, A., 'Concerning the Possibility of Phenomological Research', *Journal of Phenomological Research,* vol. 14, Autumn 1983, pp. 129–70.

28. Clarke, I., Kell, I., Schmidt, R. and Vignali, C., 'Thinking the Thoughts They Do: Symbolism and Meaning in the Consumer Experience of the "British Pub" ', *British Food Journal,* 102(9), 2000, pp. 692–710.

29. Patterson, A., Hodgson, J. and Shi, J. 'Chronicles of "Customer Experience": the Downfall of Lewis's Foretold', *Journal of Marketing Management,* 24(1–2), 2008, pp. 29–45.

30. Baron, Harris and Harris, 'Retail Theatre: The "Intended Effect" of the Performance'.

31. Harris, K., Harris, R. and Baron, S., 'Customer Participation in Retail Service: Lessons from Brecht', *International Journal of Retail and Distribution Management,* 29(8), April 2001, pp. 359–69.

32. Meek, J., 'Attention Houston, Tito Has Boarded', *The Guardian,* Manchester, UK, 1 May 2001.

33. Guiltinan, J. P., 'A Conceptual Framework for Pricing Consumer Services', Proceedings of the 7th Annual Services Marketing Conference, American Marketing Association, Chicago, 1988, pp. 11–15.

34. Harris, K., Harris R., Elliott, D. and Baron, S., 'A Theatrical Perspective on Service Performance Evaluation: The Contribution of Critical Discourse and Aesthetics', 2008, as yet unpublished paper.

35. Pavis, P. Analyzing Performance; Theater, Dance and Film. David Williams (trans), 2003, US: University of Michigan Press.

36. Oh, H., Fiore, A. M. and Jeoung, M., 'Measuring Experience Economy Concepts: Tourism Applications', *Journal of Travel Research*, vol. 46, 2007, pp. 119–32.

6

Service Design

Learning Objectives

Overall Aim of the Chapter

To provide a comprehensive outline and evaluation of research on the design of the service process and the design of the physical service environment.

In particular, the *chapter objectives* are

- to demonstrate the place of service design in the expanded services marketing mix

- to demonstrate the need to incorporate support for self-service elements within the service process

- to provide an overview of the techniques of service blueprinting and service mapping used in service process design

- to summarise the strategic and operational applications of service blueprinting and mapping

- to introduce the environmental dimensions of the 'servicescape', and the effects on customer and employee responses

- to provide a classification of physical service environments

- to summarise research on the effects of ambient conditions on human behaviour.

Introduction

When we speak of service design, we may be speaking of the design of the *process*, or the design of the *physical environment*. The earlier chapters have shown the importance of process and the physical environment (a major component of physical evidence) in the services marketing mix. The additional 3Ps – Process, People and Physical evidence – are often more prominent in customers' perceptions of services than the traditional 4Ps. (Refer back to the critical incident

Service Design
Planning of the service components that comprise the process and the physical environment.

accounts in Exhibit 2.1.) In this chapter, we summarise the main contributions to theory regarding the *design* of

- the service process
- the physical service environment.

This does not mean that P for people is being ignored. For example, it is strongly advocated that consumers should be actively involved in designing a service process 'regardless of whether consumers are privy to, or even aware of all parts of the process, their awareness of its results and evidence makes them potentially valuable participants in the design of the entire system'.[1] In a similar vein, design of physical service environments is significantly underpinned by an understanding of consumer and employee approach and avoidance behaviours.[2]

Throughout the chapter we emphasise the need to consider the extent to which encouraging customers to undertake tasks traditionally performed by service employees might be appropriate and the need to design the technologies, the virtual environment and the back-stage activities that will support self-service by customers.

Figure 6.1 shows the structure of this chapter. It links the material of Chapter 3 with the two strands of service design. It should be stressed that the two strands are not mutually exclusive. For example, the design of the physical environment of a hotel would need to acknowledge the processes undertaken by guests, who arrive (need reception area), use rooms (need easy access to rooms), and possibly eat/drink/swim and so on (need signage and access to facilities). However, by separating the two strands, we can concentrate on the essential components of each of them.

Starting from the top of Figure 6.1, the services marketing system, introduced in Figure 3.1, focused management attention on obtaining a balance between operational efficiency and marketing effectiveness. By and large, operational efficiency can be addressed through the design of the process, whereas the design of the physical service environment is concerned with marketing effectiveness.

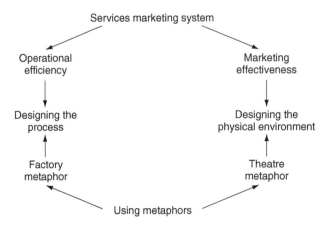

Figure 6.1   Service design: the two strands

Starting at the bottom of Figure 6.1, the application of the factory metaphor implies an efficiency goal, while the application of the theatre metaphor implies a marketing effectiveness goal – 'rave reviews from audiences'. In general, the factory metaphor provides ideas for the design of the process, whereas the theatre metaphor provides ideas for the design of the physical service environment.

📖 **It's in the News! 6.1**

Designing a Service

According to '*The Hindu Business Line*' (19 November 2006),

'The Climb of your Life' says the ticket for the Sydney Harbour BridgeClimb. Well, it may not quite be the climb of your life but it certainly is interesting and when you reach the 'summit' of the Bridge, you get a spectacular view of the beautiful Sydney Harbour, the Opera House and the Central Business District skyline.

BridgeClimb, a private organisation, organises climbing expeditions to the 'summit' of the bridge, which, at its mid point, is 415 feet above sea level. The brain behind BridgeClimb was Paul Cave, a businessman, and it took nine years of negotiations with several organisations, the government and community groups before the first public climbing expedition was launched in 1998.

The climb lasts all of three-and-a-half hours, including the preparation time when you are given climbing suits to wear complete with overalls and a safety harness that will attach you to the banister of the bridge. The preparation for the climb is an experience by itself and creates a sense of anticipation in you as you are shown safety videos and friendly BridgeClimb assistants help you gear up for the climb as if you are attempting the Everest! The experience is complete with a walk through a mock-up of the conditions as prevailing on the bridge. Included in the climbing gear are walkie talkie sets, just in case you happen to fall and are left hanging by the harness! Of course, there are headphones to help the climb leader speak to you and thankfully, a windcheater as well for it can get cold and windy as you reach the top.

The climb itself is not difficult as you walk along inclined catwalks, duck under steel girders, climb flights of stairs and widely spaced steps on the approach to the top. At one stage of the climb you will find yourself walking between two lanes of fast moving traffic and while descending you could see a train pass over the bridge right next to you, if lucky.

Expeditions are organised in small groups of 10–12 with a leader who also acts as a tour guide explaining the history of the bridge and pointing out Sydney's landmarks. Ours was a motley group of ten – six Americans, two Germans, an Australian and the sole Indian – and none of us had been on the climb before. So it was fun for all of us. At the end of the climb each of us became proud owners of a certificate certifying that we had done the 'Climb of Your Life' and a picture of the group taken at the top.

Designing the Process

As already stated, service is a process not a tangible product. It is worth reflecting, however, that in the development of many tangible products, there is usually a design stage prior to production and distribution. For example:

- a new model of car will require engineering drawings
- a house will require architects' plans
- sketches will be drawn of fashion or furniture prototypes.

When we think of a design stage, it is normally carried out with reference to a visual or diagrammatic representation of the tangible product. Let us consider the task of designing a house as an example. Architects' drawings may take the form of front, side and top elevations of the proposed building. Without these commonly understood visual references, discussions about specifications or modifications of the house would be difficult, if not impossible. Imagine using words only to communicate about plumbing, electrical supply and kitchen cupboard requirements. Words on their own, whether written or spoken, may lack the desired level of precision or be unclear in terms of context. The visual front, side and top elevations reduce imprecision and potential misunderstandings, thereby preventing potentially expensive mistakes.

For tangible products, therefore

- the design stage is an important aspect of product development. Design is sometimes synonymous with planning.
- sketches, diagrams or drawings are valued in the design stage, and may be indispensable.

Tangible products exist in time and space. In all the examples above, sketches, diagrams and drawings are used to visualise the physical aspects of the product (i.e., its existence in space, not time). Can services, which are processes, and which exist only in time, be designed, managed and changed in a similar manner to that applied to objects or tangible products? We demonstrate some of the responses to this question and explore the consequences of applying design concepts to services. Before we discuss techniques that can be used to assist in service design, it is important to acknowledge two phenomena that have a large, and growing, impact upon the design of service provision.

First, the rapid growth in the prevalence of self-service options, that enable customers to undertake tasks previously performed by employees of the service organisation, means that customers are now more aware of service processes than in the past. Secondly, the Internet is now so ubiquitous that it would be foolish for an organisation not to consider the strategic role that a website should play when designing the service process. At what point in the service process will customers access the website, what knowledge will they have at that point and what will they be trying to achieve with the website visit? Should the website be designed to encourage self-service behaviours, to provide an additional (or only) sales channel, to integrate with other aspects of the service process or merely as a source of information that customers might access? It is important to remember that websites are not the only place where customers encounter SSTs as part of service processes. Banks offer ATMs, petrol stations encourage 'pay at the pump', grocery stores are experimenting with self check-outs and airlines now encourage passengers to check themselves in either online or by using machines located near the check-in desks. Certainly the Internet, and other SSTs, can add tangibility to encourage customers to participate in service experiences or choose the most appropriate service for themselves through self-vetting processes. Passengers who check themselves in and select their own airline seats are able to 'see' the seating plan of the aircraft into which they place themselves and tourists viewing video footage of an attraction on a website can be encouraged to pre-book tickets online. Customers may also evaluate the potential full experience on the basis of how efficient and effective the self-service provision is. Indeed, the inability to perform a particular service via one organisation's website might encourage customers to book with a competitor. Currently, not all airline websites enable parents to book tickets for children travelling alone. Maybe those that do not have actively chosen not to as a strategy to reduce the number of unaccompanied minors that they carry or maybe they have overlooked this service need. We suggest that, at the very least, all service organisations need to consider the strategy behind their website and the extent to which self-service options would be appropriate within the service provision.

It is worth remembering that the 'back-stage' or 'invisible' elements of the service process do not disappear just because the customers are performing tasks themselves and may be physically invisible to the organisation. The service design will need to ensure that the organisation remains responsive and that orders received and promises made through e-service processes are fulfilled and delivered. Where self-service options are part of the service process the technologies that support that delivery will need to be designed to ensure that the customer experience is a happy one. We anticipate e-service, or SSTs becoming an important arena for interdisciplinary research for the development of service science that will combine services marketing, design and engineering (see earlier discussions regarding the emergence of SSME).

We now present two techniques that are frequently used to aid the design of service processes. First, blueprinting is described, and a stage-by-stage guide for producing blueprints is given. Secondly, we describe the technique of service mapping which is a logical extension to the blueprint. Finally we explore potential applications of the blueprinting and service mapping techniques.

Blueprinting

A technique for structural process design, called blueprinting, was developed by Shostack in 1987.[3] As we shall see, the service blueprint is a very important and effective management tool in its own right. However, in addition, the interest in blueprinting

Blueprint
A comprehensive visual model of a service process used to design and evaluate service performance.

Service Mapping
Builds on blueprinting by paying greater attention to customer interaction and provides a visual representation of the structure of the service.

- highlighted the importance of service design
- focused attention on process modelling
- encouraged the development of other diagrammatic techniques in particular, service mapping.[4]

There were already in existence techniques for charting processes or flows. For example, PERT (Program Evaluation and Review Technique) and Critical Path Analysis were commonplace visual scheduling aids for project planning, and the use of flowcharting to visualise input, output and iterative processes in computer program design was the norm. The value of the early work on blueprinting was the use and selection of the existing techniques to facilitate, specifically, the design of services.

Stages in blueprint preparation

A comprehensive visual model of a service process, in the form of a blueprint, provides the means for management more readily to identify strong and weak links in the process and to discuss the effects of potential structural changes such as greater customisation or an expanded range of services. It should be emphasised that it is not only a new service which has to be designed. It is often worth taking a closer look at the design of existing services. In each case, the preparation of a service blueprint requires a series of stages. Normally, they

1. Break down the process into logical steps
2. Recognise the variability in the process
3. Identify the 'invisible' elements in the process.

Within the context of hairdressing services, we will discuss each stage in greater detail.

1. *Breaking down the process into logical steps.*

Taking a gents' barber as an example, we can trace the steps of a typical customer from arrival at the barber's shop to his departure.

- When the customer arrives, he is greeted by the barber, who directs him to a seated waiting area unless there are no other customers. In such a case the customer will be directed to the barber's chair.
- Once in the barber's chair, the customer is asked about his requirements.
- The customer's hair is then cut in a way which (hopefully) meets his requirements.
- The barber, on finishing, will ask if the customer requires anything else (e.g. hair-care products).
- The customer will then pay and depart.
- The barber thanks the customer for payment (and possibly a tip), and in his goodbye statement infers a repeat visit.

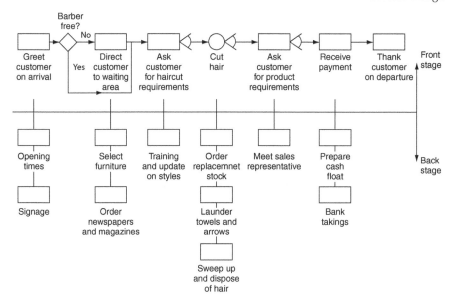

Figure 6.2 Blueprint of one-man gents' barber

Once agreement is reached on the sequence of basic steps, it is possible to represent the process visually. This is shown in the top half of Figure 6.2, and represents the element of the service that is normally in the customer's line of visibility (and within hearing distance).

2. Recognising the variability in the process.

In Figure 6.2, you will notice that in three places the symbol (a fan) appears. The fan is used to denote variability within the process. Variability can be either

- planned and controlled by the service provider, that is a range of potential actions that may be taken or
- unplanned, that is a range of potential events that might occur.

In the former case, the fan follows a rectangle. The first example is when the barber asks the customer for haircut requirements. The range of offers open to the customer is controlled by the barber. The barber may plan, for example, to offer only a limited number of options ('short-back-and-sides' or 'trim'; square neck or tapered) or to offer a wide range of the latest styles. Although customers may request different cuts, the variability in the requests is controlled by the barber. In the second example, where customers are asked whether they require any (hair-care) products, the variability of responses is controlled by what the barber has on offer on the shelves.

In the latter case, where variability is unplanned, the fan follows a circle. When the barber cuts a 'short-back-and-sides', it will not be an identical cut for all customers because of human error, and so a range of potential outcomes may occur. Within reason, customers may accept variability with a certain type of cut. There is an acceptable tolerance band within which a 'trim' or 'square neck' can fall. However, a 'trim' which more resembles a 'short-back-and-sides' would represent a deviation from tolerance standards which is unacceptable. Such deviations would be treated as quality issues and represent service failures.

It is important at this stage in the service design process to recognise where unplanned variation may occur and to anticipate potential service failure points.

3. *Identifying the 'invisible' elements in the process.*

The lower half of Figure 6.2 shows the elements of the barber's operation that are normally outside the customer's line of visibility, and how they are linked to the visible elements of the process. If greater detail is required, many of the invisible elements themselves can be represented as processes. For example, the element 'order replacement stock' is a process involving a number of stages, beginning with the initial contract with the supplier and ending with delivery and settlement of the invoice.

In total, Figure 6.2 provides a blueprint for the gents' barber. His case is somewhat unusual in that the barber himself is involved in all the visible and invisible elements and processes. He may find the blueprint useful mainly as a means of enhancing the service and determining potential future actions or strategies. In most services, however, the various contact personnel may only be involved in a limited part of the visible or invisible activities. In a theme park, for example, where seasonal employment is high, a blueprint of the whole operation provides an understandable visual reference to all employees, who may otherwise have a very blinkered view of the product offer. Newly employed or part-time staff can more readily be shown how their role fits into the whole operation, and that it is recognised to the same extent as other job roles.

Before moving on to discuss service mapping, it is worth emphasising three features of blueprint construction.

1. It is very difficult to do, even following the three stages above. It may involve a large investment in time. Apparently, Shostack herself found it very difficult to blueprint a new bank service because of its complexity. She therefore turned to a shoeshine stand service, developed the blueprint, and only then moved on to the more complex service.[5]

2. Those involved with the blueprint construction are forced to understand and discuss the basic elements of the service and to reach agreements about relative importance of elements, planned and unplanned variability and service failure points. Serious debate on such fundamentals, forcing participants to step back and take a bird's-eye view of the operation, may be considered a considerable benefit in its own right.

3. It is important that the visible element of a blueprint is constructed from the customer's perspective. Yet, in practice, service processes are often 'documented from a manager's or service designer's perspective, rather than a customer's perspective'.[6] Some suggested techniques which focus on the

customer perspective include 'service journey audits'[7] and 'service transaction analysis'.[8] There is also a need to understand where the service process begins from the customer perspective. UK supermarkets that run buses between their stores and local housing estates recognise that part of the process of grocery shopping is getting to and from the store.

Overall, the benefits of blueprinting must be weighed against the time investment.

Service mapping

Service maps build on blueprints and provide two additional features to add to management information.

- They pay greater attention to customer interaction with the service organisation.

Clear diagrammatic distinctions are made between actions of customers and of service contact personnel. In effect, more detail is provided on the visible activities in blueprints such as Figure 6.2.

- Additional vertical layers to the diagram are drawn in service maps to provide a visual representation of the structure of the service.

In particular, the 'invisible' activities are divided into those provided by frontline employees, support staff and management services.

In a service map (Figure 6.3), therefore, the horizontal axis denotes the process, going from left to right, and the vertical axis denotes the structure of the service

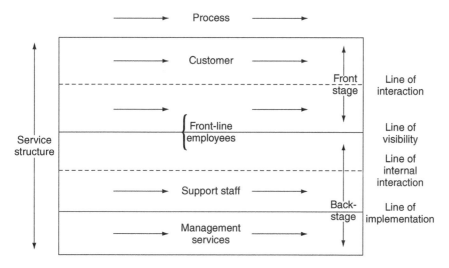

Figure 6.3   The layers and features of the service map

provided. The larger the service organisation, the greater the need to make clear the structure in order that the service logic is understood by all employees.

In the blueprinting examples, one horizontal line divides the visible from the invisible elements. Consequently, it is commonly known as the line of visibility. In service maps, the organisation structure, denoted on the vertical axis, is made clearer through more dividing lines. There are four lines in total.

1. *The line of interaction.* This denotes the distinction between the customer's and frontline employee's parts in the service encounter.
2. *The line of visibility.* Note here that whilst much of the work of frontline employees is concerned with the service encounter, which is above the line of visibility, some of their work is carried out below the line of visibility, that is, out of sight of the customer.
3. *The line of internal interaction.* This denotes the division between the frontline employees and the operations support staff. Such internal interactions normally occur out of sight of the customers.
4. *The line of implementation.* This denotes the division between operations support staff and general management services. It may be the case that the latter are located physically at a distance from the former and are not therefore directly involved with implementing the service.

To illustrate the vertical dimension of a service map (Figure 6.4), let us examine one element of a process: the payment for goods in an outlet of a multiple grocery retailer. Figure 6.4 is only a snapshot of a vertical portion of a much larger, complete service map.

Complete maps can be drawn of

- Specific services, such as that provided by a multiple grocery retailer or by a unisex hairdresser. Such maps will generally be large and complicated and the investment in time will be even greater than for blueprinting.

- Concepts. In a concept service map, general issues are highlighted, but within the layered structure. An example is given in Figure 6.5, where five service quality dimensions are considered in the row below the line of interaction. (The five service quality dimensions will be discussed in greater detail in Chapter 8.)

Applications of blueprinting and service mapping

1. *Service failures and fail-safing*

Whatever the diagrammatic form of a service design – whether it be a blueprint, a specific service map or a concept service map – one of the main aims will be to identify the potential points in the process which may result in a service failure. It is probably inevitable that on some occasion either the customer or

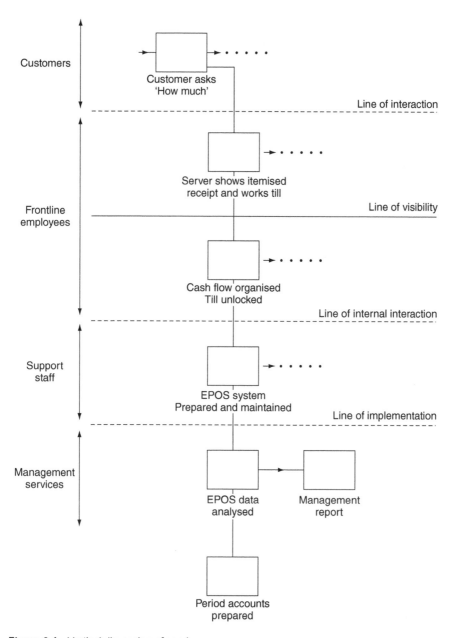

Figure 6.4   Vertical dimension of service map

the server will make some mistake. If these occasions can be anticipated, and the mistake prevented from turning into a service 'defect' and hence a service failure, then the effort spent in service design may be justified. Once points of potential service failures have been identified, fail-safes can be designed to reduce the risk of human mistakes turning into actual service failures.

Fail-safes
Simple mechanisms to minimise or eliminate errors.

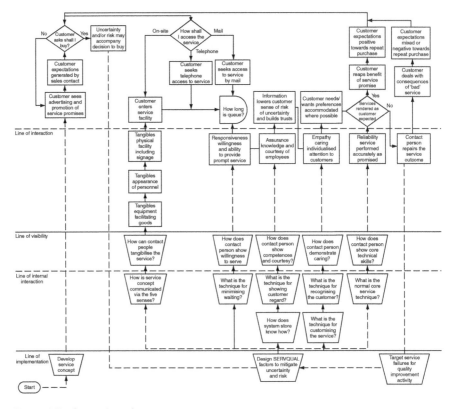

Figure 6.5   Concept service map

Source: J. Kingman-Brundage, 'Technology, Design and Service Quality', *International Journal of Service Industry Management*, 2 (3), 1991, p. 55.

In the 'Waymark Holiday' case (Case Study 5), for example, an account is given of how a holiday in Greece, at Easter, did not match the expectations of three customers. Although, arguably, the poor experience may have been largely the fault of the customers in being inadequately prepared for such a holiday, the company have responded by taking the responsibility, and introducing a fail-safe, in the form of an expanded checklist of questions to ask new customers, in order to avert the possibility of similar experiences being repeated.

Due to customer participation in services, mistakes or errors that may lead to service failures can be made by servers or by customers. Chase and Stewart[9] provide a very useful classification of server errors and customer errors, and the remainder of this section draws heavily on their work.

Server errors are conveniently described as task, treatment or tangibles.

- Task errors include doing work incorrectly or work not requested, or doing work in the wrong order or too slowly.

- Treatment errors include failure to acknowledge, listen to, or react appropriately to a customer.

Server Errors

Errors made by contact personnel relating to tasks, treatments or the tangible elements of the service.

Customer Errors

Errors made by customers relating to their preparation for, participation in, or resolution of service encounters.

- Tangible errors may be caused by failure to clean facilities or provide clean uniforms, or by failure to control ambient conditions in the physical environment.

Being aware of potential server errors is important. What is also needed, in order to fail-safe the server, is imaginative but simple means of preventing the errors reoccurring. A church minister may prevent the error of failing to mention family members by name during a funeral by always completing a pro forma prior to the service, or by going over a checklist with the funeral director. A consultant surgeon in a hospital could always talk to patients after examinations as part of a routine. Fail-safes are often simple mechanisms, but their absence can be damaging.

Customer errors can be classified as relating to preparation for the service encounter, the encounter itself, or to the resolution of the encounter.

- Preparation errors may result from the failure of customers to bring the necessary materials to the encounter, or to understand their roles in the service encounter.

- Encounter errors include failure of customers to remember steps in the service process, to follow the system flow or to specify desires or follow instructions.

- Resolution errors include failure of customers to signal service failures, learn from experience, adjust expectations or execute appropriate post-encounter actions.

The dentist's patients may miss appointments through forgetfulness. The accountant's clients may fail to produce necessary receipts. The lead violinist of the school orchestra may forget her music! Each of these are customer preparation errors, but it is obviously in the service provider's interest to devise ways of minimising the frequency of such errors through some fail-safe device, such as timely reminders or clear instructions to clients prior to the encounter. The Thai restaurant owner may prevent customer encounter errors with the lunchtime buffet feast (resulting in customer confusion and crowding) by providing diners with clear details of the routes round the buffet tables and recommended menu mixes. The follow-up customer call after a car service represents a means of ensuring that the customer has the opportunity to engage in appropriate post-encounter activities.

Chase and Stewart,[10] using a service map of the standard car service at a car dealership as a reference, identify many potential service failure points. Those which represent customer errors are denoted above the service map, and those which represent server errors are denoted below the map. Although, once drawn to the attention, most potential service failures are obvious, they are easily overlooked without a comprehensive diagram of the service design. Of equal importance to the car dealership management is that most fail-safes are relatively inexpensive to employ. The failure to notice that a customer has arrived, for example, can easily be averted by the use of a bell chain. This must be followed by the acknowledgement of the customer's arrival by a frontline employee. Such simple devices may avoid loss of business through customer frustration on confusion. Proper attention to detail such as this throughout the process is facilitated by use of the service map as a point of reference.

📖 It's in the News! 6.2

Monitoring Complaints and Service Recovery

According to the *Straits Times*, Singapore (11 February 2008),

Got any bugbears about unpleasant bank services or poor rates? Blog about it or air it in an online forum, and you just might get the bank's attention.

Ms Constance Chan, 39, a mother of two girls, was pleasantly surprised by OCBC Bank's response to her blog recounting a disappointing encounter at a branch. She recently took her daughters Tan Rae Wen, seven, and Lea Wen, three, to open Mighty Savers kids' savings accounts at OCBC. A bank teller, however, turned her away, telling her she needed to submit her children's passports, not their birth certificates, as an OCBC phone banking staff instructed her earlier. 'I looked at the kids, and they were so disappointed. I was disappointed, too. I really think that it is absurd to ask for their passports,' she wrote in her blog.

To her surprise, Ms Chan received a week later a hamper with Mighty Savers materials and toys, as well as a personal letter from Mr Nicholas Tan, OCBC head of group wealth management, group consumer financial services. He came across her blog and hurried to make amends. He quickly arranged to get the hampers hand-delivered to Ms Chan's home. This prompted her to post a blog bouquet to OCBC and Mr Tan for his gesture that, she said, 'showed that service boundary does not end once you step out of the bank's door'.

Mr Tan's swift response to Ms Chan's blog was not because of a random Internet search but a new procedure the bank implemented to monitor online feedback about its services. 'Blog monitoring has provided us . . . with feedback on the bank, especially when we launch new products or services or even premiums,' he said. Bank staff regularly sift out online information 'critical for the bank to act upon immediately, as some posts might be an indication of a latent issue that is brewing', he added.

With the Internet becoming an increasingly influential feedback channel for customers, banks such as United Overseas Bank and DBS Bank say they are now monitoring online news forums more closely. Standard Chartered Bank (Stanchart) makes an effort to respond promptly to complaints or feedback on online forums such as Singapore Press Holdings' Stomp portal. Ms Ngo Min Ying, Stanchart's general manager of customer experience, said 'these cases are usually resolved within three working days'. Banks say responding to customer online feedback is part of their efforts to emphasise better service.

They see this as a way to differentiate themselves in a keenly competitive market such as Singapore, where simply offering innovative products is not enough since rival banks can replicate the same products within hours. Other efforts to improve service include serving gourmet coffee at bank branches, OCBC's tradition of a morning greeting by bank staff, including senior executives such as chief executive David Conner, and POSB's refurbishment of its branches.

2. *Ensuring safety*

For many services, for example air travel, theme parks, and hospitals, safety of the consumer is paramount, and a significant element of the service operation. Any consequences resulting from a perceived lack of appropriate attention to safety issues are normally highly publicised. Take, for instance, the following pieces from *The Times* of 9 January, 2001:

> *Hospitals are dangerous places. Around 5,000 patients die each year from infections caught after arriving in hospital. Yet these death traps continue to accept admissions, even stacking up their customers in corridors.* [11]

> *...a damning survey [of hospitals]...that found overflowing lavatories, soiled tissues lying around the ward, carpets ripped up, and even pigeons in a canteen. A third of hospitals failed basic hygiene checks, including wards, lavatories, décor, furniture linen and 'smells'.* [12]

These are cases where there is visible evidence that the invisible elements of the service operation are not being undertaken effectively.

Clearly, a blueprinting or service mapping approach cannot, in itself, enhance safety. But, as can be seen below, with an illustration of a study of butchers' services, the linking of the consumer-centred process (the visible part of a blueprint) with the 'invisible' practices of the service providers can highlight important safety issues that may otherwise have been overlooked.

The service provided by butchers in the United Kingdom had received considerable publicity in the late 1990s especially through an outbreak of *E. coli* food poisoning resulting in fatalities. The butcher's shop at the centre of the outbreak had failed to separate raw and cooked meats, and did not provide separate knives/tools, separate tables/work surfaces, scales or vacuum packers. To understand more clearly the practices carried out by butchers, an observational study was undertaken in 1999/2000 of 91 businesses that sold both raw and cooked meats.[13]

Observation of the consumer process, which includes paying for the purchased meats, immediately highlighted the issue of hand-washing practices of the employees. Hand washing was seen not to be routine after handling money or using the cash till. Indeed, for a minority of the businesses observed, hand-washing facilities were deemed unsatisfactory, where, for example, there was no dedicated wash-hand basin, no hot water or soiled bars of soap. In all, the study was able to highlight specific areas for hygiene concern:

- the meat slicer
- the cooked meat scale pan
- the hand tap at the wash-hand basin
- the cooked meat chiller handle
- the vacuum packer
- the keys of the cash till
- a cleaning cloth used for cooked meat surfaces
- the butcher's apron.

The study had, in effect, undertaken the stages of blueprint construction outlined at the beginning of this section. The blueprint itself is an effective way of visualising the process, and the links between the visible and invisible elements.

3. *Using blueprints to identify complexity and divergence and address service positioning*

Once an acceptable blueprint has been drawn, in what ways can it aid understanding and determine potential actions?

Shostack proposed that, initially, two features of the process should be examined.[14]

- Level of complexity
- Degree of divergence.

The level of complexity relates directly to the number of steps and sequences, and the interrelationships between them. The more steps and intricacies, the greater the complexity. The degree of divergence refers to the amount of planned scope or latitude which contact personnel are given. Low divergence results in a high level of standardisation. The fans on the blueprint indicate points where varying degrees of divergences can be considered.

Figure 6.6 provides a means for an initial classification of a service in terms of the two dimensions – complexity and divergence. According to this matrix,

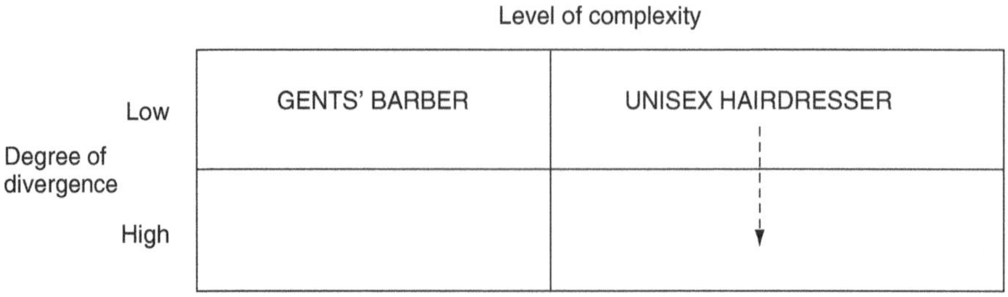

Level of complexity

Low	GENTS' BARBER	UNISEX HAIRDRESSER
High		

Degree of divergence

Figure 6.6 Classification of services according to level of complexity and degree of divergence

the gents' barber would fall into the north-west cell, that is, low in both complexity and divergence. The multi-staff unisex hairdresser is arguably more complex, because of services such as consultancy and advice, and hair-styling could be deliberately made as highly divergent, involving a high degree of customisation.

In Figures 6.7, 6.8 and 6.9, Shostack provides examples of blueprints of services which differ according to the two dimensions of complexity and

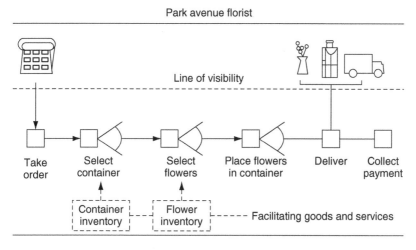

Figure 6.7 Low complexity – high divergence

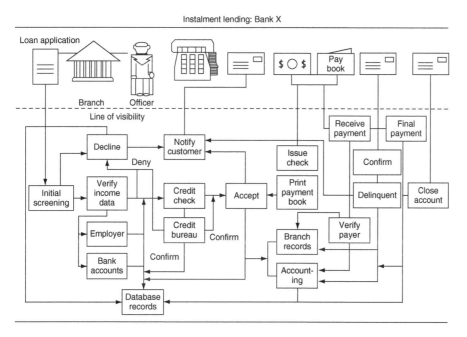

Figure 6.8 High complexity – low divergence, i.e., standardised

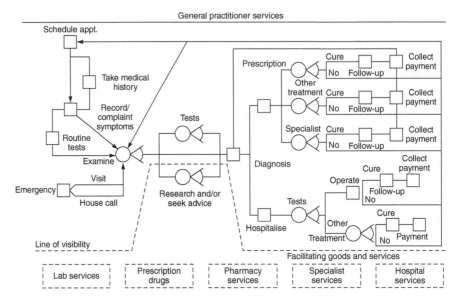

Figure 6.9   High complexity – high divergence

divergence. In each case, complexity is related to the size and number of elements in the blueprint, and divergence depends on the number of fans in the diagram.

Returning to our hairdressing examples, both the gents' barber and the unisex hairdresser can ask how they might increase or reduce complexity or divergence, and how this might alter their positioning in the market. The gents' barber, for example, could increase complexity in a number of ways. He could

- employ an assistant
- increase the range of goods to be sold
- deal with several suppliers, rather than one representative.

Each of these potential actions would result in a repositioning of his offer.
He could reduce complexity (to an even lower level) by, for example

- not stocking any goods at all
- not supplying reading material for waiting customers.

He could increase divergence by giving a greater emphasis to hair-styling. He could reduce divergence further by only offering, say, 'short-back-and-sides' cuts with two neckline levels.

Any change in complexity and divergence will reflect the barber's judgement of the current and potential customer base. The blueprint will enable him to focus on the elements of the process which affect positioning and operation.

4. *Stimulating creativity*

In our experience, the presentation of the visible component of a blueprint to a group of service providers or professionals acts as a catalyst for ideas and innovations with the service. The consumer process which underpins the visible part of the process does not necessarily have to be complex. For example, for a group of veterinary surgeons, the client experience involved with taking their dog or cat for a routine vaccination, presented as a non-complicated sequence of events (see Figure 6.10), provided the catalyst. For a group of dentists, the visible process showing the patient experience associated with a visit to the dentist for a routine check-up had the same effect.

Let us take the dog/cat vaccination process (Figure 6.10). Although the individual stages and the sequence of stages itself seem straightforward, there are many ways in which veterinary practitioners respond to the questions below the line of visibility, and creativity does not require huge changes to existing practice. Even stage 1 (ensuring that clients receives appropriate reminders) can be done in several ways – from a conventional letter to the client to a cartoon-based reminder card addressed to the pet. However, the more cheerful reminder cards only add insult to injury if the pet has died in the interim, thus highlighting another key aspect of the service (efficient record keeping). Posing the questions in the shaded area, for all the stages of the process, usually generates discussions and new ideas from groups of interested people (e.g., all employees in a veterinary practice).

Blueprints can also be used to aid *new* service development. A study of the development of nine new services identified 'lack of systematic reporting and feedback' and 'rudimentary documentation' as two of the factors contributing to problems and their symptoms in service development processes.[15] Both of these drawbacks can be overcome to a great extent by drawing and modifying the blueprint of the proposed new service as a means of communication. It can facilitate a balance between creativity and formal planning and control.

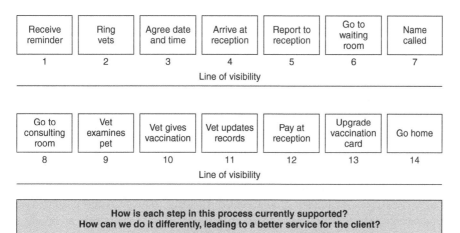

Figure 6.10   Routine vaccination of cat or dog at a veterinary service

5. *Ensuring responsiveness, fulfilment and delivery to support self-service*

The blueprinting and service mapping techniques should be particularly help-ful in drawing attention to the 'invisible' support required for self-service and e-service elements within the service process. The need to visualise the e-service or self-service elements is acute when the customer is also 'invisible'. To be effective the back-stage or back-office processes must be responsive and ensure that the organisation fulfils and delivers the service as ordered by the cus-tomer. A research study that recorded levels of responsiveness of UK service organisations to emails found a striking difference between the performance of Internet-only organisations (clicks) and those that had added the web as an additional channel (bricks), with clicks outperforming bricks.[16] By way of exam-ple, while 50 per cent of the Internet-only travel agents responded within 6 hours only 20 per cent of the brick travel agents did. Voss concluded that estab-lished organisations find it difficult to incorporate the Internet into their service process. Reasons given for this included the following:

- e-business was a small part of the business so not seen to be serious;
- an inability to cope with the different culture associated with the web environment;
- difficulty with simultaneous, multi-channel service delivery.

It also emerged that, while all the organisations interviewed had a wide range of service standards, only one had extended these standards to the online service. It appears that service processes that lack performance standards are less likely to receive management attention. Unfortunately this organisation used the same standards for Internet responsiveness as those used elsewhere in the organisation which meant that the response time for an email, being written communication, was a week!

Postcard from Practice 6.1

Planting-By-Numbers

We are a mobile landscape design company which provides a unique plant sup-ply service to the residential market. We want our service to stand out and have avoided being too serious. We want people to see us as fun and energetic. The name of our company, Landscape Safari, our services and our presentation reflect that image. Our approach is to package our time into one- or two-hour blocks and design to a formula. We have minimised the time spent on the design by reduc-ing the traditional design method to what is critical. We formulated the idea as a response to client frustrations around cost and the time required to design gardens in a small residential site. We were asked if we would walk and talk on an hourly basis by some of our clients. We would usually draw a quick A4 sketch accompa-nied by a list of plants. This service became requested more and more. We then realised that we were always using the same plants and the writing out of plant names and cross referencing from the list to the planting plan took a long time, so we decided to standardise the list that we use. Now we just include the plant numbers from the standard list on all the planting plans. This speeds up the whole process of providing clients with a design plan.

At around the same time I read a prediction that in the future gardens would be delivered and that garden centres would become obsolete. As a direct result of reading that we decided to sell plants on the back of the designs. We introduced a website and marketed around the convenience of our delivery service. A few months later a client asked me to number the plants so they could figure out what went where. This inspired us to provide this service as standard practice which we called Plant-By-Numbers.

Source: Justin Newcombe.

Designing the Physical Environment

The servicescape

As noted in Chapter 4, service managers need to consider not only the impact of interpersonal interactions on customer perceptions and behaviour, but also the impact of what Bitner refers to as the 'Servicescape'.[17] The 'servicescape' describes elements of the built environment (i.e., the manmade, physical surroundings) that constitute part of the service, as opposed to the natural or social environment – specific dimensions of the servicescape of a dentist, for example, including the lighting in the waiting rooms and the surgery, the wall decor, the signage and the temperature. Service providers demonstrate that they believe that servicescape dimensions can influence the cognitive and emotional responses of consumers to their service experience. A dentist, for example, may colour surgery walls pink in the belief that it helps to reduce the anxiety felt by patients, and may scatter small, cuddly toys around the surgery to help to put children at ease. Similarly, the supermarket operator may think that the smell of freshly baked bread pumped through the store will influence customers to buy bread. These components can potentially have as great an influence on customer behaviour as interpersonal encounters. For example, a customer may have a positive encounter with a sales assistant on entering a food store and be able to locate the ideal product, but may find waiting in a queue in a stifling atmosphere unbearable and consequently leave before making a purchase. The physical environment can also have a dramatic impact on the employee's approach to the service encounter. Research suggests that the same physical environment that can potentially affect consumers' reactions to their experience can affect the motivation and performance of service employees.[18]

Bitner presented a framework that illustrates how customer and employee internal responses and behaviours (i.e., 'approach' or 'avoid') are influenced by servicescape elements. The servicescape environmental dimensions, referred to in the model, include the following:

- ambient conditions (air quality, temperature, noise, smell, etc.)
- spacial and functional features (layout, equipment, furnishings, etc.) and
- signs, symbols and artefacts (style of decor, signage).

The model illustrates how these elements can affect the consumers' and employees' emotional, cognitive and physiological state and their subsequent behaviour.

The Physical Service Environment and Customer Satisfaction

Research, in a retail context, which examined customer behaviour in a pleasant and a not so pleasant store atmosphere, found that 'Customer satisfaction with the store was greater in the pleasant store' and 'Customers in the pleasant store spontaneously spent more money on articles they simply liked.'[19] (The pleasantness of the store was based on its condition, layout/way-finding, and information rate; that is, the degree to which the merchandise presentation was out of the ordinary, yet integrated.)

Research, in the context of leisure services such as sporting events, concluded that 'when the subjects perceived the servicescape to be of higher quality, they were more satisfied with the servicescape, and were therefore more inclined to want to go to games at the stadium', and 'What this servicescape quality/satisfaction/repatronage relationship means for owners and managers of leisure services is that careful attention should be given to each aspect of the servicescape to ensure that customers are satisfied, not only with the primary service, but also with the entire leisure service experience.'[20]

It is seen, therefore, that relationships between servicescape design and positive customer behaviours are being made in specific service sectors. Table 6.1 provides a classification of services by consumption purpose and time spent in the service facility, which highlights the types of services where the design of the physical environment is particularly important.

The more that services are viewed as hedonistic, and greater the amount of time the customer spends within the service facility, the greater the potential influence of the physical environment on customer affective responses, attitudes and re-patronage behaviour.[21]

So, whereas the design of the physical environment of a dry-cleaner may require most of the attention being given to the utilitarian service efficiency aspects, the design of the physical environment of a theme park would require

Table 6.1   Classification of physical service environments

Time spent in facility	Utilitarian	Purpose of consumption	Hedonic
Minutes	• Dry-cleaner • Taxi-cab • Post-office • Bank branch	• Barber's shop • Coffee bar • Lecture room • Vets	• Games arcade • Clairvoyant • Sauna • Children's playground
Hours	• Pre-natal class • Law office • Hospital out- • Patients • Supermarket	• Restaurant/ • public house • Airline/airport • Museum • Garden centre	• Shopping mall • Football stadium • Theatre • Leisure centre
Days	• School • Hospital • Law court • Training centre	• Hotel • Conference Centre • Health spa • Caravan park	• Cruise liner • Theme park • Holiday villa • Coach tour

much greater attention to the generation of customer excitement, fun and entertainment. Service providers in a given cell of Table 6.1. can draw on ideas of servicescape designs from other service providers in the same cell.

Additionally, those service providers that are wishing to concentrate more on consumer experiences, as outlined in Chapter 5, may look to moving from left to right in Table 6.1. For example, if an airport is to become more of a hedonic experience for customers, the airport designers could look to the kinds of physical environments which are created by the services in the far right column of Table 6.1. In Changi Airport in Singapore, for example, in addition to a very large shopping mall, the destination lounge contains an interactive science centre, a large games arcade, and a themed indoor orchid garden complete with streams, bridges, seats and tropical fish.

Physical environment design considerations

In designing the physical service environment, a balance has to be struck between enabling operational efficiency and providing marketing effectiveness through offering opportunities for customers to engage in an experience. For the services, in the left column of Table 6.1, operational efficiency may determine the design of the physical environment. The design of hospital out-patients' departments, bank branches, schools and even supermarkets are created to accommodate the main business function. In contrast, for the services in the right-hand column of Table 6.1, the design of the physical environment should encourage 'rave reviews from the customers', in keeping with the the-atre metaphor (Chapter 3). The designs of the services in the middle column of Table 6.1 are the most challenging in obtaining an appropriate balance between operational efficiency and marketing effectiveness.

Take airports, for example.

The example of Changi Airport, above, demonstrates the opportunities for air-port designs which go way beyond the utilitarian, having already succeeded in meeting the efficiency requirements of customers. In a similar vein, the com-pany responsible for the design of the Dubai Duty Free Shopping area claim that by 'combining years of duty free experience with skills of visitor attractions, we introduce "retail theatre" '.[22] However, it would be inappropriate for airports to aim for 'theatre' until customers are satisfied with the environmental dimen-sions highlighted by Bitner; that is, ambient conditions, spacial and functional features, and the airport signs, symbols and artefacts. In a study of airport depar-ture lounges, for example, Rowley and Slack[23] provided details of one particular lounge that 'did not succeed in conveying the message that the passenger was a valued customer'.

The servicescape evidence for this conclusion included the following:

- departure board not working
- insufficient space between seating areas and insufficient numbers of seats
- hot and confined space
- high level of noise, due to background music and high density of people talking and moving
- people flows crossing each other
- only two ladies' toilet cubicles
- luggage left in locations that obstruct people movement because there is nowhere else to leave it.

The design of hotels is equally challenging. Many are designed in a utilitar-ian way that has attracted criticism. 'In them, one is nowhere: in Manchester, or in Verona, in Groningen, or in Roissy... the room is a place of protec-tion and the foyer is a non-place resembling an airport lounge.'[24] The purely functional design of a hotel can prevent guests from any meaningful expo-sure to other guests, and pays no regard to the consumer being an active part of the environment. To position itself more to the right of Table 6.1, hotel designers could, for example, 'reintroduce recesses, corners and curves, fuzziness, enabling people to meet, to get together in a part-open and part-closed space that favours community encounters'.[25] Such elements of hotel servicescape designs would be driven by the aim of getting people together rather than cocooning them.

It is also important to consider the ability of the customers who will need to use the facilities. A large number of users of Waitakere City hospital in New Zealand do not find it easy to read signs in English. Responding to this community need the hospital developed a signage system which associates medical departments with colours and animals.

Postcard from Practice 6.2

Locating a Financial Planning Service in Auckland, New Zealand

We put a lot of thought into the location and the whole atmosphere of the office. We wanted to encourage our clients to visit us, rather than visiting them in their homes. We feel it conveys a more professional and stable provision which is important for financial advisers. We are neither a 'one man band' nor a large institution, but rather a boutique national practice, focusing on higher net-worth individuals. We offer a more personal service but every bit as professional as the big firms. The location on the city fringe in an old, established suburb 5 minutes drive from the centre and with easy access to all the motorways makes it convenient to access for all of our clients. We wanted an old Villa, not an office block for two reasons. First, the historic setting and ambiance is important to portray longevity and financial strength. Secondly, we need clients to open up to us. We need to understand their 'life story' and their plans for their future so that we know what their financial aims are before we can provide them with a plan – it's a sort of 'fireside chat' among friends really. A modern, clinical office isn't the right impression for us. We want clients to feel relaxed and comfortable so we wanted a homely feel.

We have a large client meeting room right at the entrance so that clients don't see the offices – with all that paper and clutter. We have nice artwork hanging too although we are planning to acquire some old photos of the area too. The meeting room has working chairs, not sofa's, around a large square table – not a desk. We can sit up to 8 comfortably although we generally have 1–1 or 1–2 meetings. Sometimes we have additional advisors like lawyers and trustees. Although we emphasise the history our clients want us to be modern too – afterall we are planning their future – so we have a 32 inch LCD screen on the wall and frequently use the notebook to present the reports and plans.

We decided to have window boxes with flowers growing rather than fresh cut flowers. We like to open the windows – better than air conditioning – and it brings the outside inside as people do with their own homes. Also, it's a talking point, with women in particular, and our wealthier clients – wealth and gardens seem to go hand in hand. My assistant is a former nurseryman so that helps to build the relationship too. Our clients see that we are real people with real interests outside just crunching numbers. We can talk about growing parsley! Building trust and respect doesn't just come from accurate and buoyant financial reports but by demonstrating that we have wider experiences – just like our clients.

Ambient Conditions
The use of scent, music and lighting within the physical environment that comprises the servicescape.

The ambient conditions

The ambient conditions of a physical service environment include air quality, temperature, noise and smells. We are all aware that service providers can, and do, manipulate the ambient conditions in service environments – air conditioning in cars and hotel rooms, background music in restaurants and shopping malls, and the smell of potpourri in craft shops. What is less well known is the effect of these manipulations on consumer behaviour in the environment. Some recent studies on the effect of smell and/or music on consumer responses can be summarised as follows.

Smell/scent

Bone and Ellen[26] provided a model of the 'conventional wisdom' of the effect of smells, scents or odours on consumers in various service environments, and then reviewed the academic research findings relating to the model. The model links three olfactory features – scent *presence*, scent *pleasantness*, and scent *congruity* (i.e., how well the olfactory cue complements other stimuli, such as music) – to the effects on the person:

- approach or avoidance
- mood (arousal and valence)
- cognitive effort

and to responses to the stimulus:

- affective and evaluative responses
- purchase intentions
- behaviour (time spent in facility, information search, variety seeking/ switching).

The relationships are believed to be moderated by individual differences and the task/content effects.

Bone and Ellen's overall conclusion, based on the existing research, was that 'the conventional wisdom is not significantly upheld in the empirical results'. For example, the research to date does not support the view that scent presence affects a retail customer's behaviour. Clearly, there is something of a mismatch, at the moment, between practitioner 'gut feel' as to the consumer responses to smell/scents and the findings from academic research. More research, particularly on-site studies, would help service providers.

Music

Oakes[27] provided a structure, which he calls the musicscape, that relates background music features – *compositional* (tempo, harmony, volume) and *genre* (classical, popular, jazz) – to internal customer responses in the service environment:

- cognitive (expectations, perceived duration)
- emotional (elicited mood)

and behavioural outcomes in the environment:

- consumption speed
- actual stay duration
- purchase behaviour.

In the musicscape, the moderating variables are believed to be customer age, gender and social class, and familiarity with the music. Research relating to these relationships suggests that:

- slower tempos tend to make consumers shop at a more leisurely pace, and sometimes to spend more money than do faster tempos
- shopper behaviour might differ according to the type of music played.[28]

However, it is again very difficult to generalise, and some studies have shown that the 'no music' option has yielded the most favourable customer responses and behavioural outcomes! At the same time, in Coventry in the United Kingdom, background music has been introduced for the *complete city centre shopping area*, with both tempo and genre being varied according to the time of day. The choice of classical music in the mornings, pop music at (the busier) lunchtime, and country-and-western music in the afternoon is presumably based on a 'conventional wisdom' view of the effects of background music on shopping behaviour. However, as with the olfactory effects, the empirical studies on the musical effects are contradictory, and situation specific, and do not necessarily support the conventional wisdom. Research has focused on the combined effects of environmental cues; that is, lavender scents with classical music, on customer responses and behaviours.[29]

The Online Servicescape: e-scapes

There is a need to learn more about customer perceptions of the online and other self-service environments in which they are increasingly experiencing services.[30] We mentioned the need to consider the extent to which self-service options might be appropriate within today's service design while blueprinting or mapping the service provision, yet relatively few research studies have considered the impact on customers of the SST and the TBSS environments. Understanding how customers perceive the SST and TBSS environment must be an imperative, as more organisations are expecting their customers to perform service tasks which used to be done by employees. As service organisations seek to increase their efficiency, in part through task performance by their customers, they need to ensure that they do not make the experience a negative one. A recent study by Curran and Meuter[31] concluded that making self-service a more enjoyable experience is a good way to get customers to adopt SSTs.

Summary

In this chapter, two separate, but related aspects of service design have been introduced – design of the service process and design of the physical service environment – both of which recognise the important people element of services.

As has been argued earlier, the process, physical evidence and people elements of the services marketing mix have significant parts to play in consumer accounts of satisfying and dissatisfying service encounters.

In designing the service process, for both existing and new service businesses, the service blueprint and its derivatives provide an informative visual aid. The applications of blueprinting include the reduction of service failure situations through fail-safing, the enhancement of core service safety, the identification of complexity and divergence in a service with a view to repositioning, and the provision of a visual catalyst for creativity in services. The design of a service process is influenced strongly by the factory metaphor, and the notion of operational efficiency (Chapter 3).

The design of the physical service environment or 'servicescape' is important to both customers and employees who frequent a service environment. In general, the environment should encourage 'approach' behaviours; that is, be comfortable and fit for purpose in the eyes of customers and employees. A useful classification of servicescapes is by the purpose of consumption and typical time a customer spends in the service facility (shown in Table 6.1). As a rule of thumb, the more time a customer typically spends in the facility, and the more likely that the purpose of the visit is hedonic, the more the servicescape should be designed to encourage affective responses in customers. Likewise, the less time a customer typically spends in the facility, and the more likely that the purpose of the visit is utilitarian, the more the servicescape should be designed for speedy through-put of customers. Ambient conditions in the servicescape, that is scent, music, lighting, can be manipulated but the effects of the manipulation of scents and music on customer responses and behaviours are not generalisable. The design of the servicescape is clearly influenced by the drama metaphor (Chapter 3) and the notion of 'experience' (Chapter 5).

We have also drawn attention to the need to learn more about the e-scape environment that customers are increasingly experiencing as they are called upon to perform elements of the service that used to be performed by service employees.

Learning Outcomes

Having read this chapter, you should be able to

- draw a simple service blueprint
- appreciate the importance of the 'invisible' elements contributing to the service process
- identify potential service failure points in a process, and plan for fail-safing or effective recovery
- link servicescape features to approach/avoidance behaviours
- classify servicescapes according to the time spent in the facility and the purpose of consumption, and appreciate the scope for transfer of servicescape ideas
- evaluate the 'conventional wisdom' of ambient condition manipulation in the light of research findings.

Discussion Questions and Exercises

1. Prepare the visible part of a service blueprint for the passenger's arrival at Auckland International Airport in Case Study 4.
2. Prepare the invisible part of a service map to support the computer repair services provided by RAD9 in Case Study 10.
3. What are the main differences between a service blueprint and a service map?
4. Can service failures be prevented through service design?
5. Examine your lecture and tutorial rooms and the student café/bar. What aspects of the ambient conditions are (dis)pleasing to you?
6. Outline how Table 6.1 allows the transfer of servicescape ideas between contexts.

Notes and References

1. Schneider, B. and Bowen, D. E., 'New Service Design, Development and Implementation', in *Developing New Services*, George, W.R. and Marshall, C. (eds), American Marketing Association Proceedings Series, Chicago, 1984, pp. 82–102.
2. Bitner, M. J., 'Servicescapes: The Impact of Physical Surroundings on Customers and Employees', *Journal of Marketing*, April 1992, pp. 56–71.
3. Shostack, G. L., 'Service Positioning through Structural Change', *Journal of Marketing*, vol. 51, 1987, pp. 34–43.
4. Kingman-Brundage, J., 'Technology, Design and Service Quality', *International Journal of Service Industry Management*, vol. 2, 1991, pp. 47–59.
5. Shostack, G. L., 'How to Design a Service', *European Journal of Marketing*, vol. 16, 1982, pp. 49–63.

6. Johnston, R., 'Service Transaction Analysis: Assessing and Improving the Customer's Experience', *Managing Service Quality,* 9(2), 1999, pp. 102–109.
7. Gyimothy, S., 'Odysseys: Analysing Service Journeys from the Customer's Perspective', *Managing Service Quality,* 10(6), 2000, pp. 389–96.
8. Johnston, 'Service Transaction Analysis'.
9. Chase, R. B. and Stewart, D. M., 'Make your Service Fail-Safe', *Sloan Management Review,* Spring 1994, pp. 35–44.
10. Ibid.
11. Wheatcroft, P., 'Sickly Hospitals are Far More Dangerous than Fragile Railways', *The Times,* London, 9 Jan, 2001.
12. Charter, D., 'Hit Squads Threat as Hospitals get Deadline to Clean Up Filthy Wards', *The Times,* London, 9 Jan, 2001.
13. Worsfold, D., 'Food Safety Behaviour in Butchers' Shops', *Nutrition and Food Science,* 31(1), 2001, pp. 13–19.
14. Shostack, 'Service Positioning through Structural Change'.
15. Edvardsson, B., Haglund, L. and Mattson, J., 'Analysis, Planning, Improvisation and Control in the Development of New Services', *International Journal of Service Industry Management,* 6(2), 1995, pp. 24–35.
16. Voss, C. A., 'Rethinking Paradigms of Service – Service in a Virtual Environment', *International Journal of Operations & Production Management,* 23(1), 2003, pp. 88–104.
17. Bitner, M. J., 'Servicescapes: The Impact of Physical Surroundings on Customers and Employees', *Journal of Marketing,* April 1992, pp. 57–71.
18. Sundstrom, E. and Altman, I., 'Physical Environments and Work-Group Effectiveness', *Research in Organizational Behaviour,* vol. 11, 1989, pp. 175–209.
19. Spies, K., Hesse, F. and Loesch, K., 'Store Atmosphere, Mood and Purchasing Behavior', *International Journal of Research in Marketing,* vol. 14, 1997, pp. 1–17.
20. Wakefield, K. L. and Blodgett, J. G., 'The Importance of Servicescapes in Leisure Service Settings', *Journal of Services Marketing,* 8(3), 1994, pp. 66–76.
21. Wakefield, K. L. and Blodgett, J. G., 'Customer Response to Intangible and Tangible Service Factors', *Psychology and Marketing,* 16(1), 1999, pp. 51–68.
22. www.haley-sharpe.co.uk
23. Rowley, J. and Slack, F., 'The Retail Experience in Airport Departure Lounges: Reaching for Timelessness and Placelessness', *International Marketing Review,* 16(4/5), 1999, pp. 363–76.
24. Aubert-Gamet, V. and Cova, B., 'Servicescapes: From Modern Non-Places to Postmodern Common Places', *Journal of Business Research,* 44(1), 1999, pp. 37–45.
25. Ibid.
26. Bone, P. F. and Ellen, P. S., 'Scents in the Marketplace: Explaining a Fraction of Olfaction', *Journal of Retailing,* 75(2), 1999, pp. 243–62.
27. Oakes, S., 'The Influence of the Musicscape within Service Environments', *Journal of Services Marketing,* 14(7), 2000, pp. 539–56.
28. Mattila, A. and Wirtz, J., 'Congruency of Scent and Music as a Driver of In-store Evaluations and Behavior', *Journal of Retailing,* 77(2), Summer 2001, pp. 273–89.
29. Ibid.
30. Ezeh, C. and Harris, L. C., 'Servicescape Research: a Review and a Research Agenda', *The Marketing Review,* 7(1), 2007, pp. 59–78.
31. Curran, J. M. and Meuter, M. L., 'Encouraging Existing Customer to Switch to Self-Service Technologies: Put a Little Fun in Their Lives', *Journal of Marketing Theory and Practice,* 15(4), 2007, pp. 283–298.

Service Employees as Operant Resources

Learning Objectives

The Overall Aim of the Chapter
To identify specific strategies used to improve the ability of employees to perform as 'operant resources' within service organisations.

In particular, the *chapter objectives* are

- to define, and explain the tenets behind, the concept of internal marketing

- to explore the use of traditional marketing techniques internally with employees

- to evaluate the usefulness of the internal marketing approach

- to explore methods of increasing job satisfaction for service employees

- to introduce SERV*OR as an instrument which enables the management to assess the contribution of the employees (alongside other influences) to the organisation's overall 'service' culture

Introduction

According to proposition nine within the service-dominant logic (SDL), 'firms that treat their employees as operant resources will be able to develop more innovative knowledge and skills and thus gain competitive advantage'.[1] This brings into focus once again the importance of effective human resource management in service organisations. The inseparability of production and consumption for many services means that customers are actively involved in the service delivery system and frequently exposed to the actions and attitudes of service employees. As we noted in Chapter 4, each interaction between customer and employee, or 'moment of truth', can potentially influence that customer's satisfaction/dissatisfaction with the service experience, and ultimately the profitability of the service organisation. In a manufacturing situation, although a dissatisfied employee may have the opportunity to deliberately produce a faulty product, normal methods of supervision and quality control would ensure that the fault is corrected before it reaches the final consumer. In a service context, the damage caused by a dissatisfied employee could be potentially much more serious. A one-minute telephone conversation with a disgruntled service operator could easily lead a customer, thinking of purchasing a skiing holiday, to switch to a competitor organisation.

In research into customer attitudes towards banks, a number of reasons why customers choose to terminate their relationship with a bank were identified.[2] Some 13 per cent of customers close their accounts because of an encounter with a rude or unhelpful employee, 11 per cent terminate because they feel that their bank is cold and impersonal, and another 16 per cent close accounts because of a general perception of poor service. All three reasons are directly or indirectly linked to negative employee attitudes and/or behaviour. Employee behaviour in services can have an equally significant positive impact on customer satisfaction. In Exhibit 7.1, a customer describes a particularly satisfactory experience with a veterinary practice – one that is almost entirely attributable to positive employee behaviour.

Exhibit 7.1   Customer Experience with a Veterinary Practice

The only reason that I stayed so long at one vet's, was the back-up staff, the fantastic nurses, who were really enthusiastic about the animals and the receptionists. They used to come out and play with the dogs and they knew all of their names. For me this is a very important part of the overall feeling, knowing that these people care.

In highly competitive service industries, such as the airline industry, where service innovations quickly get copied, the attitude and behaviour of employees can provide a key point of difference. Although British Airways introduced a range of new services for its travellers, including 'flying beds' and a 'raid the larder' flexible food offering, a statement by the Brand Manager of the airlines business class, Alison Maxwell, highlights the crucial role played by employees: '*We are proud to be innovators but these ideas do get copied so we must rely on our staff and the style and delivery of the service.*'

Service–profit Chain
A model that hypothesises how internal service quality, employee satisfaction, retention and productivity are linked to organisational growth and profitability.

The link between employee satisfaction, loyalty and productivity, and customer loyalty and company growth and profitability is neatly conceptualised in the 'service–profit chain'.[3] (The service–profit chain is covered in greater detail in Chapter 10; see also Figure 10.4.) The chain, which was developed from an analysis of successful service organisations in America, has seven components and shows how internal service quality and employee satisfaction, retention and productivity (components of the operating strategy and service delivery system) are linked to organisational growth and profitability.

Figure 7.1   Service–profit chain as applied to a retail organisation

Within the chain

- profit and growth are stimulated primarily by customer loyalty

- loyalty is a direct result of customer satisfaction

- satisfaction is largely influenced by the value of services provided to customers

- value is created by satisfied, loyal and productive employees

- employee satisfaction, in turn, results primarily from high-quality support services and policies that enable employees to deliver results to customers.[4]

The chain highlights the critical role played by human resource management in developing 'internal service quality', which in turn generates employee satisfaction and productivity and external service value for consumers. Internal service quality relates to aspects of the workplace/job design, policies for employee selection, development, retention and reward systems, but it is measured by the feelings and attitudes that employees have about their jobs, other people that work with them in the organisation, and the organisation itself. While the chain derives from the factory metaphor and focuses on improving the operational efficiency of the organisation through effective employee productivity to generate customer loyalty, the theatre metaphor reminds us that organisations need to achieve 'rave reviews' from employees by delivering satisfying employment experiences.

A simplified version of the chain, derived by the Gallup Organisation to be relevant to employees of a retail organisation, is shown in Figure 7.1.

We have already noted, in Chapter 4, that a service organisation can consider its customers as 'partial employees' and consequently develop human resource strategies to manage their contribution. The focus of this chapter, however, is on approaches put forward to *manage effectively the paid employees' contribution in service organisations.* Although, clearly, traditional human resource management

Internal Marketing
Activities which assist in the development of a customer focused organisation, reduce conflict between functional business areas and improve communications within an organisation.

SERV*OR
An instrument that enables management to assess the contribution of employee's (along with other influences) to the organisation's overall service culture.

strategies aimed at attracting, selecting, training, motivating, directing, evaluating and rewarding service personnel may be relevant to a greater or lesser extent in service organisations, we concentrate in this chapter on specific areas which we feel can potentially improve the ability of employees to perform as 'operant resources' within service organisations. First, we review the concept of 'internal marketing', which focuses on developing the 'marketing orientation' of employees. In the second section, we consider specific ways of increasing job satisfaction for service employees. We focus on employee empowerment as one particular strategy used frequently by service organisations to increase levels of both customer and employee satisfaction, and ultimately the profit of the service organisation. Finally, we introduce SERV*OR, an instrument which enables management to assess the contribution of the employees (alongside other influences) to the organisation's overall 'service' culture.

Defining Internal Marketing

There are numerous definitions of the concept of internal marketing. It has been variously described as referring to 'those activities that improve internal communications and customer consciousness among employees, and the links between these activities and external market place performance'[5]; or 'the development of an internal marketing orientation, a culture which most effectively and efficiently creates the behaviours that lead to the provision of superior customer value'.[6]

Internal Customers
Employees who provide services to other employees within the same organisation.

We can think of internal marketing as 'viewing employees as internal customers, viewing jobs as internal products and then endeavouring to offer internal products that satisfy the needs and wants of these internal customers while addressing the objectives of the organisation'.[7]

There are two basic ideas that underlie the concept of internal marketing:

1. The notion that every individual in a service organisation should recognise that they have customers to serve (both inside and outside the organisation);

2. To achieve the above-mentioned notion, all internal customers (employees) must be convinced about the quality of the service being provided, and be happy in their work.

Both ideas that underlie the concept of internal marketing focus attention on the vital role played by service employees in the service system. As our case studies illustrate, the employees of a service firm are frequently in contact with the organisation's external and internal customers. They are consequently an integral part of the image that is presented of the service and can play a key role in determining the success of the business. Berry feels that internal marketing is especially important in labour-intensive services where the performance of the employee is the product which the external customer buys. For many customers, for example, 'a rude or incompetent teller is a rude or incompetent bank'.[8] As we have already noted, with very little else that distinguishes the service of one bank from another, the quality of the people can act as a crucial point of difference.

- *Every individual should recognise that they have customers to serve.*

In order that the ultimate consumer receives a quality service, every individual and every department within the organisation must also provide and receive a quality service. Employees should be encouraged to regard their successor in the service chain as not merely a colleague but as an internal customer.[9] The provision of a five-star service for hotel customers, for example, relies on the quality being provided by all the individuals working in the supply chain. The chambermaids need to be given immaculate linen by the laundry agent, the chef needs quality ingredients from the fresh-fruit trader and well-trained kitchen assistants need to give a quality service to the ultimate customer. Every employee connected with the service organisation needs to recognise that there is someone whom he or she must serve: an internal customer. Within a traditional human resource management framework, this idea focuses on relationships between functions in the company as well as on the relationship between the contact personnel and the consumers.

In a retail environment, for example, the focus of management attention might be on improving the traditionally adversarial relationship between head office personnel; that is, buyers and store managers. Buyers would be encouraged to treat complaints from store managers about buying discrepancies with the same level of attention that they would devote to customer complaints, and provide them with the same level of service as that received by the ultimate consumer. In a reciprocal manner, store managers should be encouraged to treat head office personnel in the same way. In a qualitative study of internal marketing in a UK bank, the absence of such mutual respect was found to be a major barrier to the successful implementation of the concept.[10] Although it was acknowledged that 'support staff' in the bank should provide a level of service to front-line sales personnel, 'there was no evidence that interviewees felt that any form of reciprocal action might be necessary'. As one sales manager commented, 'I can see cash coming in when I sell a product, they don't do anything. They have to support us but the support just isn't there.'

- *All internal customers (employees) must be convinced about the quality of the service being provided, and be happy in their work.*

There are two aspects to this. First, in order to be effective and productive employees, the internal marketing approach recognises that all staff need to understand and approve of the mission of the organisation so that everyone is working towards a common goal. To achieve this, the services offered by the company need to be promoted to internal customers as well as to external customers. Secondly, Berry[11] advocates that the best way to achieve employee motivation is to use traditional marketing tools and concepts *internally* with employees. For example, just as marketers use advertising programmes to influence customers to behave in desired ways, for instance to buy a particular product, the same tools could be used to influence the behaviour of employees, for example to get them to approach external customers in a certain way. Employees are treated like customers and provided with 'job products' that satisfy their needs.[12] The people who buy goods and services in the role of the consumer and the people who buy jobs in the role of the employee are the same people. Whereas consumers exchange economic resources for goods and services, employees exchange human resources for jobs that provide among other things economic resources.[13]

Some of the traditional marketing tools that could be used internally with employees would include the following.

Market research

This traditionally involves identifying the needs and wants of consumers in a systematic manner and monitoring the impact of marketing activities on consumers. The same process can be used with employees. Service personnel can regularly be given the opportunity to give feedback to service management about working conditions, company policies generally, as well as their understanding about what comprises service quality for the customer. The information might be obtained by using questionnaires or focus groups, or in-depth interviews with employers. Although employee surveys may often need to be handled with more care than customer surveys, because of the fear of negative comeback for employees, they not only provide employees with a measure of satisfaction but also can identify early breakdowns in internal communication.

Marketing offers an array of research techniques that might not have been considered by the personnel function. For example, the critical incident technique, which has been used extensively in services to identify sources of satisfaction and dissatisfaction for customers in their encounters with employees, could also be used to develop an understanding of problem areas for employees. A survey of 1220 UK bar staff revealed a range of customer behaviours that staff found particularly unpleasant. According to the survey, more than two-thirds of those interviewed, regularly and deliberately ignored rude customers waiting at the bar to be served. According to the employees, the key to getting served quickly for customers was to have 'a good position, a pensive expression and a polite approach'. Market research has also been used innovatively with front-line employees of a DIY chain to profile the segments of customers that visited the outlets. Although profiles were generated by ten separate employee focus groups, the profile descriptors were remarkably consistent, highlighting the value of employees as internal sources of information.

Segmentation techniques

By grouping together employees with certain similarities, for example those of the same age, ambitions, previous employment and so on, the service employer is in a better position to design an appropriate service package (or job specification) for that employee. As Berry notes, internal marketing of this form is behind many of the commonly used HR concepts such as 'job share', 'flexitime', 'family-friendly policies' and 'fast track graduate training schemes' within companies. Using the theatre metaphor, the service employer should aim to create satisfying employment experiences!

Targeting

When initially recruiting employees, service providers can target suitable candidates in the same way that a successful company might target potential customers. A company with limited skills or resources might decide to serve just one or two consumer segments and therefore be selective about the people to whom it presents goods and services. In the same way, a service company might be selective about where it advertises vacancies for positions. Many of the jobs in service businesses involve constant liaison with external and internal customers and therefore require employees to possess high-level interpersonal skills. Not every interested party will possess these skills. Therefore, service businesses can use marketing techniques to match the right employee to the right job. The Waymark Holidays case study (Case Study 5) illustrates the important role played by a holiday group leader and the potential impact of getting the wrong person for the job.

Promotion

There are traditionally four basic forms of promotion available to marketing managers trying to influence the behaviour and attitudes of current and potential customers towards products and services: advertising, sales promotion, personal selling and publicity. Each form can help the organisation achieve slightly different promotion objectives. Sales promotion techniques, for example, are defined as short-term incentives designed to encourage customers to try new products or to increase short-term sales of existing products. They might include money-off tokens on products or free trial-sized packs of new products attached to a standard product. Similar mechanisms are used to motivate service employees. For example, a bonus might be given to employees who receive the largest number of customer 'thank you' letters in a month. Another alternative would be to offer incentives to employees who were prepared to swap jobs with colleagues in different positions within the organisation albeit for a short period of time. This would improve the employees' understanding of difficulties and challenges faced by others in the supply chain. 'Internal branding', for example, is the term used to describe efforts made to promoting the *brand* inside, namely to employees[14] to ensure consistency between internal and external brand messages.

All of these marketing tools could be used primarily to improve the fit between the requirements of the internal customer (the employee) and the organisation. However, if employees are to be further convinced about the quality of service being provided, as the company wants its external customers to be, other steps can be taken. Employees could experience the service and be actively involved in the formulation of marketing strategy.

It is often entirely feasible for employees to be given the opportunity to experience using the organisation's goods and services *as external customers*. This might involve giving leisure club staff unlimited access to the club's facilities, or giving staff in a DIY store a selection of new products to use. Although this occurs automatically in a number of service industries (i.e., financial services), it is still viewed as a benefit for the employee rather than seen as adding value to the organisation. Research on positive customer word-of-mouth in services continues to highlight the impact it can have on loyalty and purchase behaviour.[15] Little attention, however, appears to have been given to the potential impact of positive *employee* word-of-mouth (stimulated by product/service experiences) on organisational performance. Another alternative would be to encourage staff to shadow customers as they experience the service. For example, in an educational environment, lecturers could 'spend a week as a student' attending the full range of lectures and tutorials. Where organisations positively seek employee feedback from such initiatives, the employees are involved in the development of marketing strategy and consequently have more responsibility for the outcome and impact of customer-focused decisions. This, in turn, can result in employees gaining a fuller understanding of the company's marketing 'vision'.

All strategies that give employees the opportunity to improve their understanding of a customers experience of service provision would fall under the umbrella of 'internal marketing' activity (see, for example, It's in the News! 7.1).

📖 It's in the News! 7.1

Giving Employees a Customer Focus

According to the UK's *Sunday Times* (1 February 2004),

Bemused workers in Indian call centres are being given lessons in Chewin' the Fat catchphrases to help them understand Scottish customers. 'Gonnae no dae that', 'get it right up yiz', and 'gie's a gonk, ya dobber' have been put on the training syllabus for phone operators in Bangalore and Bombay to attune their ears to the Scottish brogue and encourage an appreciation of the country's popular culture. Alongside the Banter Boys, Betty the Old Slapper, Big Man and Neds from the hit BBC Scotland comedy series, the Indians are also being given a glimpse of the Scottish psyche through comedians such as Elaine C Smith, Rikki Fulton and Jack Milroy.

The course includes lessons in national cuisine – in particular haggis, neaps, mince and tatties and egg and chips. Saltires, Jimmy hats, sporrans and the sgian dubh (an ornamental dagger) are also explained. The young Indian graduates who man the centres, often through the night because of the time difference with Britain, are also learning about the Scots' fascination with the weather and to understand the meaning of a 'gey driech day'.

The course has been devised by Mary Rose Graham, a grandmother from Glasgow who works for Oceans Connect, a British firm that runs a call centre in Pune, south of Bombay. Graham, 64, a former music teacher who taught in Scottish secondary schools for 28 years, said: 'Being able to recognise different accents and colloquialisms really helps communication over the phone. My style of teaching is very much the old chalk and talk, and the students have to repeat things constantly so that it sticks. To reinforce things like the pronunciation of difficult town names such as Kirkcudbright and Milngavie I told them stories about the places.

Richard Coppel of Oceans Connect, which has 300 staff in India handling customer service and telesales, said the lessons in Scots culture had been invaluable. 'From speaking to our employees we know that the cultural points help as an *aide-mémoire* with language points and helps them to retain the good grounding that the course gives them. 'They are also trained to recognise a customer's mood from their voice,' he said. 'Scots tend to have a firmer tone than Indians would. If the call handlers are not used to Scottish banter, they may not realise something is a joke. 'If the Indians understand some of the cultural points that may come up in the conversation, the phone call will go much more smoothly.'

A perhaps less extreme way of treating employees is to view them as **'partial' customers**. Bowen[16] presents this as one of the strategies that service organisations should follow when trying to 'create a favourable climate for service'. At its simplest level, this would involve giving employees the same courteous treatment that the management would want the organisation's customers to receive; for instance, giving them a clear understanding of what they can expect from the service experience and help and support from various parts of the organisation. The rationale for giving employees the same treatment as customers stems from the fact that the on-site participation of customers tends to blur the distinction between the two roles. 'Employee and customer perceptions and behaviours' therefore become shaped by the same set of organisational practices and 'become strongly intertwined with each other'.

Partial Customers
Employees while acting as internal customers.

Value and Practice of Internal Marketing

Rafiq and Ahmed[17] critically appraise the value of using marketing techniques to motivate service employees. They conclude that the most valuable contribution comes from applying promotional and market research techniques internally with employees. Whilst recognising that traditional human resource management practices already include some of these, they acknowledge that marketing techniques can 'add to that array'.

Helman and Payne[18] carried out a pilot study that looked at the nature and extent of 'internal marketing' programmes in a sample of UK companies. Respondents were asked a series of questions in semi-structured interviews which related to the internal marketing programmes taking place in their organisations. Overall, internal marketing in all its forms was recognised as an important activity in developing a customer-focused organisation. Specifically, however, the research highlighted a number of other important contributions made by the approach.

- The important role internal marketing can play in reducing conflict between the functional areas of business.

For example, the customer orientation approach adopted within some retail organisations is helping to improve the traditionally antagonistic relationship between the head office functions and stores.

- The importance of effective communication in successful internal marketing.

There is a need for clear communication of the organisation's mission statement.

- The contribution internal marketing can make towards facilitating a spirit of innovation within the organisation.
- The fact that internal marketing is most successful where there is commitment at the highest level, where all employees cooperate, and an open management style exists.
- The role internal marketing approach can play in giving the organisation a competitive advantage.

Additionally, the internal marketing concept is believed to have the potential to greatly reduce the overall gap between what external customers expect from an organisation and what they actually receive.[19]

The case of EasyJet (Exhibit 7.2) reinforces some of the strengths and weaknesses of the approach.

Exhibit 7.2   EasyJet Embraces Internal Marketing

EasyJet, the passenger airline, is known to have fully embraced the internal marketing concept. The company was established in 1995 by Stelios Haji-Ioannou who, together with Marketing Director, Tony Anderson, developed a successful airline business, founded on no-nonsense values, and a strong low-price positioning to customers. The down-to-earth culture is reflected in the organisational structure which focuses on eliminating as much bureaucracy and internal hierarchy as possible. All documents are scanned and placed on a central computer system, so that everyone in the company can access them. They include mail, internal memos, press cuttings, business plans and sales data. Everyone knows what everyone else is doing, and a clear effort is made to ensure that all employees can have a say in the development of the marketing strategy. In 'easy land', the company's headquarters at Luton airport, employees are instructed to dress casually and maintain paperless offices like the company owner. This has created a system of working which has been described as 'brutally transparent in the way that information is shared between employees in all departments'.[20]

A number of problems have emerged. First, the danger of information overload. The internal customers may have to process vast amounts of information that can waste time. Second, staff can feel that they need constantly to be informed about what other parts of the organisation are doing, just in case they are asked to contribute ideas. Third, it can lead to a 'semi-chaotic culture', where, because everyone has a voice, it is difficult for staff to be recognised personally for what they have contributed.[21]

In the global service economy, it is increasingly likely that employees from one culture will be expected to deal with customers from another. This is most apparent where helpdesk facilities are outsourced. For the employees, learning to deal with idiosyncrasies of customers from a different culture can involve unusual training methods (see 'It's in the News!' 7.1).

However, 'It's in the News!' 7.1 only provides part of the story. In an earlier piece in the United Kingdom's *Sunday Times*, the problems associated with Indian employees working undesirable hours is emphasised. Stress-related disorders, slipped discs, vertigo, throat and neck problems, and marital problems because of awkward night shifts have all become more common in the call centres of Bangalore. So, although outsourced call centres are cheaper to operate, and management are striving to make them customer-focused, the long-run effect on working conditions of employees may prove to be counter-productive and even harmful. Great care needs to be exercised to create a good employee experience (see 'Postcard from Practice' 7.1).

Increasing Job Satisfaction of Service Employees

A basic premise underlying the internal marketing focus is that satisfied employees will lead to satisfied customers. As Bitner *et al.*[22] have noted, and we highlighted in Chapter 4, low job satisfaction has the potential to cause low-quality service encounter performances on the part of the employee. This, in turn, could lead to dissatisfied customers, generating negative word-of-mouth about the employees and the service firm.

The increasing use of IT within service organisations can both help and hinder employee performance and their job satisfaction. While IT systems are there to provide quick, easy access to the information that employees might need to do their job effectively, not all systems are user-friendly and some are less robust than others. IT failures and limitations can cause enormous frustration for service employees when the failures affect their performance and prevent them from delivering a satisfying experience to customers. Unfortunately it is not an uncommon experience for customers to telephone a service organisation or walk into a high street outlet (a travel agent, for example) to be told that their query cannot be dealt with at the moment because the 'system is down'. Service organisations may bemoan the immediate loss of potential sales but underestimate the impact that the failures may have on employee job satisfaction. Equally, the increasing use of TBSS by service organisations increases the likelihood that employees will be required to deal with customer complaints when those systems fail as well as the additional workload that might result from such a failure. The ubiquitous nature of the Internet also presents challenges for employers seeking to balance employee productivity with employee satisfaction. Employers are becoming concerned with the amount of time some employees spend using the Internet for personal matters during the working day. As a result, some organisations now bar access to particular websites. The most common website to be barred by organisations operating in New Zealand is TradeMe, the eBay equivalent.

Research, focusing on the determinants of job satisfaction for front-line retail customer personnel, looked at the relationship between empathy, role conflict and role clarity and job tension on the job satisfaction of service workers.[23]

The findings highlighted five 'policy concerns' for service managers striving to enhance employee job satisfaction.

1. Service employees with high customer contact need to have a very clear understanding of their role within the organisation.

Job descriptions need to be communicated to them in detail, including an indication as to what actions they can and cannot take. Increasing role clarity in this way was found to reduce the amount of conflict each employee had with others in the organisation and reduce tension generally.

2. Service managers are advised to hire individuals who are highly empathetic (i.e., able to take the viewpoint of another, either customers or fellow employees).

This is based on the contention that as employees communicate feelings of empathy to the customer, job tension is reduced and job satisfaction is increased. Although empathy is a quality that service providers can test for at the recruitment stage, it can also be developed in the work situation. J. Sainsbury's, the UK food and grocery retailer, for example, hold customer evenings at their stores where staff sit down with a group of customers and listen to their comments about the store, products and service. This enables staff to understand how customers perceive their offer, and consequently communicate feelings of empathy to the consumer.

3. Employees need to be fully trained in how to deal with customers.

Front-line employees are frequently faced with disgruntled customers who want solutions to problems caused by company policy and procedures. Although individual employees may not be responsible for the problem, they are expected by each customer to find an immediate solution to their problem. As the intensity and quantity of such conflicts increases, job tension rises for employees. As job tension rises, job satisfaction declines. Apart from developing employees' empathetic skills, service providers can use scenario-building to alert employees to potential conflict situations and give them detailed advice about how to resolve issues.

4. Clear lines of command need to be drawn up and communicated between management and employees.

When employees do not know whom to consult in order to help resolve a difficult service situation, job tension increases and job satisfaction declines.

5. Employees must be empowered by management to do whatever it takes to satisfy the customer.

Employee empowerment is considered to be a very effective strategy available to service organisations to help improve the relationship between employee and customer, and has received considerable attention in the services marketing literature. Although there are a number of different definitions of the concept, it essentially involves releasing control to the service employee at the crucial moment of contact with the customer, giving them autonomy to make decisions flexibly in response to the customers' demands as and when they occur. Workers are encouraged to think creatively about solutions to problems presented to them by customers rather than being driven by a standard functional 'script'.

Empowerment

Bowen and Lawler[24] provide a more comprehensive definition of the term 'empowerment'. They define it as sharing four organisational ingredients with front-line employees:

1. Information about the organisation's performance.
2. Rewards based on the organisation's performance.
3. Knowledge that enables employees to understand and contribute to organisational performance.
4. Power to make decisions that influence organisational direction and performance.

Research in service organisations has highlighted significant advantages in using this method to manage employees, the advantages relating primarily to increased customer satisfaction with the critical service encounter. Customers frequently recall their most satisfying service encounters as those when employees appear to have 'broken the rules' (in the customers' eyes) and responded quickly and flexibly to their particular service needs. For example, when ordering a banquet for eight people at a Chinese restaurant, the waiter takes into account the individual preferences of the party by balancing the fish and meat dishes in the banquet. This action appears to contradict restaurant policy that promotes a set menu for each group size, but greatly increases the satisfaction of the party with their experience. The customers are surprised and delighted with the waiter's flexible approach.

Bowen and Lawler[25] list six organisational benefits that arise directly from empowering service employees:

- employees will respond more quickly to customer needs during the service delivery or performance;
- employees will respond more quickly to remedy dissatisfaction;
- employees are more satisfied with their jobs and themselves;
- employees will interact more warmly and enthusiastically with customers;
- employees become a great source of ideas for service improvement and development;
- loyalty from customers who also share their experiences with others, spreading stories of good service experiences.

Bowen and Lawler[26] believe that not only do customers benefit from this approach, but employees clearly feel better about their work which results in their performing more enthusiastically and creatively. They value having a sense of control and are also more willing to give service management their view on how things should be organised to improve service performance. It is in this way that empowered employees become a great source of service ideas.

Although there are clearly advantages to empowering service employees, there are also costs that need to be considered. Five costs have been associated with empowering employees:[27]

- recruitment and training;
- ongoing wages;
- slower or less consistent service delivery;
- negative perceptions of fairness;
- bad decisions.

Because of the level of responsibility devolved to service workers, companies tend to spend more time and money on recruitment, and training as well as retaining well-qualified staff who can command greater pay. There can also be a risk of inconsistent delivery, with one service employee responding to a customer complaint in a different way from another. This may also result in slower delivery as employees elect to spend more time with customers. On some occasions this could lead directly to highly dissatisfied customers, particularly if they perceive other customers to have received 'special treatment' compared with their experiences. This could be an important drawback for organisations who empower employees, as recent research has established a link between 'perceived justice', customer satisfaction, the quality of the service relationship and loyalty.[28] Finally, organisations run the risk that employees might demonstrate poor judgement or exceed reasonable standards to satisfy customers either in the original performance of the service or in order to remedy dissatisfaction.

Research has also shown that empowerment as a strategy can be more effective in some service organisations than others. Empowerment appears to be the best approach where service delivery involves managing a relationship, as opposed to simply performing a transaction. This is clearly the situation with many of the cases described in the book. The small business orientation places the emphasis on service providers and employees establishing long-term relationships with their customers. The organisations rely on long-term clients to bring in new business and actively involve them in communication strategy and generating ideas for service development. The promotional material used by Waymark Holidays (Case Study 5), for example, includes comments from customers about their holidays. As Bowen and Lawler note, the 'more enduring the relationship (between customer and service organisation), and the more important it is in the service package, the stronger the case for empowerment'.[29]

The success of empowerment also appears to depend on the type of environment in which the business operates. For instance, it can be a very effective approach if the service is heavily influenced by uncontrollable external variables. The leaders used by Waymark Holidays (Case Study 5) are encouraged to take independent decisions about how to handle many situations, as very few problems could be anticipated in advance by the centre. While walking in the Greek mountains, one party was attacked by a swarm of bees. The tour guide had to react swiftly without consultation with the centre, and arrange for two group members to get to hospital as well as rearrange the walking schedule for the rest of the group.

Postcard from Practice: 7.1

Creating a Good Employment Experience

Jackson Russell was founded in 1844, and today the offices are located not more than 500 meters from where the firm first started operating in Auckland. The history is very important to us. We are almost an established institution in Auckland because of the time we have been here. The firm has been part of Auckland and

Postcard from Practice: 7.1   (Continued)

part of some of the long-established families in Auckland over the years. The people here have very good principles to start with, and the partners of the firm are the same. We all seem to have broadly similar common values, work habits, ethics, and quality expectations. We have a cultural commitment to provide an excellent service to our clients based upon traditional and historic service ideals. We also seek to provide a good working environment which enables all of us to deliver our work commitments while maintaining the lifestyle we have chosen. Staff frequently comment on the good working conditions that we provide.

Physically the offices were fitted out in the early 1990s. Fortunately the fit-out was of very high quality and, while the layout is obviously not a twenty-first-century design, it remains very functional and many visitors to the office comment on the comfortable professional service-type atmosphere the public areas of the firm have which we believe reflects our conservative and traditional values.

Our staff turnover is very low and for years the firm has been seen as a very good place to work. Our governance or management structure is flat and we work in an informal and at many times family-like atmosphere. Our personnel policies are designed and implemented to provide a stimulating, stable and harmonious working environment.

We try very hard to provide the best environment and are well up with the play on retention, performance reviews, flexibility of arrangements, reward, continuing legal education and other training. We took part in a working party organised by the Auckland District Law Society in 1999 which looked at introducing more flexible arrangements into the legal workplace. We are very aware of the need to be flexible with employment terms and employee expectations these days. We much prefer to treat each person or circumstance individually and as responsible employers we do our best to meet our employee needs. Consequently we avoid establishing rigid policies because they rather quickly become expectations and actually work against what we want to achieve.

In recruitment, while technical ability of applicants features prominently on a list of criteria, personality and fit within the team is also vital. We involve team members or co-workers in the recruitment selection process and this has worked well in creating a harmonious working environment. The desire to recruit with stability and harmony in mind has probably resulted in a less diverse workforce than might otherwise result. However, this 'no risk' approach has worked well for us so far.

We are embarking on a rebranding project to refresh the image of the firm and reinforcement of the firm's reputation in service and quality of advice. Business development activity and branding strategy have not been strong features of our past because we have always worked on the principle that our 'reputation has spoken for itself'. That rather complacent approach to marketing needs to change.

The rebranding project is a major event for us and we will look for more than just a change to the way we formally present ourselves. Many of our future challenges are based on either expanding our work with existing clients or working with new clients, so we anticipate the project will help us to reset our business goals and ensure that we remain a responsive and flexible firm to meet future business challenges. In addition we see the rebranding as a 'fun' part of our year in 2008 and will involve as many of the staff as is possible in the planning and implementation.

Source: Jackson Russell

Service Orientation of Organisations

As we have stressed throughout this chapter, the contribution of employees to the 'service' culture that exists within an organisation is critical. Front-line employees in particular can make a real difference by developing a deep understanding of how customers are experiencing their service (i.e., having a marketing orientation) and using their initiative to respond appropriately to customer concerns, (i.e., being empowered effectively). Many organisations find it useful to be able to measure the extent to which employees exhibit these characteristics and the contribution this is making to the overall 'service orientation' of the company.

Service Orientation
An organisational commitment to practices and procedures to deliver high levels of service quality to their customers.

Lytle *et al.*[30] devised a diagnostic tool labelled SERV*OR, which provides a measure of an organisations service orientation that companies can use to devise benchmarks and explore variations. It was tested originally in building supplies and banking services, and is being further tested for its generalisability and cultural bias.[31] Although the instrument explores ten aspects of the organisations service 'orientation', a number of dimensions directly address the employee behaviours and responses identified in this chapter. The ten dimensions are

- customer treatment
- employee empowerment
- service technology
- service failure prevention
- service failure recovery
- service standards communication
- service vision
- servant leadership
- service rewards
- service training.

Each dimension is briefly discussed.

Customer treatment

This dimension is concerned with how well the organisation is set up to treat customers in the service encounters which form the basis of customers' evaluations of service quality. Managers and employees give their levels of agreement with statements such as 'Employees go the "extra mile" for customers' and 'We are noticeably more friendly and courteous than our competitors.'

Employee empowerment

This dimension is concerned with the responsibility and authority that employees are given in order to meet customer needs in a quick and effective way. Managers and employees give their levels of agreement with statements such as 'Employees often make important decisions without seeking management approval'.

Service technology

This dimension is concerned with the utilisation of modern technology in creating a system for excellent service delivery. Managers and employees give their levels of agreement with statements such as 'We enhance our service capabilities through the use of "state-of-the-art" technology' and 'Technology is used to build and develop higher levels of service quality.'

Service failure prevention

This dimension is concerned with the capability of the organisation to proactively prevent service failures. Managers and employees give their levels of agreement with statements such as 'We go out of our way to prevent customer problems' and 'We actively listen to our customers.'

Service failure recovery

This dimension is concerned with the capability of the organisation to respond effectively to service failures or customer complaints. Managers and employees give their levels of agreement with statements such as 'We provide follow-up service calls to confirm that our services are being provided properly' and 'We have an excellent customer complaint handling system for service follow-up.'

Service standards communication

This dimension is concerned with the extent to which service standards or benchmarks are understood by all employees. Managers and employees give their levels of agreement with statements such as 'Every employee understands all of the service standards that have been instituted by all departments' and 'We use internal standards to pinpoint failures before we receive customer complaints.'

Service vision

This dimension is concerned with the clarity of pronouncement of an organisation's service goals and objectives. Managers and employees give their levels of agreement with statements such as 'There is a true commitment to service, not just lip service' and 'It is believed that the organisation exists to serve the needs of its customers.'

Servant leadership

This dimension is concerned with the extent to which leaders of the organisation set service standards by their own behaviour and style of management. Managers and employees give their levels of agreement with statements such as 'Management is constantly measuring service quality' and 'Managers regularly spend time "on the floor" with customers and front-line employees.'

Service rewards

This dimension is concerned with the link between employee service performance and compensation/reward. Managers and employees give their levels of agreement with statements such as 'This organisation noticeably celebrates excellent service.'

Service training

This dimension is concerned with the extent to which the organisation strives to improve employee skills beyond the simple but important courtesies. Managers and employees give their levels of agreement with statements such as 'Every employee receives personal skills training' and 'During training sessions, we work through exercises to identify and improve attitudes towards customers.'

The questionnaire is presented to managers and employees and the findings can be used to explore variations in behaviours and systems over time and between departments of the same company.

Summary

Successful internal marketing is based on the dual tenets that every employee in a service organisation should recognise that they have their own customers to serve, and that all employees should be convinced of the quality of the service provided. The former ensures a customer orientation throughout the support services, as well as for front-line employees. The latter requires the company mission to be 'marketed' to internal customers (the employees) with effective two-way communication systems.

The internal marketing approach has been found to have some flaws from an academic and practical perspective. In organisations that practise internal marketing, better communication, reduced internal conflict and a spirit of innovation are seen as some of the benefits of the approach. The advocates of internal marketing will look to increasing the job satisfaction of service employees in the belief that it will eventually lead to satisfied customers.

Employee job satisfaction may result from role clarification, encouragement of empathetic approaches, effective training, clear lines of command and, in particular, employee empowerment. In appropriate service environments, empowerment is seen as a strategy for increasing both customer specification and employee enjoyment. The SERV*OR dimensions (and measures) provide a valuable contribution to understanding the employees contribution to an organisation's service orientation.

Learning Outcomes

Having read this chapter, you should be able to

- explain the concept of internal marketing
- appreciate the potential benefits of applying traditional marketing techniques with employees to achieve 'rave reviews' and satisfying employment experiences
- critically assess the advantages and disadvantages of an internal marketing perspective
- understand the issues facing service organisations that are striving to increase employee job satisfaction
- evaluate employee empowerment as a strategic initiative for service organisations.
- appreciate what is meant by a service orientation and the factors that contribute to the orientation.

Discussion Questions and Exercises

1. How might 'moments of truth' influence customer (dis)satisfaction?
2. Summarise the ways in which traditional marketing tools for external customers can be implemented with internal customers.
3. To what extent do you believe that satisfied employees lead to satisfied customers?
4. Explain fully the term 'employee empowerment'.
5. Why might role clarification increase the job satisfaction of a service employee?

Notes and References

1. Lusch, R. F., Vargo, S. L. and O'Brien, M., 'Competing through Service: Insights from Service-Dominant Logic', *Journal of Retailing*, 83 (1), 2007, pp. 5–18.
2. Morves (1984), as quoted in Sargeant, A. and Asif, S., 'The Strategic Application of Internal Marketing – An Investigation of UK Banking', *International Journal of Bank Marketing*, 16(1), 1998, pp. 66–79.
3. Heskett, J. L., Jones, T. O., Loveman, G. W., Earl-Sasser Jr, W. and Schlesinger, L. A., 'Putting the Service Profit-Chain to Work', *Harvard Business Review*, March–April 1994, pp. 164–74.
4. Ibid.

5. Hogg, G., Carter, S. and Dunne, A., 'Investing in People: Internal Marketing and Corporate Culture', *Journal of Marketing Management*, vol. 14, 1998, pp. 879–95.
6. Narver, J. C. and Slater, S. E., 'The Effect of a Marketing Orientation on Business Profitability', *Journal of Marketing,* vol. 54, October 1990, pp. 20–35.
7. Berry, L. L., 'The Employee as Customer', *Journal of Retail Banking*, 3 March 1981, pp. 25–8.
8. Ibid.
9. Berry, 'The Employee as Customer'.
10. Sargeant, A. and Asif, S., 'The Strategic Application of Internal Marketing – An Investigation of UK Banking'.
11. Berry, L. L., 'The Employee as Customer', in C. Lovelock (ed.), *Services Marketing,* Kent Publishing, Boston, Mass., 1984, pp. 271–8.
12. Berry, L. L. and Parasuraman, A., *Marketing Services: Competing through Quality,* The Free Press, New York, 1991.
13. Berry, 'The Employee as Customer' 1981.
14. Ahmed, P. K. and Rafiq, M., 'Internal marketing issues and challenges', *European Journal of Marketing*, 37(9), 2003, pp. 1177–86.
15. Mangold, W. Glynn, Miller, F. and Brockway, G. R. 'Word-of-Mouth Communication in the Service Marketplace', *Journal of Services Marketing,* 13(1), 1999, pp. 73–89.
16. Bowen, D. E., 'Customers as Human Resources in Service Organisations', *Human Resource Management,* 25(3), Fall 1986, pp. 371–83.
17. Rafiq, M. and Ahmed, P. K., 'The Scope of Internal Marketing: Defining the Boundary between Marketing and Human Resource Management', *Journal of Marketing Management,* vol. 9, 1993, pp. 219–32.
18. Helman, D. and Payne, A., 'Internal Marketing: Myth versus Reality', Cranfield School of Management Working Paper, Cranfield SWP 5/92, 1992.
19. Piercy, N. and Morgan, N., as quoted in Sargeant A. and Asid S., 'The Strategic Application of Internal Marketing – An Investigation of UK Banking', 1989.
20. Curtis, J., 'No-frills Airline, No-frills Culture', *Marketing,* 9 July, 1998, pp. 24–5.
21. Ibid.
22. Bitner, M. J., Booms, B. H. and Tetreault, M. S., 'The Service Encounter: Diagnosing Favourable and Unfavourable Incidents', *Journal of Marketing*, vol. 54, January 1990, pp. 71–84.
23. Rogers, J. D., Clow, K. E. and Kash, T. J., 'Increasing Job Satisfaction of Service Personnel', *Journal of Services Marketing,*8 (1), 1994, pp. 14–26.
24. Bowen, D. E. and Lawler, E. E., 'The Empowerment of Service Workers: What, Why, How and When', *Sloan Management Review*, Spring 1992, pp. 31–9.
25. Ibid.
26. Ibid.
27. Ibid.
28. Aurier, P. and Siadou-Martin, B., 'Perceived Justice and Consumption Experience Evaluations: A Qualitative and Experimental Investigation', *International Journal of Service Industry Management,* 18(5), 2007, pp. 450–71.
29. Bowen and Lawler.
30. Lytle, R. S., Horn, P. W. and Mokwa, M. P., 'SERV*OR: A Managerial Measure of Organisational Service-Orientation', *Journal of Retailing*, 74(4), 1998, pp. 455–89.
31. Lynn, M. L., Lytle, R. S. and Bobek, S., 'Service Orientation in Transitional Markets: Does It Matter?', *European Journal of Marketing,* 34(3/4), 2000, pp. 279–98.

8

Service Quality and Customer Satisfaction

Learning Objectives

Overall Aim of the Chapter

To present the theory and practical implications relating to the concepts of perceived service quality and customer satisfaction in services.

In particular, the *chapter objectives* are

- to provide an evaluation of the similarities and differences between the concepts of service quality and customer satisfaction
- to present results showing the dimensions of perceived service quality
- to evaluate the Gaps model of service quality and the potential causes of the Gaps
- to introduce and critically assess the SERVQUAL instrument
- to examine issues associated with e-service quality
- to introduce and evaluate different perspectives of customer satisfaction
- to summarise the debates on service quality versus customer satisfaction.

Introduction

Service quality has been identified as the 'single most researched area in services marketing to date',[1] and it is maintained that, for service-based companies, 'quality is the lifeblood that brings increased patronage, competitive advantage and long term profitability'.[2] The word 'satisfaction' has been 'fundamental to the marketing concept for over three decades', and the number of academic articles on consumer satisfaction had topped 15 000 by 1992.[3] The topics of service quality and customer/consumer satisfaction have attracted the attention of both academics and practitioners who increasingly consider actions aimed at improving service quality/customer satisfaction to be an integral part of an organisation's long-term strategy.

Perceived Service Quality
The gap between customer perceptions and their expectations of a service.

Research on perceived service quality has emanated largely from the services marketing literature, whereas much of the research on customer satisfaction is to be found within the consumer behaviour literature, where the focus is on satisfaction with physical goods as well as with services. There is often some confusion regarding the similarities and differences between service quality and customer/consumer satisfaction, and this may be attributed to the different origins. Take, for example, some often quoted definitions of the two concepts.

- Perceived service quality: 'the degree and direction of the ' between consumers' perceptions and expectations (of a service)'.[4]

- Consumer satisfaction: 'a function of the similarities between the consumer's expectations and the perceived performance of the purchase'.[5]

Both definitions seem to refer to a comparison between consumers' expectations and perceptions of a service.

In this chapter, we examine, in separate sections, the concepts of service quality and customer satisfaction taking account of their different origins. In the final section, the ideas and issues are brought together to encompass current debates, areas of practical applications, and links to the following two chapters.

Perceived Service Quality

As we highlighted at the very beginning of this book, defining and monitoring the quality of a service is very different from defining and monitoring the quality of a tangible product. From an internal perspective, a manufacturer can grade pieces of fruit received from a supplier according to certain objective quality criteria; for example, weight, size, colour, texture and so on. Similarly, from an external perspective, that is, a consumer's viewpoint, a quality assessment of the fruit can be made in the supermarket prior to purchase, by touching or feeling the merchandise, albeit at a more subjective level. In both cases, the quality assessment relates clearly to the finished product. With services, in contrast, customers make judgements about the quality *of the service delivery process, as well as on the final outcome.* The independent businessman, for instance, might assess the quality of the accountant's work not only on the appearance of the final set of accounts, but also on the telephone manner of the accountant's employees and the speed with which the work is carried out.

Because a service is usually made up of both tangible and intangible components, many attempts at defining service quality have made the distinction between objective measures of quality and those which are based on the more subjective perceptions of customers. According to Gronroos,[6] for example, a service can be broken down into two quality dimensions:

1. technical quality;
2. functional quality.

Both dimensions are important to the customer. Technical quality refers to the relatively quantifiable aspects of the service; that is, *what* is being done. Functional quality refers to *how* the technical quality is being delivered to customers.

For example, with the service offered by the car mechanic, a customer might look at the machinery being used to fix the cars, and the skills and expertise of the mechanic, to make an assessment of the technical quality of the service. The general attitude and appearance of employees, in contrast, which cannot be measured as accurately as the elements of technical quality, would be components of the functional quality of the service.

However service quality is defined, most researchers agree that it has to be *defined by consumers*. In this case, as each consumer is different, we usually refer to *perceived* service quality.

Technical Quality
The quality of the core service that delivered.

Functional Quality
How the service is delivered or performed.

How Consumers Assess Service Quality

Although it may be difficult, service organisations need to take steps to monitor and improve the quality of the service that they provide. According to Lewis and Booms,[7] service quality is 'a measure of how well the service level delivered matches customer expectations. Delivering quality service means conforming to customers' expectations on a consistent basis'. Using this definition of service quality, one of the first steps before implementing a quality improvement programme involves establishing precisely which components of the service influence the consumer's perception of quality.

Dimensions of Service Quality

Service quality from the consumer's perspective is examined with reference to the pioneering work carried out by Parasuraman, Zeithaml and Berry (PZB)[8–11]. Although their research initially identified a set of ten determinants used by consumers to judge the quality of the service they receive, further research quickly reduced these to five which have become now collectively as RATER. They are the following:

1. Reliability: dependability of service provider and accuracy of performance;
2. Assurance: knowledge and courtesy of employees and their ability to inspire trust and confidence;

PZB
Parasuraman, Zeithaml & Berry.

RATER
The five dimensions of service quality: Reliability; Assurance; Tangibles; Empathy; Responsiveness.

3. Tangibles: including the physical components of the service, for example, seating, lighting;

4. Empathy: caring, individualised attention the firm gives its customers;

5. Responsiveness: promptness and helpfulness.

Using the RATER dimensions, PZB produced a conceptual framework (a Gaps model) and a measurement instrument known as SERVQUAL. The Gaps model and SERVQUAL were rapidly and widely adopted by academics and practitioners to assess service quality.

SERVQUAL
A measurement instrument developed by Parasuraman, Zeithaml & Berry, to assess service quality.

📖 It's in the News! 8.1

Service Quality – Reliability

According to the website allAfrica.com (31 January 2008),

This is definitely not a good time for operators and subscribers of GSM networks in the country (Nigeria). The bad time currently being experienced is directly traceable to the ongoing poor quality of service in the sector in recent times. Nigerians have risen up collectively to denounce poor service in all its ramifications and called for strong measures to restore good quality service for the benefit of operators.

All the operators, fixed and mobile are not exempted from the problem. But MTN's problem is peculiar. Because it has the biggest network, and with more subscribers and far more call volumes than any other network, MTN feels the heat of frustrated customers and other stakeholders in the telecom industry, more than anyone else.

In December, the Communications sub committee of the House of Representatives directed that MTN should stop further sales of SIM cards until it is assured of adequate capacity on its network. It showed that, confronted with poor service delivery by the telecom industry, rage always tends to be most directed at the biggest player, MTN.

It was in the light of the quality of service issues which customers had experienced in recent times that MTN had decided to call up journalists and show them, in robust detail, that MTN is not unmindful of the situation. Their executives stated that they fully understand what customers are going through and indeed empathize with them. 'We know that quality of service has been challenged of late and we're very empathetic to our millions of customers who may have undergone inconveniences as a result'.

Without a base station in a particular locality, it would be impossible for people in that locality to make or receive calls. Also, base stations are limited in the number of customers which they can serve so the more customers are in a particular locality, the more would be the need for more base stations to be erected. However, sometimes, customers migrate en-masse to different communities and this can sometimes put a strain on the capacity of the base stations to cope. An example of this was during the last end-of-year holiday when millions of people travelled to their villages creating problems for base stations earlier earmarked to serve a small number of people.

But while it is relatively easy to become a customer (by buying a mobile phone and a SIM card), installing the base stations which enable such subscribers to use their mobile phones is not that simple. Each base station, the company said, is accompanied by at least two generators to provide electricity as public electricity supply is unreliable and insufficient. In some instances, they added, a transformer is also added. In striving to erect as many base stations to help assuage the problem of inadequate capacity, the company they said, is actively erecting base stations on roof tops and other rather unconventional sites.

The numbers are fast growing they said. As at last December, they had about 3,400 base stations. But even this falls short of the needs of the network and the company is already aggressively implementing its plan to drive this number up by installing hundreds of additional base stations across the country in 2008.

Potential Causes of Service Quality Shortfalls: The 'Gaps Model'

In parallel with their identification of the dimensions of service quality, PZB postulated the major causes of the perceived service quality 'gap'; that is, the gap between consumer expectations and perceptions. They specified four potential causes of this gap, which they labelled as Gap 5:

- First, service providers need to ensure that management appreciate exactly what service attributes are valued by their customers and in what order. A restaurant manager, for example, may believe that customers' evaluation of the quality of the service is influenced primarily by the decor in the restaurant, and that the quality of the food and the attitude of employees towards staff are of little significance. If this is incorrect, decisions could be made about service design and delivery which could significantly affect the customers' evaluation about the quality being provided. This gap they labelled as Gap 1; that is, *the gap between customers' expectations and management perception of customers' expectations.*

- Even if management fully appreciate the attributes valued by customers, they are often unwilling, unable or simply do not care enough to put resources into solving the problem. For example, even though operators of theme parks recognise that the consumers' evaluation of the quality of their experience at the theme park is negatively influenced by the length of time they are forced to spend waiting in a queue for a ride, little has been done by the operators to alleviate the situation. This gap they labelled as Gap 2; that is, *the gap between management perception of customers' expectations and service quality specifications.*

- The research also highlighted a problem that related specifically to service delivery. Even if quality standards are correctly set in accordance with an accurate reading of customer expectations, service quality could still be substandard because of deficiencies that relate to the attitude and manner of contact employees. Employees, for example, may not have been given adequate training and support to carry out the tasks required, or they may not be aware of exactly what they are expected to do. This gap they labelled as Gap 3; that is, *the gap between service quality specifications and actual service delivery.*

- Another problem occurs when organisations promise that they will deliver one level or type of service but in reality deliver something different. This has been termed the 'promises' gap and can easily occur if an actual service experience, at say a retail store, does not reflect the implicit or explicit promises conveyed by a television advertisement. This gap they labelled as Gap 4; that is, *the gap between service delivery and external communications to the customer.*

For many service organisations, one way of closing Gap 4 is to try to develop a strong service brand. As with product branding, the strength of a service brand depends on the extent to which the brand conveys a consistent, positive and clear message to consumers about what is being offered. This is clearly a more difficult task for service organisations, given the primarily intangible nature of the offer and the reliance on variable employee interactions to convey brand messages. In theory, a clear brand should help to differentiate the service offered from the competition. As McDonald *et al.*[12] note, however, different sectors of the service industry have varied in their ability to achieve differentiation with their brands. They contrast the success of service branding in the airline industry where 'if travellers were asked to evaluate Virgin, Lufthansa or Singapore airlines according to punctuality, in-flight entertainment and attentive cabin staff, they would be very likely to talk about differences without hesitation', to the financial and insurance sectors, where very few brands have managed to differentiate themselves. The key to successful service branding involves, first, making the brands 'tangible' by manipulating the physical components associated with the service and, second, ensuring that the brand values are understood and effectively communicated to customers by all contact employees.

In essence, Gaps 1, 2, 3 and 4 contribute to the essential gap, Gap 5, the gap between consumer expectations and perceptions; the measure of perceived service quality. The Gaps model has, therefore, understandably resulted in 'follow up' research into the understanding of the antecedents of consumer expectations, and into methods of reducing Gaps 1 to 4.

Antecedents of Consumer Expectations

PZB identified four key factors that might influence a customer's expectations.

1. *Word-of-mouth communications*; for example, what your friends think about the hairdresser that you are planning to use.

2. *Personal needs and preferences*; for example, whether you personally think that it is important that sales staff wear the same uniform.

3. *Past experiences*; for example, if you are a regular user of a particular restaurant and have always been given a rose at the end of your meal, you would come to expect this treatment. However, if you had never been there before, the rose would not form part of your service expectations.

4. *External communications*; for example, advertising. An advertisement in the newspaper advising you to book three months in advance for a table at a restaurant at Christmas might lead some customers to make inferences about the quality of the food they might receive on the day.

To take a specific example, one of the authors was visiting Australia for the first time, and was booked into the Hotel Ibis Darling Harbour in Sydney. Word-of-mouth from an Australian colleague indicated that the venue was excellent. The hotel would appear to satisfy hygiene needs, with an added advantage of having a swimming pool. The person concerned had stayed in an Ibis hotel in Luton, England, and had also frequently passed the Manchester Ibis hotel with its very prominent promotion of rooms for only £39.50 per night. The website for the Hotel Ibis Darling Harbour was well developed and informative, with pictures, maps and so on. All of these sources culminate in building an expectation of the likely service experience of a week's stay in the hotel.

Methods of reducing Gaps 1 to 4

Table 8.1 summarises some of the probable causes of Gaps 1 to 4. Where the causes are relevant to *a* particular service, management can develop cures to reduce the gap.

It is worth noting that amended versions of Gaps 1 to 4 can be used to measure and monitor *internal* service quality as part of an internal marketing policy.[13]

Table 8.1 Causes of the service quality gaps

Service quality gap	Possible causes of the gap
Gap 1: the gap between customers' expectations and management perception of customers' expectations	• Lack of marketing research (inaccurate information, inadequate use of the findings) • Poor upward communication from contact personnel • Too many management or organisational layers
Gap 2: the gap between management perception of customers' expectations and service quality specifications	• Lack of clarity of goal setting, inadequate task standardisation • Lack of management commitment • Poor management of planning and planning procedures

Table 8.1   (Continued)

Service quality gap	Possible causes of the gap
Gap 3: the gap between service quality specifications and actual service delivery	• Rigid or complicated specifications • Poor internal marketing • Employee role ambiguity and/or conflict • Break-down in technology or systems support
Gap 4: the gap between service delivery and external communications to the customer	• Propensity to over-promise and exaggerate • Marketing communication not integrated between operations and the advertising, sales and human resource functions • Differences in procedures across the organisation

Source: Adapted from Gronroos.[19]

The main volume of research, undertaken by both academics and practitioners, however, has centred on Gap 5. This is because it is the 'essential' gap, but it is also the only gap that can be examined solely on data from the consumers.[14] Much of the work has applied the research instrument known as SERVQUAL.

SERVQUAL: The Research Instrument

In 1988, building on their early research, PZB published a multiple-item scale for measuring consumer perceptions of service quality, named SERVQUAL.[15] This was revised in 1991.[16] According to 'Google Scholar' in February 2008, these two papers had been cited 2942 and 2427 times, respectively, showing how influential they have been. Based on extended exploratory and empirical research, PZB identified 22 quality-related items spread among the five quality dimensions as providing a reliable and valid measure of service quality. SERVQUAL became a major research instrument used by many others.[17,18]

PZB themselves admit that, although 'SERVQUAL is a useful starting point, it is not the final answer for assessing and improving service quality'.[20] It does, however, enable an organisation to compare customer expectations and perceptions over time. For example, a theme park operator may have established during one season that the negative attitude of employees had a detrimental influence on the customers' perception of the quality of the service provided throughout the theme park. Consequently, the owner may embark on an intensive recruitment campaign to employ more highly motivated workers for the next season. The impact of the change can be monitored by a repeat survey.

The organisation can also compare the SERVQUAL score with the competitors. The results can also be used to categorise a company's customers into perceived quality segments on the basis of their individual SERVQUAL scores. Thus, the organisation may find that customers who have been with them for the longest period of time, or are all within a certain age category, assess quality on different service dimensions, and they can take managerial decisions accordingly. Finally, SERVQUAL can be used to assess the quality perceptions of internal customers; that is, different departments may want to know about the quality of service that they provide to others in the organisation.

Conceptual and methodological problems with the SERVQUAL scale

The SERVQUAL research instrument was placed in the public domain by PZB and, not surprisingly, it has been used by many researchers since its publication. These researchers, through attempting to measure service quality in a variety of service sectors, have identified some conceptual and methodological problems with the SERVQUAL scale. Indeed, criticism of SERVQUAL is becoming an academic industry in its own right. Three issues are mentioned here. The chapter's bibliographical references at the end of the chapter allow the interested reader to become up to date with SERVQUAL strengths and weaknesses:

- It is claimed[21] that SERVQUAL dimensions are not generic; that is, the applicability of the SERVQUAL scale to different service settings is questioned. In, for example, office equipment businesses, carrier services, and retailing, it was found to be difficult to apply SERVQUAL meaningfully.

- The timing of expectation measurements is of crucial importance. To use SERVQUAL implies that respondents must rate their expectations (on a scale of 1 = strongly disagree to 7 = strongly agree) and also their perceptions of a particular service, on the same scale, for each of 22 statements. Perhaps, in an ideal world, the bank customer, for example, could be interviewed before taking out an account with the bank (to assess expectations) and interviewed again three months later (to assess perceptions of the actual service). In practice this may be impossible. For very good practical reasons, respondents are often interviewed only once (after the service experience) and asked to rate both their expectations and their perceptions on that one occasion. However, Clow and Vorhies[22] have shown that 'measurement of consumer expectations after the consumption of service are biased by the experience of the customer'.

- If the gap between perceptions (P) and expectations (E) is used literally, that is, P-E, then Teas (taking expectations to be equivalent to an ideal standard) claims that increasing P-E scores do not reflect continually increasing levels of perceived quality.[23] That is, a higher P-E score does not necessarily imply higher quality. Take, for example, the situation where an ideal standard corresponded to a score of six, and a customer rated E and P each at six. The P-E score is nil. If, for pragmatic or pessimistic reasons, a customer gives an E rating of one, and then a P rating of two to a service in the same sector, the P-E score is one. Is the latter of higher perceived service quality than the former?

By 1995, these and other conceptual and methodological reservations with SERVQUAL had been well documented.[24,25] Nevertheless, SERVQUAL-based studies have dominated the empirical services quality research into the twenty-first century, and there is little doubt that the instrument gives a convenient 'kick-start' to practitioners and academics seeking to measure and monitor perceived service quality.

Postcard from Practice 8.1

Applying SERVQUAL at Arena Housing Group

As Group Chief Executive of a 15 000 dwelling Housing Association employing almost 750 people, I often wondered which of them really contributed to making our residents happy. Like many similar organisations, we had changed from being the custodians of a scarce and valued resource, where we rationed our homes on the basis of need, to a service-providing organisation needing to meet customers' expectations better than our competitors.

In other words, the market had fundamentally changed such that our residents and prospective residents had choice over both tenure and landlord. Their hand had also been strengthened considerably by the compliance expectations of a range of inspection and regulatory bodies measuring our outcomes. I came to the conclusion that we were configured like a production outfit rather than a service provider. Even worse, what most of our people were doing was producing and shuffling data rather than providing services.

We used a model of service quality (SERVQUAL) to evaluate the perceptions of management, staff and customers of Arena. We found that there was a discrepancy in customers' expectations of service delivery and the actual standard of service received by them, and this was very much at odds with the perceptions of our staff and management. When evaluating service quality, our customers looked for:

- Reliability: dependability of Arena as their service provider;
- Assurance: knowledge and courtesy of our employees and their ability to deliver;
- Tangibles: the physical components of the service and how we presented as an organisation;
- Empathy: caring, individualised attention for all our customers;
- Responsiveness: promptness and helpfulness.

In response we reconfigured how we delivered our services by employing a field force of 35 empowered Customer Service Managers who were the face of Arena, dealing directly with our customers and making the decisions that mattered. We re-engineered our support functions so that they had access at all times to our systems and to our knowledge database.

The outcome was that our Customer Service Managers created a valued long-term relationship with their customers through knowing them personally, getting things done for them by meeting their expectations and building strong bonds with key players in their communities. Our financial position improved as people stayed in our homes, demand increased and our customer satisfaction rates improved markedly.

Source: Graham Eades.

Service Quality – Its Evolution

While there are still many studies of service quality post-2000[26], service quality, as a sub-area of services marketing, is showing signs of being a less popular area of research than it was in the 1990s. For example, out of 155 abstract submissions to the 2008 American Marketing Association's SERVSIG International Research Conference, only 11 (7 per cent) were on service quality. That is not to say that its importance is diminishing. It is probably a result of reaching a saturation point in SERVQUAL-based studies. However, there is increased interest in e-service quality, and there is still much to learn about service quality with technology-based services.

E-service Quality

According to the Office of National Statistics in the UK (2007),

Internet shopping is becoming increasingly popular. A slightly higher proportion of men than women used the Internet to purchase goods or services associated with leisure, such as travel, accommodation or holidays (53 per cent of men compared with 48 per cent of women) and videos or DVDs (45 per cent compared with 39 per cent). Conversely a higher proportion of women than men used the Internet to purchase clothing or sports goods (42 per cent of women and 34 per cent of men), and food and groceries (25 per cent of women and 16 per cent of men).

According to e-commerce trade body IMRG, shoppers in the United Kingdom spent £4.98bn online in the 10 weeks before Christmas 2005, compared with £3.3bn for the same time a year earlier. In the United States, according to 'Euromomitor', online shopping expenditure in 2007 was over US$105bn, an increase of nearly 16 per cent on the previous year.

Because of the scale and dynamics of these developments, *Internet* retail service quality is a topic of contemporary importance.

Janda, Trocchia and Gwinner[27] explored consumer perceptions of Internet retail service quality and identified five dimensions, through in-depth interviews, that are most important to consumers:

- *Performance* – how well an online retailer does in terms of meeting expectations regarding order fulfillment
- *Access* – Internet retailer's ability to provide a variety of products from anywhere in the world
- *Security* – related to the perceptions of trust in the online retailer's integrity regarding financial and privacy issues
- *Sensation* – interactive features of the e-retailer's website
- *Information* – quantity and credibility of information provided by the online retailer.

The dimensions have some similarities with the constituents of the SERVQUAL dimensions, for example trust, security and credibility, but SERVQUAL was derived in the context of interpersonal service encounters, and so an understanding of Internet retail service quality is a more complex area than simply treating it as another SERVQUAL application.

When tested on a survey of 446 Internet shoppers in the United States, the five dimensions were empirically verified as distinct constructs.[28] However, while the dimensions of performance, security and information seem to be highly correlated with consumer satisfaction, it was less clear-cut with access and sensation. There is a distinct possibility, however, that the sensation dimension will increase in importance through the technological advances that have made electronic consumer-to-consumer interactions more accessible. Research in this whole area is ongoing.

Taking e-service beyond Internet shopping, Santos[29] offers a model of e-service quality that separates an incubative dimension from an active dimension, based on information gained from 30 focus groups of 6–10 members with Internet experience.

The incubative dimension, consisting of the elements 'ease of use', 'appearance', 'linkage', 'structure and layout' and 'content', refers to the service development that should take place *before* a website is launched. In many respects it is the electronic equivalent of designing the process (cf. Chapter 6). The active dimension, consisting of the elements of 'reliability', 'efficiency', 'support', 'communications', 'security' and 'incentives', is to be achieved through the period the website is active. The research resulting in the identification of these dimensions and elements is acknowledged to be exploratory. It does, however, provide a preliminary guide as to the relative importance of the elements (see Table 8.2) and, as such, gives practitioners a framework for exploring quality of their e-services.

Already, the perceptions of e-service quality are seen to be changing, as evidenced by the lower importance given by consumers to security in comparison to the attention given to this aspect in the early years when Internet fraud was a widely discussed issue. At this point in time there is still much further understanding to be gained by both theoretical and practical contributions to this global phenomenon.

Table 8.2 Dimensions and relative importance of E-Service quality

Incubative Dimension	*Active Dimension*	
Ease of Use Easy to find, use and navigate within	**Reliability** Frequency, accuracy f updating; purchasing, billing	High Importance
Appearance Use of colour, graphics, images, animations, together with size	**Efficiency** Search facilities, navigation, downloading	
Linkage Number and quality of links offered	**Support** User-friendly, help-pages, FAQs, personal advice	
Structure and Layout Organisation and presentation of website	**Communication** Contact methods, choices of languages	
Content Factual information and functions	**Security** Freedom from danger, risk, doubt.	
	Incentive Encouragement, rewards to consumers for browsing	Low Importance

Adapted from Santos.[29]

Customer Satisfaction

In the introduction to this chapter, the importance of customer satisfaction within the field of marketing was emphasised. We now examine the concept from three perspectives – the academics', the practitioners' and the customers'. References will be made to the service experiences of the Townsends in the story in Chapter 1 to illustrate the ideas.

The Academic Perspective

The origin of much of our understanding of customer satisfaction is in the field of consumer behaviour. 'Customer behaviour scholars have proposed that satisfaction depends not on the absolute levels of performance on various attributes, but rather on how the actual performance compares with the *expected* performance.'[30] Following from this approach, satisfaction or dissatisfaction will result if the performance confirms or disconfirms expectations, respectively. Thus, John or Jack Townsend would be satisfied or dissatisfied with their flight to Singapore according to whether or not the actual flight confirmed their expectations of it. Here, satisfaction is seen as a *process*. The theory, known as the expectation–disconfirmation paradigm,[31] underpinned much of the customer/consumer satisfaction research on services in the last quarter of the twentieth century.

Expectations–Disconfirmation Paradigm
When customer satisfaction is seen as a process, satisfaction or dissatisfaction will result if the service performance confirms or disconfirms prior customer expectations.

However, in parallel, the nature of the *outcome* of customer satisfaction has also received attention.[32] Satisfaction may be regarded as

- *an emotion*: an affective response to a specific service experience

  It would relate to the extent to which John Townsend was happy or excited with the flight experience.

- *a fulfilment*: the achievement of relevant goals

  It would relate to the extent to which Jack Townsend had conquered his fear of flying.

- *a state*: the level of reinforcement or arousal

  It would relate to whether the particular flight to Singapore reinforced the Townsends' views of flight travel, or whether it provided a positive or negative 'surprise'.

Measurement of customer satisfaction is appealing to both academics and practitioners. However, reservations have been expressed regarding the use of customer satisfaction surveys. They normally emphasise that the achievement of customer satisfaction should not be an end in itself. 'It's not that satisfaction doesn't matter; it matters a great deal. It's the manner, context and priority of satisfaction measurement that has become a problem. And the problem is that if we fail to link satisfaction scores to customer loyalty and profits, they all too easily become an end in themselves.'[33] There is also evidence of a 'halo effect' in measurements from customer satisfaction surveys, which may render resulting interpretations and actions unreliable.[34] Where a survey measures customer satisfaction on an attribute-by-attribute basis (such as a post-flight satisfaction survey that examines flight food, cabin crew service, in-flight entertainment, and so on), there is evidence that a high/low rating on the dominant attribute will result in positive/ negative halo effects on the other attributes. For example, Jack Townsend's delight with the in-flight entertainment may have coloured his views of all the other attributes. As such, customer satisfaction ratings on specific attributes can be misleading.

The Practitioner Perspective

As customers, we have all had the opportunity to fill in customer satisfaction questionnaires from service providers in the leisure, restaurant, banking, car rental, hotel, retail, airline and other service industries. It has been observed that 'firms spend millions of dollars on tracking customer satisfaction'.[35]

To take an example, J. Sainsbury, the UK multiple food and grocery retailer, conduct a shoppers' customer service survey – which they specify is 'part of a continual programme to ensure that supermarket shoppers receive the very best service'. The major component of the survey consists of 58 statements (on attributes associated with products and service in a supermarket) that respondents have to rate, on an 11-point scale with regard to:

- how important each statement is when shopping at ANY supermarket, and
- how satisfied or dissatisfied they are with the store's performance in relation to each statement.

In the former case, the scale is anchored by 0 = completely unimportant and 10 = extremely important. In the latter case, the scale is anchored by 0 = completely dissatisfied and 10 = completely satisfied. The statements are grouped into seven categories:

1. *Checkouts*: Example statements are 'helpers at checkouts', 'enough time to pack shopping at checkouts'.
2. *Bags/trolleys/baskets*: Example statements are 'free strong carrier bags', 'trolleys that are easy to steer and push'.
3. *Products*: Example statements are 'wide range of branded products', 'high quality fresh fruit and vegetables'.
4. *Staffed food counters*: Example statements are 'quick service at the staffed delicatessen counter', 'high quality fish from the staffed counter'.
5. *Staff*: Example statements are 'always having staff available on the shop floor', 'polite and friendly staff'.
6. *Prices/offers/promotions*: Example statements are 'clearly marked on-shelf prices', 'the loyalty card scheme'.
7. *Miscellaneous*: Example statements are 'uncrowded aisles', 'the baby-changing facilities'.

Obviously, the content and length of a customer satisfaction survey will vary according to context, and to the resources required to support the data-gathering exercise. Some customer satisfaction surveys, for instance in a small restaurant, may have as few as five or six questions/statements, relating directly to the quality of the food and the service. The example above is at the other extreme, and is no doubt very costly to administer and support, and it can be seen that the section on customer satisfaction relates to performance only and not to expectations.[36]

Firms need to assess the potential benefits from the survey data against the costs of carrying out the survey. Where firms have many outlets, such as J. Sainsbury, the benefits may include the opportunity to feed back, on a regular basis to the management of each outlet, the customer ratings on the range of attributes. The responses to relatively poor ratings, and to subsequent customer ratings, can then be monitored, with a view to increasing customer satisfaction at each outlet. The effectiveness of this benefit may depend on the level of communication within the organisation, and on the potential halo effects, and respondent fatigue, associated with the attribute-by-attribute measurement.

Most companies, however, would look for benefits associated with increased profits. Here, there is an implicit assumption that increased customer satisfaction will result in increased profit, and so the goal of increased customer satisfaction, supported by (often costly) customer satisfaction surveys is to be pursued. The links between customer satisfaction, customer retention and profitability are discussed in detail in Chapter 10. For now, it is useful to draw attention to Reichheld's 'satisfaction trap' that companies may fall into if they 'forget that there is no necessary connection between satisfaction scores and cash flow',[37] and to Piercy's reminder that customer satisfaction should not be confused with customer loyalty.[38] While firms would like to view satisfied customers as loyal customers, many customers exist who are satisfied, but not loyal ('spuriously loyal', such as those with three or more supermarket loyalty cards), and who are not satisfied, but loyal ('hostages', such as those who find costs of switching banks too high).

It is not only the service providers themselves that undertake customer satisfaction surveys. The results of formal independent customer satisfaction surveys are often publicised widely. For example, in the United States, changes in the annual Customer Satisfaction Index provide opportunities for journalists to comment on customer service and attribute blame when the index falls. According to the index, since 1994, customer satisfaction has fallen by 5 per cent in the airline sector, 7 per cent in retailing and even more in the telecommunications sector.[39] This has been attributed to the lack of ability of American companies to keep pace with the volume of demand for goods and services since 1994, and to the replacement of the 'human face and a helping hand' by virtual service using new technologies.[40] Even informal customer satisfaction surveys can be newsworthy, such as when customers were asked for their views on the initiative by London Underground to increase customer satisfaction by introducing perfumed fragrances into the stations.[41]

Satisfaction-Trap
The acknowledgement that no direct, linear relationship has been established between customer satisfaction scores, loyalty and organisational cash flow and profitability.

The Customer Perspective

What do customers understand by the term 'satisfaction', when responding to surveys by academics or service providers?

Research by Parker and Mathews,[42] that was undertaken specifically to address this question, found that there was considerable variation in the way their sample of consumers had categorised their own recent satisfactory consumption experiences with goods or services. When provided, by the authors, with possible categories, the respondents had categorised satisfaction as follows:

- 'pleasure' (14 per cent of the responses)
- 'an evaluation against what was expected' (13 per cent)

- 'contentment' (13 per cent)
- 'making the right purchase decision' (13 per cent)
- 'a feeling about the consumption experience' (11 per cent)
- 'needs being fulfilled' (11 per cent)
- 'delight' (9 per cent)
- 'relief' (7 per cent)
- 'being suitably rewarded for efforts' (5 per cent)
- 'comparing the situation with those of other people' (4 per cent).

When given an opportunity to offer their own definitions of satisfaction, eight further definitions were forthcoming, with the most popular ones relating to 'cost' (28 per cent), 'quality' (22 per cent), 'absence of dissatisfiers' (14 per cent) and 'convenience' (14 per cent).

Satisfaction clearly means different things to different people in different contexts, and there is a real concern that customer satisfaction surveys may be asking consumers to rate their level of satisfaction on scales where the constructs have no shared meaning. It has been pointed out that the implicit assumption that customers who tick the same box on a satisfaction survey have a qualitatively identical experience is wrong.[43] The scale anchors used in the J. Sainsbury example above, that is, 'completely satisfied' and 'completely dissatisfied', are open to many interpretations. Consumers being completely satisfied with, for example, baby-changing facilities, may be expressing a view on the quality of the facility, convenience, a sense of relief or an absence of dissatisfiers. Each interpretation relates to different customer emotional and cognitive states and could lead to a different management response.

Customer Satisfaction Research

Apart from surveys, how else can customer satisfaction be gauged?

There is growing support for market research techniques that encourage customer introspective accounts of their experiences, although it is recognised that they may not be appropriate in all consumption situations.[44] A good example of this approach was the use of undergraduate students given the task of writing introspective accounts on their experiences when visiting a department store.[45] Their accounts unearthed levels of dissatisfaction with the store, and the reasons for them, which were not forthcoming through the questionnaire-based surveys. Such methods, however, are dependent on the ability and willingness of customers to write their experiences in an articulate, story-telling format.

Another method is for someone in a service organisation to be a customer for a time. An excellent example of this is the account of a university lecturer becoming a student for a year in a different department of the university.[46] The different perspective – being a student rather than a teacher – demonstrated to that person the lack of relevance of many of the standard student satisfaction questionnaire components to the overall student experience.

Service Quality versus Satisfaction

Given their different origins, what is the relationship between service quality and satisfaction? 'While service satisfaction and service quality are clearly related, researchers do not share common definitions of the terms, nor is there clear understanding expressed in the literature of how the two relate.'[47]

Service Quality as an Overall Attitude

One explanation of the difference between service quality and customer satisfaction is highlighted by Bateson.[48] 'Quality is generally conceptualised as an attitude, the customer's comprehensive evaluation of a service offering. It is built up from a series of evaluated experiences and hence is less dynamic than satisfaction. Satisfaction is the outcome of the evaluation a consumer makes of any specific transaction.'

For example, imagine a customer taking a car in for a routine service. The customer's level of satisfaction with that particular transaction will relate to the level of disconfirmation between the prior expectation of the service and the actual outcome. If the disconfirmation was relatively small, or if the outcome exceeded expectations (e.g., the job was completed quickly enough for the customer to avoid the expense of alternative travel for a day), then he/she will be satisfied (or even delighted). Otherwise, dissatisfaction may be the result. The same customer, however, may judge the overall service quality of the car mechanic on a longer-term basis, and include comparisons with other car service providers in forming expectation of what can, and should, be done by the specific service provider. The service quality rating would not result from a single transaction.

PZB are quite clear about the fact that the SERVQUAL instrument, in its present form, is intended to ascertain customers' global perceptions of a firm's service quality. However, they do suggest that 'modifying SERVQUAL to assess transaction specific service quality is a useful direction for further research'.[49]

Expectations and Perceptions

Other researchers[50,51] have suggested that the difference between service quality and customer satisfaction lies in the way disconfirmation is operationalised. In particular, it may depend on how expectations are defined.

They state that in measuring perceived service quality the level of comparison (i.e., expectation) is what a consumer *should* expect, whereas in measures of satisfaction the appropriate comparison is what a consumer *would* expect.[52] An expectation about what a customer should expect, say in a particular four-star hotel, will be based not just on experiences with that specific hotel group, but will include best practice of all similar graded hotels. Conversely, an expectation about what a customer would expect of the hotel is more of a prediction based on the appearance of the hotel and previous experiences with, or word-of-mouth communications about, that particular hotel group.

The debate about different types of expectations and the difference between customer satisfaction and service quality continues. Even academics acknowledge some confusion,[53] and for customers completing SERVQUAL-related questionnaires, and service practitioners, the subtle differences may well not be appreciated. If this is the case, just what is SERVQUAL measuring?

PZB[54] still maintain that customer satisfaction is distinct from service quality. Satisfaction is thought to result from the comparison between predicted service and perceived service, whereas service quality refers to the comparison between desired service and perceived service. However, they make the point, in the current state of the debate, that 'both service quality and customer satisfaction can be examined meaningfully from both transactions – specific as well as global perspectives'.[55]

Cumulative Customer Satisfaction

Anderson *et al.*,[56] as a means of distinguishing between customer satisfaction and service quality, introduce two conceptualisations of customer satisfaction:

1. transaction-specific;
2. cumulative.

We have already considered the transaction-specific conceptualisation in the previous section. The cumulative customer satisfaction is seen to be based on 'the total purchase and consumption experience with a good or service over time', and, as such, is a more fundamental indicator of the firm's past, current and future performance. If perceived service quality is seen as a global judgement of a provider's service offering, then (cumulative) customer satisfaction and perceived service quality can be viewed as distinct because:

- customers require experience with a service to determine satisfaction, whereas quality can be perceived without any actual experience
- customers satisfaction depends on value, where value is a combination of price and quality. Thus satisfaction (and not quality) is dependent on price
- quality relates only to current perceptions, while satisfaction is based on past and future anticipated experiences.

Which is the Antecedent?

There is the possibility that practitioners may pose the question 'So what?' to much of the debate on service quality and customer satisfaction, particularly in view of the attention given to which precedes the other. Does customer satisfaction lead to service quality, or is it the other way round?

Cronin and Taylor[57] suggest that service quality is an antecedent of customer satisfaction and that customer purchase intentions are related more closely to levels of satisfaction than to perceptions of service quality. Thus, other elements of customer satisfaction – price or availability – may require greater management attention than a striving for even higher quality. Authors concerned with service profitability and the relationships between profitability, quality and satisfaction[58,59] also view service quality as the antecedent of customer satisfaction. Their mathematical equations, conclusions and managerial actions and implications depend on the assumption that service quality precedes customer satisfaction. For many years, the conventional wisdom, based on PZB's work, supported the opposite view; that is, that transaction-specific satisfaction assessments preceded global perceptions of service quality.

Summary

Issues of service quality and customer satisfaction lie at the heart of services marketing and management. Both are seen as desirable outputs of any service strategy.

Much of the qualitative work on understanding service quality which produced the five dimensions of service quality has informed academics and practitioners alike. Similarly, the 'Gaps model', which provides the basis for measurement of service quality, has been of value as an academic framework, and as a justification for the SERVQUAL format. SERVQUAL and the operationalisation of expectation measurements have been subjects of concern for researchers into service quality, but the methodology is still extensively employed. Now is the era of e-service quality, where research and practice is in its infancy.

Customer satisfaction has its roots in the 'disconfirmation paradigm'; that is, is judged in terms of the level of disconfirmation between the expectation and the subsequent experience of a service. As such, there are many similarities between the 'gap' in service quality measurement and the 'disconfirmation' in customer satisfaction measurement. This has led to some confusion over the difference between service quality and customer satisfaction, and to a greater need for an understanding of expectations.

The majority view at the beginning of the twenty-first century, however, is that service quality should be regarded as an antecedent to customer satisfaction,[60] and most of the material in the next two chapters is developed from this view.

Learning Outcomes

Having read this chapter, you should be able to

- know the distinction between technical and functional service quality and the dimensions of perceived service quality

- critically assess SERVQUAL as a generic instrument for measuring service quality

- know the most likely antecedents of customer expectations and the role of expectations in service quality and customer satisfaction theory

- recognise issues associated with the evaluation of e-service quality

- understand the implications of regarding satisfaction as a process or as an outcome

- appreciate the strengths and limitations of customer satisfaction surveys

- make informed judgements on the academic debates about service quality versus customer satisfaction.

Discussion Questions and Exercises

1. Describe recent occasions when, in a service context, (i) expectations exceeded perceptions and (ii) perceptions exceeded expectations. Explain the main reasons in each case.

2. Outline the main feature of the 'Gap model' of service quality. How might management seek to reduce Gaps 1 to 4?

3. What are the differences between perceived service quality and customer satisfaction?

4. Are customer satisfaction surveys value for money? When, and why might you choose to use another method of determining customer satisfaction?

5. Compare and contrast the SERVQUAL dimensions of service quality with those that are suggested as appropriate to e-service quality.

Notes and References

1. Fisk, R., Brown, S. and Bitner, M. J., 'Tracking the Evolution of the Services Marketing Literature', *Journal of Retailing*, 69(1), Spring 1993, pp. 61–103.
2. Clow, K. E. and Vorhies, D. W., 'Building a Competitive Advantage for Service Firms', *Journal of Services Marketing*, vol. 7, 1993, pp. 22–32.
3. Parker, C. and Mathews, B. P., 'Customer Satisfaction: Contrasting Academic and Consumers' Interpretations', *Marketing Intelligence and Planning*, 19(1), 2001, pp. 38–44.
4. Parasuraman, A., Zeithaml, V. A. and Berry, L. L., 'SERVQUAL: A Multiple-Item Scale for Measuring Consumer Perceptions of Service Quality', *Journal of Retailing*, vol. 64, spring 1988, pp. 12–40.
5. Oliver, R. L., 'Measurement and Evaluation of Satisfaction Process in Retail Setting', *Journal of Retailing*, vol. 57, 1981, pp. 25–48.
6. Gronroos, C., 'Innovative Marketing Strategies and Organizational Structures for Service Firms', in L. L. Berry, G. L. Shostack and G. D. Upah (eds), *Emerging Perspectives on Services Marketing*, American Marketing Association, Chicago, 1983, pp. 9–21.
7. Lewis, R. C. and Booms, B. H., 'The Marketing Aspects of Service Quality', in L. L. Berry, G. L. Shostack and G. D. Upah (eds), *Emerging Perspectives on Services Marketing*, American Marketing Association, Chicago, 1983, pp. 99–107.
8. Parasuraman, A., Zeithaml, V. A. and Berry, L. L., 'A Conceptual Model of Service Quality and its Implications for Future Research', *Journal of Marketing*, vol. 49, 1985, pp. 41–50.
9. Parasuraman, Zeithaml and Berry, 'SERVQUAL: A Multiple-Item Scale for Measuring Consumer Perceptions of Service Quality'.
10. Parasuraman, A., Berry, L. L. and Zeithaml, V. A., 'Refinement and Reassessment of the SERVQUAL Scale', *Journal of Retailing*, vol. 67, Winter 1991, pp. 420–50.

11. Zeithaml, V. A., Berry, L. L. and Parasuraman, A., 'The Nature and Determinants of Customer Expectations of Service', *Journal of the Academy of Marketing Science,* vol. 21, 1993, pp. 1–12.
12. McDonald, M. H. B., de Chernatony, L. and Harris, F., 'Corporate Marketing and Service Brands – Moving Beyond the Fast-Moving Consumer Goods Model', *European Journal of Marketing,* 35(3–4), pp. 335–52.
13. Auty, S. and Long, G., '"Tribal Warfare" and Gaps Affecting Internal Service Quality', *International Journal of Service Industry Management,* 10(1), 1999, pp. 7–22.
14. Sultan, F. and Simpson Jr, M. C., 'International Service Variants: Airline Passenger Expectations and Perceptions of Service Quality', *Journal of Services Marketing,* 14(3), 2000, pp. 188–216.
15. Parasuraman, Zeithaml and Berry, 'SERVQUAL: A Multiple-Item Scale for Measuring Consumer Perceptions of Service Quality'.
16. Parasuraman, Berry and Zeithaml, 'Refinement and Reassessment of the SERVQUAL Scale'.
17. Carman, J. A., 'Consumer Perceptions of Service Quality: An Assessment of the SERVQUAL Dimensions', *Journal of Retailing,* vol. 66, Spring 1990, pp. 33–55.
18. Cronin, J. J. and Taylor, S. A., 'Measuring Service Quality: A Re-examination and Extension', *Journal of Marketing,* vol. 56, 1992, pp. 55–68.
19. Gronroos, C., *Service Management and Marketing,* John Wiley & Sons, Chichester, UK, 2000.
20. Parasuraman, Berry and Zeithaml, 'Refinement and Reassessment of the SERVQUAL Scale'.
21. Vandamme, R. and Leunin, J., 'Measuring Service Quality in the Retail Sector: An Assessment and Extension of SERVQUAL', Proceedings of the 7th International Conference on Research in Distributive Trades, Stirling, UK, 1993, pp. 364–73.
22. Clow and Vorhies, 'Building a Competitive Advantage for Service Firms'.
23. Teas, R. K., 'Expectations, Performance Evaluation and Consumers' Perceptions of Quality', *Journal of Marketing,* vol. 57, October 1993, pp. 18–34.
24. Smith, A. M., 'Measuring Service Quality: Is SERVQUAL Now Redundant?', *Journal of Marketing Management,* vol. 11, 1995, pp. 257–76.
25. Buttle, F., 'SERVQUAL: Review, Critique, Research Agenda', *European Journal of Marketing,* 30(1), 1996, pp. 8–32.
26. Ladhari, R., 'Alternative Measures of Service Quality: A Review', *Managing Service Quality,* 18(1), 2008, pp. 65–86.
27. Janda, S., Trocchia, P. J. and Gwinner, K. P., 'Consumer Perceptions of Internet Retail Service Quality', *International Journal of Service Industry Management,* 13(5), 2002, pp. 412–31.
28. ibid.
29. Santos, J., 'E-Service Quality: A Model of Virtual Service Quality Dimensions', *Managing Service Quality,* 13(3), 2003, pp. 233–46.
30. Sheth, J. N., Mittal, B. and Newman, B. I., *Customer Behavior: Consumer Behavior and Beyond,* The Dryden Press, Orlando, Fla., 1999.
31. Oliver, R. L., 'Effects of Expectation and Disconfirmation on Post-Exposure Product Evaluations: An Alternative Interpretation', *Journal of Applied Psychology,* 62(4), 1977, pp. 480–86.
32. Parker and Mathews, 'Customer Satisfaction: Contrasting Academic and Consumers' Interpretations'.
33. Reichheld, F. F., *The Loyalty Effect,* HBS Press, Boston Mass., 1996.
34. Wirtz, J., 'Improving the Measurement of Customer Satisfaction: A Test of Three Methods to Reduce Halo', *Managing Service Quality,* 11(2), 2001, pp. 99–111.
35. Ibid.
36. Expectations could have been considered, for example, by anchoring the scales as 0 = fell below expectations, 5 = met expectations, 10 = exceeded expectations.
37. Reichheld, *The Loyalty Effect.*

38. 'Customer satisfaction and customer loyalty are not the same thing; and you cannot buy real loyalty that easily' (p. 40) *Market-led Strategic Change,* Nigel Piercy, 2nd edn., Butterworth Heinemann, Oxford, 1998.
39. Jones, A., 'Have a Nice Day? No Such Luck in Corporate America', *The Times,* London, 12 April 2001.
40. Schulze, H., 'Since When Did I Ask to Help Myself?', *New York Times,* New York, 27 August 2000.
41. Wendlandt, A., 'It's Sure to Get up Travellers' Noses', *Financial Times,* London, 24 April 2001.
42. Parker and Mathews, 'Customer Satisfaction: Contrasting Academic and Consumers' Interpretations'.
43. Stauss, B. and Neuhaus, P., 'The Qualitative Satisfaction Model', *International Journal of Service Industry Management,* 8(3), 1997, pp. 236–49.
44. Caru, A. and Cova, B., 'Small versus Big Stories in Framing Consumption Experiences', *Qualitative Market Research: An International Journal,* 11(2), 2008, pp.166–76.
45. Patterson, A., Hodgson, J. and Shi, J., 'Chronicles of 'Customer Experience': The Downfall of Lewis's Foretold', *Journal of Marketing Management,* 24(1–2), 2008, pp. 29–45.
46. Nathan, R., *My Freshman Year: What a Professor Learned by Becoming a Student*, Cornell University Press, Ithaca, NY, 2005.
47. Fisk, Brown and Bitner, 'Tracking the Evolution of the Services Marketing Literature'.
48. Bateson, J. E. G., *Managing Services Marketing: Text and Readings,* 2nd edn., Dryden Press, London, 1992.
49. Parasuraman, A., Zeithaml, V. A. and Berry, L. L., 'Reassessment of Expectations as a Comparison Standard in Measuring Service Quality: Implications for Further Research', *Journal of Marketing,* vol. 58, January 1994, pp. 111–24.
50. Cronin and Taylor, 'Measuring Service Quality'.
51. Anderson, E. W., Fornell, C. and Lehmann, D. R., 'Customer Satisfaction, Market Share and Profitability: Findings from Sweden', *Journal of Marketing,* vol. 58, July 1994, pp. 53–66.
52. Ibid.
53. Ibid.
54. Zeithaml, Berry and Parasuraman, 'The Nature and Determinants of Customer Expectations of Service'.
55. Parasuraman, Zeithaml and Berry, 'Reassessment of Expectations as a Comparison Standard in Measuring Service Quality'.
56. Anderson, Fornell and Lehmann, 'Customer Satisfaction, Market Share and Profitability'.
57. Cronin and Taylor, 'Measuring Service Quality'.
58. Anderson, Fornell and Lehmann, 'Customer Satisfaction, Market Share and Profitability'.
59. Rust, R. T. and Oliver, R. L., *Service Quality: New Directions in Theory and Practice,* Sage, London, 1994.
60. Sivadas, E. and Baker-Prewitt, J. L., 'An Examination of the Relationship Between Service Quality, Customer Satisfaction and Store Loyalty', *International Journal of Retail and Distribution Management,* 28(2), 2000, pp. 73–82.

9

Relationship Marketing

Learning Objectives

Overall Aim of the Chapter

To define the relationship marketing approach and outline the implications of a concentration on customer loyalty and retention.

In particular, the *chapter objectives* are

- to compare the transaction and relationship marketing approaches

- to explore and contrast the many definitions of relationship marketing from academic and organisational perspectives

- to introduce the concept of market-based relationship marketing, and its advantages and disadvantages for customers and the service organisation

- to demonstrate the internal and external relationships that constitute network-based relationship marketing

- to explore the practical implications of two customer loyalty strategies.

Introduction

A relationship marketing (RM) approach draws attention to *the importance of retaining as well as attracting customers* with the emphasis being placed on the development of long-term relationships with existing customers. The approach is not exclusive to the marketing of services. It is, however, at the heart of many service businesses, and something many of them do particularly well. As the Waymark Holidays cross-country skiing literature points out (Case Study 5), 'much of our success over the past two decades has been due to the loyalty of our regular customers, many of whom travel with us every year – in some cases, twice or even three times per season'. The hairdresser (Case Study 1) estimates that about 90 per cent of all customers have been to the salon at least five times. These organisations have been able not only to attract customers to their service in the first instance, but also to develop and maintain a series of long-term relationships with many clients that have helped to secure the survival of their

RM
Relationship Marketing

business. Many of their loyal customers act as an important referral source for new business, recommending their service to new clients.

Why is customer loyalty and retention of particular interest and importance to *service* businesses?

One reason is that it is relatively easy to copy many services (as in the travel company and hairdresser examples above), and consequently easy for customers to switch loyalties. It may take only one bad 'moment of truth' in a service encounter to persuade a customer to go to a competitor. Therefore, service businesses incur high switching costs if they do not recognise the importance of customer loyalty and retention. The development of a closer, long-term relationship with customers is particularly important in certain types of service operation: namely, when the service cannot be provided completely on one occasion; for instance, certain treatments at the dentist which require several visits, or a problem with a car which requires more than one visit to the mechanic. Similarly, if the service itself is highly intangible, the existence of a stronger relationship can be an important influence on a customer's decision to pay for the services of one provider in preference to another. If there is little tangible evidence available to assess the quality of the service on offer, customers frequently turn to the provider they have used before, whom they feel they can trust.

Another reason is that, as we have seen, there is a significant *people* element in the *services* marketing mix, and, according to Zineldin,[1] 'Relationship marketing views marketing as an integrative activity involving personnel...personal relationships, interactions and social exchange are the most important core elements of relationship marketing.' So, one would expect that an approach which has interpersonal interactions at its heart would be of particular relevance to service businesses.

Arguably, many service and other businesses have intuitively adopted such business practices without being aware that their marketing activities are being labelled as 'relationship marketing'. If so, they have adopted a marketing approach, focus and strategy which is different from that which concentrates on single sales or transactions (known as 'transaction marketing'). Relationship marketing is said to differ from transaction marketing in the following ways.

Transaction Marketing
An approach that uses 'offensive' marketing strategies to achieve a sale or transaction. Transaction marketing is differentiated from Relationship Marketing.

- Transaction marketing is about *attracting* customers using *offensive strategies* (encouraging brand switching and/or recruiting competitors' dissatisfied clients).

- Relationship marketing is about *retaining* customers using *defensive strategies* (minimising customer turnover and maximising customer retention).[2]

Service Recovery
Steps that a service provider and their contact personnel take to move a customer evaluation of the service from dissatisfaction to satisfaction.

In this chapter, we examine RM in the service sector. First we set the scene by exploring some of the definitions and features of RM from both an academic and an organisational perspective. Two themes of RM – market-based RM and network-based RM – are then explained and evaluated. Finally, strategies that have been embraced by practitioners as a means of maintaining customer loyalty – effective service recovery, and loyalty schemes – are considered in detail.

📖 **It's in the News! 9.1**

Network-based Relationships: Government/Supermarket/Primary Care Trust

According to the BBC News, 21 February 2008,

Patients will soon be able to pick up some shopping on a visit to their GP [General Practitioner/Doctor]. A supermarket in Greater Manchester is believed to be the first in England to offer doctor appointments. Doctors from three different surgeries will work from a consulting room at a Sainsbury's store in Heaton Park, near Prestwich, from next month.

It is the first phase of a £126 000 pilot by the Heywood, Middleton and Rochdale Primary Care Trust to provide extended-hours medical care. It means National Health Service patients in the area can book appointments on selected evenings and weekend days. The clinic will be staffed by doctors from private company 'Doctors in Store' during the six-month pilot, which starts on 3 March. The government announced last year that supermarkets and other private firms were being invited to bid to run GP surgeries as part of a drive to improve access to care in deprived areas.

The Sainsbury's surgery will run appointments, between 1830 GMT and 2130 GMT on Monday and Thursday, as well as 1100 GMT to 1500 GMT on Saturdays. Dr Mohammed Jiva, who runs the company running the surgery, said: 'Patients' needs are changing and so it's important that we find ways to provide a more flexible and convenient service. A number of practices in the local area have already come on board and once demand increases, we will explore the potential to roll this out to even further across the whole of Rochdale.'

The GPs will work at the store in addition to their regular hours at local surgeries in Heywood and Middleton. They will have full secure access to patient medical details and be able to make referrals or update records, just like a regular GP. Patients can book appointments through their registered GP practice. Dr Ruth Hussey, director of public health in the north west of England, said the supermarket surgery was an important development in health care.

'We know how important it is to make health services more convenient for people, especially for prevention of poor health as well as for treatment and care,' she said.

Definitions and Features of Relationship Marketing

The academic perspective

Some prominent academics refer to RM as 'the new paradigm for marketing'.[3,4] There is little doubt that RM has become a fruitful area for academic research, especially since the early 1990s. There have been many attempts to define what is meant by RM and to outline its main features. The sheer volume of academic literature on this area can be daunting, so we have picked out below some key definitions and features of RM, and provided a summary of RM indicators.

1. RM is about 'attracting, maintaining and enhancing customer relationships'[5] and 'the development and enhancement of internal and other external relationships'.[6]

   This definition draws attention to the importance of retaining as well as attracting customers with the emphasis being placed on the development of long-term relationships with existing customers. It involves changing the focus of marketing from a transactional to a relationship focus, with the emphasis on customer retention, high customer service and commitment, and quality being a concern for all. It also emphasises that RM is not only about bettering relationships with customer markets, but also about the relationships with supplier, recruitment, referral and influence markets, as well as the internal market (Chapter 7).

2. RM is about 'turning new customers into regular purchasers . . . to strong supporters . . . to active vocal advocates of the company'.[7]

   Underlying this definition is the belief that the identification and retention of loyal customers can result in significant financial benefits for the organisation, and that loyalty retention measures should be integral to strategy.[8] Reichheld believes that potentially loyal customers need to be targeted by the company right from the beginning from an analysis of the characteristics of existing users.[9]

3. RM is about 'bringing marketing, customer service and quality together'.[10]

   Here, it is argued that RM orientation involves a closer alignment between three crucial areas; marketing, customer service and quality. They are three components of strategy which may have traditionally been 'treated as separate and unrelated'. In order to be a truly 'customer-focused' service organisation, these three elements need to be integrated together within the organisation. Christopher et al.[11] argue that although companies have made efforts to measure and monitor quality within the organisation, their actions have largely been taken from an operations perspective (i.e., conformance to set requirements; e.g., BS5750) rather than from the customer-perceived quality perspective. They also argue that measures aimed at improving customer service levels have often been taken in isolation from these quality initiatives. A true RM orientation would require all three areas to be linked together.

4. RM is about 'developing mutual trust',[12,13] and 'commitment'.[14]

   Trust and commitment are features of a RM approach that have been identified by many researchers. In particular, relationships have been found between customers' trust in the service provider, and commitment to the relationship, and their levels of customer satisfaction and loyalty.[15] In certain service offers, there are opportunities for customer commitment to be mutually beneficial. For example, the personal trainer would like a customer to sign on for a 10-week training programme, ensuring customer retention over the period. From the customer's perspective a commitment to a 10-week programme can enhance the health benefits, which relate to levels of satisfaction not associated with a single training session.

5. RM is about 'the development of database marketing, interactive marketing and network marketing'.[16]

In this context, RM is about recognising that the organisation's existing customer base is its most important asset and about working to protect it at all costs. One of the major reasons why RM is attractive to service business managers is because of advances in information technology and specifically the generation of customer databases. These clearly make it easier for service organisations to identify loyal customers. Both small and large service operators use databases in this way. A video retailer, for example, holds membership details of all customers on a database and sends regular users a birthday card with a complimentary voucher for a free video.

For managers of service organisations who are adopting, or who are considering the adoption of an RM approach, the definitions and features outlined above may help. In addition, Pressey and Mathews[17] provide a very useful summary of the key indicators of an RM approach. They are the following:

- a high level of trust between both parties
- a high level of commitment between both parties
- a long time horizon
- open communication channels between both parties with information exchanged between both parties
- having the customer's best interest at heart
- a commitment to quality from both parties
- an attempt to favourably lock-in or retain the customer.

The organisational perspective

Many organisations adopt RM within a function headed 'Customer Relationship Management'. From their perspective, customer loyalty and retention is best addressed through the integration of Marketing, Customer Service and IT.

Customer Relationship Management (CRM), therefore, often involves

CRM
Customer Relationship Management.

- *Precision Marketing.* CRM is believed to be at the heart of customer communications, and is felt to be the future for direct marketing agencies. According to the Chief Executive of IBM's CRM unit, 'Most companies are now competing with more commoditised products, so the only differentiation is the customer relationship.'[18]

- *The use and operation of 'call centres'.* Call centres are central to many CRM projects. Datamonitor, in 2003, predicted that the global market for call centre components is primed for growth, particularly in regions such as India and Central and Latin America, where offshore outsourcing is already developing strongly. Call centres are being integrated with Internet online offers. Sometimes, however, CRM may be interpreted as 'customer care' and seen as a cost to the organisation.

- *The development of customer databases.* This is in line with the definition 5 above. A problem, in practice, in the development of effective databases, may be the failure of connection between IT specialists and marketers.

This can be illustrated as follows. A Social Services Department in the United Kingdom appointed a CRM software specialist group to coordinate the many databases on the people using their services. Prior to the appointment of the software specialists, the Department kept the user records in many separate hard-copy files, and this posed difficulties for the social services staff. For example, staff in the Children's Section were frustrated that files on children needing adoption, potential parents, police checks and so on were all kept separately and not speedily updated, and this slowed down the process of effectively and efficiently matching the children with the potential parents. The CRM software seemed to provide a solution to the problems. However, in practice, its implementation created a different problem. The centralisation of the data brought with it a centralisation of enquiries to the Department (a kind of mini call centre). This, in turn, resulted in potential parents being asked to wait in a queue when telephoning in, and not being able to speak directly to the appropriate member of staff in the Children's Section. Both the prospective parents and the staff in the Children's Section were being prevented by the ICT system from engaging in the essential inter-personal interactions that make the service effective.

This is by no means an isolated example. Implementation of CRM software-based systems must be managed with caution, and with the inputs of all the people who are to use the system.

Based on the perspectives above, we now provide a more detailed evaluation of two complementary elements of RM:[19]

1. *Market-based RM*: Here the focus is on customer retention;
2. *Network-based RM*: Here the focus is on enhancing internal and external relationships.

Market-based Relationship Marketing

The focus of market-based RM is on keeping existing customers rather than going out to get new ones. Customer retention is the key. Ideally, the organisation would like to treat large numbers of customers individually (and profitably).

Therefore the organisation's development and management of a customer database is central to the process.

First, however, we look at the factors that may influence a customer to stay with a service organisation, rather than defect to a competitor. Customers stay with a service provider either because they want to or because they feel they have to. It has been suggested[20] that customers who 'want to stay' behave differently from those who 'have to stay'. Those who want to stay are more likely to trust the organisation and behave in ways that have a positive impact on the organisation. In contrast those who feel they have to remain are more likely to behave in ways that may create difficulties for the organisation. They may be less co-operative when interacting with service employees and may be more likely to spread negative information if they become dissatisfied.

- 'Exit costs' may be too high.

Exit Costs
Costs that a customer may incur when moving their business from one service provider to another. This may include non-financial costs such as time, effort and 'hassle' required.

Customers are retained by some service companies simply because it is too much trouble for the customer to switch to a competitor. Maybe, it is the amount of time required that dissuades customers from defecting, even if they are not particularly satisfied with their existing service. For many years, this was given as a principal reason why customers stayed with a particular bank, even if more favourable interest rates or a wider range of services was being offered elsewhere. In the mobile phone industry, for example, switching costs associated with changing a network service may include costs in time and effort on seeking information about different providers, filling out forms to instigate the switch, and informing relevant people of the new telephone number. Sometimes, however, it is a perception of risk that prevents a customer from switching. They may feel, for example, that other companies are not as reliable as 'British Gas', even though these companies are, according to advertisements, supplying the same gas through the same pipes at a cheaper price.

- The service provider has a detailed understanding of the customer's needs.

Customers may be retained by a service provider because the provider has demonstrated the ability to do a good job for the customer, based on a thorough understanding of the needs of the customer. Such an understanding may not be easily replicated. Personal services, such as those provided by hairdressers, chiropodists, manicurists or chiropractors, may fall into this category, where customers choose their favourite employee to carry out the service, and possibly build up a strong interpersonal relationship. With professional services, such as counselling, accounting and legal services, clients, having disclosed personal details to a person whose confidences they trust and who they feel is empathetic, are likely to remain with the service. Customers are likely to return to restaurants or hotels which cater to particular customer needs for, say, children's menus, special diets or speedy service. A hotel in Zurich, for example, has opened exclusively for women.[21] The high likelihood of repatronage for female executives is due not just to the physical features (bigger and better-lit bathrooms, for example) but also to a reduction of anxiety (not feeling intimidated by dining alone in a hotel restaurant).

- Customer choice is restricted.

Often customers are tied into a service, because they have little or no choice. Commuters may have to travel by train or bus, simply because there may be no feasible alternative mode of transport to travel to work. Guarantees, which accompany the purchases of goods ranging from cars to washing machines to satellite television, involve the employment of contracted maintenance services, over which the purchaser has no choice. Even if the service levels in these situations are extremely poor, customers cannot defect to a preferred service provider.

Service organisations have responded to these factors by attempting to know their customers better through the development and management of customer databases, developing personal relationships with customers through their employees and tying in customers to the organisation with guarantees or through long-term commitments. In banks, for example, loyal and profitable customers (identified through the database) may be offered a personal bank manager whose role is to build a personal relationship with the customer, making switching more 'costly', and increasing long-term commitments through favourable loan packages covering several years. However, other banks, looking at attracting new customers, may view the high exit costs as something to challenge. For example, the Abbey National, one of the new UK banks, produced a national advertising campaign which focused on how easy it is for a customer to transfer their accounts from any bank to the Abbey National – just a signature is needed.

Market-based RM aims for customer retention and long-term relationships. However, it is not always appropriate for the two parties; that is, the customer and the organisation. From the many research projects on RM, it is clear that there are both advantages and disadvantages of market-based RM for each party. We summarise the findings below.

Advantages of market-based relationship marketing

For the customer

- Market-based RM can contribute to a sense of well-being, stability and quality of life.

The relationship with the organisation (or employee(s) representing the organisation) is something that the customer can rely on. For the elderly customer, the fortnightly visit by the mobile gardener not only results in an improvement in the look of the garden, but also provide opportunities for gardening-related conversations. For the business person, the favourite restaurant and waiter provides a safe venue for the client lunch.

- Market-based RM can make it unnecessary for the customer to incur high switching costs.

It is becoming easier for customers to switch service providers, even those, such as banks or insurance companies, where there has been a long historical commitment. Nevertheless, customers may still find it difficult, inconvenient and, in some cases, stressful to make the switch. If, through market-based RM, the existing service providers are responding to the customer's needs, the customer avoids the potential anxieties and costs associated with switching.

- Market-based RM can be part of a customer's social support system.

By encouraging and supporting 'regulars', service providers are providing the physical space for customer social interactions (as shown in the section on customer-to-customer interactions in Chapter 4). The obvious examples are pubs, bistros and coffee shops, but other service settings, such as hairdressers, launderettes, betting shops, adult learning centres, retail outlets and leisure clubs, become the meeting places for social groups.

For the service organisation

- Market-based RM can result in customers spending more.

Reichheld and Sasser[22] showed that customers, across a variety of services, spend more each year they are with an organisation. For example, if the car mechanic or dealership retains customers, the customers may pay more each year for regular 'car services' as they upgrade their cars. Similarly, wine club members will pay more as their tastes for fine wines develop. They calculated that a 5 per cent increase in customer loyalty can produce profit increases from 25 to 85 per cent.

- Market-based RM can result in lower marketing costs.

Recruiting new clients or customers is costly. For example, many leisure clubs permanently employ a person whose sole task is to recruit new members, while, according to the UK Advertising Association, businesses in the holiday travel and transport industries spend over £250 million per year on advertising to solicit new customers. In contrast, it is widely believed that the cost of retaining customers can be as little as one-sixth of that of recruiting new customers.

- Market-based RM can result in free positive word-of-mouth recommendation.

Services, because of their intangible nature, rely a lot on word-of-mouth (WOM) to reassure potential customers to make a purchase. For example, specialist holiday companies build strong relationships with segments of their customers, such as retired people, or families with very young children, knowing that recommendations from their existing customers, through positive WOM, will be perceived as credible by others from within those segments.

WOM/W-O-M
Word-of-mouth.

• Market-based RM can increase *employee* retention.

It is believed that employees feel happier in long-term relationships with customers. Face-to-face service encounters which occur on a regular basis with loyal customers, such as those experienced by hairdressers, aerobics teachers, pre-school playgroups and residential care assistants, often result in enjoyable conversation and repartee between the employees and the customers. This, in turn, can make the employee's job more enjoyable or rewarding, or, at the very least, reduce potential boredom, resulting in a reduction of employee turnover costs.

Disadvantages of market-based relationship marketing

For the customer

Some customers find that market-based RM can actually be a relationship hindrance[23] because:

• Market-based RM can be irritating.

Not every customer wants a 'relationship' with representatives of each and every service provider. If customers feel that they are being forced into such a relationship, the organisation's market-based RM moves may be counterproductive. The customer's irritation with an overly friendly service employee can be increased if the friendliness is perceived as being false and an act.

• Market-based RM can be intrusive.

Organisations will understandably wish to use their customer databases to target loyal customers with offers designed to meet their needs. Careless use of market-based RM and customer databases, however, can result in customer feelings of intrusion. RM can raise privacy issues and may bring accusations of exploitation when the relationship is one-sided in favour of the organisation.

• Market-based RM can be time-consuming.

Customers are often faced with relationship initiation processes that require time and patience on their part. Signing up for a store or loyalty card can involve tedious form-filling, and a certain amount of uncertainty and anxiety when completed online. As one non-customer[24] observed, 'I do not have a loyalty card because it saves me time from having to fill out the paperwork and doing all the rigmarole of getting one of those little cards.'

• Market-based RM can be unenticing.

Customers may simply not rate the benefits offered by the organisation very highly. The rewards for loyalty may seem disingenuous to the customer if they are difficult to redeem or do not stack up with the amount of money or time that it took to win or gain them. They may be considered as 'no big deal' and not of sufficient worth to enter into a relationship with an organisation.

Table 9.1   An example of customer relationship segmentation

Segment	Features
• Purely anonymous customers	Do not wish to provide name or personal information or participate in any of the company's individualised services.
• Anonymous customers	Are prepared to use personalised shopping services very occasionally.
• Customers who choose to access and provide information	Are happy to provide lots of personal information in the belief that they will get better deals.
• Customers who seek an individual relationship with the retailer	Cash-rich, time-poor people who are happy to have a personal shopper to advise and get products together for them.

Source: Philippe Lemoine, Galaries Lafayette.[25]

To counter this, some service organisations segment their customers according to the relationship the customers may want with the organisation, and then handle the segments differently. One such segmentation in a retailing context is shown in Table 9.1. There is the recognition, for example, of the segment of customers who wish to remain anonymous. An organisational respect for customer anonymity can pay dividends. For example, Boots, a UK multiple retailer, respects that shoppers want to be anonymous. With their 'Advantage' Loyalty Card Scheme, they do not undertake any personalised analyses of associated databases, partly because the sensitive nature of purchases of health care products. Any abuse of the sensitivities could have deterred shoppers from going to their shops. As a result, sales rose significantly in parallel with the establishment of the loyalty scheme.

At the other end of the scale, there are customers who are willing to pay for relationship services even more personalised than a retailer's personal shopper. Hillary Clinton is just one of a number of individuals who have paid for the services of a 'life coach' – someone 'at the end of the phone who will cajole, push, bully and beg you to lose weight, find a better job, or just get plain organised'.[26]

For the organisation

• Market-based RM can stifle innovation and employee creativity.

Clients may change advertising agencies precisely because the strong relationships are felt to have resulted in a dearth of new ideas, brought about by a similarity of thinking. Employees having regular, and similar, service encounters with loyal customers may feel frustrated by the lack of variety and opportunity to display different talents. This may apply to the hairdresser who sees the same customers for the same cut every six weeks, or to the driving instructor who has a slow-learning client.

• Market-based RM can raise customer expectations.

In Chapter 8, it was argued that customer satisfaction relates to customer disconfirmation of expectations of the service. Because market-based RM aims to make loyal customers feel they are being treated as individuals, or even as 'special', this may raise their expectations, making customer satisfaction progressively more difficult to achieve.

• The benefits of market-based RM 'loyalty schemes' do not always outweigh the costs.

In the United Kingdom, there has been some high-profile strategy changes, especially in the grocery retail sector, regarding the use of loyalty cards. While the leading UK grocery retailer, Tesco, achieved a high penetration of loyalty card holders (over 18 per cent of UK households in 1998), two other grocery retailers, Asda and Safeway, abandoned their loyalty card schemes, with Safeway claiming that there were too many loyalty schemes in the market for them to work any more. There are problems too with the use of the customer databases, with 'data overload' preventing organisations targeting individuals successfully with tailor-made offers.[27] Loyalty schemes will be considered in more detail later in this chapter.

Network-based relationship marketing

The focus on network-based RM is on enhancing networks of internal and external relationships.

Relationships with suppliers

As far as relationships with suppliers are concerned, there is clear evidence that organisations are moving away from a traditionally adversarial relationship to one based on mutual support and cooperation. There is increasing awareness of the benefits to be gained by working together to meet the needs of the final consumer. Waymark Holidays (Case Study 5), for example, recognises that, as nearly all their holidays use scheduled flights, strong relationships with airlines are crucial to success. The company feels that their dealings with airlines are built on 'confidence and trust' which it has taken 20 years to build up.

Postcard from Practice 9.1

Service Failure Loses Customers

As part of a telecommunication company's marketing campaign, it was decided that 'light boxes' would be distributed to 300 prime retailers across New Zealand. The 'light box' in this case consisted of an A2-size poster housed inside a glass-fronted box that was to be mounted in each retailer's window. A small bulb at the back of the light box illuminated the poster.

The aim of the light box was to advertise the company's product to the passing members of the public thus increasing the sales for the retailer and the company. The whole of the light box budget was spent on the design and printing of the poster, the purchase of the light boxes and the distribution and erection of the boxes in the retailers across New Zealand.

Soon after the distribution, problems arose such as malfunctioning light boxes, retailers requesting removal of the light boxes for various reasons and some retailers wanting payment for advertising the product.

The implications and cost of the ongoing maintenance and support had not been factored into the project and consequently the growing number of retailers' requests and complaints were ignored. This led to customer dissatisfaction amongst some of the company's best customers in an industry where competition was fierce. Some of the frustrated retailers transferred their business to the competition.

Source: Julie Nolan.

Many retail organisations in the United Kingdom are making a deliberate effort to reduce the number of suppliers that they deal with in order to develop stronger, more mutually beneficial relationships with the remaining few. By employing 'category management' and 'efficient consumer response' systems, both the retailers and their suppliers can develop a customer focus. The supermarket retailer can work with a limited number of suppliers to provide the 'Saturday night in' experience for its customers by selling popcorn, drinks, chocolates, and a 'take-away meal for two' to go with a film video. The retail buyer recognises the fact that suppliers are very much a part of the final product, and that working together with suppliers can increase the benefits to both parties. Benefits in this context have been found to include shorter delivery lead times, lower stock levels, fewer quality problems and faster implementation of design changes.

Relationships with recruitment markets

Network-based RM also involves having a closer relationship with those who supply human resources to the organisation; that is, recruitment markets. We have already highlighted, in Chapter 7, the important role played by employees in generating customer loyalty. Service organisations need to cultivate long-term relationships with the suppliers of such employees to ensure that they receive both the right quantity and quality of employees.

Some companies, for example, work closely with university departments who have sizeable numbers of undergraduates and postgraduates in business and management-related courses. The companies may provide student placement opportunities for the undergraduates, guest speakers on the course units, and real-world student projects, with an aim to assess potentially suitable service-oriented employees. Such initiatives provide mutual benefits for the relationship partners.

Relationships with internal markets

Internal marketing is highlighted as being a crucial element in network-based RM approach. Employees need to feel that they have formed a long-term relationship with the service provider and have a shared understanding of the mission of the organisation. Human resource strategies need to focus on internal markets and specifically on employee retention.

It is important, however, that such strategies are fully thought through. For instance, some companies provide support for their managers to obtain higher qualifications, such as the MBA, as a means of showing their commitment to the manager's future, and to generate a reciprocal commitment from the manager to stay longer with the company. This is in the belief that 'the longer employees stay with the company, the more familiar they become with the business, the more they learn, and the more valuable they can be'.[28] However, managers attaining new skills and knowledge through their qualification course can become frustrated (and leave the organisation) if company structures do not allow them to implement the skills and knowledge.

Relationships with referral markets

Relationships need to be developed with referral markets. Specific strategies need to be devised to reward the referral sources that generate the most business. Although, traditionally, satisfied customers are the key referral source for service organisations, other sources might include suppliers, other agencies dealing with the company, for instance, banks, and in some cases even competitors. The wedding photographer can have mutually beneficial referral relationships with the suit hire shop, the wedding-dress shop and the specialist cake maker, or the accountant may recommend that a customer should approach another firm for expert advice on insolvency if they cannot provide this element of the service in house.

Relationships with influence markets

Influence markets can also affect the strength of the relationship the organisation has with its customers. Here, Christopher *et al.*[29] refer to legislatory bodies, political groups, and trade and consumer associations. Professional organisations such as accountants, holiday tour operators and funeral services all feel that it is important to develop and maintain strong links with the relevant trade associations. This not only enables them to keep up to date with developments in the industry, but also gives a signal to their customers that they are serious about the relationship they have developed with them. Organisations benefit from building up relationships with their local newspapers. A running club, for example, can gain extensive editorial coverage showing the achievements of their members, which, in turn, can ensure a regular set of enquiries from potential new members.

Customer Loyalty

We outlined the reasons why customer loyalty is important for the long-term sustainability of service organisations in the introduction of this chapter. Here we explain how loyalty has been defined and present two strategies for maintaining customer loyalty.

What is it?

Since the early 1990s, there has been a debate about whether loyalty is a behaviour or an attitude or both.

- Behavioural loyalty is related to a customer's purchase behaviour; for example, measured by proportion of purchase, probability of product repurchase, purchase frequency, repeat purchase behaviour or monetary value.
- Attitudinal loyalty is a psychological tendency, expressed by evaluating an entity with some degree of favour or disfavour. It captures both cognitive and affective aspects.

Most academics agree that neither behavioural nor attitudinal measures *on their own* are sufficient to explain or define customer loyalty. A customer who frequently purchases Chinese 'takeaway' meals from a particular establishment (labelled as behaviourally loyal) may easily defect to a new Chinese restaurant in the area that offers a wider range of products, larger portions, cheaper prices or a delivery service. In contrast, a customer who is favourably disposed to Thai cuisine (labelled as attitudinally loyal) may purchase Chinese takeaway meals simply because of lack of accessibility to Thai alternatives.

Dick and Basu[30] offer a helpful framework that considers behavioural and attitudinal loyalty together. They look at patronage behaviour and relative attitude towards, or preference for, an organisation, and consider the following four cases:

1. *No Loyalty* – patronage behaviour *low* and relative attitude *low*.

    Commonly quoted examples of organisations that are in this position, and that do not command either behavioural or attitudinal loyalty from customers, are petrol/gas stations. Of course, such organisations may use promotional offers or loyalty cards to encourage patronage behaviour, but it is difficult for them to differentiate themselves from other organisations because the product or service offering is perceived as a commodity. It is difficult to build customer preferences in such circumstances.

2. *Spurious Loyalty* – patronage behaviour *high* and relative attitude *low*.

   Spurious loyalty normally occurs when customers are fairly indifferent to the products/services offered by players in the marketplace, and so are swayed (often temporarily) to frequent a particular organisation because of price promotions or special offers. This often happens with supermarket shopping in the United Kingdom, where many residents can choose between four or five superstores within a 3–4 mile drive, and will vary their main food shopping destination.

3. *Latent Loyalty* – patronage behaviour *low* and relative attitude *high*.

   Customers can develop preferences for a product, service or organisation, but find it hard or impossible to purchase it. For example, customers wishing to fly from Manchester (UK) to Shanghai (Peoples Republic of China) will only be offered a limited number of airlines (Emirates, Finnair, KLM, Virgin, Air France, Lufthansa, British Airways), some of which involve two or more changes. Such customers may not be able to fly with their favourite airline (say Singapore Airlines or Cathy Pacific).

4. *Sustainable Loyalty* – patronage behaviour *high* and relative attitude *high*.

   This is, of course, what service organisations are aiming for, and is sometimes referred to as 'true loyalty'. Organisations in this position are encouraged to reinforce attitude and behaviour, by developing appropriate strategies. Aspects of such strategies are now considered.

Strategies for Maintaining Customer Loyalty

Postcard from Practice 9.2

Understand What Drives Customer Loyalty in Your Business

It is important to understand that some customers deliver more profit to an organisation than others, so service needs to be targeted. This is not an excuse to lower standards to some customers but rather an incentive to up service standards to the more profitable areas of business. This requires two things to be understood. First, you must understand your business well enough to be able to identify the product lines and areas of business which are the most profitable. Secondly, you must understand what motivates your customers to remain loyal – is it the quality of the product or service, the standards of the service you provide or something else? Ask them and keep asking. If you wish your business to grow, you can then target profitable business from a satisfied loyal base.

Source: Richard Handley.

Practitioners have sought strategies for maintaining and enhancing sustainable customer loyalty. Two of the more popular ones relate to effective service recovery and loyalty schemes.

Effective service recovery

Research on the nature and characteristics of customer complaints in service organisations has revealed that those consumers who bother to complain about the service that they receive tend to be the loyal users. Although these 'complainers' may represent only a small percentage of dissatisfied customers, the service provider is usually able to identify them and, more importantly, take some action to maintain their loyalty. As we have noted already, RM is all about retaining loyal customers, not just attracting new ones. A number of researchers have offered advice to service organisations setting up service recovery strategies. Some have suggested that, as breakdowns usually occur as a result of inbuilt faults in the delivery system, organisations need to focus on service design to reduce complaints.[31] Zemke and Bell[32] highlighted the fact that different customers will have different views about how they want their problems to be dealt with, that is, different recovery expectations. The way to respond, in this case, is to design a recovery strategy that will meet the needs and expectations of each customer. Empowered employees are the best vehicle to carry out these recovery processes as they can respond flexibly as, and when, a problem arises. The study of service encounters carried out by Bitner *et al.*[33] and referred to in Chapter 4, highlighted the positive impact that employee verbal responses to service failures could have on customer perceptions of the service. They noted that 'even service delivery system failures can be remembered as highly satisfactory if handled properly'. In their study, for example, when an employee compensated a customer for a long wait in a restaurant with a free drink, or upgraded a guest's room because the original booking was not available, customers registered the incident as very satisfying even though the problem was caused by a system failure in the first instance.

A more recent study by Johnston,[34] based on an analysis of 224 anecdotes from customers in a wide range of service organisations, looked specifically at the issue of service recovery. One of the objectives of the study was to identify more clearly what constituted service failure in the minds of the consumers. The findings drew attention to some interesting concerns for service management. The situations that customers described as failures all related to something that had gone wrong during the service experience. Although the responsibility for many of the problems could be traced back to the service provider (e.g., a doctor's surgery which was running late), at least 25 per cent of failure incidents were caused by customer mistakes. This clearly presents certain managerial problems for the service provider attempting to set in place a planned service recovery strategy. Although it may be possible to identify the sorts of failure situations that might occur for one's own service, and therefore design appropriate procedures, it would be impossible to identify all the problems that the customers might themselves cause. Johnston suggests that 'the response to such a wide range of situations may lead organisations away from more prescriptive procedures to a greater reliance on the training and empowerment of individual contact staff'.

The impact that empowered employees, with finely tuned interpersonal skills, can have on the service recovery process was highlighted in the study. Johnston found that those employees who listened attentively to the customer's problem, and showed concern and sympathy for the situation, could go a long way towards placating a disgruntled customer. However, the response was most effective when the employee had the power to react flexibly to every different situation, perhaps doing something extra or totally unexpected for the customer to make amends. Research in this area emphasises yet again the crucial role played by employees in the service organisation.

In general, research suggests that effective service recovery strategies must include

- an understanding of how customers want the service organisation to handle complaints
- priority given to improving customers' waiting experience (see chapter 2)

Exhibit 9.1   Service Recovery: The Aurora Experience

Over 1700 passengers paid between £9800 and £42 000 for a 103-day cruise on P&O's cruise-ship Aurora, taking in 23 countries. The ship was due to set sail on 9 January 2005 from Southampton, England. Due to engine problems, the departure date was delayed and the Aurora left Southampton on 11 January. It developed further engine problems immediately, and returned to port for further repairs. At this point, the Aurora's problems attracted media attention, with a short trip around the Isle of Wight being linked to the prices the passengers had paid. Headlines of the form 'Jinxed cruise ship Aurora still stuck in the Solent' (*The Times*, January 12, 2005) indicated the media's stakeholding in the emerging crisis. P&O offered passengers free drinks with meals and at all 12 of the bars, and their money back if they wanted to call of their holiday. At this point 385 passengers left the Aurora.

It was not until 19 January that Aurora attempted again to set sail. Again, problems with the propulsion system caused it to 'limp back' to Southampton. So, finally, on 20 January, 11 days after the original sailing date, the cruise was cancelled and the passengers disembarked. By this time, the story was a main feature on UK terrestrial and satellite news programmes, and the cameras were on the disembarking passengers. The BBC 24-hour news programme on 21 January, for example, showed interviews of Aurora passengers who were wheeling their (many) suitcases on to the dock at Southampton. 'Surprisingly', according to the news report, 'many passengers had enjoyed their short trip', and this was supplemented with interviews that were, in the main, supportive of what the company had done in the difficult circumstances.

P&O issued the following statement on 20 January 2005:

'Passengers will be refunded their full fare with compensation of 25 per cent of the amount paid for their holiday to be used as a future credit on a cruise holiday booked before the end of January 2007' (Prynn 2005).

They had also provided free drinks/meals for the passengers, and brought in some well-known entertainers, over the 11-day period. Overall, the cancellation of the cruise cost P&O over £20 million.

Some passenger views of their experience were captured by the media

> *We have been wined and dined for free and spent 12 days on a marvellous ship. Obviously we are all disappointed, but I think the vast majority (of passengers) have been stoical and reasonable.*
>
> (Passenger James Hanley)

> *Ten days holiday in a '5-star hotel', all free – you can't ask (P&O) for anything more can you?*
>
> (Passenger interviewed on BBC News, 21 January 2005)

At the first return to port on 11 January, a spokesperson for P&O maintained that passengers had been kept fully informed and that drinks were 'being offered at dinner and at the bar free of charge'. Later, when the decision was finally made to cancel the cruise, the company issued a full apology: 'P&O Cruises apologises for the disappointment this has caused passengers and offers its assurance that everything possible was done to get Aurora's Grand Voyage under way before this difficult but unavoidable decision was taken'. The free drinks, once introduced, became an expectation of behalf of the passengers for the whole of the period of engine repair. Reputedly, 1600 bottles of beer, 1800 bottles of wine and champagne, 146 bottles of spirits and 1300 cocktails were consumed, all free, by passengers in the last 24 hours before the cruise was finally cancelled (*Daily Telegraph*, 22 January 2005). In justifying the generosity, P&Os Managing Director, David Dingle, emphasised the people on board were 'among our most regular and loyal passengers'. Explanations of the delays were regularly given to passengers, but sometimes with mixed effect:

> *If the captain came on the tannoy, you knew it would be good news, but if it was the managing director, you got that sinking feeling.*
>
> (Passenger Norma Fretwell)

An understanding of customers' evaluations of complaint handling

When evaluating a company's attempts at service recovery or complaint handling, it is felt that customers may weigh up their own inputs (e.g., time, money, emotion and energy) against the outputs associated with the recovery tactic (e.g., apology, cash compensation and replacement), and then make a judgement as to whether the recovery tactic was fair or just. Customers are looking for *justice*. Perceived justice may take three forms:[35]

1. *Distributive justice*: relates to the *outcomes* of the service recovery efforts. A problem here is that companies may assume they know what customers regard as a fair and just outcome without finding out from customers themselves. This may even lead to companies overestimating the rewards customers would accept as fair to compensate for a service failure. For example, a pizza company offered delivery within 30 minutes or a free pizza, but changed the policy to delivery within 30 minutes or $3 off the pizza, because customers regarded the former as too generous!

2. *Procedural justice*: relates to the *processes or procedures* that take place to achieve the outcome. Very often customers will engage in very negative word-of-mouth about a service organisation if they perceive that they have been treated poorly during the recovery process – if they feel that they have been passed from one service employee to another, or have not had their telephone call returned, or never been given the opportunity to speak to a particular employee.

3. *Interactional justice*: deals with 'interpersonal behaviour in the enactment of procedures and the delivery of outcomes'.[36] This relates to the *people* element of the services marketing mix. How did the customer judge the people who handled the complaint? Customers who perceive that the employees did not seem to care, nor understand the importance to them of the service failure, will be judging interactional justice in a negative way.

The extent to which the three types of perceived justice are likely to affect customers' evaluations of the effectiveness of the service recovery may depend on the factors such as the duration of the encounter, the degree of customisation or the extent of the switching costs.[37]

Offering perceived justice in service recovery methods is based on the assumption that a customer has a genuine cause for dissatisfaction regarding a service failure on the part of a service company and that the customer complaint is legitimate. However, some recent research has identified the prevalence of illegitimate complainants who seek distributive justice (e.g., compensation) from service organisations even though the organisations are not at fault in the first place. Human nature being what it is, it is of no great surprise that customers seek to fraudulently extract money from organisations, precisely because they are aware of organisations' attempts to use service recovery strategies in order to retain valued customers. Research by Reynolds and Harris[38] shows that illegitimate complaints are often perfectly rational and normalised acts for many people, although morally questionable. Are we all guilty of such acts at some time in our lives? Have we not, at some time, blamed a company for our own errors? It would seem that any service recovery strategy must include plans for dealing with illegitimate customer complainants ranging from the 'one-off complainant' to the 'professional complainants'.[39]

📖 It's in the News! 9.2

Service Failure

According to the UK's *Daily Express* (2 February 2008),

A regular customer was dragged out of a DIY superstore in handcuffs after staff accused him of stealing his own sink plug. Thomas Radcliffe, 72, had gone to his usual B&Q store to replace a worn chrome plug, and took the old one with him to ensure he got the right size. Once there, he found the store did not even stock the right ones – but that didn't stop heavy-handed staff accusing him of theft.

The great-grandfather was prevented from leaving the superstore and frog-marched by two security guards into the office. Police were called to arrest him, and he was paraded back through the aisles in handcuffs and put into a patrol car. His neighbours happened to be shopping there at the time – and witnessed the whole embarrassing episode.

At the police station Mr Radcliffe was searched, fingerprinted, DNA-tested and interviewed under caution. And only then did staff at B&Q telephone officers to confess: 'We don't even sell that kind of plug.'

Yesterday Mr Radcliffe – a do-it-yourself enthusiast who used to be a frequent customer at the store – was still waiting for an apology from the company a week after his public humiliation. 'I will never set foot in one of their stores again,' said the retired aviation inspector. 'They treated me as if I was a murderer and I have never felt so ashamed in my life.' I was handcuffed and marched through B&Q in front of all the customers.

I even saw some of my neighbours and they looked shocked, obviously wondering what on earth I had done. Everyone is going to think I am some kind of criminal.

Mr Radcliffe, in a subsequent BBC radio interview, said that B&Q had sent him an apology, a bunch of flowers and £100 of vouchers to spend in the store. He was incensed by this response which he felt was just adding insult to injury.

E-service failures and recovery

Much of the discussion above, on service recovery, is based on service encounters that are 'face-to-face'. Would service recovery strategies differ if the service

Table 9.2   Retail and e-tail failures

Failure type	Retail (%)	E-tail (%)
Policy failure	14.1	–
Slow/unavailable service	4.1	15.9
System pricing	1.8	6.1
Packaging errors	3.2	43.0
Out of stock	2.4	2.9
Product defect	33.3	12.2
Hold disaster	2.3	–
Bad information	5.1	5.3
Alterations & repairs	4.2	–
Web site system failure	–	4.5
Special order/request	6.5	3.2
Customer error	1.5	3.2
Size variation	–	3.7
Mischarged	13.5	–
Accused of shoplifting	0.8	–
Embarrassments	4.4	–
Attention failures	2.9	–

Source: Forbes, L. P., Kelley, S. W. and Hoffman, K. D., 'Typologies of E-Commerce Retail Failures and Recovery Strategies', *Journal of Services Marketing*, 19(5), 2005, pp. 280–92.

is predominantly electronic? Research on e-commerce retail service failures and recoveries suggests that modified strategies may need to be devised, as customers tend to experience different types of failure as compared with traditional retail outlets.[40] Table 9.2 compares retail and e-tail failures based on an analysis of critical incidents presented by 377 customers. Whereas product defects constitute about one-third of retail failures, they only make up about one-eighths of e-tail failures. The major cause of e-tail failures is packaging errors.

Therefore, whereas current retail service recovery efforts mainly concern distributive justice actions, such as replacements and refunds, current e-tail service recovery efforts emphasise corrections, and a concentration on procedural justice and improved processes.

Loyalty schemes

It was mentioned earlier that planned loyalty schemes (e.g., those which reward purchases) have encountered mixed success. For every Tesco 'Clubcard' and Boots 'Advantage' Card scheme that is acknowledged to be successful,[41] there are others that have been discontinued. Kumar and Shah[42] attribute these mixed fortunes to the concentration by many loyalty schemes on behavioural loyalty only. Points accrual on loyalty cards, frequent-flyer air-miles and free coffees for every ten stamps on a card are all schemes that encourage customers to return, but do not necessarily influence relative attitude to the service organisation, and therefore engender sustainable loyalty.

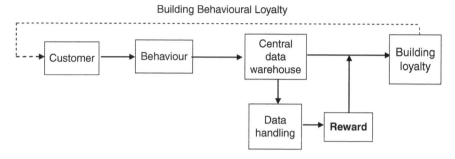

Figure 9.1   Building Behavioural Loyalty across All Customers
Source: Adapted from Kumar and Shah.[42]

Loyalty schemes, that involve the issue of loyalty cards, or the equivalent, to customers, provide the means for an organisation to capture transaction data, and ensure that all (including new) customers are aware of the rewards programme. It provides a valuable customer database (see Figure 9.1). Such a structure can provide a means for determining rewards for behavioural loyalty, based largely on what a customer has spent, and what he/she has spent it on. Rewards often take the form of money off future purchases and/or purchase vouchers for certain products that are deemed as attractive to the customer, based on past purchase behaviour. Such schemes do not make any distinction between customers, and the rewards are on an aggregate level, irrespective of customers' attitudes. Furthermore, they tend to reward past and current behaviour (rather than considering future customer lifetime values), are easily copied, and reward spending not profitability.[43] Examples of the latter are the air mile schemes that are based on the number of miles flown, irrespective of whether the flights were on the more profitable routes.

There are different views as to whether service organisations should develop loyalty schemes and programmes that go beyond the process outlined in Figure 9.1. Jang and Mattila,[44] in the context of restaurant loyalty programmes, provide empirical research that indicates that restaurant customers prefer imme-diate, necessary and monetary rewards, in contrast to points-system rewards or luxury/non-monetary rewards.

Kumar and Shah,[45] however, contend that a reward system based on Figure 9.1 should be complemented by further rewards that treat customers at an indi-vidual, as opposed to an aggregate level, if sustainable customer loyalty is to be achieved. This may be achieved through a process of customer selection, where data from the central data warehouse, and other sources such as attitude surveys, and customer profile information, is analysed with the intention of identifying those customers whose attitudinal loyalty needs cultivating and/or whose behavioural loyalty needs augmenting. Once identified, such customers can be offered individual rewards that fit their circumstances. For example, Amer-ican Express offer rewards such as 24-hour trip advisers, exclusive shopping and complimentary stays at five-star hotels to selected valued customers.[46] Key features of such rewards are that they are differentiated and relevant to the customer, not divulged in advance to customers (and therefore difficult for competitors to copy), and are only offered to customers whose lifetime values (future loyalty) justifies a positive return on investment. There is an intuitive appeal to such attempts to build sustainable customer loyalty through two tiers of rewards. However, at the moment, practical examples of the adoption of these ideas are relatively hard to find.

Summary

The interest in RM, especially in relation to service businesses, has been on the increase throughout the 1990s and the early part of the twenty-first century. There are many definitions of RM, but also a consensus on the two strands – market-based RM and network-based RM. The initial enthusiasm for RM has been tempered by the recognition that there are both positive and negative consequences for customers and organisations. Customer retention and loyalty are central to RM, and sustainable customer loyalty is generally believed to consist of a combination of high levels of repeat patronage, coupled with a preference for that service provider. Strategies for maintaining customer loyalty include effective service recovery systems and customer loyalty schemes.

Learning Outcomes

Having read this chapter, you should be able to

- define RM from academic and organisational perspectives
- outline and evaluate the features of an RM approach
- understand the focus of market-based RM, and appreciate its potential advantages and disadvantages for both customers and the service organisation
- summarise the internal and the external relationships that make up network-based RM, and apply these ideas to specific service companies
- compare and contrast behavioural and attitudinal loyalty
- discuss and evaluate the customer loyalty strategies associated with service recovery and loyalty schemes.

Discussion Questions and Exercises

1. Are the definitions of RM by academics and practitioner markedly different?
2. What is the difference between market-based RM and network-based RM?
3. Outline the main strategies that service companies can employ in order to maintain sustainable customer loyalty.
4. What do you understand by the terms 'distributive justice', 'procedural justice' and 'interactional justice'?
5. With which service organisations do you feel that you have a relationship? Why is it the case?

Notes and References

1. Zineldin, M., 'Beyond Relationship Marketing: Technologicalship Marketing', *Marketing Intelligence and Planning*,18(2), 2000, pp. 9–23.
2. Fornell, C. and Wenerfelt, B., 'Defensive Marketing Strategy by Consumer Complaint Management: A Theoretical Analysis', *Journal of Marketing Research*, vol. 24, 1987, pp. 337–46.
3. Sheth, J. N. and Kellstadt, C. H., 'Relationship Marketing: An Emerging School of Marketing Thought', Paper presented at the American Marketing Association, 13th Faculty Consortium in Services Marketing, Arizona, USA, 1993.
4. Gronroos, C., 'From Marketing Mix to Relationship Marketing: Towards a Paradigm Shift in Marketing', *Management Decision*, 32(2), 1994, pp. 4–20.
5. Ibid.
6. Christopher, M., Payne, A. and Ballantyne, D., *Relationship Marketing: Bringing Quality, Customer Service and Marketing Together*, Butterworth Heinemann, Oxford, 1991.
7. Ibid.
8. Reichheld, F. F. and Sasser Jr, W. E., 'Zero Defections: Quality Comes to Services', *Harvard Business Review*, September–October 1990, pp. 105–11.
9. Reichheld, F. F., 'Loyalty-Based Management', *Harvard Business Review*, March–April 1993, pp. 64–73.
10. Christopher, Payne and Ballantyne, *Relationship Marketing*.
11. Ibid.
12. Crosby, L. A. and Stephens, N., 'Effects of Relationship Marketing on Satisfactory Retention and Prices in the Life Insurance Industry', *Journal of Marketing Research*, vol. 24, November 1987, pp. 404–11.
13. Morgan, R. M. and Hunt, S. D., 'The Commitment-Trust Theory of Relationship Marketing', *Journal of Marketing*, vol. 58, 1994, pp. 20–38.
14. Beaton, M. and Beaton, C., 'Marrying Service Providers and Their Clients: A Relationship Approach to Service Management', *Journal of Marketing Management*, vol. 11, 1995, pp. 55–70.
15. Crosby and Stephens, 'Effects of Relationship Marketing'.
16. Brodie, J., Coviello, N., Brookes, R. and Little, V., 'Towards a paradigm shift in marketing? An examination of current marketing practices', *Journal of Marketing Management*, vol. 13, 1997, pp. 383–406.
17. Pressey, A. D. and Mathews, B. P., 'Barriers to Relationship Marketing in Consumer Retailing', *Journal of Services Marketing*, 14(3), 2000, pp. 272–85.
18. Special issue of *Financial Times* on 'Understanding CRM', Spring 2000, www.ft.com/crm.
19. Moller, K. and Halinen, A., 'Consumer versus Interorganisational Relationship Marketing: A Metatheoretical Analysis', in J. Sheth and A. Menon (eds), *New Frontiers in Relationship Marketing Theory and Practice*, Emory University, Atlanta, GA, 1998.
20. Bendapudi, N. and Berry, L. L., 'Customers' Motivations for Maintaining Relationships with Service Providers', *Journal of Retailing*, 73(1), 1997, pp. 15–37.
21. Follain, J., 'Swiss Women Book into Man-Free Hotel', *Sunday Times*, London, 18 February 2001.
22. Reichheld and Sasser Jr, 'Zero Defections'.
23. Noble, S. M. and Phillips, J., 'Relationship Hindrance: Why would Consumers not want a Relationship with a Retailer?' *Journal of Retailing*, 80(4), 2004, pp. 289–303.
24. Ibid.
25. Special issue of *Financial Times* on 'Understanding CRM', Spring 2000, p. 8, www.ft.com/crm.
26. Taylor, H. K., 'Call the Doctor', *Sunday Times Magazine*, London, 3 December 2000.
27. O'Malley, L. and Tynan, C., 'Relationship Marketing in Consumer Markets – Rhetoric or Reality?', *European Journal of Marketing*, 34(7), 2000, pp. 797–815.
28. Reichheld and Sasser Jr, 'Zero Defections'.
29. Christopher, Payne and Ballantyne, *Relationship Marketing*.

30. Dick, A. S. and Basu, K., 'Customer Loyalty: Toward an Integrated Conceptual Framework', *Journal of The Academy of Marketing Science*, 22(2), 1994, pp. 99–113.
31. Schlesinger, L. A. and Heskett, J. L., 'The Service Driven Service Company', *Harvard Business Review*, September–October 1991, pp. 71–81.
32. Zemke, R. and Bell, C. R., *Service Wisdom: Creating and Maintaining the Customer Service Edge*, Lakewood Books, Minneapolis, 1989.
33. Bitner, M. J., Booms, B. H. and Tetreault, M. S., 'The Service Encounter: Diagnosing Favourable and Unfavourable Incidents', *Journal of Marketing*, vol. 54, 1990, pp. 71–84.
34. Johnston, R., 'Service Recovery: An Empirical Study', Proceedings of the 3rd International Research Seminar in Service Management, La-Londe-les-Maures, France, May 1994.
35. Hoffman, K. D. and Kelley, S. W., 'Perceived Justice Needs and Recovery Evaluation: A Contingency Approach', *European Journal of Marketing*, 34(3–4), 2000, pp. 418–32.
36. Tax, S. S., Brown, S. W. and Chandrashekaran, M., 'Customer Evaluations of Service Complaint Experiences: Implications for Relationship Marketing', *Journal of Marketing*, vol. 62, April 1998, pp. 60–76.
37. Johnston, 'Service Recovery'.
38. Reynolds, K. L. and Harris, L. C., 'When Service Failure is not Service Failure: An Exploration of the Forms and Motives of "Illegitimate" Customer Complaining', *Journal of Services Marketing*, 19(5), 2005, pp. 321–35.
39. Ibid.
40. Forbes, L. P., Kelley, S. W. and Hoffman, K. D., 'Typologies of E-Commerce Retail Failures and Recovery Strategies', *Journal of Services Marketing*, 19(5), 2005, pp. 280–92.
41. Rowley, J., 'Building Brand Webs: Customer Relationship Management through the Tesco Clubcard Loyalty Scheme', *International Journal of Retail and Distribution Management*, 33(3), 2006, pp. 194–206.
42. Kumar, V. and Shah, D., 'Building and Sustaining *Profitable* Customer Loyalty for the 21st Century', *Journal of Retailing*, vol. 80, 2004, pp. 317–30.
43. Ibid.
44. Jang, D. and Mattila, A. S., 'An Examination of Restaurant Loyalty Programs: What Kinds of Rewards do Customers Prefer?', *International Journal of Contemporary Hospitality Management*, 17(5), 2006, pp. 402–8.
45. Kumar and Shah, 'Building and Sustaining'.
46. Ibid.

Service Profitability

Learning Objectives

Overall Aim of the Chapter

To summarise academic and practitioner research on the drivers of service profitability.

In particular, the *chapter objectives* are

- to highlight the relationships between service profitability and services marketing variables – quality, satisfaction, loyalty, productivity

- to explore macro-level links between service quality and service profitability

- to explore the trade-offs between productivity and quality in relation to service profitability

- to explore the usefulness of categorising customers according to their profitability

- to comprehend the models linking customer (and employee) loyalty to profitability

- to appreciate the statistical approaches to service profitability measurement and their applications to customer satisfaction indices.

Introduction

In an International Research Seminar in Service Management in the mid-1990s,[1] discussion at the final session focused on the relative lack of work on profitability of services. It was pointed out that only 6 of the 37 papers presented at the seminar made any reference at all to profitability and that the seminar was, in this respect, representative of research activity in Services Marketing and Management at the time. However, it was also recognised that the subject of profitability of services was becoming increasingly important, in the light of reports of companies, described by some commentators as 'excellent', experiencing severe financial difficulties.

Managers of service and other organisations were beginning to ask more questions, and seek further understanding, of the relationships between profitability and variables such as service quality, customer satisfaction, customer loyalty and productivity. Questions were being asked such as:

- Are there economic benefits to improving customer satisfaction?[2]
- What is the impact of quality on the bottom line?[3]
- What impact do customer defections have on the bottom line?[4]
- Do productivity improvements cause profits?[5]

In this chapter we will examine, in broad terms, the findings of the groups of researchers and practitioners who have brought service profitability to the fore. The chapter has four sections. We start with a look at the work that has taken a macro-level view on the links between quality and business results. This will be followed by a description and discussion of the Q, P and P (Quality, Productivity and Profitability) programme being undertaken by Gummesson and colleagues in Sweden.[6,7] We then further examine the work on the relationship between customer loyalty, employee loyalty and profitability, and the related 'Service–Profit Chain', and review some of the recent work that tests the propositions regarding the links of the chain. Finally, the results and applications of some of the quantitative studies that explore the relationship between profitability and customer satisfaction, at the company and national level, are presented.

Macro-level Links between Quality and Business Results

Results from the PIMS project database

The PIMS (Profit Impact of Marketing Strategies) project database contains measures of quality, profitability and shareholder values over several years for a large number of organisations in many different US industries and markets. The information is held at the level of the business unit for over 2500 business units.[8] Through careful interrogation of the PIMS database it is possible to examine the relationship between measures of quality and those of profitability (or other financial indicators) over a number of years. This, in turn, makes it possible to derive some quantitative indicators of the effect of quality on various financial performance measures.

The early PIMS findings on the relationship between quality and profitability were used to justify a financial investment in, and concentration on, quality improvement methods for service organisations. For example, Zeithaml et al.[9] reproduce a graph originally constructed by Buzzell and Gale[10] which showed a positive relationship between relative perceived quality and return on investment (ROI). More recent PIMS findings were graphically presented by Gale.[11] In summary, they are

ROI
Return on Investment.

1. *Superior quality leads to higher selling prices.* In particular, 'businesses that have achieved a superior quality position earn prices eight per cent higher than businesses that have been shoved into an inferior quality position'.

2. *Achieving superior quality does not mean higher cost.* In particular, 'businesses with superior quality positions have relative direct costs that are slightly lower than businesses with inferior perceived quality'.

3. *Superior quality drives profitability.* This is a logical result of 1 and 2 but, in particular, 'businesses with superior quality are three times as profitable as those with inferior quality'.

Gale goes on to examine the relationships between quality and other financial measures such as cash flow, shareholder value and market value of businesses. The interested reader is urged to consult the original article.

The results are convincing and intuitively appealing. However, caution needs to be exercised regarding interpretation and applicability because:

• The measurement of quality is extremely difficult.

The PIMS database uses one particular measure, the market perceived quality ratio that relies on identifying appropriate quality attributes for a business and assigning relative weights to these attributes. This is in addition to obtaining reliable customer ratings of these attributes for a business unit, and its competitors. The market-perceived quality ratio is highly sensitive to the weights assigned to the attributes and the sample of customers surveyed. Once the market-perceived quality ratio has been computed, business units are assigned to one of the five categories:

1. inferior quality

2. somewhat worse quality

3. about the same quality

4. somewhat better quality

5. superior quality

for the purpose of further analysis.

• The relationship between quality measures and financial indicators is not necessarily similar for all industries and sectors.

Indeed, Gummesson[12] concludes that there is no general cost–quality relationship, only specific relationships.

• Some of the earlier quality measures in the PIMS database were based on the firm's assessment of what they believe to be their customers' perception of quality, and not on the customers' actual ratings.

- The relationships do not explicitly explore the processes by which quality impacts on profitability.
- The companies in the PIMS database are large organisations and the findings may not apply to the numerous small businesses in the service sector.

Despite these reservations, the PIMS database, and the analysis of the data, will continue to provide useful insights into the relationship between profitability and quality.

Postcard from Practice 10.1

The Cost of Negative Customer-to-customer Interactions

I was in the position recently of having to choose a hotel for a conference for 100–150 delegates, and was provided with promotional information on the medium to large hotels in the area. One of the hotels, according to the brochure and web site, looked perfect: it had meeting and syndicate rooms of just the right size, very modern looking bedrooms and decor after a recent refurbishment, and was offering extremely competitive prices. Before arranging a visit to the hotel, I checked, on the 'Trip Advisor' website, to see what previous guests had said about staying in the hotel.

The first account, headed 'What a hell hole. Avoid at all costs', went on to describe how the hotel was full of young men on a stag night (bachelor party) running around naked in front of children of other guests, and that, at weekends, the hotel bar was full of prostitutes plying their trade. Another of the guest accounts specified that the hotel employees were neither willing nor able to dissuade the prostitutes from entering the hotel bar. These were not the only negative features of the hotel listed in Trip Advisor by the customers. Inconsiderate employees and poor food were also mentioned, but it was the incidents with the stag-night revellers and prostitutes that were expressed in upper-case letters. Based on 45 guest reviews, the mean overall rating was less than 2.5 out of 5.

Needless to say, I did not bother to arrange the visit, and the hotel owners/managers, unknown to them, lost out on potential revenue of £15 000–£20 000.

Source: Steve Baron.

Awards for companies investing in quality

A number of national and international government bodies make awards on an annual basis to companies that invest in quality. Many companies enter the competitions for these awards, which are perceived as prestigious, and winning an award is regarded as very important.

One of the pioneering awards was the Malcolm Baldrige National Quality Award (MBNQA), created by the National Institute of Standards and Technology in the United States in 1987. The MBNQA was set up to encourage leadership by the United States in product and process quality, something that was being challenged at the time by foreign (mainly Japanese) competition. There was a belief that poor quality was costing companies as much as 20 per cent of sales revenue.[13] The national quality award was intended to help improve quality and productivity of American companies by:

1. helping to stimulate American companies to improve quality and productivity for the pride of recognition while obtaining a competitive edge through increased profits;

2. recognising the achievements of those companies that improve the quality of their goods and services and providing an example to others;

3. establishing guidelines and criteria that can be used by business, industrial, governmental, and other organisations in evaluating their own quality improvement efforts;

4. providing specific guidance for other American organisations that wish to learn how to manage for high quality by making available detailed information on how winning organisations were able to challenge their cultures and achieve eminence.[14]

This was an award for quality of both goods and services. There is a link between investment in quality and company profitability (in Point (1) above), but it is not presented as starkly as in the PIMS literature where superior quality is said to drive profitability.

The examiners for the MBNQA rate the applicants according to seven criteria: leadership, strategic planning, customer and market focus, information and analysis, human resource focus, process management and business results. Los Alamos National Bank, an independent community bank with 167 employees, won the MBNQA for small businesses in 2000. Its quality and business achievements included high percentages of customers who were very satisfied with the service they received, and a high level of customer loyalty (with a third of the customers having five or more banking relationships), very high employee satisfaction results and correspondingly low employee turnover, high productivity levels and a commitment to the community.[15] Most of the criteria have been addressed in earlier chapters. It is interesting that the criterion of social responsibility (and its association with successful service businesses) is now being recognised explicitly.[16]

In Europe, the European Foundation for Quality Management has been responsible for the European Quality Award (EQA) since 1992.[17] The criteria, based on a business excellence model, are very similar to those used for the MBNQA. Applicants are scored on leadership (10 per cent), people management (9 per cent), policy and strategy (8 per cent), resources (9 per cent), processes (14 per cent), people satisfaction (9 per cent), customer satisfaction (20 per cent), impact on society (6 per cent) and business results (15 per cent). Foxdenton School and Integrated Nursery from Oldham UK, who won a prize in the public sector category in 2000, is a school that caters primarily for children with special educational needs. They attribute their winning formula to 'high expectations to raise achievements in pupils, learning from the people we serve, a premium on staff development, upbeat communications, involvement of all our stakeholders, promoting partnerships, and an emphasis on structuring success and building self esteem for all members of the community' – a mix of 'customer' focus, internal marketing, network relationship marketing and social responsibility.[18] Having a category for the public sector acknowledges that the business excellence model criteria can be applicable to not-for-profit organisations.

But are the private companies that meet the awards criteria those that are more profitable?

There were some doubts, initially, when one of the early MBNQA winners had to file for bankruptcy. However, there have been some recent studies which have compared stock performances of MBNQA award winners with those of the Standard and Poor's (S&P) 500 companies. The returns on the MBNQA stocks consistently out-performed the S&P 500 index, both before and after the award, and more so after the award.[19] Moreover, some of the criteria for the awards, information management, HRM and customer focus, have been found to have a significant effect on customer satisfaction and business results.[20]

Quality, productivity and profitability programme

The Q P and P programme, that examines the interactions between quality, productivity and profitability in service operations, has been advocated by Gummesson and colleagues in Sweden. The programme, which was set up in 1993, regards quality, productivity and profitability as 'triplets' with the implication that 'separating one from the others creates an unhappy family'.[21] Unimpressed by current measures of productivity in particular, the group have sought, through actual company case studies, to better understand the interactions between quality, productivity and profitability before attempting to quantify what is not yet fully understood.

A simple framework (Figure 10.1) shows the basic relationship, in financial terms, between the triplets:

1. concentration, by a service company, on productivity means that the company will look towards an effective use of resources and towards producing more for less.

2. concentration, by the company, on service quality means that it will look towards satisfying customers and, through customer retention and loyalty, increasing revenue.

3. concentration on profitability means that the company will address the combined effect of cost reduction and revenue generation. This should involve an active interest in both productivity and quality.

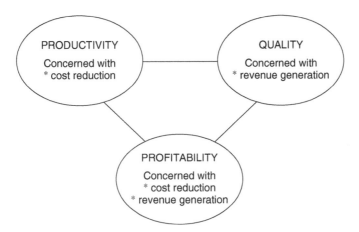

Figure 10.1 Interaction between productivity, quality and profitability

According to the framework, all three elements of the triplets are pulling in the same direction. In practice, even within a single service organisation, the interactions between the elements may be affected by a tribal culture,[22] where the different tribes – the productivity tribe, the quality tribe, and the profitability tribe – have different mindsets and do not necessarily understand one another or work together to a common aim. Expanding on Gummesson's arguments it is suggested that

- The productivity tribe are concerned primarily with issues of definition of productivity and the various mathematical formulae to 'measure' productivity. Their concern is with, for example, the number of patients seen per hour in the surgery, or the average service time per supermarket customer.

- The quality tribe are concerned primarily with customer expectations, perceptions and levels of satisfaction. Their concern is with the quality of the service encounter and with arguments regarding customisation versus standardisation of service.

- The profitability tribe, normally educated in accounting practice, are concerned primarily with the balance sheet and profit and loss statements, and on relatively short-term financial results.

Perhaps these tribal differences are less obvious in the operation of a small service business. In the case study of the dental practice (see companion website), for example, the father and son agreed on a course of action which reflected a quality, rather than productivity, approach. They have tried to ensure, for many of their patients, that time is made available for talk and explanation and a more relaxing appointment, rather than attempt to increase the number of patients per hour. Their concern for productivity is in the service support area, particularly through the use of computer systems.

However, in many larger organisations, the tribes exist and can be identified. The whole issue is further complicated by the fact that many organisations do not conform to the traditional hierarchical structure with clearly defined boundaries. Networks of communications and relationships make organisational boundaries more fluid and add to the problem of understanding the interactions between quality, productivity and profitability.

In effect, research on the Q P and P programme has caused the group to question their original findings that gave qualified support to the notions that

1. productivity improvements lead to increased profits;
2. quality improvements lead to increased productivity;
3. quality improvements lead to increased profits.

The early conclusions were based on what the group now acknowledge as 'deceptively clear' definitions of the three triplets. They argue strongly that a premature move to quantifying relationships between the triplets will fail to address the many tribal and interpersonal contributions to an organisation's operation. This may result in measuring the wrong things, or only looking at variables that are of relevance or importance to members of a particular tribe.

If many companies are regarded as networks, then quality issues are said to affect all members of a network and not just the provider and customer. Relationships in the networks take on an even greater prominence that is not reflected in the assets of a company, nor in company performance. The Q P and P group observes that the accounting tribe do not measure the profitability of *relationships*. The group therefore raises the notion of a *return on relationships*, based on a recognition of the *intellectual* capital of an organisation, as a way of assessing financial outcomes. It poses the question, 'How should we measure the return on relationships and how should we evaluate the contributions to profits from the various actors in a network?'[23]

The financial impact of customer satisfaction versus operational efficiency

Organisations that pursue customer satisfaction without regard to the cost of achieving that goal may end up over spending and misallocating resources.[24] There is currently an academic debate regarding the financial benefits of prioritising customer satisfaction (a revenue emphasis) or operating efficiency (cost emphasis) or both (dual emphasis). The cost emphasis, typically an accounting and operations management perspective, promotes an internal focus on the financial benefits derived from operational efficiencies and improvements that reduce costs. Six sigma, Total Quality Management (TQM) and statistical process control (SPC) are all examples of the cost emphasis. The revenue emphasis promotes the need to satisfy customers on the basis that satisfied customers will increase long-term revenue and profitability. The dual emphasis combines these two approaches arguing that greater financial benefits accrue from reducing costs by becoming more efficient while also increasing revenue by improving customer satisfaction. One study suggests that organisations *trying* to achieve a dual emphasis perform less well financially than those organisations prioritising customer satisfaction.[25] However, another study found that organisations that *achieve* a dual emphasis are likely to enjoy greater long-term profitability than those that favour either customer satisfaction or operating efficiency.[26] The distinction between *trying* and *achieved* may be crucial in that the financial benefits of achievement are long term while the process of achievement may be associated with greater short-term costs to the organisation.

Micro-level Analysis of Customer Profitability

The customer pyramid

The fact is that all customers are not equally profitable for service organisations. Most organisations are aware of the Pareto principle or the '80:20 rule' that a minority of customers are likely to produce a disproportionate amount of value for the organisation. If customers are not equally profitable, should service organisations treat all customers in the same way? Federal Express categorise their customers as good, bad or ugly depending upon their profitability and treat each category differently.[27] Zeithaml, Rust and Lemon[28] propose a four-tier Customer Pyramid categorising customers as Platinum, Gold, Iron or Lead depending upon the amount they spend with the organisation, the cost of servicing them and their potential to spread positive word-of-mouth. They suggest a need to use the pyramid to ensure that an organisation's limited resources are put to best use and, in particular, to ensure that the best customers are not being under-serviced. They further claim that using the Customer Pyramid will enable service organisations to increase profitability by managing lower tier customers into higher tiers, tailoring service delivery to the customer profitability level and by managing the 'lead' out of the organisation. Airlines are a good example of such management. Passengers receive different service levels depending upon the price they pay (first, business or economy class) and the amount of commitment they have demonstrated in the past through frequent flyer schemes.

Customer Pyramid Tool that enables service organisations to identify differences in customer profitability and manage.

Postcard from Practice 10.2

Client Categorisation by a Financial Planning Service

I don't reject clients or turn them away, mainly because they are generally referred to us by other contacts. However, not all of our clients are going to yield the same profit over the long term. It isn't just a matter of absolute profit either. Our smaller clients tend to have less complex financial needs than our larger clients so it helps us to tailor our services to their needs as well as to ensure that we are not spending too much time and effort on clients that don't need it and are only marginally profitable to us. We categorise clients based on their potential to influence and

Postcard from Practice 10.2   (Continued)

refer others through their networks as well as their portfolio size and potential to grow. At the top end we have 'A' clients, moving down to 'D' clients.

Client Category	Client Newsletter	No. of Client Reports	No. of Annual Meetings	Invites to Client Functions
A	Yes	4	4	Several – technical and 1 social
B	Yes	2 or 4	3	1 – social
C	Yes	1 or 2	1 or 2	None
D	Yes	1	1	None

'A' clients tend to have larger, more complex portfolios and tend to have a more sophisticated knowledge of financial matters so we lay on a couple of 'technical' functions a year where they can ask questions about the markets and currency fluctuations etc. A typical 'D' client will not have a lump sum to invest but will be a small saver focused on superannuation. There is unlikely to be an inheritance or any other circumstances that would change their potential financial situation. Consequently there simply isn't the need for the same level of service or contact that we give to 'A' clients. They are very happy with the service they get because it is what they expect from us.

Source: Phil Ashton.

📖 It's in the News! 10.1

Customer Anger at Being 'Categorised'

According to the BBC News (2 February 2008),

Angry customers of internet bank Egg have hit out at its decision to cancel their credit cards. Egg says 161,000 cards belonging to people whose credit profiles have deteriorated since they signed up will stop working in 35 days' time. But people who insist they have good records have been contacting the BBC to say they are on the list.

A spokesman for the bank said those affected were customers it no longer wanted to lend to 'regardless of their current status'. Credit cards are being withdrawn from 7% of Egg's customers who it deems to pose an unacceptably 'high risk'. This could include those who have missed repayments or exceeded their credit limit. Cardholders will be able to continue making minimum monthly repayments on their balances but will not be able to spend any more after the deadline.

The move follows a 'one-off' review after Egg was bought by US-based Citigroup for £575m last year. The 35-day notice period starts on receipt of the letter, which according to the bank also provides details of how to appeal against the decision.

BBC News website readers, however, say that they have been told by Egg call centre staff that an appeal is not possible.

But the move has triggered an angry backlash from some customers who told the BBC they received a letter informing them of the withdrawal, despite having an excellent credit history. Gillian Cox, of Farnham, Surrey, said she was 'absolutely furious' to learn her credit card had been cancelled in what she described as an 'unbelievable arbitrary action' Mrs Cox said she and her husband are 'retired, no mortgage, no debts' and 'always paid the balance off in full each month'. She added that she had contacted credit reference agency Experian who said she was marked as having an excellent credit rating, 'thus totally negating Egg's claim that this measure is about credit risk'.

A spokesman for Egg said: 'We are sorry some customers are upset after receiving notification we are ending their credit card arrangement, but they are people we do not feel it is appropriate to lend any money to.' He added: 'The decision was taken after an extensive one-off review of our credit card book following acquisition by Citigroup.'

'We can certainly understand the concerns, but even if people are up-to-date with repayments, they are people we decided we no longer wish to lend money to regardless of their status.'

Satisfaction, loyalty and profitability

During the 1990s a series of articles in the *Harvard Business Review* drew attention to the issues of customer, and employee, loyalty and their likely effects on a firm's profits. Many of the conclusions are derived from studies of businesses operating primarily within the service sector of the US economy. These same businesses have provided the examples of sales and profit figures per customer which are used in the articles.

Customer defections

In late 1990, Reichheld and Sasser[29] provided results of studies of customer defections over a range of service companies: including auto-services, credit cards, banking, insurance, industrial distribution, office building and software. They concluded that customer defections 'have a surprisingly powerful impact on the bottom line'. The results demonstrated

- how much profit a (loyal) customer generates over time.

For example, a new credit-card customer represents a loss to the credit card company of $51 in the first year, but the typical loyal customer generates a profit of $55 during the fifth year. The profit per customer of an auto-servicing business increases from $25 in year one to $88 in the fifth year.

- that a reduction in customer defections of five per cent can boost profits by 25 per cent to 85 per cent.

Based on net present value calculations of average customers, a 5 per cent reduction in customer defections would, for example, increase profits in the credit card company by 75 per cent and those in the auto-servicing company by 30 per cent.

Some of the reasons given as to why customers can become more profitable over time are:

- a reduction in operating costs per customer.

First-time customers incur a number of one-off costs; for example, checking credit-rating, adding to database. As a service organisation gets to know its customers, service can be dealt with more efficiently. This is illustrated well in the Waymark Holiday case (Case Study 5), where telephone discussions with repeat customers can more easily deal with customer requirements, without first having to establish customer walking or skiing capabilities.

- a 'trading-up' of customers over time.

Customers may wish to 'trade-up' or be willing to pay a price premium for a service they know or trust. A good experience with a financial advisor, for example, may result in customers looking to increase the investment through a person or company that they trust, or a decision to purchase more financial products.

- the free advertising they provide.

Positive word-of-mouth can result in much further business for a service organisation. It is a major factor for all the small businesses in our case studies.

An implication of these findings is that companies should go all out for customer loyalty and devise a defections management policy within a relationship marketing framework (see Chapter 9).

The link between retention of loyal customers and profitability resulted in much attention being paid to the role that service quality and customer satisfaction play in generating customer loyalty. Particular attention has been paid to two models: the satisfaction–profit chain[30] and the service–profit chain.[31] The satisfaction–profit chain (Figure 10.2) focuses entirely on the customer while the service–profit chain seeks to recognise the impact that employees and internal service quality has on external customer satisfaction.

The links in the satisfaction–profit chain are said to be asymmetric and nonlinear.[32] This means that the impact of an increase may not be the same as an equivalent decrease. Data from 125 firms within the Swedish customer Satisfaction Barometer (SCSB), based at the University of Michigan, finds that, on average, a 1 per cent increase in customer satisfaction is associated with a 2.37 per cent increase in ROI, but a 1 per cent decrease in satisfaction leads to a 5.08 per cent drop in ROI. This suggests that, on average, a decrease in customer satisfaction is two times more detrimental to an organisation than the benefit gained from the equivalent increase in satisfaction.[33] A recent study has confirmed the non-linear character of the satisfaction–profit relationships. The relationship between customer satisfaction (CS) and customer loyalty (CL) and the relationship between CL and profitability were both found to be positive. However, both relationships were positive at a declining rate above a certain point. The study also indicates a need for both customer satisfaction to reach a threshold level before it influences customer loyalty and that loyalty also needs to meet a threshold level before it impacts on profitability.[34]

Postcard from Practice 10.3

Evaluating the 'Fight the Monster' Fundraising Campaign

In 2005 the Child Cancer Foundation had a spontaneous awareness of 8% and was the preferred charity of only 6% of New Zealanders. 23 non-profit organisations ran television advertising campaigns with both Oxfam and World Vision maintaining a presence throughout the year. We could afford only 7 days. How could we develop a fundraising campaign that would stand out and convince people that our cause is more deserving of their money than any other charity? First, we arranged for everyone involved in developing the new campaign to visit the Oncology Ward at Starship Hospital (the Auckland hospital for children) so they could experience first hand what children suffering from cancer and their families endure. The 'Fight the Monster' campaign emerged which comprised TV and on-line advertising, an appeal week website, direct marketing, outdoor posters and letterbox drops.

Appreciating the need to recognise the contribution donors make we developed 'Bravery Beads'. They sold for $4 each with over 100,000 beads selling in just a week. These 'supporters beads' enabled our supporters to spread the campaign message, and their association with it, in a highly visual way.

The financial results were impressive. Public donations rose by 18% during 2006 while the above-the-line media costs reduced by 4.5%. The ROI increased to 600% from 466% in 2005. But there was more:

By March 2007 our spontaneous awareness had increased to 27% and the Child Cancer Foundation became THE most preferred children's charity in NZ. Donations from the donor base increased by 25%. The new media channels (on-line advertising and the website) produced a younger donor base. All national offices experienced a 25% increase in donations. Two significant corporate sponsorship relationships were established with Hyundai Automotive NZ and JK Kids Gear (a clothing retailer). Trelise Cooper and Greg Murphy (celebrity designers) both designed special clothing for sale through JK Kids Gear stores. Dean Lonergan Events selected the Child Cancer Foundation as his charity of choice for

Employee loyalty

Schlesinger and Heskett[35] support the attention given to the economics of customer loyalty, but in addition present a critical look at the economics of employee loyalty and turnover in service organisations. To attempt to put some figures on employee costs, turnover, revenues and profits, they quoted results from company studies. Examples are

- The US retailer Sears found, from a regular customer survey carried out in 1989, that employee turnover and customer satisfaction were negatively correlated. Stores with high customer service scores experienced lower annual employee turnover rates.

- Findings at two divisions of the Marriott Corporation suggest that a 10 per cent reduction in employee turnover would raise revenues by $50 million to $150 million (by reducing customer defections).

- At Merck & Co. it was estimated that the transactional, disruption and administrative costs associated with placing staff on and off the payroll raised the total costs of employee turnover to 1.5 times an employee's salary.

Cycle-of-Failure
Where organisations cut costs to achieve short-term goals which increase employee turnover which may have a negative impact on the organisational ability to maintain customer satisfaction and deliver good service experiences.

While such examples may indicate the direction of further studies, Schlesinger and Heskett concluded that 'the economics of employee loyalty are still largely unexplored'. They warn against what they call the 'cycle-of-failure', where companies, for short-term cost reductions, may increase employee turnover. This in turn can result in fewer, less knowledgeable contact personnel, and customers becoming dissatisfied and expressing their negative feelings. The resulting demotivating effect on staff may lead to further employee turnover, and the cycle continues.

Loyalty-based system chain

Reichheld, in a follow-up article in the spring of 1993,[36] sets out a logical framework which encapsulates the concepts of customer and employee loyalty and links them to a service company's competitive position. The chain is triggered by a will to pay employees well. It is summarised in Figure 10.3.

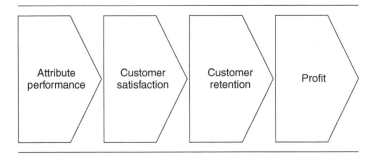

Figure 10.2   The satisfaction–profit chain

Source: Anderson, E. W. and Mittal, V., 'Strengthening the Satisfaction-Profit Chain', *Journal of Service Research*, 3(2), November 2000.

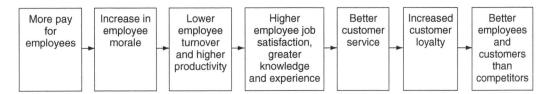

Figure 10.3   Loyalty-based system chain

The chain has an intuitive appeal, but it must be stressed that the causality links required further testing and verification over a range of firms and industries and were regarded as hypotheses at that stage of research. Reichheld himself doubted that many executives would agree to a 25 per cent pay increase to employees in order to reduce employee turnover by 5 per cent and increase customer retention, even though the resultant reduction in customer defections to the competition can increase profits considerably.

The service–profit chain

The postulated relationship between loyalty (both customer and employee) and profitability was visualised with reference to the 'service–profit chain', constructed by Heskett and his colleagues in 1994.[37] The service–profit chain showed the proposed relationships between profitability, customer loyalty, and employee satisfaction, loyalty and productivity. It is reproduced here as Figure 10.4.

Figure 10.4 is an expanded version of Figure 10.3, with profitability and revenue growth explicitly included. As with the loyalty-based chain, the links in the service–profit chain should, as the authors themselves emphasise, be regarded as propositions. They provide evidence to support each proposition and further suggest how a service company can conduct a service-audit on the elements in the chain.

The service–profit chain provided, probably for the first time, an intuitively feasible and simply visible set of links between the internal marketing and management of an organisation, the external focus on the customer and business

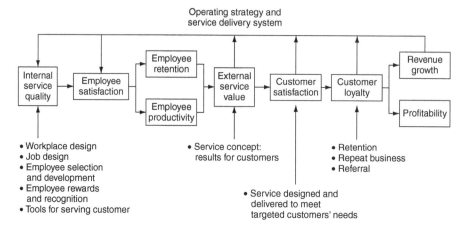

Figure 10.4   The links in the service–profit chain

Source: Heskett, J. L., Jones, T. O., Loveman, G. W., Sasser Jr, W. E. and Schlesinger, L. A., 'Putting the Service-Profit Chain to Work', *Harvard Business Review*, March–April 1994.

performance. As such it has been embraced by some companies as part of their philosophy.

Testing the propositions in the service–profit chain

Subsequent published research that has investigated the propositions within the service–profit chain has resulted in some contradictory findings, and has highlighted potential differences in the relationships between employee and customer satisfaction within different service offers. The service–profit chain may, for example, be more applicable to professional and management services, or business-to-business services, than to consumer services, such as retailing. For example, a study of the service–profit chain links within 15 stores of a leading UK grocery retailer[38] found that although there was support for many of the proposed links in the chain,

- there were no significant correlations between service value and either employee satisfaction, employee loyalty or internal capability

- there was no relationship between employee satisfaction and customer satisfaction thus calling into question the 'satisfaction mirror' proposed by Heskett *et al.*[39]

- furthermore, employee satisfaction was *negatively* correlated with the store's profit margin with the most satisfied and loyal employees working within the least profitable stores!

Although this finding surprised the academic researchers it was in line with anecdotal evidence which appears to be well known among grocery retailers. Store performance within the grocery sector correlates with store size of the larger stores being more profitable. However, employee satisfaction is higher within smaller stores. The two store types are categorised as 'achieving' and 'coasting'. With a large number of customers with diverse shopping habits, the staff at the larger 'achieving' stores tend to be more tightly monitored which creates a more stressful environment. The smaller, 'coasting' stores tend to attract local employees and customers with more consistent shopping habits, being more patient, more likely to want to interact with staff, and generally easier to manage. It appears to be easier to generate a team spirit among employees within coasting stores.

Replicating this study within 107 grocery superstores within a large multinational retail grocer based in continental Western Europe, Keiningham et al.[40] confirmed the need to consider store size. In contrast to the much smaller UK study that found a *negative* relationship, they found no correlation between employee satisfaction and store profitability within the overall sample. However, when controlling for store size they found a *positive* relationship between employee satisfaction and store profitability. Furthermore they found some evidence to support the suggestion, from the earlier study, that employee satisfaction was related to store size.

A further study among 75 stores within a home improvement chain within the United Kingdom has produced another set of results which both lend further support to some links within the chain while contradicting previous research and calling into question other links in the chain.[41] In this case employee satisfaction was positively related to employee loyalty, productivity, service value, customer satisfaction and revenue growth.

Employee loyalty may relate to either employee commitment or employee tenure.[42] Loveman, in an empirical study of the service–profit chain in the context of a US regional bank, found that

- there were significant positive relationships between employee satisfaction and stated employee commitment, but not with tenure, whereas
- customer satisfaction was positively correlated with employee tenure, but not with stated employee commitment.

Service–profit chain
A model that hypothesises how internal service quality, employee satisfaction, retention and productivity are linked to organisational growth and profitability.

In a study entitled 'From People to Profits', carried out by the Institute of Employment Studies in the United Kingdom,[43] employee commitment to a company was linked to company profitability via three routes:

1. *Directly.* The study estimated that a one-point increase in employee commitment could lead to a monthly increase of up to £200 000 in sales per service outlet.
2. *Via customer satisfaction with the service.* This is the link shown in Figure 10.4, and assumes that customer satisfaction mirrors employee satisfaction.
3. *Through a reduction in staff absence.* This relates to the costs of unwanted staff turnover.

Unsurprisingly, the study concludes that companies should invest in employees and look beyond simple measures of employee satisfaction to measures which increase employee commitment.

Overall, the service–profit chain has certainly succeeded in one of its aims; that is, to provide 'a tool for managers and students of management to use in thinking about how to improve performance of service organisations'.[44] Empirical support for the entire model does not exist and empirical support for several individual links of the chain is mixed. The main conclusion arising from current research is a need to consider the service–profit chain as a useful generic model that requires contextual modification prior to its practical application in any given service organisation. Managers could usefully research what the service–profit chain would look like for their organisation.

Statistical estimations of the relationships between profitability, customer satisfaction and quality

When companies are employing resources with a view to improving service quality or increasing customer satisfaction, the management often feel happier when they have some concrete figures showing the financial justification for such strategies. The same can be said for national or international groups that advocate the goals of customer satisfaction and/or service quality. The figures may be forthcoming if mathematical equations could be constructed which relate profitability to customer satisfaction, quality and other variables. Given that there are many problems with the measurement of quality and satisfaction, and that there are limited databases of company information, the production of equations using statistical estimation techniques presents a great challenge.

On a national and international level, we have seen the development of customer satisfaction indices to measure the economic benefits of customer satisfaction. At the level of the firm, there have been attempts to measure Return on Quality (ROQ) as a means of monitoring the financial accountability of service quality.[45]

ROQ
Return on Quality.

Customer satisfaction indices

The first attempt to derive a national index of customer satisfaction was the Swedish Customer Satisfaction Barometer (SCSB).[46] The SCSB provides yearly updates on customer-based measures of performance of Swedish firms in a variety of industries. The measures are of variables such as quality, expectations and customer satisfaction for each firm, and are based on annual customer surveys. The extensive customer-generated data and the method of weighting attributes distinguish SCSB from PIMS. For each firm, standard financial performance data such as market share and ROI are also readily available. In the spirit of PIMS, quality and satisfaction measures can be linked to financial performance measures.

In addition to estimating correlations between the variables, however, Anderson *et al.*[47] set out to provide a mathematical model (through a set of equations) which contributes to a greater understanding of the relationships between profitability, satisfaction, quality and expectations. Because of the more detailed availability of customer-based measures of the variables within the SCSB, statistical techniques were employed to estimate the coefficients of the equations.

Using ROI as the financial performance measure, their model can be represented by the set of equations below (Anderson *et al.* p. 60).

$$EXP_t = a_1 + b_{11}\,EXP_{t-1} + b_{12}\,QUAL_{t-1} + b_{13}\,TREND + e_{1t} \qquad (1)$$

$$SAT_t = a_2 + b_{21}\,SAT_{t-1} + b_{22}\,QUAL_t + b_{23}\,EXP_t + b_{24}\,TREND + e_{2t} \qquad (2)$$

$$ROI_t = a_3 + b_{31}\,ROI_{t-1} + b_{32}\,SAT_t + b_{33}\,TREND + e_{3t} \qquad (3)$$

where

EXP_t = Expectation at time period t.
$QUAL_t$ = Customer perceived quality at time period t.
SAT_t = Customer satisfaction at time period t.
ROI_t = Return on Investment at time period t.
TREND = Net effect of other variables which change over time
Values $a_1, a_2, a_3, b_{11}, b_{12}, b_{13}, b_{21}, b_{22}, b_{23}, b_{24}, b_{31}, b_{32}, b_{33}$ are coefficients to be
   estimated; e_{1t}, e_{2t}, e_{3t} are the disturbance times.

In effect, equation (3) postulates that a firm's ROI at any period is a function of ROI at the previous period, current customer satisfaction, and the trend. Equation (2) postulates that customer satisfaction with a firm at any period is, in turn, a function of satisfaction at the previous period, current customer perceived quality, current customer expectations, and the trend. From equation (1) it is postulated that customer expectations of a firm at any period are, in turn, a function of expectations at the previous period, perceived quality at the previous period, and the trend.

Extensive justifications are given by Anderson *et al.*[48] for the structures of the equations. The statistical techniques for estimating a and b coefficients are also described. To obtain a flavour of the implications of the analysis, let us look at equations (2) and (3) once the estimates of the coefficients have been inserted. They are

$$SAT_t = -.12 + .44\,SAT_{t-1} + .49\,QUAL_t + .10\,EXP_t - .003\,TREND \qquad (2)$$

$$ROI_t = -1.10 + .75\,ROI_{t-1} + .40\,SAT_t + .002\,TREND \qquad (3)$$

From (2), a 1-point increase in quality results in, all other things being equal, a 49 increase in satisfaction (from the estimate of b_{22}). From (3), a 1-point increase in satisfaction results in a 40 increase in ROI (from the estimate of b_{32}). Taken together, the two effects suggest that a 1-point increase in quality results in a $0.49 \times 0.40 = .196$ increase in ROI. This result is consistent with earlier PIMS findings.

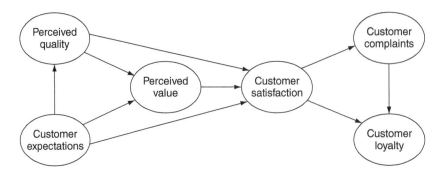

Figure 10.5 Methodology behind the computation of the SCSB, ACSI and ECSI
Source: Adapted from ACSI Methodology, University of Michigan Business School.

The equations can be used in a number of other ways, including a calculation of returns on investment due to a 1-point increase in satisfaction each year.[49] It should be stressed, however, that, as with any statistical analysis, the structures and strengths of the relationships will inevitably be subjected to further studies, and interpretations may be modified as the result of the further empirical work.

The methodologies for computing the elements of the SCSB were employed to start the American Customer Satisfaction Index (ACSI)[50] in 1994 and the European Customer Satisfaction Index (ECSI)[51] in 1997 (see Figure 10.5).

In turn, as more annual data becomes available on the indices, there will be further research to demonstrate the strength of the relationship between customer satisfaction and financial performance.[52]

Return on quality

The work on 'return on quality' is also concerned with statistical relationships between satisfaction, quality and profitability. However, the focus is different. A return on quality (ROQ) system is being developed to provide decision support to *managers of a particular business*. The aim is for managers to use the ROQ system in order to

- quantify the financial impact of quality
- identify opportunities for quality improvement
- estimate optimal expenditure levels
- reveal opportunities for spending reductions
- conduct 'what if' analyses of potential decision alternatives.[53]

The ROQ system acknowledges that while quality is an investment, it is possible to spend too much on quality (the case of a company that, in order to win an award, spent so much on quality improvements that it went bankrupt

Figure 10.6 Return on quality – chain of effects

is quoted as evidence to support this view). The ROQ system is based on the chain of effects shown in Figure 10.6. This is similar to sections of the service–profit chain shown in Figure 10.4. It must be remembered, however, that for the ROQ decision-support system, all the elements of the chain refer to a single company.

Through the use of customer survey data, internal company information and competitor financial data, sets of equations have been derived to represent each link in the chain for two test company cases. Profits can, through a series of equations, be linked to customer satisfaction or quality improvement costs.

One of the key features of the system is that it is not just an overall customer satisfaction measure which is extracted from customer surveys, but also satisfaction measures on various service processes. In one of the test companies for the system, a hotel group, it was possible to measure the impact on profits of several processes – for instance, room service, restaurant, staff, bathroom – and to further identify the impact of various features of each process. It was found that it was bathrooms, and in particular cleanliness of bathrooms, which had the most impact on profits. Further use of the system could establish whether to spend more on ensuring bathroom cleanliness, and if so how much more, and assess the potential effect of the decision on the bottom line. The same system may identify elements of the process where it is better to spend less, without adversely affecting profitability.

Clearly, decision-support systems, such as ROQ are attractive to managers. However, they are still in their infancy. Rust *et al.*[54] reckoned that 'thorough testing of the ROQ decision support system will require several years to complete'. However, the group do state that 'The ROQ approach enables managers to determine where to spend on service quality, how much to spend, and the likely financial impact from service expenditures, in terms of revenues, profits and return on investments in quality improvement...'.[55] This system, like the SCSB-based equations, relies on assumptions, one of which is that quality is an antecedent of satisfaction. Not all services marketers would agree, particularly if satisfaction is seen to be associated with single service encounters and perceived service quality is associated with a longer-term overall judgement (see Chapter 8).

Summary

Although, as was indicated at the beginning of this chapter, the subject of service profitability has probably not received as much attention as other aspects of services marketing, there are clear signs that research groups and practitioners are increasing understanding, and striving towards appropriate measures of the relationships between satisfaction, quality and profitability.

We have looked very briefly at four approaches to service profitability. The first looks at the macro-level links between *quality* and business results. The PIMS database examines relationships between financial indicators (including profit) and quality measures over time and bases conclusions on the temporal correlations. The national and international quality awards are based on scoring systems which link quality performance criteria to business results. In turn, the award-winning companies then provide a focus for comparisons in terms of quality. The second examines the relationships between the triplets of quality, productivity and profitability and is using a mainly case-study-based approach to reach a greater understanding of the triplet relationships and the value of network relationships. Linked to this approach is the measurement of the impact of a dual emphasis on organisational profitability. The third, in the form of the satisfaction–profit chain and the service–profit chain, focuses on the effects of loyalty (both customer and employee) on profitability and utilises customer retention and defection figures from a range of service industries. The fourth uses statistical techniques to provide series of equations which quantify the relationship between profitability and customer satisfaction at either the national/international or business level. We also explored the usefulness of categorising customers according to their profitability to the organisation.

There are many aspects of all four approaches which have been omitted in this brief summary. The original sources can be found in the references at the end of this chapter.

A recurring theme has been a frustration with the inability of most accounting systems to measure such variables as costs of customer–employee turnover or profit margins generated by repeat custom. As Gummesson[56] bemoans, 'An essential conclusion is that service organisations cannot be correctly assessed by studying the traditional information in the balance sheet and the cost and revenue statements of the annual report.'

Learning Outcomes

Having read this chapter, you should be able to

- summarise the results and evaluate the implications arising from work associated with the PIMS database
- outline the criteria used in awarding companies that invest in quality
- appreciate the perspectives of the quality, productivity and profitability 'tribes', and the difficulties in recognising the contribution of relationships to profitability

- demonstrate knowledge of the propositions presented in the satisfaction–profit chain and the service–profit chain, and of the work undertaken to test the proposed links in the chains
- appreciate the models and methodology behind the computations of national satisfaction indices, and company-specific measures of ROQ.

Discussion Questions and Exercises

1. Does investment in quality lead to increased profits?
2. Is quality compatible with productivity?
3. Find an example of an organisation, or industry, using the customer pyramid approach.
4. Find examples and counter-examples to the propositions represented by the links in the service–profit chain.
5. Explain the methodology behind the computations of national customer satisfaction indices.
6. Why might the concept of 'Return on Quality' be attractive to managers?

Notes and References

1. 3rd International Research Seminar in Service Management, La-Londe-les-Maures, France, May 1994.
2. Ibid.
3. Anderson, E. W., Fornell, C. and Lehmann, D. R., 'Customer Satisfaction, Market Share and Profitability: Findings from Sweden', *Journal of Marketing,* vol. 58, July 1994, pp. 53–66.
4. Rust, R. T. and Varki, S., 'Making Service Quality Financially Accountable', Proceedings of 3rd International Research Seminar in Service Management, La-Londe-les-Maures, France, May 1994, pp. 645–58.
5. Reichheld, E. E. and Sasser Jr, W. E., 'Zero Defections: Quality Comes to Services', *Harvard Business Review*, September–October 1990, pp. 105–11.
6. Gummesson, E., 'Service Productivity: A Blasphemous Approach', Proceedings of 2nd International Research Seminar in Service Management, La-Londe-les-Maures, France, June 1992.
7. Gummesson, E., 'Productivity, Quality and Relationship Marketing in Service Operations', *International Journal of Contemporary Hospitality Management*, 10(1), 1998, pp. 4–15.
8. Gale, B. T., 'Customer Satisfaction – Relative to Competitors – Is Where It's At (strong evidence that superior quality drives the bottom line and shareholder value)', *Marketing and Research Today*, February 1994.
9. Zeithaml, V. A., Parasuraman, A. and Berry, L. L., *Delivering Quality Service: Balancing Customer Perceptions and Expectations*, The Free Press, New York, 1990.
10. Buzzell, R. and Gale, B. T., *The PIMS Principles: Linking Strategy to Performance*, The Free Press, New York, 1987.
11. Gale, 'Customer Satisfaction'.
12. Gummesson, 'Service Productivity'.
13. http://www.quality.nist.gov/law.htm.
14. Ibid.
15. http://www.nist.gov/public-affairs/baldrige00/LosAlamos.htm.
16. Baron, S., Harris, K. and Parker, C., 'Understanding the Consumer Experience: It's "Good to Talk" ', *Journal of Marketing Management*, 16(1–3), 2000, pp. 111–27.
17. http://www.efgm.org/award/PressRelease.htm.
18. http://www.foxdenton.oldham.sch.uk.
19. Soteriou, A. C. and Zenios, S. A., 'On the Impact of Quality on Performance: First Empirical Evidence from the Financial Industry', Proceedings of the Fifth Conference of the Association of Asian-Pacific Operations Research Societies, Singapore, July 2000.

20. Pannirselvam, G. P. and Ferguson, L. A., 'A Study of the Relationships Between the Baldrige Categories', *International Journal of Quality and Reliability Management*, 18(1), 2001, pp. 14–37.

21. Bylund, E. and Lepidoth Jr, J., 'Service Quality and Productivity: A Post-Industrial Approach', Proceedings of 3rd International Research Seminar in Service Management, La-Londe-les-Maures, France, May 1994.

22. Gummesson, 'Service Productivity'.

23. Gummesson, 'Productivity, Quality and Relationship Marketing'.

24. Brooks, R., 'Alienating Customers Isn't Always a Bad Idea, May Firms Discover', *Wall Street Journal*, Jan 7th, 1999, pp. A1 and A12.

25. Rust, R. T., Zahorik, A. J. and Keiningham, T. L., 'Return on Quality (ROQ): Making Service Quality Financially Accountable', *Journal of Marketing*, vol. 66 (October), 1995, pp. 58–70.

26. Mittal, V., Anderson, E. W., Sayrak, A. and Tadikamalla, P., 'Dual Emphasis and the Long-Term Financial Impact of Customer Satisfaction', *Marketing Science*, 24(4), 2005, pp. 544–55.

27. Zeithaml, V. A., Rust, R. T. and Lemon, K. N., 'The Customer Pyramid: Creating and Service profitable Customers', *California Management Review*, 43(4), 2001, pp. 118–42.

28. Ibid.

29. Reichheld and Sasser Jr, 'Zero Defections'.

30. Anderson, E. W. and Mittal, V., 'Strengthening the Satisfaction-Profit Chain', *Journal of Service Research*, 3(2), November 2000, pp. 107–20.

31. Heskett, J. L., Jones, T. O., Loveman, G. W., Sasser Jr, W. E. and Schlesinger, L. A., 'Putting the Service-Profit Chain to Work', *Harvard Business Review*, March–April 1994, pp. 164–74.

32. Anderson, E. W. and Mittal, V., 'Strengthening the Satisfaction-Profit Chain', *Journal of Service Research*, 3(2), November 2000, pp. 107–20.

33. Ibid.

34. Helgesen, Ø., 'Are Loyal Customer Profitable? Customer Satisfaction, Customer (Action) Loyalty and Customer Profitability at the Individual Level', *Journal of Marketing Management*, vol. 22, 2005, pp. 245–66.

35. Schlesinger, L. A. and Heskett, J. L., 'The Service-Driven Service Company', *Harvard Business Review*, September–October 1991, pp. 71–81.

36. Reichheld, F. F., 'Loyalty-Based Management', *Harvard Business Review*, March–April 1993, pp. 64–73.

37. Heskett, J. L., Jones, T. O., Loveman, G. W., Sasser Jr, W. E. and Schlesinger, L. A., 'Putting the Service-Profit Chain to Work', *Harvard Business Review*, March–April 1994, pp. 164–74.

38. Silvestro, R. and Cross, S., 'Applying the Service-Profit Chain in a Retail Environment', *International Journal of Service Industry Management*, 11(3), 2000, pp. 244–68.

39. Heskett, J. L., Sasser Jr, W. E. and Schlesinger, L. A., *The Service Profit Chain: How Leading Companies Link Profit and Growth to Loyalty, Satisfaction and Value*, 1997, Free Press, New York, NY.

40. Keiningham, T. L., Aksoy, L., Daly, R. M., Perrier, K. and Solom, A., 'Re-examining the Link Between Employee Satisfaction and Store Performance in a Retail Environment', *International Journal of Service Industry Management*, 17(1), 2006, pp. 51–7.

41. Pritchard, M. and Silvestro, R., 'Applying the Service profit Chain to Analyse Retail Performance: The case of the managerial strait-jacket?', *International Journal of Service Industry Management*, 16(4), 2005, pp. 337–56.

42. Loveman, G. W., 'Employee Satisfaction, Customer Loyalty and Financial Performance', *Journal of Service Research*, 1(1), 1998, pp. 18–31.

43. Barber, L., Hayday, S. and Bevan, S., 'From People to Profits', *IES Report* 355, 1999, ISBN I-85184-284-5.

44. Loveman, 'Employee Satisfaction'.

45. Rust, R. T. and Oliver, R. L., *Service Quality: New Directions in Theory and Practice*, Sage, London, 1994.

46. Fornell, C., 'A National Customer Satisfaction Barometer: The Swedish Experience', *Journal of Marketing*, vol. 55, 1992, pp. 1–21.

47. Anderson, Fornell and Lehmann, 'Customer Satisfaction, Market Share and Profitability'.

48. Ibid.

49. Ibid.

50. See http://www.theacsi.org/

51. See http://www.ipq.pt/ecsi/index_in.html.

52. Yeung, M. C. H. and Ennew, C. T., 'From Customer Satisfaction to Profitability', *Journal of Strategic Marketing*, 8(4), 2000, pp. 313–26.

53. Rust and Oliver, *Service Quality.*

54. Ibid.

55. Rust, R. T., Zahorik, A. J. and Keiningham, T. L., 'Return on Quality (ROQ): Making Service Quality Financially Accountable', *Journal of Marketing*, vol. 59, April 1995, pp. 58–70.

56. Gummesson, E., 'Service Quality and Productivity in the Imaginary Organization', Proceedings of 3rd International Seminar in Service Management, La-Londe-les-Maures, France, May 1994.

11

Future Research Issues

Learning Objectives

Overall Aim of the Chapter

To outline some of the potentially fruitful areas of research for service marketers at the beginning of the twenty-first century.

In particular, the *chapter objectives* are

- to present an overview of service marketing issues that are engaging academics and practitioners at the beginning of the twenty-first century

- to identify areas and issues within the services marketing discipline where further understanding would be useful.

Introduction

Our principal aim when writing this book was to present you with a concise summary of the issues, models and theories currently recognised as representing the sub-discipline of services marketing. We have included a bank of special small business case studies to give the reader the opportunity to explore how these issues, models and theories can be applied to a realistic business situation. The 'Postcards from Practice' along with the 'It's in the News!' items included throughout this book provide examples of the daily relevance of many of the models and theories for service organisations. The topics selected for inclusion in the book broadly reflect the areas of study which have been engaging the attention of academics and practitioners from the beginning of the 1990s. However, we are conscious of the fact that in the previous ten chapters we have not been able to cover every topic in as much detail as we would have liked, and that certain of the more traditional marketing topics have not been covered explicitly at all. For example, chapters have not been devoted to discussion of some of the components of the services marketing mix, such as promoting, pricing and distributing services.

This final chapter is mainly for those of you who have been sufficiently encouraged and excited by the field of services marketing that you want to

TBSS
Technology-based
self-service options.

keep abreast with some of the key research issues of the twenty-first century. It may also be a useful starting point for those of you seeking ideas for a research project, dissertation or thesis. The chapter is presented in two sections. The first section acknowledges the pervasiveness and increasing importance of TBSS provision. The second section highlights research issues that have a more general application for service organisations. In both sections we present the issues that are already engaging academics and practitioners as well as the authors' views as to where and how research could be meaningfully employed to increase the understanding of important fundamentals of services marketing theory and practice.

Before presenting the research issues it is worth reminding ourselves of the discussion in Chapter 2 of the emergence, development and current state of the services marketing sub-discipline. It is clear that a fundamental shift is taking place with regard to the position that service occupies within both the theory and the practice of business.

Academic interest in the service sector of the economy has increased markedly since Vargo & Lusch coined the term 'service-dominant logic'[1] to emphasise that service is the basis of all marketing exchanges. Manufactured products are a mechanism of delivering a service and enable customers to choose how they wish the service to be performed and the extent to which they co-perform and co-produce the service thereby co-creating the value they receive.

The S-D logic, however, requires empirical testing.[2] In particular, empirical studies are needed on how consumers co-produce services and co-create value (through using and integrating their resources), and on understanding experiences from the consumer perspective. Lusch, Vargo and O'Brien[3] have observed that 'since value is co-created, comprehending how customers combine resources provides insight into competitive advantage'. Some preliminary studies have been undertaken and specialised colloquia have been organised to debate the ideas and develop the studies.[4] This is a fruitful area for academic research that requires practitioner involvement to move it from a theoretical exposition to a genuinely helpful framework for service organisations and customers.

SSME
The recognition of
Service Science,
Management and
Engineering as an
emerging field of study
that seeks to develop
inter-disciplinary
knowledge of service.

IBM report that services now account for more than 50 per cent of the workforce in Brazil, Russian, Japan and Germany and over 75 per cent in the United kingdom and the United States.[5] This has caused a knowledge gap and prompted a switch in focus for scientific research from resolving problems in product manufacturing towards increasing the productivity and efficiency of service provision. As discussed in Chapter 2 it is this shift in attention towards service provision from non-business disciplines (specifically science, engineering and design) that has resulted in the emergence of the new field of study known as Service Science Management and Engineering (SSME) which seeks to combine knowledge from these disciplines to support the development of more efficient service practice.

Steven Brown, Director of the Center for Services Marketing and Management at Arizona State University, in a keynote address to the American Marketing Association Services Marketing Special Interest Group in May 2001, identified *former product manufacturers* as the principal group of practitioners who are interested in the practice and theory of services marketing and management. Companies that originated in manufacturing, and became known for the physical products that they made and sold, are finding that the more profitable components of their business are the services and solutions that they provide.

In the business-to-business sector, there is a continuing trend to outsource services which had been traditionally provided in-house, in order to concentrate on core competencies. Specialist consultancy groups, together with the large (former manufacturing) companies with specialist product knowledge and access to networks, are providing the outsourced services and solutions.

The range of services and solutions offered by the large (former manufacturing) companies can be staggering. On the 'products and services' page of the IBM website[6] is a list of services and solutions offered by the company. Services are in four main groups – Business services, IT services, Training and Financing. Within each group are sub-groups of services. For example, IT services include Infrastructure, Systems Management, Networking and Connectivity, Outsourcing and Web Hosting. Each subgroup is further divided into 'service descriptions'. The solutions are also in four groups – Industry solutions, Cross-industry and alliance solutions, Government and Education. Again, within each group of solutions, there are subgroups of solutions. For example, Education includes Universities and Colleges, and Schools.

The company offers hundreds of services/solutions, at the level of the service/solution description, to clients in all sectors of the economy all over the world. IBM claims to be a global service provider, but like many former product-based companies, the change of focus from product to service-based company is difficult. Steven Brown's conference address emphasised the need for research into the management of such changes.

Consequently we believe that service provision is likely to receive even more attention from both academics and practitioners in the future than it has received in the past. We now present a number of areas that we consider will be of particular interest.

Issues Arising from Technology-based Self-service Provision

We believe there are a number of areas where research would provide support for practitioners as they develop their self-service provision. Two areas where a greater understanding of how customers experience the service would be beneficial for service organisations are service design and customer productivity.

Service design

Consistent with our approach in Chapter 6 we now summarise areas where theory could be developed to assist practitioners design the service process and the service environment.

The service process

One of the implications of the increased use of technology-based services is that the design of service takes on an extra layer, from that explained in Chapter 6, because of the increased choices open to consumers to create their own experiences. For example, do customers carry out personal banking activities at the bank branch, via ATMs, on the telephone or via the Internet? Or through some combination of all these methods? The service blueprinting described in Chapter 6 was developed primarily to represent person-to-person interactions. Clearly the process varies if the customer interacts with technology instead of or as well as the contact personnel. It is suggested that a service science approach, combining the resources of service and IT experts, is required to add the additional layer to the service blueprint.[7] As such, this represents one of the many, potential, interdisciplinary approaches to service issues that are emerging because of the ICT mediation of services.

One of the first issues that service organisations need to address when considering TBSS is the role that the Internet will play within the service provision. Table 11.1 outlines four distinct ways in which the Internet can be utilised. First an organisational website can be used simply to provide information about the service provision and promote customer participation. Such a website need not be interactive since it is not an integral part of the service provision and, in this form, would not be supporting self-service provision. In the remaining cases customers are engaged in self-service behaviours.

Many service organisations now use the Internet to increase the number of customers they can reach to purchase their products. This may be to support an existing 'bricks' based business, which is the strategy adopted by supermarkets,

Service Science
A term used to identify the emerging discipline of Service Science Management and Engineering (SSME) which seeks to integrate knowledge from a range of disciplines such as: economics, business, design, IT and engineering.

Blueprint
A comprehensive visual model of a service process used to design and evaluate service performance.

Table 11.1   Internet roles

	Current service	*New service*
New market	Use of website for online sales to gain access to more customers than would be achieved without website	Use of Internet to provide new to the world services such as online gaming and virtual worlds (Second Life); online auctions (eBay and TradeMe); social networking (FaceBook; You Tube)
Current market	Use of website to provide information to promote and support service delivery. May provide e-form or other contact details to facilitate initial contact with organisation	Use of Internet to change customer behaviours eg: Onine banking; Online booking (travel and leisure industry); texting for parking meters

or entirely 'click' based as with Amazon.com. Another common usage is to move customers into performing tasks that were previously performed by service employees. Good examples are online banking and online booking for travel and leisure activities. The final way in which the power of the Internet has been harnessed is that of entirely new services where the purpose is to connect customers with each other rather than the service organisation. Here the organisation provides a framework within which it manages customer-to-customer interaction.

Once the role of the Internet is decided it will be possible for the organisation to use service mapping and or blueprinting tools to analyse the relationship between the automated and non-automated elements of the service provision. Key to this will be understanding what back-stage processes are required to support the self-servicing customers who can easily remain 'hidden' to the organisation. We believe that it would be worth researching the skill set required for employees that support the automated self-service elements of the provision. Back-stage staff who are technical wizards may need additional training and development to ensure satisfying customer encounters or it may be more effective for service organisations to separate technical staff from customers and design a process where technical staff liaise with customer contact staff who then interact with the customer. There is likely to be a need to ensure 24/7 employee coverage which will present a number of challenges for service organisations, particularly those that may have added self-service options to their more established business. Consequently there may be a need for such organisations to design two separate service processes to ensure that they are providing effective back-stage support for the self-service provision. When the UK supermarkets first launched into online shopping provision, some were more successful than others. Much of Tesco's initial success was attributed to their decision to process the online orders through their store network, rather than through the warehouse network.

Currently little is known about e-failures and how organisations can deliver effective service recovery within the automated environment. This would be a fruitful area for future research.

Christopher Voss[8] raises a number of research questions relating to perceptions of service quality within an automated self-service environment. He points out that although the 'rhetoric of the Web suggests that service will be faster, more responsive and more personalised', we do not yet know if that is indeed what customers expect or receive. Voss found a difference in responsiveness between Internet only (click) and established (click & brick) service organisations, and concludes that the established organisations are finding it hard to adapt their service performance to the online environment. Indeed, the majority of established organisations participating in the study had yet to establish performance standards for the online environment. We conclude that there is considerable scope for research into the application and relevance of the quality frameworks developed within traditional service marketing contexts to the automated self-service environment.

The service environment

Within Chapter 6 we associated the design of the service environment with the design of the physical environment in which service encounters take place. However the move towards greater self-service provision requires service organisations to address the virtual environments in which customers are performing the self-service provision. The term 'e-scapes' has been coined to reflect this need to extend our knowledge of the servicescape. Ezeh & Harris[9] suggest that experimental methods could be used to research this area, given the relative ease with which the TBSS environment can be manipulated to explore and model customer reactions to differential online stimuli.

Customer productivity

The move towards greater self-service within service provision raises a number of issues about which we currently know very little. Will service organisations seek to develop a competitive advantage by having the most productive customers? How will the need for customers to undertake more tasks within the service process affect their perceptions of the value they gain and their satisfaction with the provision? Will service organisations seek to re-structure their pricing based upon the cost of self-service delivery and seek to charge a 'premium' for personal service? How does the concept of self-service sit within the S-D logic context of co-creating value?

If organisations can gain a competitive advantage from utilising the operant resources of their customers, then it is important to understand what would make customers more productive. It would appear to be imperative to learn more about the situational circumstances in which customers are more or less likely to adopt self-service behaviours. Are some service contexts naturally more 'co-production friendly' than others? Can service providers create processes and environments that are more conducive to, and therefore encourage, co-production? What, if any, benefits do customers get specifically from co-production? A recent study calls on service organisations to 'put a little fun' into customer lives if they wish to promote usage of SSTs.[10] Organisations would also need to know more about the nature and duration of the customer 'learning curve' and the cost to the organisation of 'training' their customers. There may be certain customer characteristics that are more likely to result in productive co-creation than others. John Bateson[11] reminds us that all service organisations have both expert and novice customers and suggests the need to manage the performance quality of these two customer types differently. Ironically, it is probably easier to differentiate experts from novices online, provided the service process includes a login and password process. Those with a login are more likely to be returning customers. Those without are likely to be novices and can be provided with more information regarding service usage.

We know very little about the impact that increasing the need for customers to co-produce the service has on their evaluation of the service provision particularly with respect to perceptions of value and satisfaction. Initially service organisations provided discounts for customers utilising online self-service provision. However, as self-service provision has proliferated it may be that some organisations seek to position their face-to-face provision as a premium service with the online provision as a 'no-frills' service. Some organisations, such as EasyJet, use online self-service as a means of demonstrating their commitment to delivering a low-cost service provision. One study found that customers who choose to participate in the service delivery process are more willing to take credit for successful outcomes and to share the blame for unsuccessful outcomes.[12] It would be of interest to know if customers feel the same when they have no choice but to use self-service options in order to receive the service.

📖 It's in the News! 11.1

Self-scanning in Retail Stores

According to the Maryland, USA, *Community Newspaper* Online, 5 Sept 2007,

More and more, self-checkouts – where customers scan and purchase items without the help of a cashier – are showing up in stores and are being used by shoppers who prefer their independence. The systems have been used in the United States since the early 1990s, but have gained in popularity over the last seven years as more affordable and user-friendly models have become available, according to Lee Holman, an analyst at technology research firm IHL Consulting Group of Franklin, Tenn. Though companies such as Home Depot and Wal-Mart have introduced self-checkout at their stores, Holman said, grocers have embraced the trend the most.

'I just like it because it gives me more freedom,' Mona Khan of Damascus said after making a self-service purchase at the Giant Food store in Germantown's Neelsville Village Center. 'If I have something I don't want somebody to see or be touching, it's more comfortable.'

'They're extremely popular,' Giant spokesman Barry Scher said. The systems can be found in all new Giants as well as stores that have undergone major renovations. They have proven so popular that the company plans to install self-scanning lanes in all of its supermarkets, he said. Shoppers in North America are expected to spend more than $525 billion at self-service machines in 2007, up from $438 billion in 2006, according to a study released in July by IHL Consulting. A poll of U.S. and Canadian consumers conducted by New York-based BuzzBack Market Research found that 77 percent were more likely to shop at businesses with self-service machines, and 55 percent said they wanted more self-service at grocery stores.

📖 It's in the News! 11.1   (Continued)

'It's really fast because I know how to use it,' said Jose Dory of Gaithersburg after using a self-checkout at Magruder's on Quince Orchard Road in Gaithersburg. 'A lot of people don't know how to use it, so I definitely take advantage of that,' he added, referring to sparse lines. Common complaints include malfunctioning machines and the difficulty of locating items that cannot be scanned, such as produce, on the self-checkout's screen.

Some shoppers are also concerned that the arrival of self-checkout could cause cashiers to lose their jobs. 'I noticed [stores] stopped hiring people, and people need employment,' said Latisha Gasaway of Frederick while finishing up her shopping at a Germantown Giant. Holman said that the companies his firm interviews about self-checkout are more interested in reassigning cashiers to customer-oriented positions, such as answering questions or carrying bags to the shopper's car, than creating a mechanized workforce, an attitude echoed by Giant and Magruder's spokesmen. Still, some shoppers enjoy the service provided by cashiers, such as Bill Morgan of Montgomery Village, who does like the efficiency of self-checkout. 'I would prefer a cashier, personally, the contact with a person,' he said as he exited the Gaithersburg Magruder's.

There is some interaction at self-checkout, however. At Giant and Magruder's stores, employees help customers bag their items, and they flit from station to station, plugging in produce codes and assisting stumped shoppers. Jordan Katz of Germantown said he prefers self-scanning and seeks out shops, such as Magruder's, that provide the service. 'There's a couple places that I shop at specifically because of self-checkout,' he said. Many shoppers said self-scanning is best used for small purchases instead of for a week's worth of groceries. 'I usually have too many items and I don't feel like it,' Dayton Ward of Boyds said as he pushed his full cart through an upcounty Giant. 'Also, I have a 5-year-old.'

Ishan Khetarpal of Clarksburg said his young sons, Sanjay and Mihir, grocery shoppers of tomorrow, love the hands-on self-checkouts. 'There's also no waste of time, generally speaking,' Khetarpal said while the trio wheeled their cart out of the Neelsville Giant. 'But there is a downside to it,' he said. 'Things have to be weighed, the produce.... When you look at it, it's not user-friendly at all. But overall, I enjoy it.'

📖 'It's in the News!' 11.2

Fast food, German-style: Dining out at Germany's Fully Automated 'Robot' Restaurant

Steve Rosenberg, writing for BBC News, Nuremberg http://news.bbc.co.uk/go/pr/fr/-/1/hi/world/europe/7335351.stm Published: 2008/04/08 07:02:47 GMT.

Germany likes to call itself the 'Land of Ideas' – and over the centuries it has certainly had plenty of them. It was Germans who invented the aspirin, the airship, the printing press and the diesel engine. But Germany has surely never produced anything quite as weird as the automated restaurant. I say 'restaurant' – but it actually looks more like a rollercoaster, with long metal tracks criss-crossing the dining area. The tracks run all the way from the kitchen, high up in the roof, down to the tables, twisting and turning as they go. And down the tracks – in little pots with wheels fixed to the bottom – speeds food. Supersonic sausages, high-pace pancakes and wine bottles whizzing down to the customers' tables with the help of good old gravity. One pot is spiralling down so fast, it looks like an Olympic bobsleigh (but it's only Bratwurst).

What's more, at the Baggers restaurant in Nuremberg, you don't need waiters to order food. Customers use touch-screen TVs to browse the menu and choose their meal. You can even use the computers to send e-mails and text messages while you wait for the food to be cooked. But all this may not appeal to those who like traditional waiter service.

Up in the kitchen, it is man, not machine, that makes the food. They haven't found a way of automating the chef, just yet. Everything is prepared from fresh. When it is ready, the meal is put in a pot and given a sticker and a colour to match the customer's seat. Then it is put on the rails and despatched downhill to the correct table. Manna from heaven, German-style.

The restaurant is the brainchild of local businessman Michael Mack. 'I wanted to come up with a complete new restaurant system,' Michael tells me, 'one that would be more efficient and more comfortable'. Replacing waiters with helter-skelters and computers is fun for the customers. It also makes financial sense for the restaurant. 'You can save labour costs,' explains restaurant spokesperson Kyra Mueller-Siecheneder. 'You don't need the waiters to run to the customers, take the orders, run to the kitchen and back to the guests.'

The restaurant has not completely done away with the human touch. There are still some staff on hand to explain to rather bemused customers how to use the technology. But what do the punters here think? Do Germans really have the appetite for automated mealtimes?

'It's another art for eating. I like it!' one man raves.

'It's more for young people than old people,' a woman tells me. 'My mother was here yesterday and she needs my son's help to order.'

Watching all this food raining down on the restaurant makes me ravenous. I decide that it is my turn to test the system. I order steak and salad on the computer and wait for it to appear. A few minutes later, a pot glides down to my table with my 'fast food' – and it is delicious. As I finish the meal and prepare to leave, one final thought crosses my mind. An automated meal doesn't only save the restaurant money, but the customer, too. After all, in a restaurant without waiters, there is no need to leave a tip . . . .

Customer 'productivity' and its impact on employee performance

The two situations described in the 'It's in the news!' items above also illustrate a range of the issues for further research related to customer performance and 'productivity'. In the scenarios above, the customer interacts with technology with little or no input from the employee. Although there is a debate as to whether the customer is replacing the employee here or if new technologies are replacing them, the fact remains that the customer is now acting as an 'employee' and their 'performance' will impact productivity, that is one customers' inability to order quickly and correctly could slow down the entire system. This scenario can be seen with self-scan checkouts in a retail environment. The idea of customers scanning their own groceries initially represented a low-cost option with a customer theoretically replacing a service worker. However, due to a lack of customer skills and knowledge (and training) traditional employees have had to be redeployed at checkouts in a 'problem solving' capacity at a much higher cost.

Despite the importance of 'productivity' research in services, there have only been a limited number of attempts in the services marketing literature (since Lovelock and Young's thought-provoking article[13]) to enhance conceptual and empirical knowledge about the *customers' contribution* to service productivity. Most notable has been the contribution from Johnston and colleagues,[14] who have highlighted the qualitative differences between inputs and outputs from an operations perspective and the counter intuitive relationships which exist between operational and customer productivity.

Conceptual frameworks which currently guide discussion of customer productivity are largely based on traditional economic frameworks and are arguably incomplete. They fail to address the full range of forces affecting both customer inputs and outputs in the context of productivity. In self-scanning, for example, the focus is on speed of throughput and convenience as the valued customer outputs. In reality, however, evidence suggests that there are many 'hidden' outputs which are also important to customers. Some elderly customers participate to get exposure to technology for the first time and many children, simply to have fun and parents to entertain children. For many service providers it is becoming increasingly important to be able to identify and ultimately evaluate these social and 'experiential' outcomes. Not only can they provide a major source of differential advantage, but they also help to ensure that the customers' service experience is a safe and enjoyable social event.

In addition, limited coverage has been given in the human resource management literature to the impact of the customers' contribution on the role and performance (and productivity) of traditional service workers. Although, the customers' contribution may initially appear to offer a lower cost base, as noted above, it has also been shown to have a negative impact on the existing work force with role ambiguity leading to job stress.[15] Customers too can find participation stressful. They are expected to possess the skills and knowledge to operate as partial employees, yet unlike traditional workers receive no formal training.

Understanding and managing customer skills and knowledge in this context has received little attention to date.

There remains, therefore, a pressing need to develop a more detailed understanding of the resources customers have (and seem willing to provide) in a service setting to achieve a desired level of output and the impact this contribution has on the role and performance of the existing workforce. In terms of SDL, there are three related propositions[16] which would be explored in this agenda.

- *Understanding how the customer uniquely integrates and experiences service-related resources is a source of competitive advantage through innovation.*

  Where do customers acquire necessary skills and knowledge to participate? As discussed in Chapter 5 there is some suggestion that customers acquire this knowledge from other customers rather than from communication efforts driven by the organisation. There is clearly a need for more research which identifies the networks of relationships customers use to accumulate resources to participate.[17]

- *Providing service co-production opportunities and resources consistent with the customer's desired level of involvement leads to improved competitive advantage through enhanced customer experience.*

  This proposition relates to the factors influencing the customers' desire/willingness to get involved in the first place. It is clear from the customer comments, noted in Exhibit 11.1, that levels of ability and willingness to become involved vary greatly between customers.

- *Firms can compete more effectively through the adoption of collaboratively developed risk-based pricing value propositions.*

  The issue of 'collaboration' in a service context includes how customer involvement relates to (impacts on) employee performance. To explore this area services academics would need to work more closely with colleagues in the area of human resource management.

Exhibit 11.1   Customer Confidence and Ability

I used the Self scan self checkout twice. I quite liked them. I have to say I did get stuck on both occasions . . . but now I know what to do. I love it when people watch you and you are doing it there fine..all happy and smiling . . . .

I have worked in shops since I was 16 years old that's 10 years but these b . . . . . . machines make me feel like its my first day! I hate them. My boyfriend insists on using them cos they are gadgety . . . .

We've got them in our local supermarket. I don't use them as man and machinery don't usually work together well, and I know that if its going to break down it will do so on me and Im the one left standing there looking like a gormless plum . . . not good.

Additional Areas for Future Research

The employment experience

In Chapter 7 we identified a need for organisations to provide a good experience to ensure that service employees deliver and perform high-quality services. We believe that research into what might constitute a 'good' employment experience would be worthwhile. We have noted throughout this book that the service sector has undergone rapid change as a result of the pervasive adoption of TBSS. This will affect the employee experience as well as the customer experience. If service employees, who previously chose careers in the service industries because they enjoy interacting with people, find the decreasing opportunity for direct contact less enjoyable, how can service organisations best reward and retain them? The increased reliance on technology within the working environment also brings with it the need to understand the impact of technology failure on service employee performance.

One of the current and most vocal concerns of business organisations relating to managing their workforce is how to attract and retain the 'Generation Y' employee. A survey conducted by Deloitte's concluded that organisations providing Gen Y employees with the opportunity to contribute their talents to non-profit organisations might gain a recruitment advantage.[18] Gen Y appear to view and evaluate employment as an experience that needs to meet their lifestyle needs more than other employee groups. They want to work with friends, or in a friendly environment. They seek flexibility and have a tendency to use technology to blur the boundaries between work and home life.[19] The current practitioner focus on the characteristics of Gen Y employees that differentiate them from other employees suggests a need for academic research to study the service marketing implications arising from the need to attract, retain and benefit from their contributions as service providers.

The working environment now looks quite different from just a few years ago with customers expecting to be able to contact service providers and access service provision 24/7. Of course this is a self-perpetuating cycle as the greater number of employees that are required to work outside of the traditional 9–5 period fuels the need for service organisations to extend their service hours to meet their demands. Does this provide service organisations with an opportunity to manage their employee work schedules to match the profile of employees with the prevailing customer profiles during the same time period and, if so, would it affect customer satisfaction and perceptions of service quality?

Another business practice that has become more prevalent is the global outsourcing of service functions. Service organisations now frequently outsource the provision of call centres that provide customer support. In some cases this takes the form of relocating to another country to benefit from lower labour costs. This practice has occurred within the UK banking market where call centres have been set up in India to service UK customers. In other cases organisations that operate globally channel all customer service support through one centre. Singapore Airlines have adopted this approach through their website and their call centre. The first option when contacting them is to select your language. Given the need for service employees to understand and empathise with their customers the added complexity created by cultural diversity is likely to impact upon the perception of service quality.

Customer switching behaviour

One aspect of loyalty behaviour that has received relatively little attention is that of customer switching. Customers may defect from, or switch between, service providers as a result of service failure events, conditions (e.g. inconvenience) or competition which includes pricing. The most influential research in this area to date concluded that service failure events were the main reason why customers switched from one service provider to another.[20] This finding led to significant attention being paid to service failure events by both academic researchers and practitioners. Much of that work has been discussed throughout this book. However, a recent study suggests that the situation is more complex than previously described in that conditions may play a more significant role than previously acknowledged and may depend on whether the service is 'located' or 'non-located'.[21] The most frequent reason for switching among non-located service providers was price, whereas inconvenience and other conditions were most likely to prompt switching among located services. Service failure events were more likely to lead customers to switch among non-located than located service providers. These findings prompt the researchers to conclude that the current focus of management attention and organisational resources directed at the service encounter may be misplaced. Such a suggestion is obviously controversial so we anticipate switching behaviour becoming a more widely researched area.

Service recovery

The role of perceived justice

We explained the concept of perceived justice in Chapter 9 as comprising three elements: distributive justice (the outcome), procedural justice (the process) and interactional justice (the impact of people). However a recent study has identified a further influence on customer evaluations of service recovery, that of macro-justice, which is associated with perceptions of collective practices at the industry level.[22] The identification of macro-justice as an influence leads the researchers to suggest that differentiating the behaviour of the organisation from competitors within an industry with a negative image would provide a competitive advantage. Alternatively, they posit that collective strategies that improve macro-justice perceptions of a service industry would influence perceived quality and trust to the benefit of all. The study found that perceived justice influences satisfaction and relationship quality as measured by trust and commitment with relationship maintenance and customer loyalty behaviours associated with higher levels of perceived justice.

Managing dysfunctional customers

The language and concepts of services marketing has become widely known and used by customers as well as service organisations. Customers have been bombarded with questionnaires asking them to evaluate the service provision and seeking information on satisfaction and willingness to recommend the provider to others. A number of service providers have even claimed that they aim to exceed customer expectations. Many service providers have developed 'customer charters' to communicate their service performance standards to customers. Customers are able to access enormous amounts of information, frequently in real time. All of this means that customers are more aware than ever of service performance standards. One outcome of the need for business organisations to continually identify and develop competitive advantages is that service performance standards can be copied. A standard which was seen as outstanding when only one organisation offered it can very quickly become a basic customer requirement of the industry. The introduction of the 'flat bed' airline seat is a good example. Originally a British Airways innovation introduced for First Class passengers in 1996, it is now a standard item for long haul flights within Business Class. As a result customer expectations are constantly changing and placing greater demands on service organisations to deliver.

However, not all customer expectations are reasonable and not all customers behave well. Such customers have been called 'Jay customers' which suggests they demonstrate similar anti-social behaviours that we associate with Jay birds. This raises a number of issues for service organisations. There is the need to identify Jay customers and manage customer-to-customer interactions to limit the impact that Jay customers might have on other, more desirable, customers. There is also a need to understand the impact that Jay customers have on the perceptions of co-customers and the ability of service employees to perform. To date this area has attracted little academic research.

As if that were not bad enough for service organisations, it has been said that we now live in 'an age of rage'[23] and that the number of angry customers exhibiting volatile behaviours has increased to the level of being common place rather than isolated incidents. Service employees, fellow customers and inanimate objects may all become the target of raging customer behaviours. Service organisations may be able to reduce the frequency and impact of these incidents through identification of the triggers for rage, training service employees to recognise and prepare for encounters with potentially dangerous customers. Employees also need to know how to diffuse a volatile situation if they have not been able to prevent it arising. The skills involved in such a process differ from those which we traditionally associate with performing a service well and are therefore additional skills that service organisations need to address. To date this aspect of service recovery has received very little academic attention and we therefore view it as ripe for future research.

Cultural impact on service recovery

Much of our knowledge of service recovery is predicated on the assumption that organisations need to have a recovery strategy to implement when service failures arise. While it is acknowledged that recovery strategies may need to differ depending upon the service failure, the need to adapt service recovery depending upon customer characteristics has received comparatively little academic attention. However, a recent article suggests that differences in customer recovery expectations when presented with similar service failures may be attributed to customer adherence to different cultural models.[24] The researchers provide the following overview of consumer cultural models and suggested diagnostics:

Table 11.2   Overview of consumer cultural models and diagnostics

Consumer cultural models	Relational	Positional	Utilitarian
A consumer applying this cultural model	. . . has a strong desire to maintain emotional ties with the provider and 'work together' to make things right after a goods and/or service failure.	invokes a suspicious and oppositional position towards providers after a service and/or goods failure.	. . . weighs future benefits of the relationship against the incurred cost (in time and effort) stemming from the goods and/or service failure.
Consumer responses to a failure	• Emotional (looking for consolation) • Anxious (e.g. sense of estrangement, betrayal, or being slighted, letdown, and hurt). • Self-attribution. • Self embarrassment. • Commitment to solve the problem. • Recovery paradox effect possible. • Willingness to forgive, absolve, and tolerate.	• Emotional (aggressive, distancing) • Caveat emptor. • Not willing to forgive. • Emotional/angry. • Tentative, skeptical, and cynical. • Recovery paradox unlikely. • Does not forgive easily.	• Provider attribution • Equity approach / homo economicus. • Inconvenient to the achievement of personal goals. • Irritated. • Recovery paradox unlikely.
Managerial diagnostics identifying cultural models. The consumer	• Expresses hurt/vulnerability. • Looks for consolation.	• Is antagonistic • Blames provider • Aggressive (I am being exploited)	• Is not emotional, firm. • Rational.

Table 11.2   (Continued)

Consumer cultural models	Relational	Positional	Utilitarian
	• Is helpful. • May blame self. • Shows understanding. • Will work with the provider.	• Is overly demanding. • Shows willingness to fight. • Suggests excessive redemption	• Expects compensation for time/discomfort. • Is very pragmatic.
Consumer's expected recovery initiatives from providers	• Sincere apology. • Show respect. • Care for the customer. • Explanation of why things went wrong. • Assert the importance to have consumer as a partner.	• Provide a range of recovery options among which the consumer can choose (sense of control). • Resist satisfying excessive demands.	• Acknowledge (take responsibility) and explain the problem. • Exchange or refund. • Compensate for time or energy.

Source: Ringberg, T., Odekerken-Schröder, G. and Christensen, G. L., 'A Cultural Models Approach to Service Recovery', *Journal of Marketing*, vol 71, July 2007, p. 210.

Once again this highlights a fertile area for research to gain a better understanding of different consumer cultural models as well as equipping service employees with the additional skills required to identify customer types and adapt their service recovery scripts accordingly.

Health services research

Health services are clearly important worldwide. They are offered in different forms in different countries. In the United Kingdom, for example, the National Health Service is a *public* service offered free-of-charge to all, with private health organisations offering an alternative at a price. In the United States, there is not a universal health care system. Around 84 per cent of US citizens have some form of health insurance; either through their employer, purchased individually, or provided by government programmes.

Whether health services are public or private, they have common, specific characteristics that make them different from other services, and very difficult to operate effectively and efficiently. In health services[25]:

- Customers are generally sick
- Customers are reluctant recipients of the service
- Customers relinquish their privacy
- Customers need the providers to understand them holistically

- Customers are at risk; they can be harmed by the service
- Clinicians (the providers) are stressed.

These characteristics make health services an 'intellectually challenging field of study'[26] where enormous sums of money are spent on something that contributes significantly to well-being.

The theatrical approach to services

The Theatre metaphor was introduced in Chapter 3. The way is still open to explore the metaphor in key service areas. For example, how can theatrical performance measurement and analysis methods inform service performance measurement and analysis? It could contribute to the understanding of the elements that constitute value for consumers (thought of as audience). How can improvisation in music (say, jazz) inform the training of service employees? This has potential to explore further the notion of the employee as operant resource.

On Research Methodology

Although it is likely that mainly quantitative research techniques will continue to be used extensively in many areas of investigation, researchers are presently being encouraged to draw on a range of quantitative and qualitative research to provide richer insights into a range of topics: specifically the use of field experiments, participant observation and more laboratory experiments. Researchers are making a deliberate effort to combine different research techniques to investigate some of the more difficult issues. Price, Arnould and Deibler,[27] for example, used both participant observation and consumer diary methodologies to gain new insights into the interpersonal dimensions of service encounters. In the latter, consumers were recruited and trained to record characteristics of their service encounters, along with their own emotional responses. These records were completed immediately after each encounter.

The services marketing academic community seem more open to encourage the application of innovative research methods. It is recognised that survey-based, quantitative studies, which still dominate the published articles in many of the academic journals, can be complemented by more qualitative studies. For example, the editorial in the first edition of the *Journal of Service Research* emphasised that many business disciplines are represented on the editorial board, which 'is also inclusive of quantitative, behavioural and qualitative approaches'.[28] In a more recent editorial in the *Journal of Services Marketing*, the appropriateness of studies that involve 'pilot studies, or "exploratory" research that offer some data to tentatively address relevant research questions, and...case studies that show the relevance or application of the topic in a specific company setting', in the early stages of a topic's lifestyle, was restated.[29]

Our rally, above, for a greater understanding of how and why people behave the way they do, would require qualitative research based on *extended observations* of the people concerned, and interpretations of their behaviour. Such studies should add richness to the data collected and uncover the subtleties in behaviour that are related to cultures or technologies.

Learning Outcomes

Having read this chapter, you should be able to

- appreciate the potential importance, to the academic and practitioner community, of the recent emergence of the field of study that has been named, 'Service Science, Management and Engineering' (SSME), and its association with the language of S-D Logic

- appreciate the need for empirical testing of the claims that underpin S-D logic to understand how consumers co-create value and how they make sense of that experience

- appreciate the importance of considering, and integrating, TBSS when designing services and the need to research the impact that increasing customer productivity, through TBSS use, will have on both the consumer and the employee experience

- appreciate the need to learn more about the impact that culture and perceived justice have on service recovery as well as the need to differentiate between 'good' and 'bad' consumers

- appreciate the potential contribution of observational research to an understanding of human behaviour in service contexts.

Notes and References

1. Vargo, S. L. and Lusch, R. F., 'Evolving to a New Dominant Logic for Marketing', *The Journal of Marketing*, 68(1), 2004, pp. 1–17.
2. Brown, S., 'Are We Nearly There Yet? On the Retro-Dominant Logic of Marketing', *Marketing Theory*, 7(3), 2007, pp. 291–300.
3. Lusch, R. F., Vargo, S. L. and O'Brien, M., 'Competing through Service: Insights from Service-Dominant Logic', *Journal of Retailing*, 83(1), 2007, pp. 5–18.
4. In particular, two forums on the S-D logic have been hosted by the University of Otago in New Zealand (2005 and 2008).
5. www.research.ibm.com/ssme.
6. www.ibm.com.
7. Patricio, L., Fisk, R. P. and Falcao e Cunha, J., 'Designing Multi-Interface Service Experiences', *Journal of Service Research*, 10(4), 2008, pp. 318–34.
8. Voss, C. A., 'Rethinking Paradigms of Service – Service in a Virtual Environment', *International Journal of Operations & Production Management*, 23(1), 2003, pp. 88–104.
9. Ezeh, C. and Harris, L. C., 'Servicescape Research: A Review and a Research Agenda', *The Marketing Review*, 7(1), 2007, pp. 59–78.
10. Curran, J. M. and Meuter, M. L., 'Encouraging Existing Customers to Switch to Self-Service Technologies: Put a Little Fun in their Lives', *Journal of Marketing Theory and Practice*,15(4), 2007, pp. 283–98.
11. Bateson, J., 'Are your Customers Good Enough for Your Service Business?', *Academy of Management Executive*,16(4), 2002, pp. 110–20.
12. Bendapudi, N. and Leone, R., 'Psychological Implications of Customer Participation in Co-Production', *Journal of Marketing*, vol. 67, Jan 2003, pp. 14–28.
13. Lovelock, C. and Young, R., 'Look to Customers to Increase Productivity', *Harvard Business Review*, vol. 57, 1979, pp. 168–78.

14. Johnston R. and Jones P., 'Service Productivity: Towards Understanding the Relationship between Operational and Customer Productivity', *International Journal of Productivity and Performance Management*, 53,(3), 2004, pp. 201–13.
15. Hsieh, A-T. and Yen, C-H., 'The Effect of Customer Participation on Service Providers' Job Stress', *The Service Industries Journal*, 25(7), 2005, pp. 891–905.
16. Lusch, Vargo and O'Brien, 'Competing through Service: Insights from Service-Dominant Logic'.
17. Baron, S. and Harris, K., 'Consumers as Resource Integrators', *Journal of Marketing Management*, 24(1–2), 2008, pp. 113–30.
18. http://www.deloitte.com/dtt/press_release/0,1014,cid%253D152753,00.html.
19. http://www.time.com/time/magazine/article/0,9171,1640395,00.html.
20. Keaveney, S. M., 'Customer Switching Behavior in Service Industries: An exploratory study', *Journal of Marketing*, 59(2), 1995, pp. 71–82.
21. East, R., Grandcolas, U. and Dall 'Olmo Riley, R., 'New Evidence on the Reasons for Switching Service Providers', *Marketing Theory into Practice: Proceedings of the Annual Academy of Marketing Conference*, Kingston University, London, England, July 2007.
22. Aurier, P. and Siadou-Martin, B., 'Perceived Justice and Consumption Experience Evaluations: A Qualitative and Experimental Investigation', *International Journal of Service Industry Management*, 18(5), 2007, pp. 450–71.
23. Grove, S. J., Fisk, R. P. and John, J., 'Surviving in the Age of Rage', *Marketing Management,* March/April 2004, pp. 41–6.
24. Ringberg, T., Odekerken-Schröder, G. and Christensen, G. L., 'A Cultural Models Approach to Service Recovery', *Journal of Marketing,*vol. 71, July 2007, pp. 194–214.
25. Berry, L. L. and Bendapudi, N., 'Health Care: A Fertile Field for Service Research', *Journal of Service Research*, 10(2), 2007, pp. 111–22.
26. Ibid.
27. Price, L. L., Arnould, E. J. and Deibler, S. L., 'Service Provider influence on consumers' emotional responses to Service encounters', Proceedings of the 3rd International research Seminar on Services Management, La-Londe-Les-Maures, France, May 1994.
28. Rust, R. T., 'Editorial, What Kind of Journal is the Journal of Service Research?', *Journal of Service Research,*1(1), 1998, pp. 3–4.
29. Martin, C. L., 'Editorial, Completing Your Life with JSM', *Journal of Services Marketing*, 15(2), 2001, pp. 78–81.

Case Studies

1

Joe & Co. Hairdressing

History and Background of the Business

Joe & Co Hairdressing, owned by Anthony Keates, was established in August 1990 in Leek, in the north Midlands of England. Given the 'up-market' position of the salon relative to competitors in the Leek area, Anthony could easily have used his own name for the hairdressing business. He chose instead, however, to adopt the nickname 'Joe' in the title, which was originally given to him by his teammates in his local Sunday morning football team. Although 'Joe & Co' was set up in 1990, Anthony had owned a salon in Leek between 1981 and 1986. He subsequently gave this up to take up a teaching career in hairdressing. While he enjoyed the experience of teaching, and learnt a lot in four years about different types of hairdressing businesses (by visiting trainee students on hairdressing placements), he felt he still had too much to offer as a practising professional hairdresser to stay in teaching full-time. He decided to open up a new business in a different part of Leek. In 1990, despite the four years' absence from full-time hairdressing, Anthony used his knowledge of the community and old contacts to build up a strong customer base for the new salon. He found that 15 per cent of the customers he had dealt with in 1986 appeared on his doorstep as clients for the new business.

The present salon operates with two part-time female stylists, Anthony himself and two junior staff who are learning the profession. Details of the range of services offered are given in Figure CS1.1. The salon opens five days a week and closes on a Monday. Two stylists work each day. They each have eight clients booked for an appointment every day, working to a target of one client per hour. The restriction on the number of client bookings was a deliberate policy decision by Anthony who feels that only by allowing each client this amount of time can he guarantee that they will receive what he considers to be a 'necessary' level of customer service.

PRICE LIST

PERMANENT WAVING SERVICES

(not including any other service)

	Joe Acid	Alkaline	Pip/Bev Acid	Alkaline
Top Perm	£14.00	£10.00	£13.00	£10.00
Three Quarter Perm	£16.50	£14.50	£15.50	£13.50
Full Head Perm	£20.00	£17.50	£18.00	£16.00
Technical Winding	Upon application			
Long Hair	upon application			
Le Coiffeur (exclusive)	£25.00		£23.00	

LADIES

	Joe	Pip/Bev
Restyling (inc. Wash and Dry)	£16.50	£13.50
Cutting (inc. Wash and Dry)	£14.00	£12.00
Trimming (by prior arrangement)	£7.50	£7.00
Blow Drying	£7.00	£6.00
Setting	£7.00	£5.00

GENTS

	Joe	Pip/Bev
Cutting (inc. ash and Dry) (Dry cutting by prior agreement with Bev only)	£7.50	£6.50

COLOURING SERVICES

(not including any other service)

		Joe	Pip/Bev
Permanent Colour: Full Head		£13.50	£12.00
Roots		£10.50	£10.00
Colourbath		£8.00	£7.50
Semi Permanent Colour		£5.50	£5.00
Highlighting/Lowlighting: Cap	Full Head	£13.00	£12.00
	Part Head	£10.00	£10.00
Highlighting/Lowlighting: Essi meche. foils			
Full Head		£20.00	£20.00
Part Head		£14.00	£14.00
Roots		£16.00	£16.00

CONDITIONING SERVICES

Le Coiffeur Conditioning Treatments from £3.00
All prices inclusive of styling products and refreshments

Figure CS1.1   Ranges of services offered by Joe & Co

Every customer deserves to be greeted with a cup of coffee, have their coat taken and receive a quality haircut in a professional environment. You cannot do this properly if you are always worrying about finishing one client's hair to get another one through the door!

He does not do any advertising for the business as the client book is always full.

The Salon

From the outside, the salon looks professional. The exterior and interior decor has a distinctive black-and-white theme with a simple but effective painting on the door stating 'Joe & Co Hairdressing'. The window has not been deliberately designed to attract passing trade as all new customers come from recommendations made by existing clients.

Inside, there is a black-and-white marble floor with black cushioned chairs for customers. The staff wear black trousers and waistcoats and white shirts or blouses, and coffee is served in black-and-white mugs with the Joe & Co logo on the outside.

Plants are placed strategically around the mirrors in the salon to enhance the perception of a clean, fresh working environment. The physical environment has been deliberately designed to create the professional image that Anthony considers to be such a critical part of good customer service.

The Customer Profile

The majority of customers are female aged between 30 and 60 years. According to Anthony, what they all have in common is that they appreciate a good cut! This was confirmed by a regular customer who described the cutting side of the service as the best in the area. Although the salon is technically unisex, only about 10 per cent of customers are male, and very few are teenagers. Anthony attributes this largely to the attitude of these particular client groups towards hairdressing. With only eight appointments per stylist available each day, appointments have to be carefully scheduled and planned by clients in advance. As they leave one appointment, regular clients are encouraged to book their next six weekly appointment. The system makes it very difficult for anyone just to turn up in the hope of getting an appointment. They can expect to have to wait at least six weeks to get in for a haircut. In Anthony's experience, men and younger fashion-conscious women are rarely prepared to wait that long. The technical 'cut' of their hair is just not that important to them.

Anthony considers each of his clients as 'long-term' prospects. It is important that he establishes a good relationship with them from the very beginning so that he can 'manage' the development of their hair. Although many clients may not feel that they have changed their style very much since they have been visiting the salon, Anthony knows that in comparison to how they looked since first attending, many of them are significantly different. Many clients have been with Joe & Co since the business opened in 1990. Customers who do not stay are usually those who were not prepared to wait for an appointment. As the majority of customers know each other well (having been recruited by personal recommendation), they chat easily while having their hair cut. As Leek is a small rural community where almost everyone is interested and involved in community events, the salon acts as a focal point for debate and 'gossip'. The atmosphere in the salon is consequently very relaxed and informal.

Restrictions on Growth

Anthony has been operating the strict 'appointment only' system for over a year. It was originally set up because the stylists were so busy that clients were having to wait too long in the salon itself between appointments. Although the system ensures that all clients receive the full attention of each stylist for at least an hour, and clearly generates strong customer loyalty, there are negative aspects to the policy. As well as the obvious frustration felt by clients who are unable to get extra appointments for special occasions or change appointments at the last minute, Anthony himself feels personally frustrated at times. In one sense he is a victim of his own success. 'Although having such a regular group of customers means that I am always busy, it is difficult to keep interested in the technical side of the job, with familiar clientele.'

He attends hairdressing seminars and keeps up to date with the latest fashion styles by reading magazines and journals, but he feels at times that his creative talents are being stifled by the system. Whilst he has the full range of hairdressing qualifications, as well as a hairdressing teaching qualification, he feels that, for his personal development, it is important to experiment with new styles and deal with new faces on a regular basis. One way to do this would be to move away from Leek and join a number of different salons in a large city. There he feels he would have the opportunity to compare his cutting skills with those of fellow professionals and gain recognition from them, as well as from clients. As a hairdressing professional, Anthony feels that this is an important component of his work. He is not motivated solely by money. As long as he can make enough to live comfortably, it is much more important that he enjoys his job. He is keen to have the opportunity to develop his own professional skills and expertise by working with some of the top hairdressers.

Another development option might be to open a second salon in another area. As Anthony explains, the difficulty here would be finding suitably qualified staff to work for him. He is conscious that his clients keep returning to the salon because of the particular skills and personalities of individual stylists. It is unlikely that they would stay loyal to Joe & Co if Anthony, Bev or Pip left to work in a second shop in a new location. Although the three stylists have very different personalities and strengths, they all have their own group of regular customers who expect their particular 'brand' of hairdressing service. Anthony, for example, attracts clients who are mainly interested in the technical quality of their haircut. He spends most of the time allotted concentrating on the detail of the cut itself. Pip and Bev have more outgoing personalities and allow time within the service to talk to customers, giving them a slightly different service 'experience'.

It appears to be very difficult to attract suitably qualified stylists to work in a salon of this type. Anthony recently advertised for a new stylist to take up a 'chair' in the salon on particular days of the week. For the rest of the time he/she might travel to work in different locations. Anthony felt that this would present an ideal opportunity for a motivated hairdresser to build up a loyal customer base without having to incur the overheads associated with actually generating your own premises.

A third development option might be to act as a representative for one of the leading hairdressing manufacturers, calling on other hairdressers and giving them technical advice on how to get the best out of their products.

Staff Development

As well as his personal development, Anthony is conscious of the need to train and develop the junior staff in the salon. He feels that one of the advantages of working for a smaller business, and operating a system that allocates an hour to each client, is that trainees can get hands-on experience in all aspects of the hairdressing business. He has the time to talk to the trainees about each aspect of the haircut as he works on each client. Even though the training may be good, however, he does not expect the young trainees to stay with Joe & Co for very long. Because of the dynamic nature of the hairdressing business, he feels that young people should be travelling around, building up their experience and learning new skills and techniques from professionals all over the world. He sees hairdressing as a very exciting and challenging career for young people who are prepared to dedicate themselves to reaching the top.

Competition

There are a number of other salons in the town of Leek and the surrounding area, but Anthony does not feel that these present serious competition to his business. He has more clients than he can manage at this point in time and feels that he must be doing enough to satisfy them for this to be the case. Although he recognises that the other salons provide a service for males, younger people and passing trade, he does not consider these to be the types of clients who would appreciate his particular offer. He finds it difficult to hide his frustration with customers who don't appreciate the quality of a good haircut. He treats every style like a work of art describing himself as a perfectionist who takes pride in the technical quality of his work.

The Future

Anthony is confident about his skills as a hairdresser, but he does not feel that he handles the business side of things as well as he might if his objective was to make as much money as possible. Although he sells his own hairdressing products in the salon, with the Joe & Co logo clearly inscribed on the bottles, he does not think that it is fair to 'push' customers into buying them just so that he can make more money. They are the products that they use every day in the salon, and if customers ask for his advice then he recommends them as he feels they are quality products, but it is totally up to the individual client what they buy.

Prices for services are laid out on the pricing card (see Figure CS1.1). However, Anthony likes to retain a certain amount of flexibility with the prices charged. For example, he explains, 'If I do not feel that a client's hair has taken as long as it should for the price charged and treatment received, I will reduce the price accordingly. I suppose that this would not be considered very good business practice but then . . . '.

Whilst each client is treated as a long-term prospect, Anthony does not have a clearly defined long-term strategy for the business. He does not feel that he or his staff have the necessary expertise to offer other services to customers as some other hairdressers are beginning to do. These may include, for example, make-up advice, colour consultancy, skin-care treatments including sunbeds and facials. His main problem at the moment is working out how he is going to fit in all his regular clients for a haircut before Christmas!

2

George Ball & Son, Funeral Directors

History of the Company

In 1870, George Ball was a joiner working in the Heaton Moor area of Stockport, a town six miles south of Manchester in the north-west of England. As part of his trade, he made coffins of solid wood and people came to him for these in particular. In those days it was a basic need to have a coffin as it was normal for the deceased to be kept at home prior to a funeral, rather than be taken to a chapel of rest. George's wife was the local nurse and midwife and it was part of her duties to 'lay out' people who had died; that is, wash the body and prepare it for the funeral. Because of their dual roles, a funeral business evolved. George and his wife began to hire horse-drawn hearses from the Parish Borough Carriage Company.

At the time there were many small funeral directors, even within a couple of streets of each other, but nearly all the funeral services were additional to the main business. As well as joinery/building businesses, furniture shops with skilled cabinetmakers would also make coffins and 'undertake' the services required for burials. George Ball, however, was the first funeral director in Stockport to provide a chapel of rest. George passed the business on to his son, also called George, who in turn passed it on to his son Sidney Ball in 1954. The company is now run by Margaret Arnison, Sidney's daughter, who took over in 1978 when her father retired at 65, and the family business is now in its fourth generation. It operates as a sole trader, not as a limited company. Until three years ago, Margaret's husband was running a building business in conjunction with the funeral business.

The Current Premises

The business is located, since February 1994, at a former print works which was refurbished by Margaret's husband. It is next door to their previous premises and, in addition to having 'loads of space', is ideal because of the access for vehicles to the back of the building. The business has now got its own fleet of vehicles, complete with GBS personalised number plates, an option which was not available to them (because of lack of access to the rear) at the previous address.

On entering the front door, there is an office to the right and an interview room to the left. Towards the rear of the building are two small chapels of rest separated by a curtain. When the curtain is open the combined space of the two chapels of rest is large enough for a service to be held. Some people prefer a service here to one at a church.

Further back is a garage for the vehicles and a workshop/storeroom. The latter has a stock of coffins, many accessories and an engraving machine. Nowadays it is very rare to have solid wood coffins. Large joinery firms started making coffin sets (i.e., sides, base and lids) to various sizes, and moved on to making veneers. George Ball & Son have not made their own coffins for the last 25 years. It is economically sensible for them to order coffins rather than make them. Also the regulations to protect the environment, with regard to cremations, are very strict; great care has to be taken to ensure that the correct glues, varnishes and finishes are used.

They own another smaller office in Heaton Norris, three miles away, which they purchased five years ago. This office is not always manned but is always operational with a telephone transfer to the main Heaton Moor office. It contains a small chapel of rest, a facility that is needed in Heaton Norris. A series of takeovers and closures of funeral businesses had left people in the area without a conveniently located chapel of rest.

The Staff

There are three full-time staff working for the business: Margaret Arnison herself, another funeral director, Nick Luty and Margaret's 21-year-old son Daniel. Margaret and Nick split the funeral directing between them, supported by a part-time lady who runs the office. Daniel takes on a whole range of duties including office work, driving, and coffin preparation. Margaret's husband, Bill, also helps out with any building work, such as the recent refurbishment, and 'covering' the office when needed.

Staff working in a funeral business do not require any qualifications or registration by law. People can start up a funeral business with no training or experience whatsoever, and some do. This used to cause problems for the image of funeral businesses in general. According to Margaret Arnison, it is not so much of a problem now as anyone proposing to start up a funeral business would require substantial financial backing.

George Ball & Son, with over 120 years of experience in the business, are very aware of the importance of having the right staff, who are fully trained, to work in such a sensitive area. They insist that the staff are 'straight as a die, discreet, and aware of the regulations so that they don't overstep the mark in any sense'. There is a qualification available – the Diploma in Funeral Directing – that is run under the auspices of the National Association of Funeral Directors (NAFD). Training and Education in Funeral Services (TEFS), which incorporates NAFD, is currently taking on board the National Vocational Qualification (NVQ) framework for the award. This move introduces a test with a number of practical competencies associated with the job; for example, fitting out a coffin and cleaning the car, which are basic skills, but ones that really matter in the job. The practical competencies support the other tested area; the knowledge of procedures. Knowing the regulations and the appropriate forms to be completed is vitally important. When someone rings in to say a relative has died, there are many standard procedures to go through before the body can be moved to the chapel of rest. Failure to apply the procedures can lead to problems with the coroner if the death was believed to have occurred in suspicious circumstances.

In general, staff need to be ultra-flexible (they can be rung up in the middle of the night), good with people (they have to deal with doctors, ministers, families, old people, young people) and be confident on the telephone. If someone rings up, a member of staff must clearly and confidently establish what kind of funeral is required from people who are anxious and distressed.

The Service

George Ball & Son deal with approximately 250 funerals a year. In a given week, there can be as many as 12 funerals. Unlike the situation half a century ago, there is now no discernible seasonality in demand. Whilst there are many technical, logistical and procedural elements to the service, they acknowledge that they offer the first line of bereavement counselling. They are 'looking after people at a very vulnerable time; getting them through the first week when they don't want to make any decisions but certain choices have to be made'.

There is much to bereavement counselling and every occasion is different. On the day everything must be right, and it must be right first time. There is no second chance. The funeral director must listen carefully to what has happened – was it a sudden death or long illness? Was it a tragedy or a relief? – so that he/she can take the background into account when planning the details of a funeral which takes the form that the bereaved would prefer. In most cases, the longer-term bereavement counselling must be taken on by someone else. People do not always want to keep seeing the funeral director after the funeral itself. On occasions, however, someone who is on their own will call in regularly for help or just a chat, and the staff will always make themselves available even though the main business has finished.

At the time of the first contact with the funeral business, people need to be put at their ease. In particular, they need to know that the first decision, often taken at a time of great stress, need not be final. They can change their mind if they want to. Information about available alternatives needs to be given in a clear and sympathetic way. The funeral director will also need to be able to respond to worries about all the 'red tape' that has to be gone through. The bereaved find probate – the process of officially proving the validity of a will – particularly confusing and an intrusion into their private financial circumstances. To be able to explain the procedure and, often more importantly, why the procedure has to take place is a further skill required of funeral directors, even though probate is not directly their responsibility.

It is clear that 'no two funerals are ever the same'. Margaret Arnison sums up the company's attitude to bereavement counselling and the provision of a funeral service as follows:

> It's making the families know and feel that whatever they ask is normal for them, and that it's no trouble for us, even if we have to pull out all the stops to make it happen.

There are many examples of them carrying out this philosophy. They range from requests to dress the deceased in a particular way – even in thermal underwear to keep out the cold – to making special arrangements for transport and equipment. One lady, for example, requested a white coffin and white limousines. The limousines were hired from a company that has wedding cars. On another occasion, four grey Rolls-Royces were brought in from Huddersfield, 50 miles away, at the request of the widow of a businessman who had always been a 'showman'. The HRH number plate on the Rolls-Royces added to the occasion. The funeral caused quite a stir and the occasion suited and helped the family to remember the deceased in an appropriate way. It was just the right touch.

There have been occasions when George Ball & Son have made arrangements for a body to be flown home quickly, when a relative has died abroad. Although there is a repatriation service available, based in London, it is more costly and does not offer an individual service. Margaret Arnison can recall a situation where, after a phone call on a Saturday from the deceased's mother, the body of the daughter was in Stockport, flown from South Africa, by the following Thursday. To do this involved teamwork and knowing what to do, and making use of networks of contacts who are members of the NAFD.

Teamwork

Teamwork is of paramount importance in providing the service. Not only must individuals in the business work as a team with a common philosophy – all being willing, for example, to pick up relatives and drive them to the registrar or to the chapel of rest – but the business must form a team with other 'players' such as ministers, doctors and grave diggers. Funerals are likened to a jigsaw. On the outside are the fixed elements – the time, the place, the minister – and there is a picture in the middle which makes it right for the particular customer. The elements of the picture may include a special piece of music played at the service or a reading by a long-standing friend.

At one funeral, a reading was given by the schoolfriend of the deceased, who managed it in a very composed manner. However, the minister had a copy of the speech in case the school-friend found the occasion too much. One lady had expected only a few people to attend her father's funeral. However, Margaret Arnison received a phone call from the 'Normandy veterans' to say that the deceased was an ex-member of their association. After many subsequent phone calls between Margaret, the minister and the veterans, they were able to provide a union flag, poppy wreath (each provided by George Ball & Son), a tape of the last post (provided by the veterans), and a guard of honour at the service. The family were overwhelmed by the simple tribute and the kindness of the veterans.

It is clear that, where such teamwork is essential, an oversight by one of the team can cause a problem with the funeral service. This may happen, for example, if flowers have not been ordered or the wrong hymns are played, or family names are forgotten in the service. Through experience, fail-safes and contingency plans can be devised to prevent such mistakes happening more than once.

A 'popular' image of a funeral service is governed by what is seen by those attending a funeral. Some people perceive the funeral directors as driving up on the day of the funeral, being on hand for an hour or two, and departing. They wonder why it can cost £900. They do not see, or understand, what is happening behind the scenes, and do not take into account that the business is 'open' 24 hours a day, 365 days a year with premises to be run, 'bone fide' staff to be employed (e.g., coffin bearers), and the responsibility and effort to be applied to getting things right for the customer. It is probably not appreciated by most that there is a considerable amount of expenditure on the premises alone, as refrigeration or cooling systems need to be in place because of the type of building, and hoists need to be installed for the many lifting jobs in compliance with Health and Safety regulations.

Orders have to be made for coffin sets, sometimes in special sizes, and the coffins must be prepared. Handles and other accessories have to be attached at the workshop and engraving applied. All these tasks require training and skills. Virtually all the accessories and the gowns are obtained from a single supplier.

Methods of Payment and Record Keeping

Customers normally do not pay the funeral business directly. Payment is made through the customer's solicitor. George Ball & Son do not accept credit cards and receive payments mainly by cheque and cash. Their bills are made up in two parts: the funeral services and disbursements. Disbursements are the payments made by the funeral business on behalf of the customer to cemeteries, crematoria, ministers, churches, doctors and so on. At any point in time, George Ball &

Son have laid out very large amounts of money on behalf of customers prior to receiving payment. As Margaret Arnison says, 'Disbursements can be horrendous.' Some 50 per cent of the bills are paid within two months, but in some cases it can be as long as two years before the bill is finally settled. Often delays in payment are out of control of the family of the deceased, who can be very embarrassed about them. Some solicitors do not rate funeral payments at the top of their list of priorities. The funeral business is, in effect, offering an interest-free money-lending service.

At George Ball & Son, records of orders, invoices, payments and all other details are kept in a manual system. They have contemplated computerisation, and are not averse to it, but currently hold the view that the business can be managed efficiently without computer databases. All the order forms from past funerals are kept in a filing cabinet in the office. It only takes a few minutes to locate a particular file, even one going back many years. This is required when, for example, a family is using the business for a second or subsequent time, and the previous file(s) are consulted as a reminder of the circumstances of the earlier death(s). It is recognised that such a system could be computerised but because the scale of the business is manageable – 250 new files per year – and the investment in time to create a database is considerable, the manual system is being kept. In contrast, the Manchester Crematorium has recently been computerised with over 200 000 funeral records, from 1892 to the present, on their database.

Making Contact with Customers

Most business comes from recommendations or tradition. Recommendations can be made via some very involved routes – 'the nephew of a person who died worked with the son of the man whose funeral we had just done'. There are also many families who, by tradition, use George Ball & Son for their funerals.

The nature of the funeral business makes it different from most others, from a marketing perspective. A funeral is infrequent (people may only make contact with the business once or twice in a lifetime) and is something that is a necessity, not a choice. Other businesses where customer contact is infrequent, but where the customer exercises a choice, can use mainstream promotional tactics, with special offers. Clearly, such tactics are inappropriate for funeral services. When *Yellow Pages* ring up saying how advertisements will encourage business, Margaret Arnison is not impressed.

They do advertise in the *Yellow Pages* and the *Thompson's Directory*, but believe that people will normally look for their telephone number in there, not use them as a means of making a choice. They always advertise in the local free paper, the *Heaton Guardian*, and have done so for many years. Again, the main purpose is to provide easy access to their telephone number, as people in the district will know it will be in the free paper. They also place advertisements in the various church magazines in the area. Such magazines are funded by the advertising revenue.

George Ball & Son are one of the nominated funeral directors for the largest UK prepayment plan, 'Chosen Heritage' (see next section and appendices). Such plans are now becoming popular and the company will be assured of regular business in the future through this scheme.

In general, people will use either a private family firm or the 'Co-op' for their funerals. The Co-op, or Co-operative Society, operate under their own name, or under the name of groups which they have bought out in the past. In Manchester, for example, there are very few family businesses left. Most funeral businesses are operated by the Co-op in one guise or another. In contrast, in Stockport, local membership of the NAFD is made up almost entirely of local family businesses (approximately 17 in all). Margaret Arnison is secretary/treasurer for the NAFD in Stockport. The Co-op has a presence in Stockport but no longer contributes to the local association of the NAFD. The family businesses can usually offer a lower price than the Co-op, but do not have the brand name or the regional/national catchment area.

'Chosen Heritage' Recommended Funeral Plans

Chosen Heritage Limited, who have operated since 1986, run a pre-arranged scheme where funeral plans can be paid for, in advance, by single payment or by 12, 24 or 60 monthly payments. In conjunction with the charity Age Concern, they offer special discounts for people aged 60 and over. Most of the 70 000 subscribers to the scheme are from the South of England. George Ball & Son is the nominated funeral director for the South Manchester area. This entails a much larger area to service than Stockport alone, and there are about 500 Chosen Heritage members on their list. An extract from the Chosen Heritage brochure, outlining the benefits of such a prepayment plan, is included in Appendix 1.

Three types of plan are offered – The Simplicity Plan, the Traditional Plan and the Heritage Plan. Nominated funeral directors must be capable of offering such plans to the highest standards. Details of the three plans are shown in Appendix 2.

As part of the scheme, Margaret Arnison would like to produce some literature about George Ball & Son. She has been talking to representatives of Age Concern who wish to promote the scheme, and believes that they could work together on this, as well as on an introduction to the company with details on how to find them. There would be more general information on how people can cope with grief and the willingness of the company to listen. By working together on the literature, the local branch of Age Concern and George Ball & Son can jointly provide information of specific relevance to South Manchester members of the scheme.

Service Quality

We establish the needs of the bereaved, and then are as flexible as we can be to meet those needs.

Service Quality for the company consists of the successful application of listening skills (to establish needs) and flexibility (to tailor the service, where possible, to meet the needs).

Customers are sometimes very surprised and appreciative of the flexibility. Some funeral directors still tell the customer *when* the funeral is to take place. George Ball & Son, as a matter of course, ask which day would be best, and whether morning, lunchtime or afternoon is preferable. They have found that some people find even this aspect incredible, as they have just been told a date and time in the past. Flexibility such as this may not cost any more to provide. Indeed, the business operates at a charge that is lower than that of most large organisations. What may be different is the ethos. Margaret Arnison insists that 'service is the first order of the day – the lads know that as well – we aim to do whatever the customer wants plus that bit extra'.

Fellow members of the NAFD believe that funeral directors should be client-oriented, providing customer-based services, and Margaret Arnison means to ensure that such a policy is carried out in practice. She has considered the possibility of applying for BS 5750 (ISO 9000) approval, but has doubts whether the business is big enough to warrant an application.

The Future

The business will stay as a family business, building on over 120 years of tradition and experience. People's expectations of funeral services are changing and they are responding accordingly. Much of their business is gained through personal recommendations or family loyalty. If the Chosen Heritage scheme really takes off in the north-west of England, the company may need to expand to accommodate the extra business, whilst maintaining the strengths of the personal customer service currently being offered.

Appendix 1

Some of the Benefits of a Chosen Heritage Plan

☑ Firm arrangements are made and understood in advance – avoiding future concern and distress for your relatives.

☑ A guarantee that, if you join today, the funeral is paid for at today's price. Whenever the funeral is actually required. Whatever the prices are at the time.

☑ Total security – your funeral payments are placed in National Funeral Trust, with Barclays Bank PLC as Custodian Trustee.

☑ Plans may be paid for by a single payment or in easy instalments. Suitable for those of any age – with no health questions.

☑ Available throughout England, Wales and mainland Scotland (also available in Northern Ireland – please ask for separate brochure).

Appendix 2

Burial Option

If you require burial instead of cremation, the Traditional and Heritage plans will cover the funeral director's services as itemised. In addition, because burial fees vary so widely, a contribution equivalent to the value of the cremation service fee prevailing at the time of the funeral will be made towards the burial fees. The current value of the Burial Contribution is shown on the enclosed application form.

Traditional®

The Traditional Plan is designed for those who require the customary features of a traditional funeral, whatever their religion. Either cremation or burial (see Burial Option below) can be selected.

■ Confidential and sympathetic advice on the social and legal aspects to be considered when arranging a funeral.

■ Helpful information and counselling if required on the religious ceremony and other matters.

■ Guidance on the certification and registration of death.

■ Removal of the deceased from the place of death within England, Wales and mainland Scotland to the funeral director's premises.

■ Preparation and care of the body in accordance with the wishes of the family.

■ High-quality oak-veneered coffin.

■ Viewing by the family at the funeral director's chapel of rest or other convenient place.

■ Provision of a hearse and limousine to start from the house (calling at a local church for a service if required) and then proceed to a local crematorium or cemetery.

■ Funeral director and staff attending as required, before, during and after the service.

■ Guidance to the religious and other authorities on the wishes of the deceased and relatives.

■ Complimentary 'return thanks' cards and full listing of floral tributes.

■ Cremation Service Fee to cover the cost of a service at a local crematorium, the minister's fee and cremation medical certificates (or Burial Option).

Heritage®

The Heritage Plan provides all the elements of the Traditional Plan, together with the following additional features, to complete the highest quality service

Figure CS2.1   Range of services offered by George Ball & Son

- A coffin of solid hardwood (instead of oak veneer).
- Conveyance of the deceased to a local church the evening before the service, if required.
- Provision of two limousines (rather than one).
- An obituary notice, placed by the funeral director in a local weekly newspaper.

Simplicity®

The Simplicity Plan provides an economical option for those who require a very basic cremation funeral, including only the essential features with the minimum of ceremony.

- Guidance on the certification and registration of death.
- Removal of the deceased from the place of death within England, Wales and mainland Scotland to the funeral director's premises.
- Care of the body prior to cremation (facilities for viewing are not included).
- Simplicity coffin.
- Provision of a hearse to meet the family at a local crematorium (the plan does not include a funeral procession from the house, or attendance at a church service).
- All necessary staff for the service.
- Cremation Service Fee to cover the cost of a service at a local crematorium, the minister's fee and cremation medical certificates.

Figure CS2.1   (Continued)

King's School Band Programme

Background

King's School is a leading independent day primary school for boys from Year 1–Year 8 (5–13-year olds). The school is situated in the suburb of Remuera in Auckland City, New Zealand. Established in 1922 the school sits on a ridge overlooking Auckland Harbour and caters for 680 boys. The ethos of the school is to reach the full potential of all boys in our care with an aim to 'develop the individual talents of each boy...for life'.

The school needed to consider how to fill the shoes of the Director of Music who resigned from King's. One applicant [Emma Featherstone] for the post used her interview to 'pitch' her ideas, beliefs and dreams. She drew attention to research that demonstrates how teaching children instruments before puberty has a significant impact on their general academic ability and social lives. While working in Hong Kong, Emma had previously created a music education programme to support her passionate belief that music should be learned as a practical subject rather than as a theoretical subject with children actually playing instruments to understand music. Emma 'sold' the opportunity to develop a unique programme that would benefit the boys and the school. Coincidentally, Emma's work in HK was known to the Head Master through a mutual friend, so he knew what could be achieved if the programme went ahead. He shared the vision. Emma was offered job on the understanding that she would establish and develop a similar programme at King's.

The Programme

The band programme is mandatory. Every boy is required to choose and learn to play an instrument. Every boy is on the same playing field but with no expectation of their playing ability. The purpose of the programme is to learn about music through playing an instrument and performing: experiential rather than theoretical learning. In terms of playing ability, boys are encouraged to just see how it goes. Some boys with special learning needs have had a huge success in music but would never have been given the opportunity to learn an instrument within an 'opt in' system. Such boys generally have to spend more time on basic learning skills which reduces the time available to pursue opportunities such as playing instruments. Often the boys who appear on the learning support register turn out to be among the best instrument players. The mandatory nature of the programme means that these boys are able to progress and achieve skills that would not be available to them otherwise.

Gathering Internal Support for the Programme

Emma started the programme with the full backing from the Headmaster and the School Board. The importance of this support cannot be overlooked given the huge task to be undertaken.

Colleagues

There were two groups of music colleagues. First the full-time teaching, administrative and senior staff at King's. Secondly the itinerant music teachers contracted to provide private music lessons for the boys outside of the formal and structured music education curriculum. The reaction from the two groups differed. The first group were Colleagues incredibly supportive and excited. The idea of the programme created a lot of 'buzz'. They want what is best for the boys and the school community and they could see the potential for the programme before it had even begun. Some thought the idea might be a challenge too far and were concerned that it might be en masse craziness but all were very supportive and wanted to make it work.

The reaction of the itinerant staff was patchy. Some were supportive but most were not. Knowing that the new programme would involve the boys learning to play instruments, they thought they would lose clients for private lessons. Knowing that the new programme was based on band instruments they feared that the importance of strings would suffer within the school. It was perceived as an attack on their livelihood. They wrote letters to the Headmaster outlining their fears. Meetings were held and assurances were given that their contracts would continue but still around one-third were not won over at the beginning. Four years on the number of students taking private lessons has gone from 150–285 which is almost one-third of all the boys which demonstrates that their fears were not warranted. However, there remains one who still struggles with the notion of the programme.

Curriculum

Music education is compulsory at primary and intermediate level within New Zealand. Previously the arts curriculum had been split between drama, art and music with music having 1.5 hours per week. Class band is now an hour per week with year group band having an additional hour in second week, so 3 hours over

2 weeks. The boys are split into different groups depending on the area of study and literature. Boys who join King's in Year 7 (post-primary school) are a bit behind those boys who have been with the school for their primary education. This requires additional consideration to ensure that they maximise their learning and because being at King's is all about being part of a team and community. Playing in a band for music education is not the same learning as one-to-one private lessons. So, to ensure that all the boys can perform in the same band they all learn the same literature (music) but the Year 7 starters get easier practical work. Boys who find it hard get moved onto easier instruments such as drums and provide the bass beat. Their attitudes have changed and our attitudes have changed towards them. More able boys play the melody, but all make a significant contribution to the performance of the band. This approach works better than putting boys into groups comprised of learners because boys don't want to be associated with not playing well. The whole point of the programme is that they learn about music, not what it is they can't do.

The music is chosen based on what is happening during the year that the boys can relate to. The year 2007 was the year of the Rugby World Cup so they learned the anthem which was Jupiter. The boys will be learning music linked to the Olympics during 2008. They ask to learn theme music to popular shows like Pirates of the Caribbean and Family Guy. The teachers aim to learn pieces that reflect a range of styles, from big band music through to lyrical and sacred music, each year.

Facilities – The Lighthouse

About the same time as Emma's interview, King's had committed itself to the building of specialist facilities for art, science and ICT which would also provide a better space for the library. Although there had not been a plan to accommodate specialist music education, Emma quickly jumped on this opportunity to enhance music education with a dedicated music suite. The Headmaster and School Board backed her request. A significant redesign with considerable additional costs for the design and soundproofing of an entire music suit including a state-of-the-art recording studio was required. The Lighthouse building opened during the second term of 2007 which was the third year of the band programme. The space provides more options for splitting up the classes in order to cater for different learning styles as well as dedicated rehearsal space.

Challenges Encountered when Establishing the Programme

Band was chosen because orchestra is not renowned for full school participation. Woodwind and brass instruments lend themselves more to children. They are easier to hold and manage on a large scale.

Colleagues

Prior to joining the school, Emma met with her new team to explain the programme and their role to ensure success. They were excited by the clear direction to be achieved and the fact that they were going to teach boys teaching music by playing which is an unusual approach to music teaching. This enthusiasm was important because they needed to engage in significant professional development to upskill themselves. They needed to play all the instruments! Although this was a bit of a challenge Emma met with no resistance. They started to take the instruments home and did their own 'homework'. Emma treated them like a class, so they could experience what it would be like for the boys.

Day-to-day management of the boys

Emma's experience in HK had taught her that the key to mass music is classroom management – to be a classroom manager first and a musician second. At the beginning of each year Emma encourages the boys to set their own rules based on what they need to learn and have fun while bearing in mind the need to be disciplined enough to perform. The rules on the wall for 2008 are

1. Respect the individual performer
2. Be prompt
3. Listen and play when appropriate
4. Practice 30mins a week
5. Be a team.

Launching the Programme to Boys and Parents

The key stakeholders in the success of the programme were the boys. They needed to be convinced that this was going to be fun and good for them. Secondarily, the parents. The details of the new band programme were revealed to current students and in-coming students and their parents on one night towards the end of the school year. This was no easy task. A total of 450 boys and their parents finding out that next year they would be required to play an instrument and participate in a band! Obviously there was a need to ensure that all the boys, and their parents, accepted the idea.

Considerable effort was made to ensure the event went well. Emma sought the involvement of the most accomplished players and 'cool' looking boys at King's College (the senior school) knowing that the younger boys look up to the boys at the college. They talked about what they liked about their instruments to the audience and then they played their instruments. The younger boys were blown away with the playing. After that the boys were encouraged to try out whichever instruments they wanted to have a go with to see which ones they were able to get a note from. Ensuring that the boys had the opportunity to hear and try out the instruments was critical to the success of the programme. Research into musical instrument selection research demonstrates that people are more likely to be successful if they like the timbre of instruments and if they are able to pick them up and play them on the first attempt.

The scale of the programme enabled the school to provide the instrument rentals and music for an additional cost to parents of only $100 per term. Private lessons remained an extra cost but not necessary except for boys taking on a brass instrument who were required to have private lessons for the first semester. This is required to ensure embouchure is formed correctly by the brass players. So boys were encouraged to select two instruments in case parents could not afford the additional lessons.

Out of the 450 families who attended the first 'band night' event, only four or five were concerned with the idea behind the programme. Their concerns were that their son already played an instrument and that they would have to start back at scratch with another instrument which might affect their progress in the other instrument too. It was agreed that these boys would play percussion as part of the band programme. The boys thought it was great because they saw percussion as 'cool' and the music staff had the benefit of the most able musicians keeping time for the rest of the group. Another concession was that those parents were not charged for the instruments. However, those concerns were only raised in the initial year. Now all parents want their boys to belong to the programme.

Performance

A big part of the programme is the emphasis on performance. At end of term 2, it is important for the community to come and hear what the boys have been doing. They may only know three or four notes but they must have the discipline of performing: look good, sit still, stand and perform and so on. They are provided with a specific purpose: to perform for your parents to hear. Every boy performs also at the end of year concert. Performing ensures that the boys put into practice what they have learned, provides a purpose for their learning, and an opportunity to evaluate their achievement. It is also a great thing for the school community to come and support. The performances are recorded so the boys can see what they did, reflect and talk about it and learn from the whole experience. Often they are just amazed that they managed to all stand up, sit down, start and stop together! That really motivates them to continue.

Managing the Logistics

Two instrument firms were initially approached. The supplier was chosen because they were able to guarantee a turnaround for collection and delivery of repairs within 1 or 2 days and their instruments were of better quality. The King's contract is a big contract for the supplier because the school hires and buys instruments on the biggest scale within New Zealand. There were a few hicups in the beginning. Financially they were not prepared for how big an account it was and the repair and return systems were not as accurate as the school expected. After withholding payment for 6 months until it was resolved the contract runs well now. Emma deals with the chap from the repair workshop directly and liaises with one person for purchases. The school Bursar deals with the accounts. The programme has necessitated an additional internal tracking process for the instruments and payments within the King's system.

Future Challenges

The programme in now in its fouth year. Initially it was designed as a 3-year programme for Years 6, 7 and 8. The challenge is to ensure that the boys who joined the programme in Year 5 remain motivated and continue to learn in Year 8. Fortunately, the opening of the Lighthouse building with its dedicated recording suite enables the programme to develop around composition and arrangements. They boys can now play what they write. So, using software and the recording studio the boys can develop arrangements and then compose over top of those arrangements with the instrument they can play.

Measuring Success

It is hard to measure success in a robust way as there are no tests administered to the boys. However, there is no negative feedback relating to the programme.

Music education is not assessed in the same way as Maths and English, for example. However, the feedback from the boys, parents and the whole school community is positive. The school now gets invitations to play with the New Zealand Symphony Orchestra and leading solo artists. They have been invited to tour Australia. The point of the programme is success on a large scale – the whole cohort – not the individual achievements of a boy. Auckland Grammar School tests new boys in English, Maths and Music intelligence for streaming purposes. This year there are more King's boys in the A stream at Grammar than ever before. This may be due to the programme.

Neil Shroff, an ex-principal at Point View School Auckland, undertook a review of music programmes in schools within the UK and NZ during a sabbatical in 2006. This resulted in a glowing report for the band programme at King's: 'I observed many impressive programmes in the UK and NZ but nothing bettered that which I saw at King's School.'

Case Study developed with Emma Featherstone, creator of the Band Programme and Music Director at King's School, Remuera, Auckland.

Discussion

To what extent were the operant resources of the separate groups of people necessary to the success of the Band Programme at Kings? Through what processes was the commitment and support of these separate groups achieved?

4

An Individual Experience of Arriving at Auckland International Airport

Introduction and Background

The case is based on the personal experiences of an individual traveller during one particular travel experience. As it represents one person's feelings and perceptions, and cannot possibly be a comprehensive overview, it is written in the first person. Nevertheless, it is felt that a view of the service from a traveller's perspective is of interest and value. Whilst the account is of an actual experience, some details have been omitted, and the names of all individuals have been changed.

The traveller, Terri, is a British citizen who lives in New Zealand. She is a frequent traveller in and out of Auckland airport so was already familiar with the arrival process at the International Terminal. The case demonstrates how familiarity with a service provider and service process can influence expectations and the way in which an individual experience is evaluated against previous experiences. On this particular occasion, Terri was returning home to Auckland after visiting the United Kingdom. She was travelling with her 11-year-old son, Gregory. The case starts when the plane lands at Auckland airport.

Getting to Passport Control

As usual it had been a tiring journey coming 'straight through' from Heathrow with a 5-hour stop at Singapore. Having been travelling for around 30 hours, not including the trip to Heathrow, I was hoping for a quick sprint through passport control, baggage claim, customs control and into the taxi waiting to take us home. So far the travel had been easy enough without any undue delays and, being Gold members of the Star Alliance, the shower and light meal in the member lounge at Singapore had provided a much needed opportunity to refresh and stretch during the long journey.

During the long walk from the plane to the passport control hallway, I noted the 'Kia Ora' welcome signs and all the warning signs related to prohibited goods including the ubiquitous 'last chance to discard your fruit' above the numerous bins placed for the purpose of collecting banned items. I remember how odd, and rather threatening, I found these notices on my very first trip but now, as a resident, I am reassured by the way that New Zealand protects its natural environment so robustly. However, casting a critical eye, the signs and messages definitely appear unwelcoming and rather menacing with their emphasis on fines to be imposed, especially since those messages are so poorly communicated to passengers before they get here.

Seeing someone clutching beautiful bouquets of orchids, clearly purchased from the lovely stand in the middle of Singapore's Changi airport, I realise that they must be first time visitors to New Zealand. They do not realise they will not be able to bring those in. I remember making a similar mistake myself and mentally note how complicated it is to travel internationally these days, with the need to keep on top of the different rules for each country. I recall buying the smallest size the first time I bought those orchids as gifts for my family in the United Kingdom and being pleasantly surprised when customs at Heathrow treated my request to declare them as a joke! Now I confidently buy orchids at Changi on the way to the United Kingdom but never on the way back to New Zealand.

Passport Control

As we climbed down the steps into the passport control area, I noted that the hallway looked incredibly crowded. I had never encountered so many people in this area before and immediately realised that this was going to be a long wait. Travelling under a British passport, and noting that the 'all passports' queue appeared much shorter than the 'New Zealand passports and Residence Permits' queue, I wondered whether we might opt for the shorter queue, but didn't want to risk being sent back to the longer queue. As I considered this the loud speaker announced an apology for the queue and explained that three planes had landed within the last hour which had placed stress on the system. The announcement went on to say that all of the passport control stations were manned and they were moving people through as fast as possible. I was surprised at how clearly I had heard the announcement, even though my ears had not yet 'popped' back to normal after the landing. I immediately felt reassured, rather than anxious at the potential wait. Waiting is a far less frequent experience in New Zealand than it is in England due to the much smaller population. However, the New Zealand systems are built around the 4 million population, so there are times when even a small number of additional people can have what appears to be a disproportionate impact. Three planes an hour sounds a very light number of passengers for the airports we have travelled from to get here but clearly not a number that Auckland is used to processing.

Gregory takes one look at the queue and dives into a seat at the side shouting that he'll see me when I get to the desk! Great, now I don't even have anyone to talk to as I wait. I watch him pull out his portable play station (PSP) and settle down. The queue moves slowly. An official appears to help manage the flow of people into different chained off areas so, hopefully, I check which queue I should use and was told to stay where I was. I did. Forty minutes later my mobile rang. It was the taxi driver wanting to know if I was there. He knew the flight had landed over an hour ago but also knew that a late arriving flight was causing problems. I assured him that he would have plenty of time to get a coffee before I would emerge. The apologetic announcement acknowledging and explaining the situation was repeated several times during the long wait and I noted that everyone seemed resigned to the situation with good humour, there was no evidence of anger or intense frustration. Many people were chatting cheerfully on mobile phones.

At last Gregory bounded up and we reached the end of the queue. I was extremely surprised to find the immigration officer in a good mood. She was polite and cheerful and the processing questions were not rushed nor did the officer neglect to welcome us home something which I had noticed as part of the 'script' since I had become a 'permanent resident' rather than a visitor. It is a small thing but such a nice friendly way to greet people and so typically 'Kiwi'.

Baggage Collection

Once through passport control, Gregory quickly found two trolleys for the baggage which had clearly been circulating around the carousel for some time. Passing the concession stand offering free hot drinks, I thought it was a shame that no one had thought to circulate a tray of free drinks just a few yards away on the other side of passport control. Within a few minutes we had spotted all of our bags and loaded them onto the trolleys. I could see the beagle dog on the scent for fruit being carried in illegally and noted that the handler appeared more aggressive than usual yelling at everyone to place their bags on the floor for the dog to inspect. I recalled what a shock I had had to find a dog sniffing my handbag on our first trip but now it all seemed quite normal and I am more surprised that similar precautions are not taken at Heathrow to protect the United Kingdom. Only two more stages to go before getting into that taxi. Gathering ourselves and our trolleys together, we joined the rapidly growing queue for the Bio-security processes.

Bio-Security

As usual I had filled in the entry documents in the departure lounge at Singapore and, having had a bad experience previously, read and re-read each of the questions very carefully before ticking the 'no' boxes. I know from bitter experience that there is an automatic $200 fine just for 'forgetting' that you have a banned item, or not realising that an item is banned and should have been declared. Fines rise rapidly into the $000s if the officer believes that the act is a deliberate one.

As usual I was more than a little anxious at this stage. I know I've brought chocolates back before but I wasn't sure if the shelled nuts from Marks & Spencer would prove problematic. So, to be safe, I had decided to say yes to food products and declared them now. While I was relieved to find that they were ok my anxiety levels had not dropped. If anything I was getting hotter and more uncomfortable as we were assigned a line for the X-ray machines.

X-Ray

I placed the cases on to the X-ray conveyor and desperately hoped that they find no inconsistencies between the contents and my declaration. I think my anxiety arises from the time, several years ago, when the X-ray found Gregory's football boots. I had forgotten that he had packed them and so thought nothing of ticking the 'no' box for bringing in 'studded shoes'. I recall vividly the officer hauling me to one side to ask if I had packed any studded shoes, my saying no, and his request to open the case. The horror of finding the shoes was awful. I was overcome with feelings of guilt and shame! I felt as bad as I imagine a drug trafficker would feel when caught red handed. The shoes were checked and, to my great joy, the studs were found to be clean, with no evidence of mud. I had always thought that it was this pristine condition of the shoes that allowed me to escape the fine for 'forgetting' but I never wanted to find out. It was an embarrassing and most uncomfortable moment that I never want to repeat and even though it had been a genuine error on my part the memory continues to cause me anxiety whenever I go through this process. Nothing problematic this time though so, with the cases once again loaded onto the trolleys, we head out to find the taxi driver.

Discussion

To what extent do Terri's previous experiences influence each subsequent encounter within the arrival process?

5

Waymark Holidays

Background

...we are celebrating 20 successful years as a tour operator. We have always specialised in walking holidays, and although we have expanded our operations into many different countries, we still prefer to concentrate our attention on the activity we know best – walking.
('Walk with Waymark', 1994 Holiday Brochure)

We try to give our customers the best value for money, by making sure that they go on a holiday that's just right for them...70% of our business is from regular customers who come back.
(Peter Chapman, Director, Waymark Holidays)

Waymark Holidays was founded in 1974 by two people, Peggy Hounslow and Noel Vincent, who had been running the holiday side of the Ramblers' Association for several years. Peggy Hounslow was the Managing Director of Ramblers Holidays and Noel Vincent was Managing Director of 'Wings', another subsidiary of the Ramblers' Association. They both wished to have more freedom to organise holidays their own way, so they left Ramblers and set up their own company, Waymark Holidays, which operated initially from a bedroom, then from a cellar, and finally from a ground-floor office in Fulham, London. In 1991, the company moved to its present office on the second floor of a two-storey office block in Slough, 20 miles west of London. Waymark Holidays is a specialist direct sell tour operator offering two related types of holiday: walking holidays and cross-country skiing holidays. In 1993, they sold 2400 walking holidays based on their 'Walk with Waymark' brochure, and 1800 cross-country skiing holidays, based on their 'Cross-Country Skiing with Waymark' brochure.

Peggy Hounslow and Noel Vincent retired in 1984, and the company is now run by three director/shareholders, Peter Chapman, Martin Read and Stuart Montgomery, supported by four full-time salaried salespeople and three part-time administrative/clerical staff.

The UK Tour Operators Industry

Between April 1990 and March 1991, the four largest UK tour operators – Thomson Holidays, ILG Travel Ltd, Owners Abroad and Airtours – accounted for 65.5 per cent of the 13 million holidays sold (Key Note Publications Ltd, 1991). The largest tour operator, Thomson Holidays, trading under the names of Thomson Holidays, Horizon Holidays, Portland Holidays and Sky Tours, accounted for 4.3 million holidays (33.2 per cent). ILG Travel Ltd went into receivership in March 1991 but the level of concentration has not changed significantly as Airtours has been the major beneficiary of ILG's collapse.

A further 25 operators, offering between 46 000 and 320 000 holidays per year, account for 16.3 per cent of the volume, whilst the remaining 18.2 per cent is shared between an unspecified number of small operators offering 45 000 or less holidays per year. Waymark fall into this latter group with 4000 holidays per year. For every holiday Waymark sells, Thomson sells 1000.

Polarisation of Service Operations of Tour Operators

The largest operators, such as Thomson and Airtours, are competing on price and volume. They measure their customers in millions and sell holidays primarily through the intermediary of a travel agent. They employ charter flights, and may own their own airline. For example, Thomson owns Britannia Airways, Owners Abroad owns Air 2000 and Airtours owns Airtours International. These tour operators will normally service their short-haul business through charter flights on their own airline.

They strive for efficiency in the processing of bookings by becoming highly computerised. For example, nobody, not even a travel agent, can telephone Thomson to book a holiday – a direct computer-to-computer access is required to do this. No telephone number is given on any Thomson holiday brochure. Computerised booking systems are accurate and efficient and the customer in the travel agency can have immediate feedback on availability of hotels and flights and guaranteed bookings 'on the spot'. The only personal service which customers receive is that offered by the travel agent employees.

At the other extreme, Waymark Holidays sell direct to the customer, offer a specialised service in a niche market, and make a positive effort to discuss, on the telephone, special requirements by customers for their holiday. They offer a highly personalised service, and are prepared to talk to customers at length even though it is more expensive to operate such a service in such low quantities. According to Peter Chapman, customer enquiries can range from the very general, 'What's the weather going to be like in Austria next June?', to the very specific, 'I went with you to Sardinia last year, and am considering Samos [Greece] this year. Will I like the hotel?' Other calls may request general advice, 'I would like a more strenuous holiday than last year. What do you suggest?' or 'How many people are already booked on the holiday? What are their ages?' Virtually all their customers pay by cheque. Some overseas customers may pay by credit card, for which they are charged an additional £15 per person.

As Peter Chapman's quote at the beginning of the case shows, Waymark get to know, personally, many of their customers, some of whom book Waymark Holidays two, three or four times a year, and these customers are often on first name terms with the Waymark representatives. Nearly all the holidays use seats on scheduled flights with, for example, British Airways, Swissair, Austrian Airlines, Scandinavian Airlines or Lufthansa.

At Waymark, they feel that the middle-sized tour operators, who are not big enough to compete on price and volume with Thomson, Owners Abroad and Airtours, but are too big to offer personal services and specialisation, may find it a struggle to position themselves in the future in the highly competitive market.

Waymark's main competitors are other small tour operators offering specialist walking or cross-country skiing holidays. There are 10–12 companies who offer walking or 'soft adventure' holidays; for example, 'Ramblers', 'Headwater', 'Inn-Travel', 'Exodus' and 'Explore'. None of them offers a precisely comparable programme to Waymark but there are some considerable overlaps. They all use direct-sell methods, believing that the ability to direct customers to the right holiday would be lost if the holiday was just being processed by a travel agent. 'The travel agent is just interested in making a booking, not if it is the right holiday for that person.' Selling direct to the customer also saves on the commission to be paid to a travel agent. On the skiing side, there are fewer competitors, with only two or three operators offering cross-country skiing holidays. Waymark deliberately keep out of the downhill skiing holidays offered by the middle- to large-size operators. They have also rejected the urge to offer what are perceived to be related specialist holidays such as cycling, canoeing or horse-riding. As Peter Chapman observes, 'We don't know anything about them. We don't want to branch out into things we don't understand. We are all enthusiastic about walking and cross-country skiing and that's all we want to do.'

Features of a Waymark Holiday

Customers who book a holiday with Waymark will be struck by two features in particular which are not present on a more conventional package holiday offered by the larger tour operators.

First, all holidays are graded according to how strenuous they are felt to be. Figure CS5.1 shows the grading criteria specified in the 'Walk with Waymark' brochure. A similar section appears in the 'Cross-Country Ski-ing with Waymark' brochure. Waymark employees are extremely concerned to ensure that customers choose a grade of holiday that is suitable. In addition to the information given in the brochure, they take a lot of time discussing, by telephone, the suitability of a particular holiday for a customer. There have been occasions where, if the Waymark representative does not believe that a customer is physically capable of a holiday, the booking will be refused. They know from experience that if someone goes on a Grade 3 holiday, but is only capable of Grade 1 walking, that person will struggle and the experience is bad for all concerned. The Waymark philosophy is summed up by Peter Chapman: 'You've got to deliver what you promise. I'd rather turn a booking away than accept it and make a mess of it.'

Grading of holidays

We grade our holidays from 1 to 5. Among mountains, distance is a poor guide; hours of walking and amount of ascent are better indication of how strenuous a holiday will be. Bear in mind, though, that these are rough estimates: on some days the hours of walking and amount of ascent may exceed these figures. Also remember that hours of walking exclude stops for refreshments and so on. Sometimes a combined grade is shown, for example 'Grade 3/4'; this means that some days will be at Grade 3, other Grade 4.

Choosing a grade. Bad or even hot weather can make a holiday more strenuous. Even at Grades 2 and 3, bad weather in mountains can mean walking across snow; we also emphasise that mountain paths abroad can be much steeper than in British hills, and that there may be some degree of exposure at times on high mountain paths. Bear in mind that the walking at higher grades tends to beat a faster pace than at lower grades. So please compare the holidays with your own experience, and don't try something too tough for your first time abroad. If you are in doubt, we are always ready to help you choose a holiday within your capabilities.

Grade 1. Walking mostly on paths, sometimes rough underfoot, about four hours a day. Ascent in general each day less than 300m. Good walking shoes would do but take boots if you are used to them.

Grade 2. About five hours a day. These holidays may be in hill country, or at mountain centres, mostly on paths. In hill country there may be some longer days on modest gradients. Ascent in general each day less than 500m. On a continuous walking tour it is essential that you consider your ability to walk every day except when a rest day has been planned – a weak link spoils not only your own but everyone's holiday. boots advisable.

< indicates that most of the walking on these Grade 2 holidays is in mountainous terrain where paths are often steep; please consider this when booking. Ascent in general each day up to 1000m.

Grade 3. About five/six hours a day walking, sometimes off paths, and occasionally scrambling*. Be prepared for steep ascents and descents. Ascent in general each day up to 1000m. Boots essential.

Grade 4. About seven hours a day walking, some scrambling*. Across the snow-line at times. Steep ascents and descents perhaps for 3–4 hours at a time. Ascent in general each day up to 1500m. Boots essential.

Grade 5. Long days of about eight hours' walking, with scrambling* in big mountains and remote terrain. Often above the snow-line and across glaciers. Ascent in general each day 1500–2000m. Boots are essential, and ice axe, crampons and climbing harness are often needed – see holiday description for details.

Scrambling* means that hands as well as feet are used for ascent or descent. Previous experience is not necessary for easy scrambles although a good head for heights will be required at Grades 3, 4 and 5. On most of our holidays at Grade 4 and 5, the leader will carry a rope in case it is needed for security, but none of our holidays involve technical climbing.

Mountain Hut Tours. For these you have to carry a full rucksack which slows the pace and increases the grade and we have to be satisfied that you have sufficient previous experiences such as walking in big mountains and carrying a full pack. If in doubt try our Stubai Alps holiday, which combines one week at a centre with another on a hut tour.

Sightseeing and Wildlife. Some holidays are particularly well suited for visiting places of interest and viewing wildlife. Where this is mentioned in the text, time will be allowed for sightseeing but it does not lower the grade of walking on other days.

Figure CS5.1   Grading of Waymark Holidays

For their many regular customers, who are already familiar with, and realistic about, the gradings, discussions may centre on moving up a grade, or on the weather in a completely different location. For the new customers, Waymark have to base their initial advice on information contained on the booking form, where customers are asked to give details of previous walking experience, if booking a holiday of Grade 2 or above (or of any previous skiing experience, for the cross-country skiing holidays). Sometimes, the Waymark staff must politely inform customers who have, for example, been trekking in the Himalayas, that they have Grade 2 experience, and would be ill-equipped to take a Grade 5 holiday in the Alps. The two experiences are very different physically. A more common piece of advice is to regular walkers in the United Kingdom, who frequent Scotland and the Lake District where it is generally cool, that walking on a sunny day in Switzerland can be much hotter and that, on their first visit, they should avoid a Grade 4 or Grade 5 holiday.

Secondly, customers on a Waymark holiday will be members of a party or group of walkers/skiers for the whole period of the holiday. Parties, of up to 16 people per holiday, have the services of a leader appointed by Waymark (see below). The compatibility of the group members is an important aspect of the total holiday experience, as evidenced by some of the customer telephone calls to Waymark. People will say that they are booking another holiday because they had an enjoyable group experience last year. The walking was good, but it was the people who made the holiday memorable. They will ask about ages of other group members, the gender mix and whether it is mainly singles or couples.

In the past, Waymark made some attempt to 'manage' groups, for example to balance the sexes, but now they would just rather give general group details and leave it to the customer. On occasions they may advise a potential customer that he/she is 20 years younger than the rest of the party, or that he is the only male in a group, but this is to point out a possible problem rather than dictate the group make-up. On very rare occasions, a customer may write to complain about not being warned of the structure of the group. For example, one lady commented that on a particular holiday she was the only single person, and that in the evenings most couples went to their rooms leaving her at a loose end. Such an experience is unusual as most Waymark customers, single or not, enjoy the wider group camaraderie.

Specialised Services

As a small company dealing directly with customers, Waymark is sometimes in a position to offer specialised services to individuals or groups. For example, a customer may ring to say that he is on a business trip to Scandinavia and would like to add on a skiing holiday at the end of it, so he only wants the back-end of the advertised holiday. Or another may ring to say that, as her daughter lives in Switzerland, she would like to fly out three days earlier to stay with her before joining the party.

Such requests can often be accommodated. If it can be done, it secures a booking and the customers remember Waymark. Giving personal service like that, it is felt, leads to satisfaction and a high probability of a repeat buy in the following year. There are occasions when holidays may go wrong. Waymark will seek every means to recover such situations. Peter Chapman recalled a case of a party who were on a 14-day tour of Mont Blanc, staying in mountain huts. The leader of the party was not performing well and had lost confidence after some navigational errors at the beginning of the holiday. His stress was clear to the whole party and he was encouraged by the group to telephone Waymark. Waymark had to act quickly to save a potentially embarrassing situation. To solve the problem they (i) brought the leader home and asked a willing customer to take the balance of funds for the hut accommodation (almost £3000), the maps, and to keep the group going for a day, and (ii) tracked down another leader by radio telephone who was just finishing a tour in Austria and asked him to take the train from Innsbruck, through Switzerland to Geneva and meet up with the other group. The new leader took over and the remainder of the holiday was very successful. Waymark paid each member of the party £50 compensation, and received several complimentary letters thanking them for acting so quickly and praising the professionalism of the replacement leader.

Another case where Waymark was able to act quickly was when a customer had left an airline ticket in a taxi. To save embarrassment, the customer had bought a new ticket at the airport by credit card and not told anybody. The taxi driver handed in the original ticket to Swissair who contacted Waymark. The customer was booked on a remote holiday in Italy and the leader confirmed that he was actually there. Waymark agreed to ask Swissair if the customer could have his money back. Swissair was understanding and gave a credit card refund before the credit card bill had to be paid. So it cost the customer nothing. The problem would never have come to light but for the honest taxi-driver; but when it did Waymark was able to act.

Relationships with Hotels and Airlines

Waymark believe in long-term relationships with airlines and hotels, just as they nurture long-term relationships with customers. By such means 'everyone knows what they are expecting and what they can deliver. If you keep changing holidays, hotels and airlines, there's always the opportunity for things to go wrong.'

Waymark prefer to deal with small hotel-keepers in each country. They believe that the similarity in attitudes, business practice and preferences for such hoteliers far outweighs any national or cultural differences. Small hotel-keepers in France, Greece or Austria all like to be treated fairly and plan well in advance. Like Waymark, they also have many faithful customers who return every year. To build up a long-term relationship, Waymark will start small and then put in more groups per year if it is popular. Small family-run hotels are preferred by Waymark customers, many of whom stay in five-star hotels on business, because of their character and charm.

Clearly some holidays have 'product lifetime', and after a promising start begin to 'fade' after three or four years. Eventually such holidays have to be phased out.

Some are a failure from the outset. Many holidays, however, have been operated successfully for 15 years or more, operating on virtually the same formula throughout.

It is also important for Waymark to build up strong relationships with airlines as nearly all their holidays use scheduled flights. Their dealings with the airlines are based on 'confidence and trust' built up over many years. A Waymark representative may need to ask British Airways, for example, for 20 seats on a high-season date next year. British Airways' positive response will be based on their experience with the company. They would not wish to reserve 20 seats a year in advance to a company who may return them, unsold, a month in advance. According to Peter Chapman, 'Having a track record of doing what you say you are going to do is extremely important if you want to get seats on a busy day. We definitely benefit from having 20 years in the business and treating people right that is, as we would like to be treated.'

Information Technology

Waymark have a computerised mailing list and invoicing system. Unlike the larger operators they do not have a computerised reservation system. They have decided not to do so in order to maintain flexibility and variations in holidays as part of their service. Such flexibility would be difficult, if not impossible, to offer through a computer programme. They use a manual ledger with relevant information, for instance, 'Coming home two days later', on each customer booking, and that is easily kept and understood.

Because many airlines are moving to computerised bookings, particularly for low-volume tickets, Waymark have to use a viewdata system, 'FASTRAK', to make such bookings. Without the system they could not book APEX tickets with many airlines. As the airlines become more computerised, even routine information on passenger details, for example, names and ages, will have to be input directly to their computer and Waymark's current practice of sending such details by fax will no longer be acceptable to them.

Party Leaders

Each party on a Waymark holiday is in the charge of a leader. Waymark use about 200 volunteer leaders. They tend to be people in early retirement or those who take two or three weeks of their own holiday to be party leaders. The basic requirements of a leader are: (i) must be a keen walker and knowledgeable about navigation and safety in the hills (the number one priority is that a leader can take people out and bring them back safely); (ii) must speak the language of the country they are in, as most hotel managers who deal with Waymark do not speak English; (iii) must be a caring person who is doing the job because he/she wants to give people a good holiday; and (iv) must have common sense and the initiative to cope with the unexpected.

Every year, a few new leaders are appointed as replacements, or for new destinations. Waymark will interview them, take up references and check their credentials. Through the interview questions, Waymark need to know if the person takes a caring attitude and will look after customers. They wish to reject candidates whose first priority is to have a free holiday. A disappointing leader can affect the enjoyment of a holiday. A good leader will ensure that 'the personal service we give in the office is carried through into the "field"'. Whilst other companies make leaders attend extensive training programmes, not only in navigation but also in, for example, how to organise a country dancing evening, Waymark have chosen not to. Their philosophy of long-term relationships extends to leader appointments and many leaders have been with them for all 20 years.

Leaders are given quite a lot of initiative. For example, in Greece where holidays are on a 'bed and breakfast' basis, leaders have the money to buy evening meals and will choose restaurants and arrange good value deals. They will choose the itinerary of walks from notes provided by Waymark and are free to investigate other suitable walks. If there is any crisis, a leader will be expected to offer three or four possible courses of action to the Waymark office rather than saying, 'I've got a problem. What can I do?'

Peter Chapman reckons that there are about 20 real 'stars' with big fan-clubs. Piles of unsolicited mail are received about such leaders, extolling the virtues of putting in the extra ounce of effort, preparing well beforehand, keeping the party well informed and explaining what is going on. Conversely, where a leader is disappointing, Waymark has very rarely received a telephone call during the holiday from concerned customers. In some cases a replacement leader may have to be flown out.

Publicity and Promotion

Of the 30 per cent of customers who are new each year, half come through responses to media advertising/public relations and the other half through personal recommendations. Regarding the latter, it is known that many walkers belong to rambling clubs and when people are rambling they talk about holidays. Waymark have benefited from such word-of-mouth, but are very aware that bad news about a holiday will also gain a wide circulation.

They pay to advertise in the national 'quality' press – *The Daily Telegraph*, *The Independent* and *The Guardian* and in specialist magazines such as *The Great Outdoors*, *Trailwalker* and *Country Walking*, and have used these publications for many years. They believe in the public relations benefit of persuading a journalist to take one of their holidays and write about it. Figure CS5.2 contains extracts from an article in *The Daily Telegraph* on 1 January 1994, about the cross-country skiing holiday to Lapland and Murmansk. Such an article generates more telephone calls than a paid advertisement.

We met for breakfast at a five-star hotel in Helsinki. The 61-year-old Wakeling twins first caught the eye. In a beaver-tailed Davy Crockett hat, and a home-made waistcoat of patched reindeer, rabbit and fox, Derrick looked every inch the backwoods trapper stepping from the pages of Jack London. Derrick is psychic and lives in Suffolk, where he makes jewellery.

Edwin (the elder, by half an hour) lives at the foot of Cairngorm and knows as much about reindeer as any Lapp, having managed a herd there for years. Ach, Aviemore's so polluted now,' he told me apologetically, 'I'm not sure I can stay there. But where else would I live?'

My fellow trekkers were certainly a diverse bunch, as varied in age and occupation as you could imagine. The journey may smack of macho romanticism, but attracted as many women as men. Toni, an agronomist and pillar of the West Yorks Cross-Country Ski Club, was sure the trip would be too arduous for her husband and left him to water the plants.

A DTI civil servant, Richard, accompanied by his wife Anne and student daughter, were our new-kit contingent – new skis, sleeping bags, clothes, packs . . . no doubt even their toothbrushes were new. Anne and Richard take turns to choose holidays. This year was Richard's turn. Fine-boned Anne looked as fragile as a teacup and slightly nervous.

A chemistry lecturer from Sheffield University came with his wife. A cancer research epidemiologist brought her boyfriend. Jackie, a teacher at a Bristol comprehensive, was the only one of us with the sense to bring a supply of alcohol.

All these people were regular Waymarkers, as they call themselves, although few had tackled cross-country ski tours in regions as remote as Lapland . . . Our guide, David Lane, completed the group. A cartographer, orienteer and professional group leader at an activity centre in the Highlands, he oozed competence.

By the end of that first breakfast, at least we knew we would not lack conversation while huddled around the camp fire hundreds of miles from the nearest television set. . . . Everyone found something useful to do. The chemistry professor fetched ice and water from the lake. The psychic silversmith split logs, which the DTI man carried. The agronomist made tea. For any outdoor task we had to wear skis, or sink waist-deep in soft snow. . . . After a two-hour pancake-making competition, the civil servant and I skied across to the sauna, stoked the stove, threw water on hot coals to get a good sweat running before the roll in the snow without which no visit to the Arctic would be complete. After a few rolls and sauna re-entries, the tingle factor was quite high enough, and we decided to forgo the Finnish sauna's traditional climax, flagellation by birch branches. Even Waymarkers recognise limits to masochism. . . . We exchanged addresses before parting and promised to keep in touch. Holiday friendships usually prove as durable as footprints in the sand, but *we* felt confident that ours would last. That may be the most satisfying souvenir of our Arctic adventure.

We have kept in touch, too, discussing plans for a return visit to Lapland. Once you get a taste for adventure, there is no denying the call of the wild.

Figure CS5.2   Extract from *The Daily Telegraph*, 1 January 1994

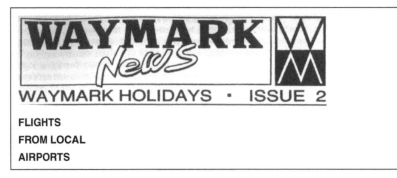

Figure CS5.3   'Waymark News'

We are always grateful when customers take the trouble to write in with suggestions and queries. One of the favourite topics is the question of why we can't make more use of local airports instead of concentrating on Heathrow and Gatwick.

Sometimes the answer is simply that no direct flights exist from your local airport to the foreign destination. Often if such flights do exist they are charters and this opens up the whole debate over whether we should use scheduled or charter services for our customers-in using scheduled services rather than charter flights. Advantages such as:

- scheduled timetables are fixed many months in advance
- scheduled services offer more convenient departure and arrival times
- scheduled services suffer from fewer delays
- scheduled services have shorter check-in-times
- there is better on-board service with scheduled flights.

The only significant disadvantage is that the vast majority of scheduled services to overseas destinations fly out of Heathrow or Gatwick, with even the fast-growing Manchester airport still some way behind.

On balance, because we know that our customers appreciate the benefits of scheduled flights, we use them wherever there is a direct service; and only use charters when destinations are not served by direct scheduled flights. This applies to our holidays to Corsica, Crete, the Pindos in Greece and southern Turkey. For these holidays there are flights from both Gatwick and various local airports.

For holidays using Munich, Zurich and Geneva airports the situation is better and we can regularly offer flights out of Manchester as well as Birmingham-and for Munich we can also offer flights from Glasgow.

One alternative-although we recognise this would add to the cost of your trip-might be to take a connecting domestic flight with British Midland or British Airways, which we can organise on your behalf.

Please call us if you would like further details.

LATE

AVAILABILITY

If you still haven't got your summer holiday planned, don't panic. We still have places on a number of trips, many of which depart later in the season so there is plenty of time to prepare. Here is just a sample of what's on offer: (Brochure page number in brackets).

- KERRY (4) 7 nights: 31 July, 28 August, 23 October.
- WICKLOW MOUNTAINS (5) 7 nights: 24 July, 4 September.
- TOUR THROUGH SAVOY (*) 14 Nights: 29 August, 12 September.
- St SAVIN (9) 7 nights: 4, 11 September.
- GORGE OF THE ALLIER (10) 14 Nights: 4,11 September.
- BRITTANY (12) 7 & 8 nights: 11, 19 September.
- SOUTHERN CEVENNES (13) 7 & 10 nights: 18, 25 September.
- MILOS (14) 14 nights: 24 September, 8 October.
- MOUNTAINS & SEA IN CYPRUS (16) 7 & 14 nights: 27 September, 11, 24 October.
- WESTERN TAURUS (17) 15 NIGHTS: 20 September.
- SENDAS (20) 7 & 10 nights: 8 August, 22 August, 26 September, 3, 24, 31 October.
- JIMENA DE L FRONTERA (20) 7 & 10 nights: 30 September, 10, 24 October.
- TOUR IN ANDALUCIA (21) 7 & 10 nights: 26 September, 17 October.
- TRINS (24) 10 & 14 nights: 10 July, 7, 21 August, 11 September.
- AROSA (26) 10 nights: 14, 27 August.
- TOUR D'OISANS (32) 14 nights: 17, 31 July, 14 August.
- PEAKS OF THE PYRENEES (33) 14 nights: 22 August.

WAYMARK HOLIDAYS: ☎

Figure CS5.3 (Continued)

Regular customers are automatically on the brochure mailing list. People who ask for a brochure for the first time get two brochures, the second in 12 months' time even if they did not book a holiday. If they do not book on the second occasion they are taken off the mailing list. Regular summer customers receive a newsletter in May/June (see Figure CS5.3), and this always produces another 'mini-surge' of bookings for about a month.

Service Quality and Customer Expectations

Peter Chapman believes that service quality is about trying to understand what a customer wants from his holiday and then delivering it. He does not believe that Waymark will have a satisfied customer if they have not understood at the beginning what he/she wants. To emphasise this point, he can recount a case when three ladies were very dissatisfied with a holiday on a Greek island at Easter. They had booked late and taken an available holiday. It became clear that they had expected a fortnight in the sunshine in a standard hotel, and had never been to Greece before or on a walking holiday. The weather was poor and wet and the hotel owner forgot to heat the water some days. The ladies complained about the basic hotel and sought compensation for the holiday. The other members of the group felt that such compensation was not necessary, as the weather and Greek hotel idiosyncrasies were not Waymark's fault.

Waymark, however, feel that they should have better gauged the ladies' expectations through questioning their hotel preferences. As soon as they had established that a room with modern bathroom facilities and plenty of hot water was important, they could have advised against a Greek holiday. They have a number of questions which may be used to assess customer expectations; for example, 'Do you want a strenuous or easy walking holiday?', 'Do you want a comfortable hotel, or are you prepared to rough it?', 'Do you want guaranteed sunshine, or do you wish to go into the mountains (where it may be sunny or it may be wet)?'

Finding out what the customer wants is not enough if it is not delivered. Waymark personnel are all located in the same office and communicate regularly with each other. By this means, potential problems can be solved internally before they get to the customer stage. They process thousands of details of information and get it right at least 99 per cent of the time. This is important because getting one small detail wrong can affect delivery and ruin someone's holiday.

Like other operators, no single individual employee looks after all aspects of a customer's holiday. Different employees are responsible for different airlines and different groups of hotels. The smallness of the Waymark set-up is believed to be important in maintaining communication on hotels and airlines bookings, especially for the personalised requests.

Market Research, Trends and the Future

Two very large box-files contain the unsolicited mail, from customers, and the responses from Waymark representatives. This is one of the reasons why Waymark can monitor customer likes and dislikes. Many letters are motivated by customers' wishes to assist Waymark's future planning. For example, the overall holiday is highly praised apart from one small hitch that the customer wishes to draw to their attention. Many customers send photographs of their holiday. Waymark run a photograph competition and pay £20 for each photograph subsequently published in a brochure. The senders of the three best photographs are offered the opportunity of a free deposit for their next holiday.

More formal market research is carried out by sending approximately 10 per cent of customers a questionnaire. Holidays are chosen at random and all customers on that holiday will be included in the survey. Questions cover such areas as the food, the leader, the brochure, the service provided, reasons for booking the holiday, and what future holidays are being considered. One question, in particular, yielded some interesting results. When customers were asked, 'In which other countries would you like to see us operating?', about 50 per cent said they would like a holiday in Ireland. This surprised the Waymark staff who felt that, with Ireland being close to Britain and easy to get to, people would not want to book through a tour operator. Nevertheless, they put Ireland in the brochure and it has been successful. They now believe that, because of the relative lack of good maps and a network of footpaths in Ireland, the services of a leader with such knowledge is the key factor in the customer choice.

Eastern Europe is the second most frequently requested destination. Way-mark are reluctant to offer holidays in many eastern European destinations at this time because the standards of services and hotels are being compared unfavourably by customers with those in western Europe. They are 'soft-pedalling' in eastern Europe at the moment, hoping that in five to ten years' time the levels of service will be comparable to those in, say, Switzerland.

Customers are becoming more demanding each year, as their expectations rise. The travel industry in general has a poor reputation for delivering brochure promises, and customers are made more aware of their legal rights. Whilst Waymark's record on delivering promises is excellent, they have noticed some trends in customer expectations over the last five to ten years. For example, it is now very difficult to sell rooms without private facilities, whereas ten years ago such rooms were generally acceptable for walking holidays. Also, more and more people are demanding flights from their local airports, rather than London. People are turning down a holiday if they cannot fly from Manchester. A few years ago, customers would be delighted by a Manchester flight. Now they want a Manchester flight and are demanding that they don't have to wait two hours at their destination for the other people to arrive from London!

Over the last five years, there has been a trend for people to look to Waymark for walking holidays in the southern European destinations of Greece, Italy and Spain, as opposed to the 'heartland' of walking holidays; that is, the Swiss and Austrian Alps. Some middle/large tour operators are now offering 'lakes and mountains' brochures, and between them it is estimated that they may take 200 to 300 Alpine bookings from Waymark.

Waymark is not unduly worried, as the trend has served to flatten out their summer season. Instead of having a very large peak of bookings in July and August of each year, they now have a flatter pattern of booking extending from March to October. Holidays in the Alps are still booked mainly in July and August, but there are now significant bookings in Greece and Spain in the 'shoulder' months.

And finally . . .

> We have always believed it is right to concentrate on what we do best, and although our activities now cover many countries, we still specialise in cross-country ski-ing. Much of our success over the past two decades has been due to the loyalty of our regular customers, many of whom travel with us every year – in some cases twice or even three times per season – and for this we extend our sincere thanks.

> (From 'Cross-Country Ski-ing with Waymark)

6

Landscape Safari

Background to the Company and the People

Landscape Safari aims to deliver an efficient, practical, informative and creative mobile landscape design and installation service within the Auckland area of New Zealand. Landscape Safari was started by Justin Newcombe in 2000. He had always enjoyed gardening. As a child attending a small country school he had involved himself in horticulture and agriculture. While completing a Fine Arts degree at university he undertook a number of part time gardening jobs and then worked with a landscape architect for 2 years after University. There he learned to draft and gained valuable industry experience. He now considers this to have been a very lucky break.

Justin started the business with no capital at all. He borrowed an old car from his mum. Only one door worked so he spent much of his time greeting clients after emerging from the passenger door! He made all his own signs in the beginning and the main tools of his trade were the pencils and paper he used to sketch the designs. The lack of the 'trappings' that surround many larger businesses never bothered Justin who was determined to be different. Even now he still does most of the designs on-site in the company van.

Landscape Safari is positioned as a down-to-earth company with a sense of humour, rejecting the pompous positioning associated with many design-orientated companies. He also had an interest in systems. He had identified that companies could lose a lot through the systems and processes within the business, so he took a different approach to that used by other landscape designers. He found that streamlining the processes to allow people to either take it or leave it created an attractive proposition that people were really open to.

In addition to Justin the Landscape Safari workforce comprises two teams with three guys in each team. One group does the planting while another group, who are large Tongan men, do all the hard landscaping. Being able to offer a full range of landscaping services, without the need to contract out, increases the profitability of the business. After some bad experiences with using advertising to recruit staff, Justin now uses word-of-mouth and looks for attitude rather than qualifications. Although punctuality is important so is flexibility. He acknowledges that landscaping attracts people who like being outdoors and tend to enjoy surfing and tramping so he recognises their need to fit their working commitments around those pastimes but he also expects them to accommodate the business needs to turn up if there is a job to be done. He now asks around at nurseries and follows up leads from other landscapers. If he sees someone he thinks is being undervalued on a site then he might ask them.

In the early days Justin used radio advertising to promote the company and found that the first three days of advertising generated 80 jobs. This was the same amount of business as he had done the whole of the previous year using just the yellow pages, word-of-mouth and his own signs. He had booked and paid for 2 weeks advertising but had to ask the radio networks to stop playing the ads because he couldn't cope with the business it generated!

The Website

This was only created only 2 years ago in response to requests from clients who wanted to see a website when the Internet was becoming something everyone had access to. It now provides an important 'shop front' which enables people to get a feel for what the company does, who does it and what they can expect when buying the services.

It also describes the services clearly which also provides a fall back position in case of customer queries at a later date.

Interestingly for a small company Justin also uses a standard script that he reads out when people telephone in so that he knows exactly what has been said, and promised, in case of any later disputes.

The plantshop service is also on the website. This allows customers to track their expenditure when ordering plants online. Justin then telephones all clients after receiving their orders. This is an important point of contact and provides an opportunity to set size expectations depending upon the time of year. Although the plants are sold depending upon the size of the containers the actual plant size will depend upon the season.

The Clients

Although the range of clients include TV celebrities, schools, really big houses and little rental houses the majority of clients are within the middle-income bracket who will buy some plants and get some construction. The top end of the market prefer greater design individuality and time than the Landscape Safari process provides. Money is often an issue for clients so many get a design and then do it themselves. Justin will try to give them as much information as possible and the feedback is that his clients really appreciate that additional time and advice. Many of the clients return when they move or want to update their garden design. The cycle for repeat purchases seems to be 3–5 years.

The Services

Responsive to Customer Needs

The website www.landscapesafari.co.nz claims that the team at Landscape Safari aim to provide customers with a landscaping service that is:

- mobile;
- quick;
- convenient;
- great value.

Landscape Safari wants customers to enjoy the process of having their garden designed by them and has innovated a new approach to the process of designing, and delivering a landscaping service to clients. They provide a variety of service packages that can be bought separately or as a combination depending upon requirements. Customers can purchase a garden design, buy plants online for delivery, or purchase the full design and installation package. Being able to separate the elements out also provides customers with the opportunity to spread their financial costs.

The big money is in building the gardens but the plant service delivery is probably the future. Only about 1 in 10 new clients would build the whole garden with the remaining 9/10 buying the design service and then installing it themselves. The full service rate among repeat clients rate is much higher, around 80 per cent. In terms of profitability around 70 per cent comes from construction, 20 per cent from plants and 10 per cent from design. In terms of pricing the policy is to put a straight 40 per cent mark-up on everything. The labour rate for planting is a straight $33 per sq meter plus the plants.

Design services

The Landscape Safari website provides details of two design packages. Each of the packages, one hour or two hour, come with a range of options which enables the service to be tailored to customer requirements and the price (Figure CS6.1) they are prepared to pay for the service.

Package	Availability	Cost
One-hour package	Between 10am & 3pm Monday to Friday	$165.00
Two-hour package	Between 10am & 3pm Monday to Friday	$280.00
Peak one-hour package	Before 10am & After 3pm Monday to Friday	$180.00
Peak two-hour package	Before 10am & After 3pm Monday to Friday	$340.00
Saturday one-hour package	Between 10am & 3pm Saturday	$200.00
Saturday two-hour package	Between 10am & 3pm Saturday	$385.00

Figure CS6.1   Design package prices

1) One Hour

Our one-hour package is priced at an unbeatable **$165**. This price is inclusive of GST but maybe **subject to travel** depending on your location.

This option is available between 10am and 3pm, Monday through Friday.

Outside of these times the cost of this package is **$180**. Saturday appointments are charged at **$200**.

2) Two Hour

Our two-hour package is competitively priced at **$280**. Again this includes GST but may incur a **travel fee** as per location.

This option is available between **10am** and **3pm, Monday to Friday**. Outside of these times, the two hour consultation is charged at **$340**.

Saturday's are charged out at **$385.00**.

The website suggests that these design prices are competitive and will provide customers with cost savings that can be used to purchase plants with the added convenience that the plants will be delivered straight to their door. This provides an effective link into one of the other service innovations, the 'plant by numbers' system.

In addition to the pricing for the design service the company provides information on how the service will be performed:

- That an on-site meeting will take place at the client's garden;
- That the design will take account of particular client requirements including practical considerations, space and privacy issues, preferred aesthetic and ongoing maintenance;
- That, unless otherwise specified at the time of booking the appointment, the design will not be to scale but will include the basic geography of the site and particularly any hard landscaping features that interest the client, for example retaining systems, paths, fences, pools, driveways, water features and planter

boxes. If a scale drawing is required the additional costs are specified on the website;

- That the design will include recommended material specifications
- That the design comes complete with an itemised plant list which enables clients to take advantage of the convenient Plant-By-Numbers system.

Further information, along with photographs, is also provided to give potential customers an idea of the style of the garden designs: 'Justin Newcombe has designed over 4000 gardens in the last 7 years and is now focusing on creating art gardens. These are gardens drawn from Justin's contemporary art practice and have a notional edgy feel. They include explorative drawings & plans and are conceived in a "Landscape as Sculpture" context. Plans cost $1.70 + gst per ^{2}m and conditions apply.'

Plant-By-Numbers

Once customers have a design they can purchase plants from Landscape Safari to be delivered to their door at any time. It is not necessary for the company to do the installation of a design. A key element in the success of this service is the catchy title and the way in which the service is conveyed to customers which stresses the convenience and reliable results: 'Using our great Plant-By-Numbers System you can literally plant by numbers. It's just like paint by numbers but you use plants instead of paint. We deliver the plants straight to your door. Each plant is numbered to correspond with your drawing and plant list. This way you can plant your own garden and have a professional looking result every time. You don't have to know what any of the plants are, you just match the numbers on your plants to the numbers on your drawing and list. It's that simple!' The online order form (Figure CS6.2) is more than just an order form. It also provides good photographs and relevant, useful information relating to planting, care and growth of the plants. All of which add value to the basic plant-ordering service.

Installation

Landscape Safari offers a comprehensive installation service which is positioned as a convenience for busy gardeners: 'everything from tiling, retaining, decking and masonry, section clearing and planting can be achieved without you having to lift a finger.' Fixed pricing is applied to all installations so that customers know how much the service will cost before agreeing to go ahead. It is also possible for clients to do the planting, using the Plant-By-Numbers system, themselves after Landscape Safari have completed any site clearing and hard landscaping installation.

Browse plants/products: 1-10 | 11-20 | 21-30 | 31-40 | 41-50 | 51-60 | 61-70 | 71-80 |
Other products/specials

Code	Plant	Size	Price	Quantity
1	**Acer Palmate** This is the Japanese maple . It is a small deciduous tree with coloured foliage ranging from iridescent green to scarlet red a must have for any serious Japanese garden but can also be used in a range of other styles . It is a good choice for a domestic garden as it is not to big at maturity . [Plant Care Tip]	95 litre	$150.00	☐
2	**Bangalow Palm** Native to Australia the Bangalow palm grows naturally next to stream beds in wooded gullies .It grows up to 18m high ,has a very tidy trunk with a handsome crown . It prefers a sheltered aspect but will adapt over time to windy or hot conditions so long as it has a good water supply.	40litre	$150.80	☐
3	**Butia Capitata** Native to southern Brazil, Uruguay and northern Argentina . the Butia is an elegant silver palm with a feather type crown . Each frond has an exaggerated arching in the foliage so that the tips of the frond point in toward the trunk. It grows up to 6m.	3m high	$650.00	☐
4	**Chamaerops Humilis** A survivor of the ice age this palms has evolved to be especially hardy and versatile. Instead of growing in a single stem habit it grows small trunks from the base on which a tight clump of hand shaped fronds appear . growth varies from plant to plant and environment to environment , but a 3 m canopy is not out of the question . They will perform in very sandy condition but can also be planted into very heavy soils and do well in pots.	20 litre	$160.00	☐
5	**Citrus Lemonade** A well behaved small lemon with classic yellow fruit . Good looking and productive can be worked into a variety of garden styles. A strong fertilizer and watering programme is important and keep the drip line free of foliage and grass.	45 Litre	$65.00	☐
		45 L Lime tahiti	$65.00	☐
		45 L Lemon mayer	$65.00	☐
6	**Cyathea smithi** This is the silver fern (New Zealand s National symbol) It has delicate emerging fronds and dose better in sheltered conditions .If grown in optimum environment it is capable of reaching 5m.	3.5 Litre	$12.00	☐
7	**Dracena Draco** From the Canary islands this stunning piece of plant sculpture has a single trunk with strong branches supporting a canopy of upright sword shaped foliage . Ideal for pots and raised planters as well	5 Litre	$30.00	☐

Figure CS6.2   Online order form

	as being a great asset in any garden a proven low maintenance performer			
8	**Eugenia Ventinates** A fast growing hedging tree with a green, yellow and rogue foliage . The small leaf form allows for trimming into strong geometric shapes . It is a popular hedging plant and a favourite with topiarists . It is a very hardy subtropical plant however dislikes clay soil and is also susceptible to air born pest damage such as Pysllid.	**5 Litre**	$17.50	☐
9	**Feijoa Mamoth** The Feijoa is cultivated primarily for its fantastic fruit but also can become a dense hedge . This native of South America also has a pretty flower and can be trimmed into an attractive ornamental . Considering the quality of the fruit it is amazing how little care the need and what variety of conditions they will withstand.	**5 Litre**	$30.00	☐
10	**Kentia Palm** This is one of the most attractive and hardest palms. It has an attractive foliage and tight distinctive rings around the trunk it grows in full gale force wind and maintains its handsome form . In its native environment of Lord Howe Island they will even grow in between the high and low tide mark .	**60 litre**	$195.00	☐

Press **Add Plants To Order** to save your selection   Add Plants To Order

Figure CS6.2 (Continued)

Plant Supply

Landscape Safari has one supplier for plants. Having all lines coming out of one nursery means that they do not have a storage depot or staff and systems to process orders in and out. The nursery undertakes the delivery to Landscape Safari's clients provided the delivery constitutes a reasonable amount of plants. This means that the cost of deliveries in excess of $600.00 are borne by the nursery and where the order is under $600.00 a delivery charge is passed onto clients. Prior to delivery the nursery labels the plants with the Plant-By-Numbers labels. The company has put a lot of effort into selecting a nursery with very high standards because they are aware that people are often wary about buying from the internet. They are determined that their clients will have a good experience in order to attract repeat business.

Adding Value

The website is a gardener's dream. It includes a lot of beautiful photographs and a number of case studies as well as extensive practical information on popular gardening topics such as lawn care and roses.

The Future

There is no need to advertise on the radio any more. Justin would only consider that now if he wanted to really expand and pump money into it the business but that is not what he wants to do. He's really happy with it and does not want to take on all the pressures and stresses associated with expansion.

Last year he had the opportunity to build a garden for a cancer hospital in Nepal. Justin did a radio interview about the cancer hospital project. Caught short for a stand-in presenter for the show the next day, the producer telephoned him back to see if he would do it. Now he has a contract as the stand in for the main presenter on the weekly 'Kitchen & Garden' show. Although the main purpose is not to generate business for Landscape Safari, the number of website hits increase substantially after each of the shows. As a result of this media success Justin has now developed a garden programme for television too.

The Auckland Herald ran a two-page spread on the company last year. They liked the whole zany landscaper angle. Although there was no indication of significant new business being generated Justin feels that the media exposure is good for business because it makes clients feel comfortable when doing business with Landscape Safari.

Discussion

What aspects of the Landscape Safari process do you imagine might differ from another landscaping service?

To what extent do you think the Landscape Safari service process has been designed to ensure a good customer experience?

To what extent do the 'back-stage' processes support the 'front-stage' experience?

7

Waterstons, Business Analysis and Computer Consultancy[1]

Background

Waterstons was founded in 1993 by Sally Waterston as an Information Technology (IT) Service Provider, based in Durham in the north of England. The business originally focused on the provision of independent advice on computer-based accounts for small-to-medium sized enterprises (SMEs). By the year 2001, it was providing business analysis and computer consultancy services for SMEs in manufacturing, distribution, production, accounting, retail and catering and industrial services.

Waterstons service offer is summarised on the website (http://www.waterstons. co.uk) as follows:

Waterstons aim to provide a complete and independent IT service to companies in the medium enterprise sector. With our approach you get the right people at the right time while avoiding the need to recruit, train and retain skilled IT staff.

In the early days, as the business grew, clients demanded more and more complex technical services and Waterstons recruited staff to respond to clients' needs. Mike Waterston and Ajaib Singh joined the company in 1994, forming a tripartite partnership. They now employ a further 38 staff, offering independent, expert assistance with selecting software, advice on making the best use of established legacy systems, help to get the best out of the internet, support for desktop, server, WANS and LANS, security against attack by hackers and viruses, retail, manufacturing and distribution consultancy, systems development and systems integration, website design and business-to-business applications, facilities management and disaster recovery, networks and email. Increasingly they found there was a need for supporting clients IT infrastructure on a daily basis and formulated the Facilities Management group.

Developers and facilities management staff are Microsoft certified, Novell, Lotus and Cisco specialists. Business analysts are trained in accounts and have first-hand experience in their respective industry sectors. Waterstons won the 'Fast 50 Technology' award in March 2001, as their three consecutive years of

58 per cent per annum growth put them in the top 50 fastest-growing technology companies in the north of England. Two months later, they won a national Microsoft award. Their IT solution for the National Salvage Group came top in the Enterprise Agility Category.

Waterstons was originally located in rented accommodation above a franchise garage. From using only part of the space, they eventually took over all the space, and they finally outgrew the space. In May 2001, they relocated in purpose-built offices in Belmont Business Park, just off the Al Motorway in Durham.

The Nature of the Business

Waterstons place high value on independence, and on the quality of their independent advice. This is reflected in relationships that are conducted in an open and unbiased manner. Indeed, many of the company's early clients are still with them. They tended to be small enterprises whose IT spend was limited, and who did not have dedicated IT resources in-house. Many of them used a wide portfolio of services offered by Watersons. Watersons also offer 'hand-holding' support to clients who wish to upgrade their IT services. The consultants are careful to identify the 'right' IT solution, and will not sell solutions that cannot be delivered.

Waterstons' employees are highly valued, and recognised for their knowledge, experience and contribution. Before an offer of employment is made, potential recruits have to meet most of the existing staff to see how they 'fit in'. Finding staff with the right mix of skills and willing to locate in the north is challenging; many IT professionals with relevant experience tend to be based in south-east England. Senior management adopt a philosophy that is based on employee empowerment and trust. There is a flat organisational structure, split into divisions, with each division having a team leader and the other employees known as 'consultants'. Mike Waterston is a firm believer of 'management by walking around' and has instilled a company culture that drew on ideas from Tom Peters, Peter Drucker and Warren Bennis.

The business normally falls into one of three categories: consultancy, facilities management and software development.

Consultancy

Consultancy is offered to clients who wish to assess their IT needs. Consultants at Waterstons take on clients in the role of a key account manager. They work with a client to analyse the IT systems and strategies to identify the current adequacy and effectiveness. Normally the consultants would identify the specific needs and opportunities within clients' businesses and facilitate the development of either a new 'off-the-shelf software package or a customised solution. Comprehensive project management services are provided to ensure implementation of the solutions, and other factors connected with project completion. Where a company has already made substantial investments in IT, consultants can help businesses to get more out of them.

Facilities management

The facilities management service is offered to clients that do not have the resources to provide total in-house IT expertise. Waterstons provide day-to-day tactical network support with up-to-date IT knowledge and capabilities. Flexible contracts allow clients to use the consultants when needed. Waterstons support the University of Durham Business School (UDBS) in this capacity; for example, Ray Knox, the IT Manager at UDBS, values the technical competence of the Waterstons staff, their flexible approach to the different cultures within UDBS and their very high work ethic.

Software development

The development team can provide solutions where bespoke software is required rather than 'off-the-shelf' packages. The software may range from simple databases to company-wide management systems and include email and Internet. The team can also provide support services to systems implementation in the form of data transfers and other bespoke work.

Growth and Development of the Business

Accommodation and communication

Waterstons has achieved tremendous growth since its inception. When the business started, it only occupied one room of the three available above the franchise garage, and so communication between staff was relatively easy. As the business grew, and more people were recruited, they expanded into the other two rooms. At this stage, staff were divided physically, and communication became more difficult. Indeed, when the Development Section was formed in 1998, it was separated from the Facilities Management and Consultancy Sections by a wall. The 'management by walking around' policy was adopted in recognition of the physical division of the sections. As a further response to the need for clear communications, Waterstons set up an intranet that contained newsworthy items and monthly financial information.

Nevertheless, staff in the development section were often referred to as the 'back-room boys' or 'the techies'. Despite their own perceptions of working in the back room, direct client contact has always been essential on all projects and contact was occasionally carried out by email or presumed not necessary. Indeed, some clients had written to Waterstons to ask why they had not heard from them on certain projects, and Mike Waterston has had to ask the development section to visit clients on a regular basis.

The original office led to serious overcrowding and, as the number of employees grew, a 'hot desk' policy became necessary within the facilities management section. With the move to new offices in 2001, Waterstons hoped to alleviate many of the growth-related accommodation problems, but are aware that as the new offices are on two floors, there may still be problems with internal communications.

The client base

The clients that Waterstons served in the early days of the business were typically small enterprises with a limited budget for IT and no in-house experience. Clients with no IT knowledge were heavily dependent on Waterstons to provide IT skills in all areas from help with Microsoft Office to the design of complex databases. The time required to service 'small' clients properly and the amount that they are able to pay means that the margins from small clients are small and often negative. Highly skilled and expensive people were often required to sort out jobs which only require very basic skills (mainly due to the nature of the relationships between staff and clients). The nature of relationships with clients means that also the opportunity of earning higher rates elsewhere is lost. Margins are better for medium-sized businesses.

The dilemma for Waterstons is that they have ongoing relationships with many small clients from the early period and yet they need to increase the annual spend of clients to maintain profitable growth. One way of maintaining growth would be to devise a strategy for moving the focus of Watersons' activities from small to medium-sized enterprises. Such a strategy would have to be managed extremely carefully – the opportunity of increasing earnings must be weighed against potential lost business from long-standing small business clients.

Client contact and handovers

During the period up until the move, Waterstons used key account managers as points of contact between major clients and the organisation. The majority of key account managers worked in the consultancy section, with a few from the facilities management section. The largest and most important clients were handled by one of the three partners. For major consultancy projects, Sally Waterston was normally the key account manager. Key account managers have to ensure that they are in close contact with major clients on a regular basis, especially during a consultancy project, or through project management of an installation. There were, however, no set procedures that provide guidelines for the key account managers as to the regularity of client contact, neither was there a formal review. It was left to the discretion of the individual.

Clients viewed the service offered through contact with the partners very highly. They described Sally Waterston's service as excellent, and it is unlikely that all members of the consultancy team can provide the same service experience for clients as Sally. Differences in client service experiences could arise from the lack of formal procedures to follow during a consultancy project or from a lack of contact by members of the consultancy section with the more important clients. It may have required the key account manager to bring in other staff to work with the client as the project develops. Sally Waterston managed the Suncrest account, for example, but once the project moved from consultancy to facilities management, staff in the facilities management section deal directly with the client. Such a hand-over means that clients obtain a different 'Waterstons relationship' depending on the individuals involved. The management of clients' expectations during handover is known to be very important.

Developing the Company Culture and Awareness

At Waterstons, principles of excellent service are transmitted through the company via its culture; that is, influenced by the values held by the partners. For example, staff in the development section speak of 'going the extra mile' for the client. In 1998, a 'customer perception' survey, carried out by Waterstons, confirmed that clients were generally satisfied with the service received. Such surveys have been repeated in a less concentrated manner each year, with similar findings. Waterstons has established a reputation for the quality of its service, but getting an initial meeting with a potential client is still a challenge. Proposals have been submitted, but then rejected because the honest evaluations of resources and costs required for a project (based on an assessment of value for the client) had not matched clients' price expectations.

At Waterstons, only a few people hold knowledge pertaining to some of the key aspects of the company's operation. The partners acknowledge that the absence of a middle management layer within the company impacts on the manner in which critical decisions are made regarding its operation. Employees are generally keen to take on challenging assignments that allow them to develop their competencies and feel rewarded for their achievements, but the gap in the management structure is a hindrance. There is a perceived gap in the transference of service delivery knowledge that could ultimately lead to employee disillusionment. Mike Waterson is aware of this issue and has a plan to resolve the situation within the next year.

Watersons has many informal relationships with other service providers and retailers in the north of England, whose referrals can often lead to additional business. However, in some cases, where the relationship is only, as yet, weak, Waterstons may simply be one of a number of IT consultants that are given the opportunity to submit a quotation for the work. This happened recently when a graphic design company, known to Waterstons, had won a contract to provide a consumer e-commerce website design for a well-known jewellery retailer. The graphic designers approached Waterstons, as well as other software developers, to quote for the IT work to support the e-commerce site – mainly bespoke software to be created by the development section. Watersons did not win the contract in this particular case.

The company intranet reflects their openness with clients. There is a customer feedback page which includes comments from customers good or bad. Clients can also access any employee via the telephone, and calls will always be handled and dealt with within three rings and it is often by one of the three partners.

Company Philosophy and Values

At Waterstons, we place high value on our independence and on the quality of our independent advice. Our people are valued and recognised for the breadth and depth of their knowledge and experience, their ability to establish good working relationships, and their total commitment to customer satisfaction.

The company statement above is endorsed by the National Salvage Group (NSG), a client of Waterstons. NSG needed seamless and efficient communications with a complex network of members and customers. Waterstons used the latest Internet technology to link together all the different systems used by the national network of salvage agents and the insurance and fleet management companies with whom NSG do business, thus enabling NSG to increase their business significantly.

According to NSG's General Manager, 'The system is truly groundbreaking, and is already making a significant impact on police forces, insurance companies and NSG members across the country. Waterstons did a fantastic job developing NSGenius for us.'

Note

1. This case study was written by Norman Gordon, Yves Hausammann, John Robinson and Chris Storey, and adapted by the authors.

8

Coloring Ring Back Tone: Adding to the Chinese Consumer Experience[1]

Coloring Ring Back Tone (CRBT) is a relatively new music-related service for the mobile phone. It is very popular in some Asian countries, such as Japan, South Korea, Singapore and China, while in the United Kingdom and other European countries, this service is not widely used (in 2007).

What is CRBT?

CRBT is a service in which the receiver of a phone call *selects and pays* for personally chosen music (or messages) to be heard by *callers*. It is different from a conventional ring tone, which is only heard by the receiver and those in the immediate vicinity of the receiver. Without the CRBT service, the caller would only normally hear a standard mechanical ringing sound. The caller who phones a CRBT subscriber will hear a customized sound (about 15 seconds of popular music, or humorous voices, say) while waiting for the receiver to answer (Figure CS8.1).

Different forms of CRBT customized sounds include:

1. Music and song, which could be classical or popular.

2. Jokes, humorous story plots, or songs with lyrics changed. For example, when you call a boy aged 18, maybe you will hear a ring-back tone such as: 'Is that a beautiful young lady? If it is, do not hang up; but if not, please call me later...'

3. DIY, in either of the two forms above. These forms must be uploaded to the service platform of mobile network operators, and then be subscribed by the users.

CRBT is flexible. It can be changed easily, which means subscribers can keep pace with the latest pop music/songs. Also, users can set different CRBTs for different group of callers, and even set different CRBTs for different times of a day. Callers may hear different songs when calling a CRBT subscriber between 10.00 and 12.00 than they hear between 20.00 and 22.00. Subscribers can also choose different songs/messages depending on who is calling. For example, they could let colleagues hear a melody of classical music when they call, while close friends could hear a funny message. Furthermore, CRBT is not actually stored in the users' mobile phones but sorted in the operators' service platforms (see below), and so users need not worry that CRBT takes up too much of the mobile phone's memory space.

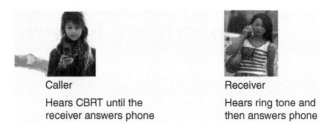

Caller
Hears CBRT until the
receiver answers phone

Receiver
Hears ring tone and
then answers phone

Figure CS8.1   Visual display of CRBT

The Impact of CRBT in China

CRBT was first introduced into China in May 2003, and has developed very fast since then. According to *2006 China CRBT Market Analysis Report*, provided by Analyses International Research & Consulting Company, at the end of 2004, the market scale of CRBT in China reached about 0.9 billion Yuan (around US $ 0.12 billion, according to the exchange rate on 25th July, 2007), compared to that of SMS (Short Message Service) which was approximately 10 billion Yuan. By the end of 2005, CRBT became the third largest value-added mobile service in China (the first two are SMS and IVR (Interactive Voice Response)), with users exceeding 60 million. At the end of 2006, the number of CRBT users in China reached over 88.5 million, and the market scale was over 1.56 billion Yuan. Going from zero to a market worth over 1.56 billion Yuan, took CRBT only about three and a half years, which was far beyond the expectation of mobile phone operators.

The CRBT Business Model

The mobile phone market in China is largely dominated by two large operators, namely China Mobile Communications Ltd. (referred as China Mobile hereinafter) and China United Telecommunications Ltd. (referred as China Unicom hereinafter). China Mobile is the largest GSM (Global System for

Mobile Communications) operator with 301 million mobile phone subscribers in December 2006 (www.chinamobilehk.com), followed by China Unicom which has more than 142 million subscribers, including nearly 36.5 million CDMA (Code Division Multiple Access) subscribers during the same period (www.chinaunicom.com.hk).

Both operators face a decrease of ARPU (Average Revenue per User), as a result of recruiting more new low-end subscribers. To counter this, they are continually introducing new value-added mobile services, such as SMS, MMS (Multimedia Message Service), mobile gaming, mobile Internet, ring tone and so on to ameliorate the situation. Given their dominant market positions, the two mobile operators have significant negotiating power over third-party SP (service providers) and CP (content providers) to dictate the terms of cooperative agreements. However, the operators are dependent on SP and CP to continuously provide content and create new innovative services in order to drive revenue growth. One reason is that the in-house service creation skills of these operators are inadequate, and another is that the operators' strategies are to focus on the construction, operation and maintenance of mobile network, and to act as a platform of service and a charging centre, leaving the task of designing and providing new services to SP/CP. This has been proved to be a very effective business model in Korea and Japan.

CRBT subscribers access their selection through the service and content providers and download their selections from the SP/CP. The SP/CP liaise and deal with record companies and other copyright owners. (The SP/CP charge handling fees to China Mobile and China Unicom, but pay subscription fees to the operators. The mobile phone operators then offer a subscription fee (1–3

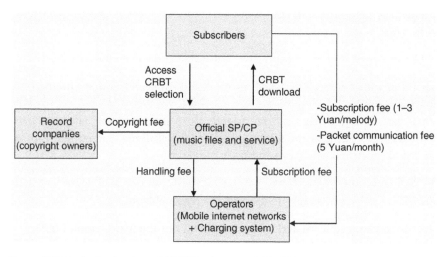

Figure CS8.2   Basic structure of CRBT business model in China
Source: Adapted from Takeishi and Lee, 2005, p. 297.

Yuan per melody) and package fee (5 Yuan per month) deal to the CRBT sub-scribers, who are given the opportunity to download music from the internet via computer or via mobile phone.)

Subscribers pay fees to operators, which include two parts; one is subscription fee (generally speaking, 1–3 Yuan/melody), the other is Packet communication fee (both China Mobile and China Unicom set it at 5 Yuan/month) (Figure CS8.2). The Packet communication fee is paid totally to operators, while sub-scription fee will be relocated between operators and the SP/CP. First, operators give subscription fee to the SP/CP, then the SP/CP pay handling fees back to oper-ators. (China Mobile sets the rate of handling fee at 15 per cent, which means SP/CP will have to pay 15 per cent of the subscription fee back to China Mobile, while China Unicom sets it at 30 per cent.)

Why has CRBT become so Popular in China?

The following indicators of CRBT popularity in China are based on research car-ried out by Hui Zhong, a former MBA student at the University of Liverpool, with Chinese mobile phone users in Shanghai, and with representatives of the two mobile phone operators and two SP, also in Shanghai.

The mobile phone users

Research took the form of two focus groups undertaken in July 2007; one with 10 people in Shanghai, China, and the other with 8 people, in Liverpool, UK. The two groups comprised a mix of gender, age, and heavy/light/non-users of CRBT.

General findings about adoption of CRBT from consumers' perspectives were as following:

• CRBT was perceived as an expressive, enjoyable and somewhat useful service.

'When I change a new CRBT, I will inform my good friends and invite them to call me to listen to it.'

'It is very funny, when I call my friends I can listen to their favourite new songs, also they can hear the song I love when they call me. Sometimes, I think it is just like a virtual music community.'

'Using CRBT helps convey some information (such as the type of music I love).'

• CRBT was perceived as easy to use and at a reasonable price.

'CRBT is very easy to learn and to use, but this is not the main reason I use it.'

'If there are some SP providing the same CRBT, I will compare the price and quality and then perhaps choose a cheaper one...but generally speaking, the price varying between 1 and 3 Yuan is reasonable.'

- Intention to use CRBT was relatively high.

'I love challenge. If the service is a little complex, I will feel proud that I can learn it more quickly than my friends and then teach them how to use it. My friends always ask me for the latest news about CRBT, or how to use it, or the hottest CRBT.'

But a minority view:

'If a mobile service is complex, I will probably not try it, because I don't want to spend too much time on it'.

- Interpersonal Influence was perceived as high whereas External Influence was perceived as moderate.

'People of my age are not easily influenced by advertisement and reports on mass media. We will think about it, doubt it and then make our own decision.'

'I was first attracted by my friend's CRBT. Then I talked about it with her and tried it...I have recommended it to some of my friends. They like it and use it now!'

- Both Perceived Value and Subjective Norm are key drivers to use CRBT.

'My using CRBT is influenced a lot by my friends, because I don't want be out of the circle. On the other hand, I find that it is worth using.'

- Perceived Enjoyment and Perceived Expressiveness played essential roles in adopting CRBT.

'I use the sports-related songs, like *We Will Rock You*, during World Cup period, and those who call me will realize at once that I love football, and maybe they will talk with me about the football match of last night for a while.'

Main segment differences are

- Younger people had much stronger Intention to Use CRBT.
- Older users perceived CRBT as less expressive and enjoyable.
- Younger users perceived CRBT as more easy to use, and priced more reasonable.
- Older users' adoption is less influenced by Subjective Norms.

The Industry Representatives

Research took the form of in-depth interviews of 30–60 minutes with product managers of China Mobile and China Unicom, and with Sales Managers of two of the top 10 SP in China. The interviews were carried out in July 2007.

From providers' perspectives, characteristics of CRBT contributing to its success can be listed as following:

- No special requirements of handsets
- No conflict with other mobile services

- Attractive content
- Affordable price.

The successful marketing strategies/practices were agreed as:

- Mobile-marketing is the most important promotion; cross-sale of CRBT and picture download has been proved to be efficient.
- Internet is the most frequently used channel to purchase CRBT, because of its convenience, especially for young users.
- Integrating the advertisement of CRBT into entertainment programs on radio and TV, and mini concerts are creative ways to market CRBT.

The burning question: can CRBT succeed in the western world?

Note

1. This case has been extracted and adapted from an MBA Dissertation at the University of Liverpool Management School, written by Hui Zhong, 2007.

Reference

Takeishi, A. & Lee, K-J. (2005) 'Mobile Music Business in Japan and Korea: Copyright Management Institutions as a Reverse Salient', *Journal of Strategic Information Systems*, vol. 14, 291–306.

9

Jackson Russell

History of the Firm

Jackson Russell, the second oldest law firm in Auckland, New Zealand, was founded by Frederick Ward Merriman in 1844. Merriman was an important early citizen of Auckland, being a Member of Parliament (1854); Provincial Law Officer; Crown Solicitor and vice-president of Auckland's first Law Society (1860). He was also a prominent member of the Masonic Lodge and took part in the local dramatic society activities as well as being secretary of the chess and whist club.

Jackson Russell has always been located within the CBD of Auckland. Back in the 1870s a feature of the offices was a large offsite strongroom. This was accessed across a yard (which became a watercourse in wet weather). Here all the deeds baskets were kept together with the heavy ledgers all bound in calf. These had to be carried daily to the offices and heaved up to the sloping wall desks where Jackson Russell's clerks sat on high leather topped square stools – a scene most reminiscent of Dickens's stories.

Legal offices of the time were very different from those of today in other ways. It is reported by George Sanders, an employee of 64 years who started as office boy, became the first typist and eventually rose to be the firm's accountant that at this time office boys had to report for work at 7.15AM. In Winter their first job each day was to chop the wood, fetch the coal, and light the fires. Sander's last job of the day was to buy a cigar for Mr Russell at 5.45PM.

During his 58 years in practice Samuel Jackson drew wills for a number of Auckland's first benefactors – Edward Costley, Dr E J Elam and James Dilworth. The money left by Costley was of immense benefit to small struggling charities, making them into well-established institutions – the Public Library, the Auckland Hospital, the Parnell Orphanage, the Sailors Home and the Auckland Institute. Dr Elam's bequest paid the salary of the director of the Elam School of Arts which functioned in a room lent by the Town Council. James Dilworth who died in 1894 left the residue of his large estate to find the school which bears his name today to educate boys in need of help.

Over the years many Auckland solicitors have trained in the firm. A number of them went on to establish firms that still carry their name today. They include Ronald (later Sir Ronald) Algie, who was a member of the staff in the 1920s and Leslie (later Sir Leslie) Munro. Algie later became the full-time Professor of Law at Auckland until entering into politics and becoming speaker of the House of Representatives. Munro later became editor of the New Zealand Herald, Ambassador for New Zealand at Washington, and President of the twelfth session of the General Assembly of the United Nations. He was also a Member of Parliament for Waipa.

A feature of the history is the long-term relationships developed with clients. Many of today's clients are proud to claim third and fourth generation relationships and commercial connections exist with some of Auckland's earliest enterprises.

The Current Practice

Jackson Russell is now a medium-sized law practice with eight partners and more than 20 staff which includes staff solicitors, legal executives, accounts clerks, secretaries and a practice manager.

The firm now practises from modern offices located in the outer fringe of Auckland's Central Business District and close to the courts. Car parking is available for clients – once the site of Auckland's historic 'Grand Hotel'. The current offices were architecturally designed in 1992. There is a lot of wood panelling and muted colours. The atmosphere is one of quiet professionalism. The office area is planned around the legal service teams comprising: commercial; family and litigation (affectionately known internally as 'the Rockstars').

The majority of client meetings take place in the meeting room which is immediately in front of the lifts and reception area and ensures that clients are not exposed to the offices or storage areas. The meeting room is lined with photographs of key members of the firm dating back to the founders. The use of the meeting room for client liaison requires a booking system which means that clients are rarely exposed to other clients during their visits.

The majority of client interactions take place in their offices as this is deemed to be a more efficient use of time, and therefore cheaper for clients, than having lawyers visit them. One exception to this is the arrangement with the student's union at Unitec (a Higher Education Institute located in Auckland, New Zealand) where the initial contact is made on site at Unitec. The reason for the arrangement is to build business by reaching new clients that would not otherwise do business with Jackson Russell. The firm recognised that a higher education provider would represent approximately the same number of adults as a small New Zealand town so, given their focus on private clients, the arrangement facilitates the development of relationships with younger adults with the hope that it may endure.

The People

There are currently eight partners; three associates; four solicitors; one law clerk; two legal executives. The fee earning team are supported by seven secretarial staff, two accounts clerks, a receptionist and a practice manager.

Retention of staff who are not partners is an issue for the firm, so much effort goes into recruiting the right person for each vacancy. It is now common practice to include several team members, both professional and support staff in the selection process to ensure a good fit with the team. Jackson Russell pay market rates for support staff but accept that their rates are not at the top end. Consequently they seek to make the firm a good place to work and are currently considering how to improve the working experience as part of a strategic review.

The employment contract specifies that those who work at Jackson Russell are expected at all times to have a standard of dress and behaviour appropriate to a professional services office.

Continual professional development centres around keeping up to date with the law rather and comprises two elements. First, the professional staff are expected to participate in seminars run by the Auckland Law Society. Secondly, the firm runs internal seminars to facilitate the sharing of knowledge and ideas.

The Service

Jackson Russell is a general practice law firm offering a full range of high-quality, cost-effective legal services (Figure CS9.1). Using an airline comparison, the firm sees itself as providing a 'business class' service. They believe that clients, particularly commercial clients, associate a 'first class' legal service with much larger firms with large departmental teams which enables them to respond immediately to their client's demands. Such clients expect responsiveness 24/7. Many clients do not appear to be aware of the breadth of their service provision and so they plan to list all of their services on the back of all their business cards.

Clients are greeted by the receptionist when they arrive and offered a drink. There are comfortable seats with magazines. The majority of meetings will take

Business advice	Civil litigation
Commercial property	Company restructuring
Employment law	Environmental & planning
Estate planning & trusts	Family law
Finance	Insolvency
Intellectual property	
Media law	Mediation and alternative dispute resolution
Probate and administration	Residential conveyancing
Rural conveyancing	Sales & acquisitions of business
Subdivisions & property development	Wills

Figure CS9.1   Range of services offered by Jackson Russell place in the meeting room next to reception away from the office areas and so the lawyers will come to meet the clients in reception. The aim is to achieve a minimal waiting period for clients.

Clients are provided with a standard letter (Figure CS9.2) that outlines the service process they can anticipate.

JACKSON RUSSELL

Est. 1844
Barristers • Solicitors • Notary Public

9 Princes Street, Auckland, New Zealand
PO Box 3451, Auckland 1, DX CP20520
Fax Litigation 09 309 9648 Fax Commercial/Property 09 309 0902
Email enquiry@jacksonrussell.co.nz   Telephone 09 303 3849
www.jacksonrussell.co.nz

Name   21 January 2008
ADDRESS

Dear Name

OUR TERMS OF ENGAGEMENT

1. It was a pleasure meeting with you on *1*.
2. Firm policy requires us to write to you as early as possible after being engaged setting out the basis upon which you are retaining us.

Description of Services

3. You have asked our firm to act for you in connection with your *2* *[give outline of major points of instructions, action envisaged and advice given]*.
4. Our firm is committed to serving you professionally and ethically. We make the following commitments to you:

   - We will hold strictly confidential all communications with you, and all information which we receive from you during the course of our dealings. We will not reveal your confidences without your agreement.

   - We will undertake your work conscientiously. In turn we will need your full and timely cooperation to help represent you.

   - We will work with you to develop an understanding of your expectations. We will work together to establish goals and deadlines that meet your needs.

   - We will communicate with you and keep you informed about the status the work we do for you. Your telephone calls will be returned promptly. We will send to you copies of significant correspondence and other documents.

Lawyers

5. Zandra Wackenier/Johanna Robertson will have primary responsibility for your matter. Zandra/Johanna will use other lawyers and legal assistants in the firm where in her professional judgment this is appropriate in order to expediently handle your file or in the interests of your work being done at a cost effective level.

Figure CS9.2   Letter of instruction

6. Our firm's schedule of hourly rates for lawyers and other members of the professional staff is based on experience, specialisation and training. (Zandra Wackenier's present hourly rate is $220 (excl GST) (Johanna Robertson's present hourly rate is $270 (excl GST).

3

Legal Aid Option

7. You wish to apply for a grant of Legal Aid. If Legal Aid is granted the writer's hourly rate will be $125/$140 (GST inclusive). In the event that Legal Aid is not granted you will be charged at the private rates outlined above.

Fees

8. Our fee will be based on time spent by the lawyers in our firm on your behalf and the criteria laid down by the New Zealand Law Society. The time spent by us on your behalf for which you will be charged will include:

- Personal and telephone attendances on you
- Correspondence with you
- Attendances upon solicitors acting for the other party
- Considering the law and facts of your case
- Reading and considering incoming letters, papers and documents in your case
- Preparing papers for the Court
- Correspondence with third parties
- Instructing enquiry agents and experts
- Attending Court on your behalf
- Time spent on travelling

Time for Account and Payment Estimate

9. It is difficult in family matters to give an accurate estimate of fees, however, we will keep you informed on a regular basis as to the time spent on your matter.

10. Generally accounts will be sent to you bi-monthly. Payment is due within 14 days of the account being rendered. For your convenience, we accept Visa or MasterCard for payment.

11. If your accounts remain outstanding after 60 days no further work will be undertaken by any lawyer of the firm until appropriate arrangements are made to bring the account back into good standing.

Disbursements

12. Disbursements include expenses such as Court filing fees, barrister's fees, toll calls, faxes, photocopying, travel expenses, couriers and the fees of agents who serve documents and who conduct investigations, searches and registrations. You are responsible for reimbursing our firm for disbursements. Disbursements may be included with our accounts or may be billed separately. Firm policy requires us to obtain from you funds in advance for significant disbursements.

Settlement Moneys

13. For property and financing transactions where payment of moneys is due by you, we require cleared funds for the correct amount to be deposited with us no later than the morning of settlement.

Termination of Legal Services

14. At all times you have the right to terminate our services upon written notice to that effect. We reserve the right to terminate our services at any time upon written notice (subject to our ethical obligations).

15. In the event of termination you are responsible for the value of recorded unbilled time plus disbursements to the date of termination.

Figure CS9.2   (Continued)

Privacy Information

16. Over the course of your involvement with us we may collect and hold personal information concerning you. Failure to provide us with information may preclude us from providing services to you or limit the quality of the services provided.

17. Information concerning you will be used by us to provide legal service, to obtain credit or other references, to undertake credit management and to inform you of issues and developments that may be of interest to you. You authorise us to obtain from any person any information about you necessary for those purposes, and you authorise any person to release information to us that we require for those purposes.

18. Information concerning you will be held at our office. Under the Privacy Act 1993 you have the right of access to, and correction of, your personal information held by us.

19. The Financial Transactions Reporting Act 1996 requires us to collect from you and retain information required to verify your identity.

Communications

20. We do not accept liability for loss arising from non-receipt of any communication, including computer email communications.

Agreement

21. If we do not hear to the contrary, we will assume that you accept the above basis of retainer and we will provide our services on those terms.

22. If you have any questions or concerns regarding these policies, we would be pleased to speak with you at any time at your convenience.

On a personal note, I am very pleased that you have selected our firm to represent you. I look forward to working with you and shall use my best efforts on your behalf.

Yours faithfully

Figure CS9.2   (Continued)

There is a desire to become more proactive but they are aware that some clients are suspicious of when lawyers make the first contact given the perception of cost associated with the use of a lawyer's time. The firm sends out client newsletters three times a year to encourage clients to contact them. Also, whenever a law change arises that requires clients to reconsider their legal situations they send letters out. They generally receive a positive reaction to such letters. While clients may be aware of legal changes through the media receiving a letter from their lawyer appears to generate a perception that the matter is important because the lawyer has bothered to write so it is something they need to deal with sooner rather than later.

'Back-stage' Processes

The philosophy adopted by the Practice Manager is that the role of support and administrative staff is to provide a 'seamless' service to the professional staff (the lawyers). It is his view that the lawyers should be able to get on with their job without having to worry about anything else. Therefore the Practice Manager is primarily responsible for ensuring that the internal systems, processes, procedures and staff provide an integrated and pro-active support system. Part of this support system is ensuring that they hire the right people to work at the firm.

There is a move towards measuring more of the internal processes, on the basis that what gets measured gets done. There is also an increasing focus on producing more management information reports relating to fees earned, fees billed, payments received and tracking debtors.

Some of the lawyers appreciate the frustrations that clients can have with form filling so there is a move towards the lawyers and support staff completing forms for clients to check through.

The Clients

While there is definitely a focus on the development of long-term relationships with individuals rather than targeting large business clients, the work does not necessarily split easily into private or commercial client work. Some of the larger clients for whom they do considerable commercial work are still considered to be 'private' clients because of the importance of the original relationship between individuals. Also, given the presence of very few large private business organisations, doing business in New Zealand invariably involves SMEs with decision-making vested in a very small number of individuals.

The nature of the relationships are more personal which may lead to the law firm to over state its focus on private client work in preference to commercial client work. However, there is no doubt that the firm seeks to build and maintain long-term relationships with individuals that will generate business across a range of legal matters. This was one of the main motivators behind the decision to provide legal services to staff and students of Unitec. The focus was very much on the long-term benefits rather than any dramatic increase in short-term business.

Evaluation of Success

Jackson Russell has recently surveyed their staff to determine motivations for continuing to work at the firm. The leading responses were: flexibility and independence of the work; the nature of the work they do; the working culture and environment; income. The main criterion used for evaluating their success has been how comfortable the partners have been with the satisfaction they gain from their work and the quality of life that the salaries have provided. These factors have taken precedence over the actual bottom line figures.

Jackson Russell does not survey clients or otherwise actively seek feedback on their service provision. When issues do arise they appear to relate to client perceptions of their access to lawyers and the responsiveness of lawyers to them, rather than fee issues.

In terms of productivity, lawyers are measured in terms of number of chargeable hours spent on a matter, the number of hours billed to the client and the amount the client actually pays. The firm aims to ensure that the person allocated to each client task is the most appropriate in terms of the complexity of the task. Consequently, a partner may delegate more routine tasks, or a whole matter, to an associate or other team member rather than doing it themselves. In doing this they seek to reduce the hourly cost to the client where possible.

The Future

The key challenge facing Jackson Russell now is succession planning. Five of the eight partners plan to retire within the next five years. The need to plan for this situation is generating much discussion within the firm particularly around the need for greater strategic planning. Is there a need to consider the financial bottom line more than in the past? In which direction should the firm go? This will determine how new partners and professional staff will be recruited. There may be a need to recruit staff with particular experience to support more specialised work, even to support the provision of a 'general' legal practice. Consideration needs to be given to what constitutes a general practice in the twenty-first century in terms of both legal and service provision.

Of course the biggest concern with so many partners retiring is how to retain their clients within the firm. The lawyer–client relationship is frequently a one-to-one relationship, even within commercial departments. While this is a strength when seeking to deliver a highly tailored and personal service, it presents a huge challenge for Jackson Russell at this time.

Discussion

How could Jackson Russell benefit from the implementation of relationship marketing strategies to minimise the negative impact of partners retiring?

10

RAD9

Background

RAD9 Computer Services (RAD9) provides information technology support business for Small to Medium Sized Enterprises (SME) and Home Computer Owners based in Auckland, New Zealand. They help customers solve computer problems by providing fast, professional service people with an innovative suite of service plans and packaged 'service products'. Their long-term vision is to be Australasia's number-one computer service business in their chosen market of SME and Home users. This will be measured using the number of customers, technical staff and offices rather than financial results which are often difficult to compare as most competitors are also private companies.

They have nine staff and six contractors in New Zealand. They are in the process of developing a franchise model and have successfully opened their first retail outlet.

Target Market and Customers

RAD9 concentrate on targeting and delivering to two target markets;

Small and medium-sized enterprises (SME)

This is defined as 10–100 staff businesses that have at least 20 per cent of their personnel using Windows-based computers. The key attributes of these customers include

- They usually have a formal management structure in place (board, GM or CEO)
- They do not currently have internal IT resource and prefer to outsource non-core activities
- Often, the business owner, Director or Manager is from a corporate background
- Computer systems' reliability is important or critical to the business' operations

The key benefits RAD9 provides their business customers are: gaining control of IT costs, having reliable and well-maintained systems. Having guaranteed support service levels from experts with great depth of experience and knowledge, their business customers can focus on their own business growth without the need to worry about IT.

Home computer owners

Although this category is very broad the following attributes have been identified;

- Own a computer that is usually over 6 months old
- Medium-to-high socio-economic status based in Auckland
- They prefer to get expert help rather than 'do it yourself'
- Male or female usually over the age of 25 and living in Auckland

RAD9 believes that home computer owners seek a fixed price with professional, guaranteed service levels which include a fast turnaround of 2–4 business days. Most of the competition either do not estimate timeframes or quote 1–2 weeks. Finally, RAD9 provides a 'No Fix, No Fee' policy on all Home PC repairs completed in their workshop.

Competitive Situation

RAD9 categorise their competition into three groups; Freelance, Mid-sized and Large IT firms.

Freelance

Although it is very difficult to quantify the freelance IT contractor market because there is no requirement for qualifications, and there is no governing industry body, RAD9 believes that freelance IT contractors make up the largest proportion of the competition. They base this on the frequency with which they come across freelance contractors when bidding for new business. They estimate that there are over 200 freelance IT support contractors in Auckland alone. Freelance contractors have the benefit of low overheads and low start-up costs enabling them to provide their services at lower rates.

RAD9 seeks to differentiate their provision from the freelance category through the guaranteed response time, managed helpdesk and nine full-time staff.

Mid-sized

Mid-sized IT support firms are categorized as 3–10 staff. RAD9 falls into this category. A mid-sized IT support firm has the ability to support larger business customers and has less operational risk than a freelance IT contractor. Mid-sized IT firms also have higher overheads. There are three key competitors within this category. RAD9 differentiate themselves from other Mid-sized firms through the provision of advanced 24×7 monitoring, guaranteed response times, specialist services and industry partnerships. These qualities are often found only in large IT firms such as those shown below (Figure CS10.1).

Figure CS10.1   RAD9 industry partners

Large competitors

Large IT firms have 10+ staff and are less numerous than other categories. Their size provides economies of scale, reliability and an ability to take on very large clients. Most large IT firms focus on business customers with 50+ staff. Since RAD9 focuses on 10–50 staff clients they believe that they operate 'under the radar' of the larger firms. While they very rarely bid for the same business clients RAD9 are conscious that as the larger, more lucrative corporate market becomes ever-more saturated; large IT firms will look closer at the lower end. So, although large competitors are not immediate competitors for RAD9 they may become competitors as the market develops and competition intensifies in the future.

Marketing overview

The Management team at RAD9 has always had a 'no salesmen' philosophy for the business. The intention has always been to ensure that the technical consultants act as account managers and that new business leads are generated through strong referrals and well executed marketing. They find that securing referral business has been relatively easy and they attribute this to their commitment to providing a good service. However, they have found that the delivery of well-executed marketing is a challenge with slim budgets and limited availability of spare cash.

   RAD9 has tested and measured the effectiveness of many different forms of marketing but without a doubt the most effective vehicle has been the website. Consequently marketing concentrates on website development and activities that promote awareness of, and visits to, the website.

Website Marketing – RAD9's Story

In 2004, RAD9 was a small IT firm doing just about anything for a buck! While developing websites for clients they also developed their own but invested little time and minimal effort to ongoing development. The result was that the website provided virtually no new leads and RAD9 felt that their failure to fully embrace the internet fully for their own marketing use was not helpful for customer perceptions of their organisation. This led to a strategic decision to stop developing websites and, instead, find an industry leader to partner with. They invested around $4000 in website design with roughly $100 per month of ongoing hosting and software costs. The website is very simple to navigate through both forwards and backwards. The ongoing investment is around 80 man-hours per month for content development and several more hours in market research. They are fully committed to a 'test, measure and tweak' philosophy. The new www.rad9.com website was launched.

Website Design: Building Confidence Through Content

The following components have been designed into the website format to increase the confidence of the website visitor and to further differentiate RAD9 from competitors:

- Customer testimonials
- Partner Affiliations
- News page
- Customer Case Studies.

Website Design: Pathways to Results

The website also has a highly defined *conversion pathway* (Figure CS10.2) designed with the purpose of compelling the visitor to phone the 0800 RAD-911 free-phone:

1. Capture Attention and Match Prospect's Problem: Home Page or Landing Page
2. Identify Resolution for Problem: Secondary Content Page/Sub Page
3. Remove Risk, Compel to Act: Secondary Content Page and Contact Page.

Although the website has a range of designated entry-points all paths lead to either the 0800 number and a call to action or to the Contact Us page. They believe that defining effective conversion pathways has been critical to their success.

The Benefits of Getting Good Conversion Rate <u>Before</u> Promoting your Website

When launching our website, we understood that to achieve a good visitor to lead conversion rate would ultimately save us money in promotion.

We tested various forms of conversion pathway over the first 3 months of the website going live. We finalised on the model illustrated on this diagram as it generated a much higher level of sales leads than other methods chosen.

Key win aspects for Conversion Rates;

- ☐ Sub-headline with 'No Fix, No Fee'
- ☐ Long copy on Conversion Page
- ☐ Adhering to 'maximum 3 clicks rule'
- ☐ Comprehensive contact details
- ☐ Pricing displayed

Due to this method, when we decided to increase expenditure in promotion, we had more confidence that the increased visitors would equate to increased sales.

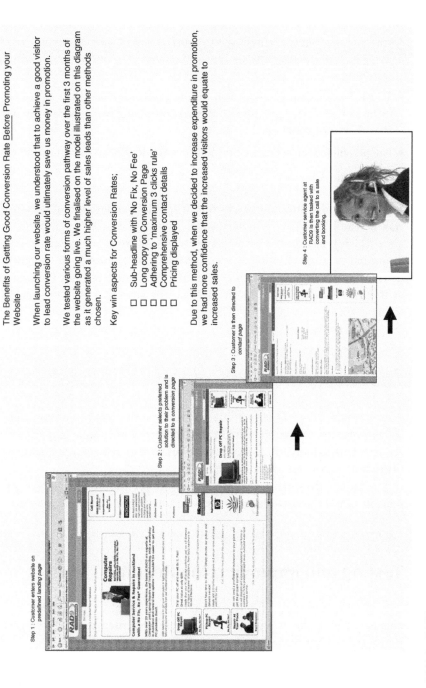

Step 1 : Customer enters website on predefined *landing page*

Step 2 : Customer selects preferred solution to their problem and is directed to a conversion page

Step 3 : Customer is then directed to *contact page*

Step 4 : Customer service agent at RAD9 is then tasked with converting the call to a sale and booking.

Figure CS10.2   RAD9.com conversion pathway

Promotion (Getting Visitors to the Website)

Promotion activities include

- Passive branding on all outbound material (e.g. email signatures, letterhead, invoices, statements and customer operational reporting highlighting the website)
- Search Engine Optimisation: identifying keywords that target customers were using to find service providers and then optimizing the website content to suit these keyword searches
- Pay-per-click: Search Engine Promotion was undertaken using Google Adwords and Google Adsense. Google AdWords

Soon after launch it was apparent that Search Engine Promotion (pay-per-click) was incredibly effective. When the RAD9 advert is clicked, then RAD9 is charged a fee which is based on a bidding system. All Adwords advertisers place a maximum bid on their chosen keywords. When their keywords are searched upon in Google, the advertiser with the highest maximum bid has their ad shown at the top. If someone clicks on their ad, the advertiser is then charged for a 'click'.

The Results were Immediate!

After a couple of weeks of running the new website and promotion campaigns RAD9 were enjoying an increase in the number of telephone enquiries for their services. Furthermore, these phone enquires were extremely well qualified taking little effort to convert into customers.

The Initial investment was about $50–80 per month on Google Adwords marketing and the new clients generated more than double that amount.

Testing and Improving the Results!

Armed with a testing and measurement philosophy, they made bi-weekly changes to both the website and the Google advertisements and budgets. Each time a change was made they measured;

- website visitor numbers
- website conversion rates (phone enquires and emails created by website)
- sales conversion rates (new customers and sales generated by website leads).

Testing identified the following key win factors;

- Headlines that matched keyword searches provided best results (e.g. for a customer searching for 'Computer Repair', the best headline is 'Computer Repairs').
- Headlines that included locality increased conversion rates (e.g. 'Auckland Computer Repairs' is the best headline).
- Body copy that included pricing improved conversion results by about 25 per cent
- Body copy that reversed risk improved conversion results by about 300–400 per cent).

It was apparent that the cost of market research was low and totally controllable so Google Adwords became the preferred research method for testing print advertising as well.

The Outcome

After six months of testing, RAD9 had learnt exactly what customers were looking for and what made them pick up the phone and call. Using the measurement tools provided by Google, and their website reporting tools, they averaged 5:1 return on ongoing marketing costs and easily gained a return on the initial website investment.

Financial results

Average phone leads per month	450
Average sales per month (from website leads)	$6604
Average monthly website marketing costs	$950
Monthly website fixed costs	$258
Return on website marketing	**$5396**
Return ratio	**5:1**

Figure CS10.3   Statistics April 2006–March 2007

Non-financial results

Marketing

The ability to gain instantaneous results from the website testing process enabled RAD9 to fast-track new initiatives and ideas before investing in other marketing such as print or advertising. They now test headlines, body copy and also calls to action with minimal financial investment and can add a new campaign in around 5 minutes. They also test different geographical regions.

Selling websites

Having seen the positive impact that a professional website marketing pro-gramme generates convinced RAD9 to offer that service to their clients through becoming a licensed reseller of Zeald.com website solutions which is a little like the 'I liked the razor so much I bought the company' scenario!

Branding and sales conversion rates

As the RAD9 website (Figure CS10.4) is frequently listed on the first page of Google searches, it is not uncommon for customers to be aware of the

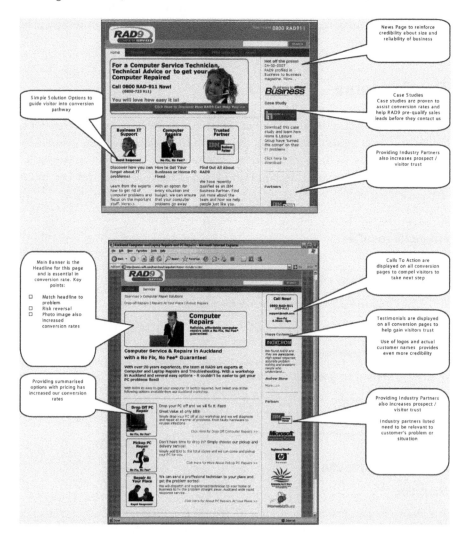

Figure CS10.4   RAD9 website

name before they come into contact with the company through networking or customer referrals. This familiarity greatly increases their ability to convert customers.

Cost reduction and control

As they no longer have to make many changes to their website advertising, they do not have to utilise valuable staff time in marketing activities which results in low overheads. When they need to increase new business leads they simply increase expenditure on Google and have confidence in the return rate.

Staff recruitment

The website have proved to be a significant tool for attracting new job candidates.

Other opportunities

Other opportunities have arisen as a direct result of being found online. RAD9 has developed exclusive partnerships with several key vendors and has an opportunity to become a service centre for a major personal computer brand.

News and PR distribution

RAD9 use the website to showcase any publicity the company receives by providing a link and article on our News page within hours of publication.

11

Living in the Cyber-society

After the long weekend break Rebecca was full of energy. She went into the office early to avoid the normal traffic jam after a public holiday and to catch up on her work. Logging into her computer while sipping her coffee she scanned her work email inbox for any pressing matters and was relieved to find no obvious dramas. Opening her personal email address in a new window she browsed through her messages. Lots of spam, e-jokes, advertisements from different companies marketing all sorts of goods, from perfumes to cheap Rolex imitations. She sent a text message to a few friends about a sale at Ezibuy starting on Thursday with 20 per cent discount on most summer clothes. They could meet at the mall, have a coffee and shop together.

Next she logged onto the BBC Radio 4 website to listen to the news and browse the programmes for the day to see if there was anything worth listening to from a marketing perspective. Then she browsed the New Zealand Herald online to catch up with the latest local news. It is so convenient to read the paper this way: scanning for the most interesting articles and then opening only the links she wants. The entertainment page was dominated by the Golden Globes awards, and a couple of movie titles caught her eye. She went to YouTube to search for their trailers and check them out. Yes, she decided they were worth seeing this weekend.

It was still only 8AM so she had time to do her shopping before the first meeting. After arriving home late last night from her weekend away, Rebecca had not had time to buy groceries and the fridge was nearly empty. She logged onto her personal shopping list on the Foodtown website and, after adding and subtracting a few items, she sent through the online order knowing that it will be there when she gets home tonight.

The main task today was to select the candidates for the vacant position and call them for an interview. She glanced over the cover letters of the 33 applications. Four of them sounded promising, so she googled the candidate names on Ringo, MySpace, Facebook and Linkedin to see what information she could find on any of them. She had heard of an employer hiring a person who sounded great at the interview but proved to be a thief with quite a history. One candidate's name and profile popped onto the screen with a link to her MySpace account. The photos on the blog were quite graphic, and the comments had a profane and insulting connotation. Rebecca vigorously crossed that name off the short list.

One of Rebecca's colleagues and friend arrived with a box of freshly baked muffins. They chatted about their long weekend trips and soon other people joined the discussion passing round their mobiles to share photos of their escapades. Later Rebecca downloaded a few photos from her mobile and uploaded them to the computer so she could share them with her friends. She will put them on Facebook tonight and send the link to her family with short, funny comments. Since she created her account a year ago, more than 65 friends and 32 colleagues have joined her network. She checked her page for upcoming events uploaded by her contacts and found that the Malaysian group had invited everyone to Albert Park to celebrate the Festival of Lanterns to acknowledge the Chinese New Year. She quickly forwarded the invitation to a couple of other friends, and RSVP'd: 'Will b there, C U soon. LOL'. Then she grabbed her report and rushed to the meeting.

Rebecca was first to jump off the seat and return to her office once the meeting was over. For the last 10 minutes of the meeting, she had been trying to get her mind off the online auction for a flashy new blackberry phone which was due to end around now. She had kept that mobile phone on her watchlist for the last 5 days and the price was too good to pass it by. She logged into her Trade Me website but found that, with two minutes to go, another buyer had put in a higher offer than she was willing to pay. Searching Trade Me for similar items she found another one with a buy-now price she could afford so she went ahead and bought it. Receiving the automatic email from Trade Me with the buyer's payment details almost instantly, Rebecca logged into her National Bank account and made the payment.

At 3PM a new email popped onto her screen, 'Cheap Flights on Sale – one day only'. She quickly opened the new link which took her to the Qantas website – up to 40 per cent off flights and accommodation packages to Australia – perfect for a long weekend getaway during winter. Checking upcoming public holidays she found the Queen's Birthday weekend in June. She checked flight availability and found two tickets available at the advertised discounted rate to the Sunshine Coast. Logging onto Skype, she searched for her best friend, who was online. After a few quick lines of chat they agreed to book. Rebecca completed the online booking form, opening another window to log into her bank account to find her credit card number. After a final check that all entered details were correct she submitted the e-form. Immediately the e-ticket appeared on the screen. She printed it and forwarded copies to her friend and to her personal email address.

The office was starting to empty. As she cleared her desk, Rebecca's mobile buzzed. It was a text message from a friend, 'Dinna out 2nite?'. She browsed the Internet to find restaurants in the CBD which had received good feedback recently. One looked interesting. The photos of the food and its location looked appealing and the prices were reasonable. Noticing that they offered a discount for booking a place online, she completed the e-form and printed out the confirmation slip before leaving the office.

Discussion

Identify and discuss the ethical issues that arise as a result of the pervasive availability and usage of the Internet and other technology-based services today.

This illustrative case study was adapted from a case prepared by Corina Crisan, Unitec Business School.

Glossary

Accommodation	The need to design services to be convenient for customers to access, participate in and consume.
ACSI	American Customer Satisfaction Index.
Ambient Conditions	The use of scent, music and lighting within the physical environment that comprises the servicescape.
ATM	Automatic Teller Machine.
Back-stage	Service elements that are invisible to customers and are frequently undertaken by non-contact personnel.
Blueprint	A comprehensive visual model of a service process used to design and evaluate service performance.
Business-to-Business Marketing (B2B)	Marketing activities involving two business organisations that do not involve individual consumers.
CEO	Chief Executive Officer.
Co-consume	Customers frequently experience service provision at the same time as other customers. Other customers can influence critical aspects of the service provision and affect the way in which one customer evaluates the provision.
Co-create	The inseparability nature of service provision means that customers frequently play an important part in the creation, delivery and performance of the service.
Consumer Marketing (B2C)	Marketing activities aimed at individual consumers.
Contact Personnel	The people who are the point of contact between the service organisation and customers.
Core Service	The service that customers pay for and frequently comprises the intangible element of the service experience.
Critical Incident	Point of service situation that gives rise to customer evaluations of the experience as either particularly satisfying or dissatisfying.
Critical Incident Technique	A research method that identifies sources of satisfaction and dissatisfaction for customers in their encounters with contact personnel.
CRM	Customer Relationship Management.
Customer Compatibility	Customers with similar tastes and behaviours.
Customer Equity	The focus on customer profitability into the future as well as the present.
Customer Errors	Errors made by customers relating to their preparation for, participation in, or resolution of service encounters.
Customer Expectations	The ways in which customers anticipate the service performance and outcomes.

Customer Experience Gap	The gap between that which customers want and what they feel they actually received.
Customer Perceptions	Customer views and opinions.
Customer Pyramid	Tool that enables service organisations to identify differences in customer profitability and manage accordingly.
Customer-to-customer Interactions	Encounters between two customers during the service.
Cycle of Failure	Where organisations cut costs to achieve short-term goals which increase employee turnover which may have a negative impact on the organisational ability to maintain customer satisfaction and deliver good service experiences.
Degree of Divergence	The amount of planned scope or latitude which contact personnel are given.
e-form	A form available on a website for customers to complete to email their comments or contact details to a company.
Employee Empowerment	The ability of employees to adopt a responsive approach to ensure customer satisfaction.
EQA	European Quality Award.
e-scape	The environment in which customers access self-service technologies.
Essential Service Element	Physical elements essential to the service but which cannot be purchased separately by the customer.
Exit costs	Costs that a customer may incur when moving their business from one service provider to another. This may include non-financial costs such as time, effort and 'hassle' required.
Expectations– Disconfirmation Paradigm	When customer satisfaction is seen as a process, satisfaction or dissatisfaction will result if the service performance confirms or disconfirms prior customer expectations.
Experience Marketing	The creation of a memorable episode based on a customer's direct personal participation or observation.
Experiential Marketing	The creation of a memorable episode based on a customer's direct personal participation or observation.
Fail-safes	Simple mechanisms to minimise or eliminate errors.
Front-line staff	Contact personnel who customers will encounter during the service provision.
Front-stage	Service elements that are visible to customers.
Functional Quality	How the service is delivered or performed.
GST	Goods and Services Tax. The New Zealand equivalent of the UK's VAT (Value Added Tax). Currently 12.5% of the price paid.
Helpseekers	Customers that actively seek information from other shoppers.
Heterogeneity	The variable nature of service performance or delivery by contact personnel.
HRM	Human Resources Management.
Inseparability	Consumption by the customer at the same time as the service is produced, performed or delivered by contact personnel.
Intangibility	The inability of services to be seen, heard, smelt, touched or tasted in the same way that products are used or consumed.
Internal Customers	Employees who provide services to other employees within the same organisation.

Internal Marketing	Activities which assist in the development of a customer focused organisation, reduce conflict between functional business areas and improve communications within an organisation.
JSM	Journal of Services Marketing.
Level of Complexity	The number of steps and sequences within a service and the interrelationships between them.
Loyalty-based Systems Chain	Hypothesis that paying employees well will increase customer loyalty.
Marketing Channels	The logistical process and parties involved in getting a product or service from production through to consumption.
Marketing Mix	The 4 Ps: Product; Price; Place and Promotion.
MBA	Master of Business Administration.
MBNQA	Malcolm Baldridge National Quality Award.
Moments of Truth	Each service encounter provides customers with the opportunity to evaluate their service experience.
Operand Resources	Organisational resources which are subjected to actions which consequently create value, that is, components parts that are combined in a particular way to manufacture a product.
Operant Resources	The knowledge, skills, capabilities and competencies that an organisation can draw upon to create value including those of their customers who co-create value. The current focus on operant resources as a result of the Service–Dominant Logic debate highlights the importance of the people involved in value co-creation.
OU	Open University.
Outlay	All financial and non-financial costs incurred by customers when accessing, participating in and consuming services many of which are in addition to the price paid to the service provider for the service product. These include costs of travel, time involved and psychological costs.
Partial Customers	Employees while acting as internal customers.
Partial Employees	External Customers who's participation in the service process is actively managed and motivated by the service organisation.
Perceived Service Quality	The gap between customer perceptions and their expectations of a service.
Peripheral Service	Service elements that support the delivery of the service paid for. Many peripheral services provide the tangible elements of the service experience.
Perishability	Services cannot be stored and are therefore time-sensitive and subject to peaks and troughs in demand.
PERT	Program Evaluation and Review Technique.
PIMS	Profit Impact of Market Strategies.
Proactive Helpers	Customers who go out of their way to offer information or advice to other customers.
PZB	Parasuraman, Zeithaml & Berry.
RATER	The five dimensions of service quality: Reliability; Assurance; Tangibles; Empathy; Responsiveness.
Reactive Helpers	Customers who readily respond to other customers seeking information or advice.
Repatronage	Returning to a service provider used previously.

Repeat Purchase	Returning to a service provider used previously.
RM	Relationship Marketing.
ROI	Return on Investment.
ROQ	Return on Quality.
Satisfaction-Trap	The acknowledgement that no direct, linear relationship has been established between customer satisfaction scores, loyalty and organisational cash flow and profitability.
SCSB	Swedish Customer Satisfaction Barometer.
Server Errors	Errors made by contact personnel relating to tasks, treatments or the tangible elements of the service.
Servicescape	The physical built environment in which service encounters take place.
Service Design	Planning of the service components that comprise the process and the physical environment.
Service Encounter	Occurs when customers directly interact with any aspect of the service delivery system.
Service Experience	Services are experienced and evaluated as a series of processes which, while frequently intangible, leave concrete impressions and memories.
Service Failure	Dissatisfaction arising from an unanticipated service outcome or performance.
Service Mapping	Builds on blueprinting by paying greater attention to customer interaction and provides a visual representation of the structure of the service.
Services Marketing Mix	The 3 additional Ps: People, Process and Physical Evidence making 7Ps in total.
Service Marketing System	A model that integrates the Marketing, Operations and Human Resource business functions.
Service Operations System	Activities and processes that generally occur back-stage and are therefore invisible to the customer.
Service Orientation	An organisational commitment to practices and procedures to deliver high levels of service quality to their customers.
Service Package	The way in which peripheral service elements are combined with core services and delivered to customers.
Service Performance	The way in which contact personnel provide or deliver the service to a customer.
Service Product	The combination of the core and peripheral service.
Service-profit-chain	A model that hypothesises how internal service quality, employee satisfaction, retention and productivity are linked to organisational growth and profitability.
Service Recovery	Steps that a service provider and their contact personnel take to move a customer evaluation of the service from dissatisfaction to satisfaction.
Service Science	A term used to identify the emerging discipline of Service Science Management and Engineering (SSME) which seeks to integrate knowledge from a range of disciplines such as: economics, business, design, IT and engineering.
Service Scripts	These are frequently used to standardise the customer experience by ensuring that contact personnel know what behaviours are expected of them. Some service scripts specify words as well as behaviours to be used when interacting with customers.
Service System	The bringing together of resources such as people, technology, organisations and information to co-create and deliver value with and for customers.

Servuction System	A model that identifies benefits customers gain from their interactions with visible elements of the service experience and places the customer within the service delivery system.
Service Transaction Analysis	A service design technique developed by Robert Johnston that encourages quality evaluations of individual transactions within service processes from a customer's perspective. The purpose is to improve customer service experiences.
SERV*OR	An instrument that enables management to assess the contribution of employee's (along with other influences) to the organisation's overall service culture.
SERVQUAL	A measurement instrument developed by Parasuraman, Zeithaml & Berry, to assess service quality.
SMEs	Small-to-medium-sized enterprises.
SSME	The recognition of Service Science, Management and Engineering as an emerging field of study that seeks to develop inter-disciplinary knowledge of service.
SST	Self-service technology.
TBSS	Technology-based self-service options.
Technical Quality	The quality of the core service that delivered.
Technology-based services	Services that rely more heavily on customers interacting with machines than with contact personnel.
Transaction Marketing	An approach that uses 'offensive' marketing strategies to achieve a sale or transaction. Transaction marketing is differentiated from Relationship Marketing.
Unacquainted Influencers	Strangers who influence customer evaluations of the service performance.
WOM/W-O-M	Word-of-Mouth.
Word-of-mouth	Information provided by one customer to another customer or potential customer.

Index